DEMOCRATIC NATIONAL CONVENTION 1992

D92

The Governor Who Gave
Georgia HOPE

What they are saying about Zell: the Governor Who Gave Georgia HOPE

Anyone who wants to understand the positive role political leaders can play in our lives should read Richard Hyatt's insightful biography of Georgia's Zell Miller, one of the nation's most effective sitting governors.

Dan T. Carter, author of *The Politics of Rage*

It would be difficult to write a biography which captures the fascinating and turbulent life of Zell Miller. Richard Hyatt has written a superb story of the man who has turned out to be the most popular governor in the history of Georgia.

James Carville, Political Consultant, author of *We're Right, They're Wrong*

Zell Miller's political record extends over three decades and includes the lottery, repeal of the sales tax on food, and HOPE Scholarships. The lives of all Georgians have been affected. For those who have questions about him as a person and a politician, this book supplies answers.

Jack Bass, co-author of *The Transformation of Southern Politics*

Zell Miller's pride, strength, and integrity shine forth in Richard Hyatt's highly readable account... A deserving book that befits its deserving subject.

Rosemary Daniel, author of *Fatal Flowers*

Richard Hyatt's new book certainly captures the Zell Miller I know—fiercely independent, Marine tough, and incredibly focused.

Billy Payne, President & Chief Executive Officer
Atlanta Committee for the 1996 Olympic Games

In this time of confusing politics and values, it is an inspiration to read how Governor Zell Miller, from the mountains of North Georgia, rose to the governor's chair, with the traditional ethics of his kin and neighbors and a belief in the efficacy of education, and made a real difference in the lives of the people of Georgia.

Dr. Loyal Jones, Former Director of the
Berea College of Appalachian Center

This is an extraordinary book about an extraordinary man who had the vision and raw courage to do extraordinary things for the people of Georgia and the nation. It is a story that should be read over and over again. This book is a story of great drama.

Congressman John Lewis

The Governor Who Gave
Georgia HOPE

by
Richard Hyatt

Mercer University Press
Macon, Georgia 31210
1997

Zell: The Governor Who Gave Georgia HOPE
The Biography of Zell Miller
Richard Hyatt

Mercer University Press
6316 Peake Road
Macon, Georgia 31210

Jacket Photograph: Ken Hawkins
Cover design: Jim Burt
Book design: Jay Polk
Inside jacket photo: Joe Maher

∞The paper used in this publication meets the minimum require-
ments of the American National Standard for Information
Sciences—Permanence of Paper for Printed Library Materials,
ANSI Z39.48—1984.

Library of Congress Cataloging-in-Publication Data
Hyatt, Richard, 1944-
Zell: the governor who gave Georgia HOPE/ by Richard Hyatt
p. cm.
Includes bibliographical references and index.
ISBN 0-86554-577-4 (alk. paper)
1. Miller, Zell, 1932-   . 2. Governors—Georgia—
Biography. 3. Georgia—Politics and government—1951-   . I.
Title.
F291.3.M55H93   1997
975.8'043'092—dc21
[B]   97–18269
CIP

Table of Contents

Dedicated to the memory of Billy Watson,
a man who loved Georgia—its newspapers and its politics

PREFACE

Kaitlin was seven. Full of life and full of questions. She wanted to know where her Daddy had been that day, why he came to see her so late. Saying I had been in Atlanta all day wasn't enough. She asked why I hadn't taken her along. When I said I couldn't, that I had been with the governor, that demanded a definition. "What's a governor?" she asked.

First graders aren't ready for textbook descriptions, but she already knew something about presidents, though she sometimes got confused and referred to a chief executive she called George Lincoln. She was, however, acquainted with Bill and Hillary Clinton. When she saw one of them on television or in the newspaper, she talked about them as if they were old family friends. Someone even sent her one of those official photographs of Clinton. That seemed to be the best place to begin my lecture.

"You've told me about Bill Clinton being the boss of the United States, well, the governor is the boss of Georgia. The governor's name is Zell Miller," I said. I told her I was writing a book about Zell Miller. That didn't impress her. It was his name that fascinated her. I spelled it out slowly ... Z-E-L-L. She repeated the letters after me, and even now she brags she can spell his name. Wanting her to know more about her governor, I began to describe him and what he did. None of those things would mean much to a child, so I searched for something she might remember when she saw him. I finally thought about his missing finger.

"He doesn't have this finger," I told her, stretching out my hands on the bed next to her, folding under my left index finger. This fact interested Kaitlin more than anything else I had said about him. "How did it get cut off?, she asked. I told her I'd ask him. "Is it all gone?" she asked. No, I said, part of it was still there. "I want to see it," she said. Not tonight, I said. It was getting late. Time for prayers. Time to be asleep. Time for a final question.

Kaitlin sprang up in bed and spread her own fingers out on the covers, just as I had done, folding down the index finger on her left hand as if it had gone away. She was concerned, and her face showed it. "Dad," she asked, "how does Zell count to ten?"

She's not the first person to ask questions about Zell Miller. People have been asking questions about him for years. From the beginning, ever since he came out of the North Georgia mountains to be a state senator, he has provoked questions. That was nearly four decades ago, and some of those questions still have not been fully answered. Many Georgians cannot remember when he wasn't in the news and when he wasn't in office. He was lieutenant governor longer than any other person who has held that office. He is nearing the end of two historic four-year terms as governor of Georgia. But questions linger.

I've been asking him questions since 1975. I heard his first inaugural address as lieutenant governor and wanted to know more about this man. With a photographer in tow, I came to his office and we sat in a pair of Brumby rockers. I wrote an article about him for the *Columbus Ledger-Enquirer's* old Sunday magazine. Like most folks who came to write, I spent as much time dealing with the mountains, baseball and country music as I did his politics or what he knew. Later I would ride through the mountains with him, stopping to see the names written in the cement at the Rock House his mother built. There would be many stories about him under my byline – including an election day piece in 1994. I was waiting for him in Young Harris when he and Shirley came to vote and was in the ballroom of the Colony Square Hotel early the next morning when he celebrated his second term as governor. That was an assignment created for what *might* be written as much as what *was* reported. I was there with him in case Zell Miller was defeated, ending a colorful but unrequited career in Georgia politics.

After more than twenty years of writing about him, I began this biography with a sense that I knew Zell Miller. I had an outline. I knew who I wanted to interview. I had a publisher. I certainly knew how the story would end. The subject was willing so I assumed we would produce a book without incident. Until the phone rang in Rick Dent's office.

Dent is the governor's press secretary. His office is deep within the capitol. Earlier that morning, I had checked in with Toni Brown, who keeps up with Miller's appointments. Without thinking, I had given her a sheet of paper on which I had written down my interviews for that week. "If he has even fifteen or twenty minutes free this week, I'll be around Atlanta every day and any time we can spend together would be helpful," I told her. She said she would pass the message on to Miller, and as I left she also told me where several people's offices were in the capitol. Dent's wasn't one of them, but that gave Toni a clue where I was going. She had followed my trail to Dent's office.

"The governor wants to speak to you," Dent said, motioning me around to the back of his desk. He excused himself. I've never asked him if he knew what was about to happen. He could have gone out to get a cup of coffee, or he may have rushed into a bomb shelter.

Toni was on the line when I picked up and the next voice I heard was Zell Miller's. "What are you doing?" he screamed. "You're wasting time talking to these people. They're clueless. You're spending all your time in Young Harris. You ought to be working on my accomplishments as governor. That's why you're doing a book." There was some more rumbling and roaring. All from him. I just listened. As we hung up, I was so shell-shocked that I tangled my feet up in a mass of cords on the floor and jerked out of the wall the wires leading to Dent's phones, modems and computers.

Later that week, back in Columbus, the governor and I exchanged a set of messages by FAX. It was more of the same. "I am concerned that this will be 'Miller Lite,' all fluff and pointed toe cowboy boot stuff at the expense of substance," he wrote in one message. He wanted a book of substance that chronicled his terms as governor—the lottery, HOPE Scholarships, teacher raises, Two Strikes and You're Out, bootcamps and economic development. He pointed to other books on other governors and how those biographies centered only around the time when the subject was Georgia's chief executive. "I have a real concern that one cannot flesh out something through interviews until you have a skeleton to build that flesh around. The skeleton is Miller's record as governor," his message said, speaking of himself in an unusual third person.

My message back to him essentially became the focus for the book that follows. I assured him that this would not be a book that dealt only with boots or George Jones or Mickey Mantle, and that it would not attach him with a label like "hilllbilly intellectual." At the same time, however, I wasn't going to ignore the significance of the experiences he had on his way to the governor's office.

"Because you have been around for so long and because people like me have written so much about Zell Miller, Georgians think they know you. They don't," I replied. "No one to date has explained why you are the governor you've become. You have been a governor-in-training since you first left Young Harris for the Georgia Senate. You didn't step down from a corporate boardroom and decide to be governor on a whim. You were born into politics, then every step of the way for thirty years you prepared for that oath of office. That is part of your journey."

For me, that bombastic phone call and the biting messages that followed were an initiation into a fraternity that is not exclusive. People who deal with Zell Miller accept his tirades and go on. When the wind stops blowing, the storm passes. He did have a point, of course. His time in office has been exceptional. A variety of forecasters and pundits agree that he will be considered one of the greatest governors in Georgia history. The things he has done deserve to be reported and remembered.

But as that inquisitive seven-year-old asked, "How does Zell count to ten?" Unlike anyone else, I would tell her. His is a singular style. He marks his own trail. He has had to improvise that just as he has had to shape and reshape a life and a career that has survived changes of time and politics. Not the zigging and zagging that opponents have accused him of, but the kind of changes known only to a survivor. For when you get to the core of this man, it is unaltered. The values and the issues haven't changed, only expanded.

His is a background that will not be repeated, for he is a product of a time and place that has faded. He has been a part of the transition between the Georgia that was and the Georgia that is, the politics that railed on the stump and the politics that smiles into a camera, the politician that remembers when the faces of leadership were only white and only male. To understand Zell Miller the elected official, you must understand the man and all that is part of him, starting with the uncomfortable boy who, finding himself in a strange city, gave away peanuts and stole Coca-Colas off the back of a truck waiting at a traffic light. To understand the politician, you must know where he has been and what he has felt, even the night he spent drunk in a rural jail. To understand the person who loves a catchy lyric and hitting behind the runner, you must know the professor who stopped just short of a Ph.D and wants once again to welcome students to Political Science 101. To understand the governor who has worked so hard for education, you must know the child born into a home obsessed with learning and educating. These things are Zell Miller, and they are the reasons behind his accomplishments as Georgia's 79th governor.

So, this is not a book that deals only with the years he has spent living in Georgia's Governor's Mansion, though I have attempted to put those years into perspective. This is not 400 pages of accomplishments and explanations, but certainly I have recorded what he has done and highlighted many of these things in detail. I will leave the textbook examinations to a political historian. This is not meant to be an academic look at his administration, but a narrative story of the man who has carried out a career unlike any other. This is a work that examines why Zell Miller has centered on the issues that have been part of him from the very beginning. It will, as its story unfolds, provide a look at contemporary Georgia, for he has been a central figure in the transitional process that is moving the state toward a new century.

A book such as this is not the work of one person, though only one name appears on the cover. At the back of the book is a list of the people who graciously offered time and insight over parts of two years. For that I am grateful. But as might be expected, some people contributed more than memory and opinion. They deserve special mention.

Steve Wrigley is not a name known to the public and until I began this project we had never met. He is Miller's chief of staff, but he could be described as the governor's alter-ego. He has a Ph.D. in history, but over the years has gained even more of an education in both Zell Miller and in Georgia politics. He took my calls when he was busy, and he opened the door to ideas I might not have explored without him.

Terry Kay is known to the public through books such as *Dance With the White Dog* and *The Year the Lights Came On*. Like me, he is a recovering sports writer, but he is also a friend who, when I desperately needed to talk about the craft of writing, was there to help get the first words from my mind to my fingers.

Toni Brown answered so many phone calls from me that she finally asked why I thought I needed to identify myself. She is the governor's appointment secretary, but to me she became a source for telephone numbers and addresses. I used her instead of Directory Assistance and she never complained.

Paul Begala is a voice on the phone and a person who is comfortable using his keyboard and his FAX machine. We talked to each other's answering machines so often without making contact that I finally sent him a list of questions. He responded with nine single-spaced pages of answers that were both encouraging and revealing. I can see why Zell Miller wants him to do his eulogy.

John Greenman is the publisher of the *Columbus Ledger-Enquirer,* a newspaper I began calling home in 1972. He didn't flinch when Kirby Godsey, the president of Mercer University, called and asked if the newspaper could lend Mercer a staff member for two months. Greenman found a way even when there was no precedent.

Billy Winn is the editorial page editor of the *Columbus Ledger-Enquirer.* As a reporter and editor, he was there when many of the events I described in this book took place. His eye for detail and perspective helped, but not nearly as much as the late-night support he offered a friend in need.

Elizabeth Romey provided much of the research foundation that went into this project. She is a student at Simon's Rock College in Great Barrington, Massachusetts. Her early perceptions of a man she had never met sounded interesting in the beginning and proved useful in the end.

The Mercer University Press family took me in for nearly two months. Kirby Godsey had the intuition to know that this book would not be finished on time without an extraordinary idea so he made it possible for me to move to Macon for forty-seven crucial days. Once there, Dr. Cecil Staton, Jr., Amelia Barclay, Marc Jolley, and all of the MUP staff adopted a homeless writer into the family. Johnny Mitchell, senior Vice President, was in Atlanta opening doors and was on the phone every day with information and encouragement. Nancy Stubbs took on the tedious chore of transcribing hundreds of hours of taped interviews. Each of them deserves a share of this completed work.

Edna Herren never had the opportunity to read this book— she died in 1994. She was Zell Miller's teacher and mentor at Young Harris College. Years later, she was my instructor in freshman English at Georgia State University. She sent him on his way to the governor's office. She sent me to remedial English.

Finally, there is Zell Miller. He's a self-confessed control freak—a fact he warned me about after our experiences via phone and FAX. But without his desire to make this book, it would not be so. I was able to drive into the garage at the governor's mansion and pack up volumes of irreplaceable scrapbooks. He and Shirley not only located valuable photographs but catalogued them as well. He calmly answered question after question, some more than once. When time became an issue, he invited written questions and answered them in detail—often as if he knew what my followup questions would be. With him, I learned more about state government, state politics and state history than I would by reading a textbook or registering for a course. I learned about presidential politics and the way a person is elected. I learned about education and about the Georgia mountains.

More than anything, I learned about Zell Miller—the subject I thought I already knew. I thought he was a loner until I saw the tears of his loyal friends as they talked about him. I thought he was cold and distant until I heard him tell about the gifts his twin grandsons had made for his 65th birthday and how he would always regret that Shirley had to put aside her career for his. I came to marvel at his youthful energy and the excitement he still has for life—after a visit with baseball legend Ted Williams, he sounded like a child who had just met a hero. I saw him interrupt an appointment in his office so he could meet with a legislator whose son was a brand-new member of the Marine Corps. I came to laugh at the interjections he would offer when he thought I was engaging in pyscho-babble instead of being a straight-ahead biographer.

Looking back on his story, it is tempting to consider overblown words like destiny. His birth, his childhood and a mother who posed her son in front of the statue of a mountain neighbor who became governor. His feeling of being out of control and the discipline he found in the Marines. His time in the classroom and his original venture into politics. His runs for Congress. His jobs with Lester Maddox and the Democratic Party. His election as lieutenant governor, the amendment that allowed a governor to succeed himself, and his ill-fated run against Herman Talmadge. These are components of Zell Miller. Individually, many of these events were disappointments. Collectively, they prepared him to be the governor he finally became.

Paul Begala has given in to those same temptations. That was one of the ideas the political consultant shared with me in a lengthy message he transmitted in March of 1997. It was a message about the subject of the biography, but it also was an admonition to the author: "In terms of his character, his personal story is so compelling, so Lincolnesque, that I think it would make a helluva movie—tragic and heroic and inspirational. The circumstances surrounding his birth, his upbringing in Young Harris, his first foray into the big city of Atlanta, and subsequent tailspin. Landing himself in Parris Island and turning his life around forever. Not a bad yarn, I'd say. Don't mess it up."

I hope I haven't.

Richard Hyatt, May 1997

1

A DREAMER AND A DOER

Her chair was hard naked steel but Birdie was soft and small. Her feet were planted firmly on the antiseptic floor of the nursing home. With frail forearms resting on the arms of the chair, Birdie Miller was in the room, even if her mind was somewhere else, remembering some other times. She was thinking, and she was rocking, swaying against the narrow seat belt that locked her into the chair.

On the drab walls were pictures of her father, her husband, her daughter and her son, who at the time was the lieutenant governor of Georgia. Scattered around the spartan room were simple artifacts that only she could make important when she told their story. All her life she had worked, like a man, folks said. Now she was resting, sitting peacefully in a wing of the hospital in Hiawassee, Georgia.

It was a dreary, wet Saturday, accompanied by a cold that chewed at the face of anyone who went out in it, as only mountain weather can. Zell Miller, her only son, came down the hall but stopped short of her room. Before he and his friend went in, Miller peeped around the door. Seeing her there gnawed at him. This was Birdie, proud, independent Birdie, a survivor, a single parent before anybody put the two words together. Deciding she needed to be in a home was the hardest decision he had ever made. His mama ought to be at home, in Young Harris, in the house she built a rock at a time and a hand at the time. Only now she sat in that chair, looking at the tile floor over folded hands.

Ed Johnson walked behind Miller. He was in Clayton visiting his own grandmother and, as he often did when he was in North Georgia, he called Young Harris. Miller was there for the weekend so Johnson, then a young lawyer in Fayette County, drove over the mountain to see him.

They had become friends when Johnson worked in Miller's first campaign for lieutenant governor in 1974. Johnson, just out of law school, was the only person authorized to speak for the candidate. They became more than friends, more like teacher and student. It was then that Johnson met Birdie Bryan Miller, already a woman in her eighties and a person he could not forget. So when he got to Young Harris that Saturday, he asked Miller about his mother and said he would like to see her.

Johnson followed Miller as they went into the room. Birdie's face lit up immediately. She recognized the young lawyer and was glad to see him. She asked him to pull a chair close to her. All the time, she was talking. "Zell's over at North Carolina with his grand-daddy," she said.

Finally, she looked up at her son. "I don't believe I know you," she said.

Miller took her hands and spoke softly, smiling a smile reserved only for her. "Yeah, Mama, you know me," he said, gently stroking her hand.

It was only after the three of them had been talking for some time that she suddenly recognized her son. It was as if a switch turned on the light in her mind. She called him by name. She was giving him all the news, the way she always did when he came home.

"Jane came to see me this morning," she said. Miller laughed. His sister lived in Birmingham.

"What did you do, Mama?"

"We went shopping," she said.

"How did you keep from getting wet? It's been raining cats and dogs for the last three days and it hasn't let up all morning." She looked up at him and it was clear that she had really heard him.

"Zell Miller, it don't rain where I go." He didn't answer. He just hugged her.

That's not the picture of a man who before his career in public life is ended will have served as the first or second most powerful man in Georgia government for 24 years. Nor does it seem to be a man who sleeps at the White House, impatiently fires school boards with the single stroke of a gubernatorial pen, and who has a temper so legendary that his staff measures his outbursts on what they laughingly call "The Zell Richter Scale."

Georgia thinks it knows him.

They know he's a history teacher. They know his flat, nasal voice, a mountain voice that one minute recites the lyrics of a country songwriter and the next moment quotes a political philosopher. They know the toes on his cowboy boots are pointy, and that he has hung out with Mickey Mantle and George Jones, and that he helped elect Bill Clinton. They know that all he ever needed to know he learned in the Marine Corps, because he told them so. They know that he helped bring to an end the legacy of Gene and Herman Talmadge in a campaign for the United States Senate so bitter that when it was over you couldn't tell the winner from the loser. They know that he is a politician who has lost as well as won.

Georgia knows that as governor he installed a lottery in a state where many people considered prohibition of gambling the Eleventh Commandment. They know that he created and named the HOPE Scholarship, an ambitious plan to spend that lottery money on college tuition for young people—in a state that historically measured schools by their football teams. They know that his friend Mr. Clinton had adopted a similar program of scholarship at the national level. They know he unsuccessfully tried to take down the state flag with its Confederate Stars and Bars, and that over the years he has habitually argued with Speaker of the House Tom Murphy and his lamp-sized cigar. They know that he has attracted industry and high-tech jobs to a state that only a few generations ago depended on one-horse farms and cotton mill villages for its livelihood.

But Georgia—like so many of Zell Miller's friends and colleagues—knows only what political writers, campaigns ads, and stump speeches have told them about the man voters twice elected governor. They've been served a six-pack of Miller Lite, given a momentary glimpse at the more obvious attributes of Miller, ignoring the complex side of this complex and fascinating individual. Many have labeled him a hillbilly intellectual without realizing that he has spent as much of his life in the shadow of the capitol in Atlanta as he has in Towns County in the shadow of the Appalachians.

They may not have paused to consider that Zell Miller is, in all likelihood, the last Georgia governor who will bear scars from The Great Depression, who listened to accounts of World War II on the radio, who knew a world without television, who lived in a county with one paved road, knowing nothing about something called an Information Super Highway. They may not realize that he is a political survivor, who was part of a state government that was all white, all male and all Democratic and that he played a part in changing those things. They may not know that he held office when Georgia's public schools were kept open and when rural and urban votes were finally equalized by the abolition of the state's County Unit System. They may not remember that in 1994, when he was elected to his second term as governor, most of his Democratic peers around the country were washed away by a Republican waterfall.

Georgia doesn't know him much better than he knew his father, Stephen Grady Miller, a revered college professor who passed out just before his first period history class at Young Harris College and died three days later, March 12, 1932—seventeen days after the birth of Zell Bryan Miller. Grady Miller was just forty years old.

It was an event that would shape and narrow Zell Miller's life.

"Wherever I went, there was the ghost of Grady Miller," he says.

Even now, should he meet someone who knew his father, or took a class under him, Miller will ask questions, seeking to put some flesh on a person who has always been an aberration.

First and foremost, Grady Miller was a teacher. He was a product of Choestoe, a Cherokee Indian word for "the place of the dancing rabbits." It was an intriguing, obscure mountain valley between Blood and Slaughter mountains. Now almost forgotten, it was a place that over the years produced two justices of the Georgia Supreme Court, a United States District judge, two college presidents, a state school superintendent and an assortment of teachers, preachers and professors. Even a poet, Byron Herbert Reece, a melancholy genius, would, like several of his Choestoe neighbors, eventually find his way to Young Harris College. Years later, many critics recognized Reece as the greatest creator of the literary mountain ballad this country has produced.

One of Reece's ballads, "I Know a Valley Green with Corn," was published in "A Song of Joy," a 1952 collection of his works. It put into words what his poetic eyes saw in that North Georgia valley.

> *I know a valley green with corn*
> *Where Nottley's waters roil and run*
> *From the deep hills where first at morn*
> *It takes the color of the sun*
>
> *And bears it burning through the shade*
> *Of birch and willow till its tide*
> *Pours like a pulse, and never stayed,*
> *Dark where the Gulf's edge reaches wide.*
>
> *There, while the twilight spends its dream*
> *Of light and shadow both, the whir*
> *Of bats and cry of doves will seem*
> *A very liveness of the air*

About a house the ivy's foot
Creeps slowly up to hide the eaves
And wreathe the chimney, dark with soot,
Into a colonnade of leaves.

And one will loiter in the yard
Soft shadowed by the last of day
As if she waited for a word
From lips three thousand miles away

That yearn to speak against her hair
But, dumb behind the palm of space
Tauten to trembling, while there
Darkness obliterates her face.

Zell Miller's ancestors were among the earliest settlers of the valley that Reece described. Thompson Collins, his great, great grandfather, arrived in the 1830s, coming from North Carolina. He went to Habersham County and waited for the Indian territory to open up. He died in 1858 and is buried in the old Choestoe Cemetery, where five generations of Miller's relatives are buried. In 1861, the ninth of his ten grandchildren, Jane Melinda Collins, was born near Walasiyi Gap, an area the Cherokees named for a frog that legends said was so large it could hop across mountains. It was later renamed Neel's Gap, for the highway engineer who laid out the treacherous road.

Jane Collins's older brother, Francis Jasper "Bud" Collins, was one of Choestoe's most prominent residents. He was a merchant, a farmer and a cattle trader. He was also a member of the Georgia General Assembly. Despite his success, he never wore any store-bought clothes, even preferring homemade socks.

Her father was Francis Collins and she had an uncle, Thompson Collins, who was among the area's more unusual characters. Around 1875, two men paid him to have his mules help haul a wagon to the top of Tesnatee Gap, a very steep grade. On the way up the mountain, federal revenue agents appeared and the other fellows disappeared. When "Uncle Tom," as he was always called, refused to identify them, he was sentenced to prison in New York—for the wagon his mules were pulling was loaded with barrels full of moonshine. Years passed. Folks thought he had died in prison. Then one day, he just appeared out in the front yard. He had walked all the way from New York.

"I've slept in many a fence corner and cut many a stick of wood for food," he said. "If ever a stranger comes by, he is welcome to sleep in our house and share my food." When he died in 1917, his headstone was inscribed with these words: "A poor man's friend."

At the age of twenty-four, Jane Collins married William J. "Bud" Miller. Like her father, he was a school teacher. He was also a widow with six children, and together they had nine more. Among them was Stephen Grady Miller.

Bud Miller was also a leader. For more than twenty-five years, he was superintendent of the Sunday School at Salem Methodist Church, never missing a Sunday for thirty years. It was a community that stuck together, and its glue was the church and education, two institutions that were hard to separate for the Baptist church often served as a school house and town hall. Only two congregations were represented in the valley—Methodist and Baptist. It was a community equally divided between sprinkling and immersing. Both were baptized in pride. For example, when an uneducated local fellow was sent to represent the area in the Georgia Legislature, he wanted to hide the fact that he knew very few words. "What's the altitude of your county?" he was asked. He thought a minute. Then he said, "I'm not sure, but it's mostly Baptist."

Bud Miller was a teacher who stressed elocution and hard-boiled beliefs. Reading materials in his class included such directives as "Drunkards are worthless fellows" and "Love for trifling amusement is derogatory to the Christian character." Miller was paid twenty dollars each of the months he conducted class. Young people were expected to work plowing, pulling fodder, or working a sawmill.

During the rest of the year, Bud and Jane Miller ran a country store that like most in that era sold good conversation as well as any item a Choestoian might want. There was medicine and there were farm implements. There were clothes, and Bud Miller knew every regular customers' size. There was no charge for the opinions and the philosophy.

As much as anything, Bud Miller was known for his regular attendance at church. Getting there was not easy. Before he could pack up the family, there was stock to feed, then there was a three-mile trip over muddy roads with his two youngest children straddling the mule with him—one in front of him, the other in the rear. Older kids followed on foot. As if the ruts in the road weren't bad enough, there was also the Nottley River to cross—without a bridge. Old-timers remembered a snowy Sunday morning when people who lived near the church felt the wind whistling off the mountains and said, "I bet Uncle Bud won't make it today." About that time, they saw his mule coming across the river, his children trailing behind. Even at church, he encouraged children to learn and to participate. He built a wooden platform in the grove near the church for students to deliver memorized speeches. His love and respect for education were passed on to his children—particularly Grady and Verdie—both of whom became teachers.

Since there was no formal academy for the children in Choestoe, Bud Miller decided to send his children to Young Harris College. Like most of his neighbors, he was born with a large dose of pride, so borrowing money was not a consideration to him. He always paid cash, but he did lend money to others, and he set aside the interest on one loan to be used to pay for his children's schooling. They went one at a time—tending to the crops, teaching school or working in the family's general store when it was their quarter out of class.

In those years, you didn't need a college degree to be a teacher. All a person needed was to pass an exam. So, even while he was attending Young Harris College, Grady Miller was teaching. His first real position was at Pinetop. It was a typical one-room school that sat at the head of Stick Mule Creek. Every day, he rode his mule all the way from Choestoe. At Young Harris he was an outstanding, active student. He was a champion debater for the Phi Chi Society and president of his class, graduating in 1912. Later, he would earn both a bachelor's and Master's degree from the University of Georgia. During World War I, soon after graduating, he enlisted in the Army and served twenty months overseas, extending his tour so he could attend King's College at the University of London.

In 1919, Grady Miller returned to this country and his mountain home. He took a position at Young Harris College, this time as a teacher. So did a talented artist from South Carolina by the name of Birdie Bryan.

The mountains were not Birdie's natural habitat. She was born September 2, 1893, on a rambling farm near Saluda, South Carolina. Her mother died when she was small, but her father remarried and the family continued to grow. Her father was not an educated man, but he wanted his children to have what he did not. Birdie was a tree-climbing tomboy and an obvious artist. She could run faster and work harder than her brothers and sisters and most of her friends. And when she wasn't running, she was drawing and sketching. Her doting father made sure she graduated from Summerland College in Batesburg, South Carolina and even sent her to New York City to study at the Arts Students League. City life was something new to her. So were the nude women she was expected to sketch. So were the loin-clothed men who came to her classes to model. By the time she came home, she had learned to hide her blushes when the scantily–clad models arrived.

When she graduated and returned to Leesville, South Carolina, jobs were scarce. New York had piqued her taste for adventure, and after unsuccessfully looking for jobs in the area, she applied for a passport so she could become a canteen worker overseas. World War I ended before she could be hired. She learned, as creative people have always known, that often there is little demand for art or artists. That is, unless a person wanted to teach. Hungry for a chance to prove herself, Birdie Bryan noticed an advertisement in an educational journal that said an art teacher was needed at Young Harris College in the Georgia mountains.

She got the job, and in the fall of 1919 she got off the train in Murphy, North Carolina, an hour late arriving from Asheville. A stage–coach was waiting to take her to Young Harris. Students were crammed into the coach and the impatient driver was obviously unhappy that she had made them late. With the two large mules pushed to a gallop, they started down the winding road to Georgia, six hours away. After they arrived, shaken and dusty, the school's newest faculty member was given a hot meal and a room in the dormitory.

The next morning at breakfast, she met two other new faculty members—Verdie and Grady Miller. This sister and brother combination would be a part of her life for years to come. One would be her best friend. The other would become her husband. They arrived at a difficult time for Young Harris. The college president, J. L. Hall, was serving without a salary, but there were still mounting financial problems. The economy in the South was at a low ebb. At the college, the fees for room, board, and tuition were low but the costs of food and furnishings were high.

Verdie Miller became Birdie's roommate. They lived in a dorm room and could eat their meals in the college dining hall. The new art teacher was not paid a salary but was allowed to recruit students who were charged two dollars a month for lessons. Music teachers worked under the same arrangement. Attracting eight or ten students, she soon was making as much as twenty dollars a month.

One of her first students was an eight-year-old orphan boy who was allowed to live in the girls' dorm. He yearned to study art, but he didn't have the fee. Birdie Bryan taught him anyway, and years later he became a significant Southern artist. For years, his former teacher had a Leroy Jackson original hanging in her home. On the back, Jackson had signed it to "My dear friend, Mrs. Grady Miller, through whose kindness and that of her late husband a beautiful world was opened up to me."

At the time, since he hadn't been out of the Army long, Grady Miller had just one suit, so his first year as a teacher he sometimes wore his Doughboy uniform to class. No one noticed, for few people there had much of a wardrobe. When they weren't in class, Grady, Verdie, and Birdie were together. Soon, the history teacher's and the artist's friendship turned into a romance. Not even the fact that during the following year Birdie Bryan had to return unexpectedly to South Carolina to care for her family cooled their budding relationship.

Figuring he could not marry and have a family on his meager pay as an educator, Grady Miller joined a friend in the jewelry business in Gainesville, Georgia. He was lured back to the classroom the next year by Dr. Joseph A. Sharp, a former president of Young Harris, who had been named to a similar post at Emory College at Oxford, a small Georgia town where Emory University began before moving to Atlanta. In 1921, the Millers married and moved into an apartment on the campus of the small Methodist college. That was a pattern from which they never escaped. In eleven years of marriage, they always lived in college quarters, never owning a home of their own.

Neither Sharp nor the Millers were happy at Oxford, and in 1922 trustees, alumni and friends were trying to lure Sharp back to Young Harris. One Saturday afternoon, Sharp and Miller were engaged in a game of Rook when Sharp laid down his cards. "Grady," he said, "will you go back to Young Harris with me?" Before another card was dealt, Miller said he would.

All of them were glad to get back to the mountains and to Young Harris College. Sharp returned for his second stint as president and named Grady Miller as his dean. They would prove to be a good team. For the school, it was a time of growth. One college historian called Young L.G. Harris the "founder" and Sharp the "builder." Back at home, Dean Miller blossomed in the classroom, teaching a variety of subjects—from history to political science to psychology to ethics and education. He was a professor whom students of that era remembered.

"We feel that it won't be necessary to cross the ocean for a year or so. We have already been taken on a perilous tour under the able guidance of Dean Miller. I think we can say of the forty countries:

'We know we've been there,' "Margaret Jane Allison wrote in a 1927 edition of *The Enotah Echoes,* the school newspaper.

Another 1927 article told of Miller asking his history class what was "Livery and Maintenance." Mr. Howard McGhenty answered that it was "a method of raising sheep."

Often, Miller himself wrote for the paper. "Young man, don't go groggy over girls, religion, words, arts or politics. They are all good in moderation but bad if you get an overdose," he wrote in 1929. "Get a hold of yourself, for a man who masters himself can more easily master the things about him. Avoid the path of least resistance. Control your temper," he wrote in 1931.

For the young married faculty couple, the campus was the center of their social life. When their daughter, Jane, was born on January 11, 1926, the event was front page news in *The Enotah Echoes.* A year later, it was noted that "a most delightful event for children of the community was an Easter Egg hunt given by Mrs. S. G. Miller for the Junior Missionary Society. Eggs were hidden in the meadow near Cupid Falls." A 1928 article was as flowery as the times: "Professor and Mrs. Mann along with Dean and Mrs. Miller and little Jane, laying aside all cares and sorrows, sallied forth and did enjoy a royal feast of wieners and marshmallows on the rock near Cupid Falls."

Grady Miller's interests extended beyond the theory of the classroom, however. As a student at Young Harris, he had founded the school's first political group, and he continued to follow politics at both the local and state levels. After finishing his advanced degree from the University of Georgia in 1926, he decided to get personally involved. It was an involvement that brought him to the mainstream of Georgia politics.

Miller had often advised young people in his classes to "Stop messing with the side–show and come on under the Big Tent," and in the fall of 1926 he announced as a candidate for the Georgia State Senate.

The Enotah Echoes reported the results.

"Professor S. G. Miller, Dean of Young Harris College and one of the best–educated men of this section, was overwhelmingly elected to the State Senate on November 3. Mr. Miller had no opposition in the Democratic Primary, but Republican leaders got busy and Mr. S. A. Deavers of Union County competed as the Republican standard bearer in the general election," the paper reported in a front page article.

The popular professor won by 856 votes and went to Atlanta representing Towns, Union and Rabun counties. In the Georgia Senate, Miller was greeted by E.D. Rivers, who was serving as President of the Senate. Years before, the Arkansas native had been one of Miller's Young Harris students. Even in school, the outgoing Rivers was interested in politics and had told friends he would one day be governor of Georgia.

In 1930, Rivers was embarking on his second race for governor. Roy Harris of Augusta—who would be a force in state politics for years to come—had managed Rivers' first campaign in 1928. This time, he asked Grady Miller to take the job. Though the one-term senator was well known in the mountain region, he was not able to help his candidate over the state and Rivers finished behind Richard B. Russell. In 1936, with Roy Harris again as his campaign manager, Rivers would at last be elected governor, defeating the Talmadge candidate in a bitter race that would be a harbinger of another race decades later, involving another Young Harris graduate and a Talmadge.

Sharp died in 1930 and his wife was named acting president with Miller directing the academic affairs of the college. Supporters pushed for him to be named Sharp's successor. Instead, the Board of Trustees turned to another Young Harris graduate and another native of Choestoe, Dr. Thomas Jackson Lance, who had been superintendent of schools in Waynesboro, Georgia. Back in the secluded valley, his Sunday School teacher had been Bud Miller, Grady's father. Lance was well known in the area. His grandfather, a Methodist preacher, had been murdered and thrown into Wolf Creek after delivering a pulpit-pounding sermon at a church in Union County against the evils of alcohol.

In his family memoirs, T. J. Lance talked about Grady Miller and the events that occurred in 1930: "(He) became one of the shining lights of the mountains of Georgia, indeed of the whole state … I spent twenty-one years as a student, teacher and president of Young Harris College and as far as I have been able to discover, Grady Miller was the most popular man who ever served in that wonderful school either as a teacher or an administrator. He should have been elected as president when I was, in 1930. However, there were two factions in the college faculty … It was impossible to elect (him) at that time."

That conflict was not between Lance and Miller, however, and they continued to serve together. Their families were also growing. The Lance family welcomed a son, Bert, on June 4, 1931 and on February 24, 1932, the Millers had their only son, Zell. The two infants were beginning a life that would be full of criss-crossing paths.

That winter, before Zell was born, Grady and Birdie were gathering wood for the fire. She was inside the house and he was passing logs through the window. For a moment, he stopped. "Where would you bury me if I died?" he suddenly asked. "Why just as close to Dr. Sharp as I could get you," she answered.

While she was still confined to her bed after giving birth to Zell, Grady Miller took cold that settled in his ear and developed cerebral meningitis. That was what caused him to pass out before history class that morning in March of 1932. His condition soon worsened. The lone doctor in Young Harris could do nothing, so Grady was rushed by ambulance to Atlanta. Lance went with him since Birdie was not able to travel.

Three days later, with Lance by his hospital bed, Grady Miller died. Birdie Miller wasn't able to attend her husband's funeral either, but she did as she had offhandedly promised. She buried Grady in the Old Union Cemetery only a few yards from Sharp, his Young Harris friend. Grady Miller's son was seventeen days old.

The Rev. Claude Haynes had known Grady Miller as a student and as a fellow faculty member. He remembered when he left for World War I. "I saw him the day he went away to fight for his country and the day he returned," Haynes said. "He was interested in the welfare of the nation. He was not only willing to die for it, but he lived for it."

More than anything, Haynes' message recalled Miller the teacher. "I too, sat at his feet and learned not so much the facts of history as to glean from him a philosophy of life .... He had that coveted ability to show an interest in every student and to cause them to be interested in their work. He was not only a teacher of books but a developer of character. As an administrator in the office of Dean, he was unassuming, but as a citizen of the town put it, 'He was the balance wheel of this institution,' " Haynes said.

Lance also praised Miller: "He did a magnificent piece of work for Young Harris College. He was teacher, dean and a friend of students. His work of raising standards of scholarship was widely recognized."

That spring, when the college held its commencement, a special service was held in the school chapel. The Rev. W. T. Hamby, chairman of the school's board of trustees, was in charge. The speaker was Charles Reid, a future Chief Justice of the Georgia Supreme Court and chairman of the state Democratic Party. He was, appropriately, one of the boys from Choestoe.

Years later, in a 1986 edition of the Young Harris school paper, a member of the Class of 1932 remembered Dean Grady Miller. "I doubt any other person in the world can give you the feeling that he did when he urged you to 'Get under the Big Tent,' " wrote the Rev. Tim Hollbrook of Bremen, Georgia.

His life and career had ended, but his influence continued. E. D. Rivers, his one-time student, was elected governor in 1936, defeating the Talmadge machine in the process. Rivers quickly moved to improve public education, providing free textbooks for Georgia's children and extending the school year to seven months. Whether Rivers would have included Grady Miller in his education-minded administration is obviously long-distance speculation. But along with the governor, Young Harris graduates William H. Duckworth, chief justice of the Supreme Court, and M.D. Collins, state superintendent of education; Miller would have had many friends and contacts in Atlanta.

Bert Lance, son of Dr. T. J. Lance, went on to play a role in Jimmy Carter's career serving as director of the Department of Transportation while Carter was governor of Georgia and as budget director when the Georgian was President of the United States. Lance was a candidate for governor in 1974, the same year Zell Miller first ran for lieutenant governor. They had shared a desk in the first grade back in Young Harris and they could have shared the state capitol in Atlanta but Georgia voters instead elected State Rep. George Busbee of Albany.

Lance says his late father—who was a member of the Georgia Board of Regents that clashed with Gov. Gene Talmadge in the 1940s—often spoke of Grady Miller. "My Dad always complimented Zell's father on his political skills," Lance says. "He said Grady Miller had a better understanding of the political process than anybody he had ever known—and he was around a lot of political figures."

Such was the legacy inherited by Zell Miller. It has been part of him for as long as he can remember. Grady Miller had left behind only memories and two children. He owned no land, no home, no furniture. An insurance policy provided $1,000 in cash and fifty dollars a month. He had ninety dollars in cash when he died. There were also debts and expenses and when all were paid, Birdie Miller was left with very little.

With a six-year-old daughter and a baby boy less than three weeks old, people assumed Birdie Miller would go back to South Carolina to be near her own family. Her father said if she came home, he would build her a house. She told him she was staying in Young Harris. Her family helped them when they could. Her sister in Louisiana, Eva Lou, would often send the struggling family money. "We called her Aunt Woo-Woo and every once in a while, she'd send a fifty–dollar check. It was a big deal," Miller remembers. Aunt Mary in Greenville, South Carolina, would send clothes. She had a son, Claude, about the same age as Zell but much heavier. "The clothes she would send were nice—except too big. What was terrible," Miller recalls, "was that in Greenville they wore knickers. I absolutely refused to wear knickers to Young Harris School."

People who knew Birdie and Grady Miller say he was the dreamer, but she had the dream this time. She wanted her family to have a house. She bought a plot of land as close to the campus as she could find for $198. It was full of rocks and broomsedge. Drawing her own simple plans, she explained to builders that she had about $700 and that was all. In 1932, there were more workers than jobs and she soon found laborers willing to work. But before the workers came, Birdie Miller had work to do herself.

As an artist, she had a picture in her mind of a house built out of the smooth rocks she had seen in the creek at the foot of Double Knobs Mountain. The rolling water had washed the rocks smooth. And they didn't cost anything. A neighbor, Callie Nichols, agreed to let Birdie have them. During the spring and summer of 1932, with little Zell rocking in Mrs. Nichols' lap, Birdie began hauling rocks. She was a New York trained artist, but those creative hands were being used to scoop rocks from a cold mountain creek. Stones she selected were piled up high then hauled by sled to a nearby dirt road. On Saturdays, a truck from the college carried the stones to the lot they now owned.

Finally, there was a house. Almost, anyway.

She ran out of money after there was a roof, windows and a single finished room. Everything else would have to wait for many years. Zell would be a senior in high school before they had running water and an indoor toilet. The first night they lived there, a stray dog marched in the doorless house, and ate their butter out of a dish. The house was always drafty, even after Birdie was finished. TVA electricity came when Zell was nine years old. Years later, when she had finished the upstairs and it had a wood heater, not a fireplace, Birdie would often rent that space out. That meant the family was relegated back to the colder area downstairs, an assignment that irritated the younger Miller. To her son, being warm was something that came to be cherished—and still is.

Even after they were in the unfinished house, she was busy— making a large garden, digging out a fish pond, planting shrubs and flowers. She became known for her flowers which she sent friends and neighbors on every special event. Sometimes her children wished their mother was like their friends' mothers, mothers who didn't have muscles or gnarled hands.

But Birdie Miller had a purpose. "She wanted Jane and me to grow up where people knew our Daddy," Miller says. "As far back as I can remember, if we met someone who knew him, she'd ask that person to tell us about him. Naturally, his old students would say great things about him."

Grady's sister, their Aunt Verdie, lived in a dormitory room on campus. She stepped in, probably feeling a responsibility since she was the children's nearest relative. Over the years, she took them to Miller reunions at Vogel State Park and all over the area to visit their relatives on the Miller side of the family. Jane, Birdie, and Verdie would be crowded onto the seat with Zell hunkered down in the little space under the back window. Birdie, too, made sure they knew about their father. An early lesson was about what he had gone through to get an education.

By the time Zell was eight years old, she had taken him and Jane on the eight–mile path that led from Choestoe to Young Harris. They had climbed the trail past Trackrock, a large stone that Indian legend said bore the footprints of animals. Some said the Cherokees themselves had carved out the markings.

"As a boy, I was told that live creatures left their prints in those rocks while the earth's surface was still soft," Miller has said. Either way, he remembered the rock, the taxing trail and the lessons that Birdie delivered that day.

Single mothers like her were a novelty in Towns County. For most of Miller's life, there was only one other family in the community headed by a mother. At home, he took it for granted. This was the only way he knew it. His mother, at various times, sold magazines, worked for the college in a variety of jobs, was a substitute teacher at the elementary school, sold pieces of her art and on election day was a poll worker. Whatever she was doing, she was busy. For a short time, she worked at the post office. Her son remembers when she stormed into the house after giving her superiors at the local post office a verbal lashing. "I'm quitting," she said at home. "I'm not gonna put up with that rotten politics."

She also continued to be creative. "I remember her making small, wooden plaques and selling them. I've got two of them now at the Governor's Mansion. They had mountain scenes, painted in oil. She'd set up an assembly line at home. She'd sand one piece of wood. She'd outline the mountains on another. Then she'd paint one. She'd have ten or twenty of them going at a time," he says.

People in town saw how hard she worked. One day her son came home from grade school with a question. "Mama, what's a Trojan?"

She told him, but she wondered why he wanted to know. "Because," he answered. "The principal said Mrs. Miller works like a Trojan."

But her son was never alone. "My mother taught me to look at Young Harris College as my family," he says. "The village looked after me. When the neighbors on either side of us killed a hog, they brought us hog meat. There was always milk and butter from somebody."

Zell's Aunt Phoebe and Uncle Hoyle lived next door and, growing up, he ate as many meals with them as he did at home, since his mother worked by her own schedule and paid no attention to what other people considered dinner time. To the college and the town, Zell Miller was always there and some of the people spoiled him. Others must have resented him. "I'm sure that to some of them at the college, I was a nuisance. We didn't have running water and when I was a teenager, I often went to the campus to take a shower while the other students were at supper."

This was his world and at the time it seemed large. "The members of the board of trustees, why, they were like gods to be in awe of," he recalls. "I can remember Ed Rivers coming up to Young Harris in a big black car. I was in awe. He was *the governor*. I thought I could see him through the window of the car. I kept looking. Then Mama introduced him to me. I was speechless. *The governor.*"

Men like the governor weren't often around, but it seemed the specter of Grady Miller was. At times his young son was almost jealous of his dead father's memory. When people told him how great his father was, it was as if they were saying Zell was insignificant, that he would never be anything as great.

"I knew my Daddy was special, and I knew what he did as an educator was special. My Mama raised me with certain expectations. To be something. Like I had a destiny to fulfill. It was a heckuva lot of pressure to put on a kid and in another way, it was a challenge," he says, looking back.

With both came resentment. "If I did anything good, it was the genes of Grady or Birdie," he says. "Anything bad, and it was me messing up. It was something to live up to for a kid."

His father had been a graduate of Young Harris College and he would surely be. His father had been a champion debater and he was expected to be one. His father was a teacher and maybe some day he would inspire students. His father was in politics and had been elected a State Senator, and one of these days maybe his son would also be something big.

To the son he left behind, Grady Miller loomed larger than life. He was a figure in a history book, like a statue to be admired on the courthouse lawn. Every good deed of his was recorded and duly reported. Every feature was chiseled. Not a hair was out of place. He was permanent and he was perfect.

"Anytime I met somebody who knew my Daddy, I picked their brain trying to find out who this man was. All I know about him was what I was told and everything I was told was something very positive," he says. "Later on, my own sons saw their Dad in his underwear. They saw their Dad have too much to drink. They saw their Dad use profanity. They saw their Dad fuss at their Mama when he should not have. They saw all his flaws—and I hope they saw some of his good points, too. See, I never saw a flaw in my father. He was a ghost, a saint, someone I had to live up to."

Then there was Birdie . . . always working . . . never sitting. Grady was on a pedestal and she was in the creek with mud over her shoes, picking out just the right stone. Her son didn't have to ask anyone about her. He knew she was unique. And he knew if he asked people, he'd find out everyone agreed.

"Even as a child, I knew that the town people thought my Mama was very special. She was a different kind of woman than those folks had ever seen," Miller says. "They knew the story. They had seen her get those rocks out of the creek and build that house. They saw how she worked."

Invariably, in a child's mind, there were comparisons. "My father was evidently a scholar, a dreamer. He was a teacher, a reader, a writer. I always contrasted him with my Mama. My Mama was a doer. She didn't read books. She knew it was important to read to me, but she never just sat and rested or gossiped like other folks did. She was always working. She was a doer."

For the last years of her life, Birdie Miller's health got worse and worse. For awhile, the family tried to take care of her themselves. Finally, they listened to the advice of her doctors and put her in the nursing home. The woman who had worked so hard for her family now depended on someone else. She had been a woman with muscles, but those muscles slowly went away. Her unmistakable laugh was no more. Her quick-witted tongue produced gibberish. She could no longer care for herself. The time came when she could no longer keep herself clean. "She once did the same for me," Miller said. "This is my responsibility now."

Even in that dreary room in the nursing home—only a short time before her death in 1986—in her wandering mind she was still doing. And though he was no longer a child, she was still Zell Miller's mama, a mama who, if she had been able, would have given him a world where it didn't rain.

2

SIN, SCHOOL, AND STEREOTYPES

"It's seven miles from any known sin," a Young Harris College catalog once said of the strait-laced Methodist school that has been locked away in the North Georgia mountains since 1886. At the time that description was coined, it might have been close to the truth.

Those were different times and different mountains. Even sin would have a hard time getting to the Towns County school. The few roads that were cut out of the hillsides were unpaved, narrow, and winding. No one imagined the romance of spreading a quilt for an afternoon picnic, with sound effects provided by a gurgling stream. No one took time to breathe in the view of sweeping valleys or noble peaks. It was an uncomplicated generation that couldn't decide whether it needed electricity and wondered why folks would want plumbing down the hall when it was down the hill. It was an era when the locals bowed their heads and prayed to a simple, earthy God instead of a real estate developer who read blue–prints instead of the Good Book.

These were the mountains Zell Miller came to know. They were hard, cold, and unforgiving. Nothing came easy. Nothing could be taken for granted. Nature wasn't motherly, it was a threat, whether it was unrelenting weather or stubborn rocky soil. Hills were to be climbed, not admired. Streams meant floods, not frolic.

People sired by this melding of time and place are innately proud. It is a pride born of survival. Their neighbors faced the same obstacles, so they are to be trusted. Anyone who didn't face them is an outsider. The world they live in is manly, in the sense of toughness, not gender. Emotions are filed for another day. Words are pondered. Time isn't valued; it is always there so why get in a hurry. Their common traits evolved from who they were and from the immutable place they lived, a place fiercely isolated from an outside world that thrived on change.

Young Harris the village and Young Harris the college brought with it not only these things but a separate conflict that pitted the people of a town that valued work against a campus that valued learning. It was more an unspoken feeling than a declared war but it was there all the same. They were two parallel worlds, thrown together between two mountains. One didn't understand the other. One was suspicious of the other.

Zell Miller walked both sides of that road. He was born into the college, but he lived in the town. His late father had been a teacher. His mother could have taught and his aunt always did. From the day he was born, the college grounds were his backyard and his playground. The faculty was his family at a time when nothing was said about extended families. He was welcome and he knew it.

At the same time, he prayed, played, and studied with people who were not connected to the college. He also learned from them, but it wasn't done in the classroom, it was an education more than could be found in books. He learned about the outdoors by watching Uncle Hoyle set steel traps. He learned about playing ball from Charlie Jenkins and Arnold Keys. He came to know which filling station was Democratic and which was Republican. He could go with his mother and worship with the Methodists, even help her fill the tiny Communion cups with grape juice. Or, he could go with his buddies to the Baptist church, where the fire and brimstone was hotter and the singing was more emotional. It was comfortable. These are things he can't escape.

"Young Harris is a major part of what I was and what I am," Miller says.

Novelist Terry Kay came out of Royston, Georgia, the little town where Ty Cobb learned to sharpen his spikes. The author of the acclaimed *Dance With the White Dog* and *The Year the Lights Came On*, Kay's deeply personal stories depict people and places similar to this part of Georgia. He is well acquainted with Miller. The Georgia governor was even the basis for a character in one of his books.

Not that Kay can claim a first-person understanding of Young Harris. "I'm a hill person," he says, "not a mountain person." It is a distinction heard often in that part of Georgia. His rural background provides insight, however. So does the fact that his brother John is a Young Harris College graduate and for thirteen years pastored Sharp Memorial Methodist Church on the college campus where the chimes are named for Grady Miller.

Kay, the writer, said if he had to use one word to describe mountain people it would be that they are proud – embracing a feeling and attitude that he underscores by lapsing into country dialect: *"We's as good as anybody."*

"It's a pride in what they do and who they are. They might be offended by that, and the word might not set well with them because of the admonition that 'Pride goeth before the fall.' But it is in them, the kind of pride that comes from isolation. Pride that comes from survival being the first order of business. *I survived the winter. I survived the summer. I survived bad crops. I survived the boll weevil. I survived the put-downs. I didn't take charity.* Those things are important, because when you say them you also are saying, *"I did it on my terms. I did it on my own."*

From the beginning, people who settled in the hills originally known as the Cherokee Mountains had to do it on their own. Most of them were Scotch-Irish people who had been driven out of Northern Ireland and Scotland. After reaching America, they moved as far from the coast as the hostile Indians and French would allow. Finally, they reached the peaks and valleys of the

Appalachian Mountains. On their heels came other groups of dissatisfied Protestant immigrants.

Settling in such an isolated locale, they clung to the customs, character and values they brought with them. Cut off from the changes that were going on around them, they became a microcosm of 18th Century culture. They valued their freedom and their inborn spirit. They had loyalty, generosity, dignity, faith and an abiding independence. They also loved the mountains they found in that new land. "Hit's rough and raggedy, but hit's home to us-uns," they would say in their traditional dialect.

Obviously, the mountain range where they settled had taken its name from the Indians who lived throughout the area. Those mountains are among the world's oldest. Geologists estimate that base rocks there date back a billion years. They aren't the tallest in the world, but eight peaks do measure over 4,000 feet. DeSoto, on his expedition through the Southeast, decided against a trip through those mountains. Pioneers who did come were a robust group. Their hardy journeys became part of lore, rhyme and lyric.

A homily of the time depicted a trip to Rabun County: "Go one day by railroad, the next day by horse and buggy, a third on horseback, a fourth day on foot, and then on all-fours until you climb a tree. And when you fall out, you'll be in Rabun County."

A popular verse once told of the first white man who ventured through Rabun Gap. Between the lines, it portrays the prevailing attitude about the Indians who had called the area home. It was repeated by *The Atlanta Constitution's* Pulitzer Prize winning editor Ralph McGill in his 1959 book, *The South and the Southerner.*

> *"Let's lay down boys, and catch a nap,*
> *We got to rest up to make the Rabun Gap.*
>
> *The first white man to cross the Gap*
> *was a Indian tradin' chap*
>
> *Cherokee's hidin' behind every rock*
> *and the flint lost off his old flintstock.*

Know a Indian girl in the Rabun Gap.
She's got chillun as calls me Pap.

So let's lay down boys, and catch a nap.
It's goin' to be fun when we're through the Gap."

Towns County was even more remote and isolated. Gold had been discovered in the mountains in 1828, but that was near Dahlonega to the south in the foothills. The gold rush had little impact up in the craggy mountains. Indian territory had already been shrinking. They were confined to small strip of land that covered North Carolina, Tennessee, and Georgia. By 1839, the entire Cherokee nation was being relocated. Their tragic removal to Oklahoma became known as "The Trail of Tears."

With the Indian influence diminishing, the territory became more attractive. In late 1832, a 319–square–mile area was carved out of Cherokee country. John Thomas, whose descendants still live in the area, was asked by the Georgia Legislature what the new county should be called. "Union," answered Thomas, "for none but Union men reside in it."

Those weren't fighting words then, but thirty years later, they were. As tempers simmered leading up to the Civil War, it was apparent that the residents of North Georgia were not as passionate for the Confederate Cause as their neighbors to the South. In 1860, less than three percent of the slaves in the states worked North Georgia land.

Mountaineers had little in common with the plantation owners to the south of their state where cotton and slaves dominated agriculture. For that reason, when the time came to cross the line in the sand, many people in North Georgia were anti-Secessionists and anti-Civil War. In 1861, Towns County Representative John Corn refused to sign Georgia's Secessionist Act.

Governor Joe Brown, himself a product of that area, was told that his neighbors were not fervent Rebs and that "the blue mountains of Georgia are being filled with Tories and deserters." When the time came to fight, the people of North Georgia were generally loyal to the Confederacy. After the war, however, unlike the rest of the state they erected few memorials to the Lost Cause. That experience further alienated the mountain region from the rest of the state.

Remembering an old-timer who came out of that generation, Ralph McGill wrote about the feeling. "There are two Georgias and many Souths," a mountain resident named Pop Lacey told the late editor. "People in the cotton South had slaves and they didn't learn how to work. Ever since they have been complaining about things and figuring life's been hard because their grand-daddy lost a war."

Young Harris College emerged out of that same background.

The Rev. Artemus Lester was a circuit preacher who rode to his scattered Methodist congregations on the back of a mule and never in his life owned an automobile. In 1884, he was assigned by the North Georgia Conference to a remote mission in Towns County in McTyeire, a small farming town that later became Young Harris. The tiny village wasn't hooked up to the rail line and didn't even have the means to provide an elementary school education. As part of Rev. Lester's mission, he decided to establish a school. It first opened in January of 1886 in a small and abandoned storehouse that belonged to the town physician, Dr. J. H. Stephens.

John Logan was among the local students on that first day of class. He grew up in Brasstown Valley, a mile and a half from the site of the present college. Fifty years later, as the college celebrated its anniversary, he recalled that shivering day for the Wesleyan Christian Advocate. Logan said that the most prized moment in his life was the founding of that tiny college. In 1893, he reached his goal, receiving a degree from Young Harris College. Wrote Logan:

"The sun was shining beautifully that morning. The road was frozen several inches deep, and when thawed was almost impassable. I made this one–and–one-half mile journey on foot. The 'automobile' of those days was an ordinary horse and buggy or an old-time ox wagon. It was nothing unusual for the front axle to scrape the road. Walking was preferable. Old Cedar and Double

Knobs were in their glory that morning. Draped in their polar ermine they seemed to smile upon a lonely lad on his way to gratify the highest ambition of his young heart. Our small clan soon gathered. I say clan advisedly, for Young Harris students are noted the world over for their brotherly love for each other. The very day this institution of learning was born, this spirit of love also came into being. God grant that it may never die."

A year after its founding, the Young L. G. Harris Institute, as it was formally called, was chartered by the Towns County Superior Court. (A court order officially changed the name to Young Harris College in 1957.) In the beginning, the school would have three grades—primary, academic and collegiate. It could issue certificates of proficiency and charge one dollar per month for tuition and one dime each month for incidentals.

The school was named for Harris, an Athens judge and former state legislator who had become a successful insurance company executive. Though he never personally visited the campus, Harris was an early benefactor. A college history said Harris' primary interest was education—"particularly the education of poor boys and girls. The mountain youth of Georgia interested him."

In those early years, it was a school that cared as well as educated. When the boys' dormitory burned in 1931, everyone was told to gather in the chapel so they could see who was missing. The roll was called one name at a time. When the last boy was accounted for, President Joseph Sharp broke down and wept.

Also by design, it was a school that could carry mountain students all the way from the first day of school through four years of college. It would not become a junior college until 1912. Even at the time of its founding, its tuition was too low, and despite the support of the Methodist Church there would always be shortages.

By design, the Methodist school was also strict. There was always a banister running down the middle of the chapel. Boys sat on one side; girls sat on the other. Its early list of rules included demerits for cheating on exams, or for drinking, smoking, fighting, or possessing a deadly weapon. To that list of understandable transgressions was added such sins as being absent from prayers, writing notes to girls, receiving a note without permission, and engaging in extended conversations with the opposite sex.

Similar rules would be part of Young Harris student life for many decades—including the time of Zell Miller. The only concession would be that future school administrators might waive the rules on Sunday afternoons so males and females could socialize.

None of this should imply that Young Harris students were without sin. Hardy students of past generations often found ways of getting around rules, just as their descendants would later. Going off campus to smoke a cigarette, students would throw down an unsmoked butt so someone else could finish it. That was known as "shooting the duck." Passing notes from palm to palm was known as "passing snow." Often those notes would invite a member of the opposite sex to sneak away for a walk to Cupid Falls, a favorite gathering spot for students.

As a professor, Grady Miller had sought to allow boys and girls to talk on campus even though he was concerned about them "pairing-off." He also helped start *The Enotah Echoes,* the school newspaper. Through that newspaper students could write not only about campus life, but also about their own experiences. An article in 1927 showed how isolated the students could be from the world around them. The student wrote of a trip to a faraway place. His making it sound as if he were describing an adventure in an untamed, foreign land. His story was about a trip to Florida. He called it "the chin whiskers of the United States" and said it was inhabited "by Indians, Americans, White Men and what they call 'feed bag tourists' or 'tin-canners' who live on camp grounds."

How could that student long ago know that generations later the people he wrote about in Florida would get even with him for what he wrote. Descendants of the "tin-canners" would come to the mountains to build chalets that teeter on the hillsides of Towns County and the surrounding area.

Ralph McGill wrote about the arrival of the tourists many years ago. He told the story of a fellow who came to Nacoochee Valley and reckoned the reason the Lord made all the piled up mountains between there and North Carolina was to hide hell.

"Now we know better," McGill's friend said. "We know it is to attract the tourist folks."

With the visitors and the outsiders came mistrust. Mountain folks heard their distinctive accents and their folksy phrases mimicked, and their natural ways became the punch lines of jokes. Such attitudes made them even more quiet and standoffish. Stereotypes and myths were common. Knowing that visitors were laughing at them when they got home, locals began to see the newcomer as an intruder. Often the label was well deserved.

Moonshine became one of the symbols outsiders used to describe mountain life. If a person believed the myth, everybody in the hills operated a still and had a jug on the table at every meal. Many did, of course. The legend that says NASCAR drivers are descendants of men who learned to drive fast while hauling illegal brew is basically accurate. On Sundays mountain moonshiners would go to dirt tracks and try to outrun each other instead of the federal agents. But for all its accuracy, it was a stereotype that survived long after its day.

Before the myth of "Thunder Road" and moonshine came the comic strip "Lil' Abner." It depicted a mountain family that fit all the stereotypes. One of the characters was even a typical, bombastic Southern politician. Years later, Zell Miller would write letter after letter to the editor of *The Atlanta Constitution* asking that the comic strip "Snuffy Smith" be removed.

"Snuffy Smith" was a popular comic. In daily newspapers across the country, every day, every panel, old Snuffy was having to avoid those pesky revenuers. Later, when the television sitcom "The Beverly Hillbillies" became Nielsen's number one TV show, viewers saw the Clampett clan take their illegal habit from the Ozarks to California's private domain. When their chores were done, you could always see Jed and Granny sitting by the cement pond enjoying a swig of 'shine.'

This myth isn't new. In 1885, a New York reporter wrote about a friend who tasted the demon brew in Tallulah, Georgia. "He feels as if he were sunburned all over, his head begins to buzz as if a hive of bees had swarmed there," the reporter wrote, "and when he closes his eyes, he sees 600 million torch-light processions all charging at him, ten abreast."

Making moonshine was not the only stereotype, of course. Most of them inferred that mountain people's intelligence was inferior. The novel *No Time for Sergeants* and the movie that followed was the story of a Georgia mountain hick who was forced by his draft board to go into the United States Air Force. He was kind of slow thinking, but as was often the case he was sly, outsmarting the psychiatrists and even the generals.

Andy Griffith made his film debut in the movie, opening the door for his legendary television series. Mayberry was a ficticious North Carolina town and on the fictional map it was near the hills. Often, to the dismay of Deputy Barney Fife who was scared to go there, Sheriff Andy Taylor went into those hills to visit his friends, the Darlings. It was through the Darlings that the sheriff met Ernest T. Bass, a demented mountaineer who would come down from the hills and throw rocks through the windows of pretty town girls he wanted to court.

The Darlings were pickers and grinners as many mountain people are said to be. Sheriff Taylor enjoyed sitting down and playing his guitar and joining in on some good old bluegrass music. Two of the Darling boys were world-class pickers. They never said a word and when the camera zoomed in for a closeup their eyes were hollow. The message was clear: they weren't too bright.

Leave it to James Dickey, a native of Atlanta, to take that image to its lowest point. "Deliverance," the poet's only novel, came out in 1970, but it is the 1972 movie that most people remember. Starring Burt Reynolds, another Georgian, it was the story of suburban Atlanta professionals who decided to test the North Georgia rapids in a canoe. The river is fictional, but Dickey later acknowledged it was the Chattooga, a river that flows near Young Harris. If a person in the theater didn't know their Georgia geography, they would have thought the characters were going to a Third World jungle instead of on a two-hour trip.

In *The New Georgia Guide,* a lengthy look at the state published by the University of Georgia Press and the Georgia

Humanities Council, writer-historian John Inscoe talked about Dickey and about Lewis Medlock, the only character in his book who knew anything about life in the north Georgia outdoors. "Dickey provides what must be the most demeaning characterization of Southern highlanders in modern literature and much of the power of his novel – and the film – lies in his descriptions of the alien and hostile world of the north Georgia mountaineers. 'These are good people,' Medlock tells his companions. 'But they're awfully clannish, they're set in their ways . . . Every family I've met here has at least one relative in the penitentiary. Some of them are in for making liquor or running it, but most of them are in for murder. They don't think a whole lot about killing."

As Dickey's story goes, Medlock was right. Not only were some of his fictional buddies killed, the city guys squealed like a pig as they were sexually attacked by the locals who, in the words of the script, "don't think a whole lot about killing."

As brutal as those scenes were, the one most people remember is that of the boy, the banjo and the porch. Was he a product of mountain inbreeding, or like the Darling boys, was he supposed to be just plain stupid, a bucolic idiot savant? We will never know. All we remember are his hollow eyes and his anemic complexion. But damn, he could play. Mountain folks are like that, you know.

Did Dickey relent? Hardly. "Thinking about that area always gives me the same feeling of excitement and fear," the author said, "a feeling spurred by being in an unprotected situation where the safeties of law and what we call civilization don't apply . . . There are men in those remote parts that'd just as soon kill you as look at you."

In a coincidental response to stereotypes such as Dickey's, educator Eliot Wigginton began his Foxfire project at a private academy near Dillard, Georgia. He began to record local legends and to learn and teach crafts and skills that were almost forgotten, such as quilting and pottery.

"Deliverance powerfully reinforces a stereotype we have been fighting for years, that of the hick with his liquor still, ignorant, depraved, stupid—sometimes laughable," Wigginton wrote in a 1972 issue of his Foxfire magazine.

From projects such as Wigginton's evolved the antithesis of James Dickey as pseudo-mountain crafts became prevalent. This was what one scholar called "the invention of Appalachia." Nevertheless, it called well-deserved attention to talents that otherwise would have been lost. It also gave respect to artisans who had for too long taken for granted their inherited skills.

Misconceptions have not gone away. While the Western hero takes on the stoic stature of a Gary Cooper or a Clint Eastwood, the mountaineer is a laughable Jethro Bodine or is a moronic banjo player. For Zell Miller, it has always been a paradox.

"Mountain people were fiercely independent and one of the ironies of history is that while the cowboy, another type of frontiersman, has been glorified, the mountaineer, the first frontiersman, has been ridiculed and caricatured in the image of Snuffy Smith," Miller once wrote.

For the people who knew Miller's mountains, these are feelings that haven't gone away. It's not just a punchline, it's an attack. On their land. On their surroundings. On them. It's that pride again.

"If you were not born in the hills, you'll never understand. You'll be an outsider. Maybe it's genetic. Maybe it's environmental. I don't know. But it's real," says Terry Kay, who tells the story of a tenant farmer who lived near his family in north Georgia.

"They were good people and good friends. Wallace Carey played football at Royston High School and every day after practice he'd walk all the way home. One day my mother was driving home and she saw Wallace walking on the side of the road. She stopped and said 'Come on, I'll give you a ride.' Wallace turned her down. 'No, ma'am, I'll get your car dirty.' That's pride," Kay said.

That's the brand of pride Zell Miller still has. Especially about his home. "I don't know how to explain it. Most folks from my generation feel that way. It's where I'm comfortable. I'm kind of uncomfortable anywhere else. I'm part of those mountains. It's where I'm supposed to be. It has a permanence about it," he says.

Years ago, Stephen Vincent Benet, the author of "John Brown's Body," forecast a change to such permanent things. He could see a world that had no room for the pioneer.

"One need not weep romantic tears for them, but when the last moonshiner buys his radio, and the last lost rabbit of a girl is civilized with a mail order dress, something will pass that is American and all the movies will not bring it back," he wrote.

Benet's vision was correct. Mountain people today not only have radios, they have satellite dishes. From channels delivered by those dishes women can order store-bought dresses. Something has passed, and the mountains of today are not the same mountains. Gut-level emotions have not changed, though. It is said today that the best way to make a Georgia mountain resident mad is to shoot his dog or tell him you're from Florida.

Young Harris itself has, so far, escaped the invaders, but down Georgia 76 in Hiawassee, the Towns county seat, there are condos, cable and change. The old life has given way to the new. There are many well-traveled highways, including Georgia Highway 515, Zell Miller Parkway, a project that some of his old friends fought against. So, instead of retiring to Florida mobile home developments decorated with artificial palm trees, retirees from all over the country are flocking into north Georgia. The region's slow-paced history has given way to what supporters and residents alike trust is controlled progress. Many of these things have come about on Miller's watch and with his guidance. Miller tries to keep this in perspective. "Of all the great things that have happened and are planned, all are dwarfed by the enduring grandeur of the mountains themselves," he says.

Along with progress comes growth. Many of the people moving there are senior citizens. In Towns County alone, twenty-four percent of the 6,754 residents are sixty-five years of age or older, according to the 1990 United States Census. The median age in Towns was forty-three in 1990—the oldest in Georgia and the only county where the mark has passed the age of forty.

As the area becomes a retirement haven, the work force and the economy are changing. So is the political base—in a part of

Georgia that has always had a strong two-party tradition. That was never more evident than in 1994 when Zell Miller was seeking his second term as governor. He received sixty percent of the vote in his home county of Towns but lost neighboring counties such as Franklin, Murray and Whitfield—counties he had carried four years before.

Mindful of those changes, a reporter from Columbus went to Towns County for election day that year. He had planned to spend the night before in Young Harris. He couldn't wake up the sleeping motel manager, and had to check into a place down the road in Hiawasee. As the sun came up that Tuesday, he made his way back to Young Harris. Looking around him as he drove, he was surprised to see the roof tops of pricey condos hanging on the hillsides. When he visited the area years before and Zell Miller had toured him through his childhood history, those places weren't there. Neither were many of the people who would be voting in the mountains that day. That's why the newsman had come. Before he went to bed that night at the Colony Square Hotel in Atlanta, the reporter would either write about a governor getting re-elected or about Zell Miller's final day in politics. He wouldn't write the ending. Georgia would—at ballot boxes all over the state.

Stopping for breakfast at a small cafe across from the Young Harris College campus, the visitor listened to locals who were enjoying politics with their eggs and country ham. Those who hadn't voted were on their way and those who had were warning folks that, though it was early, there was a crowd at the grade school where Young Harris goes to vote. The reporter was finishing his last cup of coffee when a man and woman came in and went to the nearest vacant table. Everybody seemed to know them so he decided to disturb them before their breakfast got to the table, to see what people were saying about the hometown candidate. Walking to their table, he introduced himself, said he was from the newspaper in Columbus and that he'd like to ask some questions about the election. They looked at each other and asked him to repeat his name. He did, and casually asked if they were Zell Miller supporters. "Today will be the first time I've ever voted for him," the woman said.

Before he asked any more questions, the couple introduced themselves. They were Red and Jane Ross. They had never voted for Zell Miller before because until recently they had lived in Birmingham, Alabama. Like so many others, they had retired to the mountains. Only, this was home for them. When they returned, Red Ross opened up a shop not far off the main highway where he repaired golf clubs. And by the way, Jane Ross told the embarrassed reporter, she was Zell Miller's sister.

The reporter laughed and joined them for a few minutes before he had to excuse himself and go to the school house where Miller soon would be arriving. Jane Ross, like her mother and her aunt, had been a school teacher. She told the reporter about visiting her younger brother at the governor's mansion in Atlanta. She shared memories of when the school debates stirred up so much attention at the college across the road. She asked him if he had ever seen the house their mother built. She told him that both of Zell's boys lived there in Young Harris, that Matt was on the city council and Murphy was the only lawyer in town. When their breakfast was delivered, the reporter was ready to leave. He said his good-byes and after Jane Ross's stories he took a detour past the fabled rock house that Birdie built before he went to the elementary school.

Like the old fellow at the cafe had warned, there was a crowd milling around the school. The Columbus reporter wasn't alone. Several other news people were there, even a cameraman from a nearby cable TV company. Someone announced that Zell and Shirley would soon be there and hearing that some people who had finished voting stayed around to see them, adding to a growing crowd in back of the building. There was a self-appointed greeting party there, composed of the local state representative and a former House member who had retired to the hills. Off to the side was a group of old men who made leaning on the back of a pickup look natural.

Without warning, a commotion broke out in front of the school house. People gathered around to see the governor. Growing up there, his family didn't even own a car. Now he had come by plane to the airport in nearby Blairsville. With his first administration winding to a close and a second term up to the voters, he came back to cast his ballot for governor. He certainly could have gotten an absentee ballot, but election tradition requires candidates to get out early and cast their own votes—secret of course. He was running against Guy Millner, a Republican, and the founder of the Norrell Agency, a business that provides temporary help. It was Millner's first time on a ballot and if money would insure votes he seemed to have a bright future in politics.

Miller went around to the back door of the school like everybody else. But first he had to go over to that pickup. "You know who this man is?" Miller asked the out of town reporter. "This is Hoyle Bryson. You should have seen him hit a baseball." Bryson is Miller's uncle and he fed Miller many a meal at a time when there was no airport nearby. An unmarked aide motioned to the governor that they needed to stay on schedule. First there was an impromptu news conference at the foot of the steps. Then it was time for him and Shirley to go in. Trailed by a noisy entourage of reporters and photographers, he went inside, saying good-bye to his uncle and hello to his sister.

He was the governor of Georgia. He was voting in the precinct his mother once managed, in the schoolhouse where his grandchildren were in elementary school, across the highway from the school that awarded him two diplomas, down the road from the childhood home. His name headed the Democratic Party ballot that morning. The President of the United States called him by his first name.

Standing in line, a Young Harris voter glanced at the mob and had one question.

"Which one's the governor?"

3

SCHOOL DAYS AT THE VARSITY

After awhile, they came to expect him. Every morning, there he was. Before the doors opened. He was shy. He didn't say much. He stayed out of the way. He would just show up, find the morning newspaper, then read it all—starting with the sports pages. He got there before the hungry customers. Before men in funny paper hats barked out orders in a language that might as well have been foreign.

Whattaya have? Whattaya have? . . . Two naked steaks and a NIPC! . . . Walk it through the garden! Whattaya drinking? . . . Two dogs walking and a large PC! Whattaya have? Whattaya have?

Other kids went to school. Zell Miller went to The Varsity. One by one, the flamboyant carhops would show up and the kid would join them. He liked their style. In his whole life, he had never been around African-Americans and they fascinated him. When they started pitching pennies at the line, he joined them. If they played ball with a bunch of Georgia Tech students, he wanted to play. He wasn't in school, but he was getting an education you couldn't get from books.

He was ten years old. His sister Jane, six years older, had graduated from high school and she convinced her mother that the two of them ought to get jobs in Atlanta. It was wartime, 1942, and they were hired to make buckles for gas masks at Southern

Aviation Company. The factory was on North Avenue, near the Tech campus.

For Birdie Miller, this move was a chance to get out of debt. The loan she had secured to buy that rocky land gnawed at her. She didn't like being beholden to anyone. She may not have been born a mountain person but she shared their obsession for independence.

A kid in the fifth grade didn't share those needs. Young Harris was his world. The only trips he had ever taken were to South Carolina, to visit his mother's family. He couldn't imagine living anywhere else—much less a big place like Atlanta. It might as well have been the Emerald City.

Miller had never seen a train, and the only buses he saw were loaded with college students. His mother didn't own a car and not many people he knew had an automobile. He lived next to the only highway in town, the highway between Blairsville and Hiawassee. It was a road so lonesome that a boy could take a piece of chalk, draw the lines for a game of hop-scotch and, while he and his friends played, they would never be disturbed by a passing car.

On his face is a reminder of those days and that road. "There was a deep open ditch between the road and our house. I was on my tricycle going down the steep hill and I couldn't stop. I ran off in the ditch, hit a rock and cut myself bad. Mama picked me up and took me inside. Nobody thought about stitches then and I've still got that scar between my eyebrows. The point is, you could ride your tricycle right out there on the highway," Miller says.

When the talk of moving to Atlanta began, he was a fifth-grader at the old Young Harris School. It was a four-roomed building, heated by a pot-bellied stove. Students paid seventy-five cents a year for heat or else brought a load of wood. The bigger boys chopped the wood between classes. There was no cafeteria. Students brought something to eat in brown paper "pokes," or in lard buckets that had holes punched in the lid. Some of the kids went home for lunch. Miller soon decided to tote his lunch since that meant more time to play games on the school grounds with his friends.

There was an outdoor toilet much bigger and nastier than the one at home which intimidated the five-year old Miller the first time he used it. He was so scared that he ran to his house so he would be in more familiar surroundings. When his teacher, Mrs. Maude Potts, reported him missing, Principal Frank Erwin sent out a search party. They finally found him at home.

Bert Lance was one of Miller's elementary school classmates. His father was the college president and the two boys had become friends long before they started to the first grade in Mrs. Potts' class. "Zell is my lifelong friend," says Lance, now a banker in Calhoun, Georgia. "We shared one of those double desks in the first grade. I remember I had a chance to skip the second grade and go directly to the third grade. I would not go. Not if Zell wasn't going."

It was a good place to be a boy. Arnold Keys would get the young guys together to play baseball. Miller's next–door uncle, Hoyle Bryson, could teach the finer points of fishing and hunting. At night, you could snatch lightning bugs out of the darkness and lock them away in a fruit jar. Maybe once or twice a year, there would be a trip in the back of a truck to Murphy, North Carolina for a western movie.

Sure, it was fun. But for Zell Miller, barefoot in his overalls and his cousin's cutdown shirts, it was also safe. People there at home knew Grady Miller. A lot of them had sat in his classroom, he was their Dean. They knew the story of Birdie and her house and her kids. They knew Aunt Verdie, and Jane, and Zell. Outside the Towns County line was a world that threatened a ten year-old boy who had spent all his life amid people and places he knew.

Outside was Atlanta. Not suburban Atlanta. Downtown Atlanta. Up the street was the Fox Theater with its twinkling marquee and enough seats so that a young boy figured the entire town of Young Harris could sit down together and watch a movie. Streetcars clattered down the tracks and you could hear car horns blowing all night long. It was another world, one where Zell Miller would be living without a net.

The family's first apartment in Atlanta was at 920 Cypress Street. His mother enrolled him at the Clark Howell Elementary School on nearby 10th street. "They laughed at me and the way I talked," he says. "I was laughed at for calling the brown paper bag in which I carried my lunch a 'poke,' and for saying I was 'toting' it rather than carrying it." Two days later, he came home and told his mother that he was quitting. "I refused to go anymore," he says. "I was that uncomfortable."

They soon moved to another apartment at 728 Spring Street just blocks away from The Varsity, a drive-in restaurant which even in 1942 was an Atlanta landmark. Birdie found them a place in a house with four apartments and one bathroom. Having one bathroom didn't bother them. At least it was inside the house. Jane slept on the couch and Zell in the bed with his mother. The roof over the bed was so low that you couldn't stand up on one side of the bed. You had to crawl across the bed to get out.

His mother told him that since they had moved, he would be going to Williams Street Elementary School. Reminding him how important an education was, she took him to the new school. Again, he didn't feel he fit in, that the other kids were looking down on him .

This time he stayed two weeks and this time he didn't tell his mother that he had quit going. "I just plain hated Atlanta. That first year, all I could think about was going home. I was not a happy camper and I gave my mama a real hard time. I was extremely uncomfortable anywhere but Young Harris," he says.

Zell Miller spent most of that school year on the streets of Atlanta. Not long after they arrived, Birdie took a job at the Bell Bomber Plant, a huge operation that after the war became Lockheed. It was in Cobb County, near Marietta, which in those days was not an easy commute. She had to leave very early to catch up with her carpool. Jane was also working, and from her job she went directly to the Georgia Evening School, the forerunner of Georgia State University.

Zell Miller was on his own.

He was a street kid, a latchkey kid before there were latchkey kids. That's when he made The Varsity his headquarters. Founded in 1928 at the corner of Spring Street and North Avenue, this drive-in restaurant was a haven for Georgia Tech students who studied engineering only a block away. On fall Saturdays, it was tradition to have a couple of chili dogs before crowding into Grant Field to watch the Yellow Jackets play football. Coca-Cola's international headquarters was not far away, and The Varsity claimed to be the world's largest consumer of bottled Cokes.

At the crowded Varsity, the young Zell could lose himself. No one compared him to Grady. The carhops soon adopted the soft-spoken youngster. They were a lively group. Since they were in competition for tips, many of them took on trademark personas and outrageous images. It was a group that later graduated Atlantan Nipsy Russell from the drive-in lot to the network television stage as a comedian. These fellows became the insecure boy's buddies.

He would play pitch with them for hours—either a ball or pennies. We'd pitch at the line all the time," Miller says, referring to a penny-ante game of chance where people tried to throw their coin closest to the line.

One time he won enough money gambling—about five or six dollars—"that I went down to Reeder & McGaughey, a big sporting goods store close to Five Points, and bought a fancy pair of basketball shoes. They cost four dollars and something. My mother wanted to know where I got the money and I told her a lie. I said I saved it. I couldn't tell her I won it gambling."

Not all of his time was spent wagering. Next to The Varsity was a vacant lot and Miller would join the carhops and the Tech students on the softball diamond. He had the confident hands of an infielder, he discovered. Sometimes he headed for Piedmont Park and went swimming. Other days, he might go to the Fox Theater where he could lean back and look at the stars flickering on the ceiling and take off his shoes and squish his toes into the lush carpet. Discovering a lasting love for movies, he came to love the escape he found in Hollywood's version of reality.

"I didn't have an anchor," he says. "I left that in Young Harris." The mountains were an anchor, but in her own way so was Birdie. She was making more money than she ever had in her hard-working life, only she was sending as much as she could back to the bank in Hiawassee to pay off the note on their land. Sometimes she couldn't stretch the money she and Jane were making from week to week. When she needed money, Miller would do what he could to help, sometimes selling coat-hangers he had collected to a laundry on Techwood Avenue. He worked at Planter's giving out free peanuts and had an Atlanta Journal paper route every afternoon, riding his bicycle through the neighborhood near the Tech campus.

"One day, carrying the paper, I wrecked my bike," he remembers. "I went into the old Biltmore Hotel on West Peachtree Street and this man took one look at me and said, 'You're hurt. You've got a broken arm.' He wanted to know where I lived and I told him I lived three blocks away. He couldn't understand that my mother wasn't going to be home for awhile so he took me home. I waited there for hours, it seemed, until she got home. I was hurting. She took me to Crawford Long Hospital that night and they put it in a cast."

Not everything about that year was bad. There were Sundays at the Grant Park Zoo and picnics at Piedmont Park. There was a memorable meal at the Biltmore Hotel and once at Davison-Paxon's, later to evolve into Macy's. They bought some smoked salmon at the spacious store on Peachtree Street and put it on a charge card because they had no cash to go to a grocery store and it was two days until payday.

On Sundays in the spring, Birdie took her children on streetcar adventures through the city. In those years, they were an adventure since the cars jumped the tracks as often as they stayed on them. They would ride to the end of the line, all the way through Buckhead or out toward Emory University. They would admire the lush dogwoods that turned the neighborhoods into Technicolor displays. They would look at the stately old houses that dated back to another era. When the trolley reached the end of the line, they would turn the backs of their seats around and ride back to their miniature apartment.

Miller still remembers those Sunday afternoons and the unspoken lessons Birdie was delivering to her son and daughter. "My mother would tell us 'Work hard, save your money and you can have a house like that.' Looking back, I find it very significant that she said 'work hard' not 'Those rich folks don't pay enough taxes' or 'We're not as good as they are.' "

Sometimes on a summer night, when there was money in Birdie's pocket, the three of them would walk to Ponce de Leon Ball Park to see the Atlanta Crackers play. Back home, he had loved playing ball and he worshipped his Uncle Hoyle, who everybody in the mountains knew had once played minor league baseball. But the baseball Miller was seeing now was different. These were fellows whose names you could find in the box score in the next morning's *Constitution*.

Without knowing it, he was developing a passion that would never leave him. Only the stately magnolia tree that guarded centerfield of Ponce deLeon ball field remains and there's a parking lot where the diamond used to be, but five decades later Miller still remembers the players he saw that season. This was more than twenty-five years before major league sports came to Atlanta and, at the time, nobody really cared. There was no TV, so the only thing they knew about those big leaguers was what they read in the paper or saw on a newsreel. All folks in Atlanta cared about was whether the Crackers were good enough to beat those hated Birmingham Barons.

The Crackers were the New York Yankees of baseball's minor leagues, winning pennants year after year. More than that, for a ten-year-old like Miller, there was a mystical charm about what he saw, smelled and heard at the old wooden ball park. There were banks of lights that gave the night a smoky hue. There was the aroma of buttered popcorn. There was the hawking of the vendors coming through the stands and the unintelligible chatter of the infielders. What he saw on the diamond was magical. The infield looked as if it had been manicured with a pair of tweezers.

Graceful centerfielders would climb a bank that terraced up in straight-away center and snag flyballs before they were lost in that magnolia tree. In rightfield, behind the tiers of colorful fences, was a railroad track. Train engineers would slow to a crawl so they could see a few pitches as they passed. One night, a Cracker power hitter slammed a homerun into a freight train that was creeping in the right-field darkness. The next day, a sportswriter said it was the longest ball he had ever seen hit—that it went all the way to Nashville. Down the left field line sat Zell Miller.

"I never took a street car. I always walked down Ponce de Leon Avenue to the park, just across from that big Sears store. I never sat under the grandstand. I would sit in the left-field bleachers. Everybody out there would be betting. You could put up a penny and if it was a fly ball, you got five. I guess I was continuing my education," Miller laughs.

Miller would become a lifelong student of baseball and the unpredictable characters who played the game. Later he would be a baseball coach himself. But for a young boy searching for an identity of his own, baseball had a value that went beyond the nuance of a hit-and-run. It taught him to read the paper everyday, to pore over box scores, to delve into game stories, and to distinguish between a monotone sentence that lay flat on the page and another that had a well-turned phrase. Mainly, baseball belonged to him—not the late dean of the college and not to his mother and her house of rocks.

In a boyish way he was conquering Atlanta, and without knowing it he had begun to conquer a ghost that had followed him since he was seventeen days old. People on Spring Street didn't know who Grady Miller was—or care. They didn't know where Young Harris was—or care. They didn't even care that this boy they kept seeing alone on the downtown streets was not in school.

Looking back at the events of that year, Miller knows his life could have gone in another direction. Left alone in a city, a youngster without direction might not have survived. Says Miller: "I look around at kids in trouble all the time and I think, 'There but for the grace of God go I.' "

That school term long ago, he proved to himself that he had an ability to face things and not run. There would be other times in his life when he felt inferior and uncomfortable—some of them in that very city. But after that year, he knew he could make it. He had come to Atlanta and he had survived. Without knowing it, Zell Miller was slowly growing into Zell Miller.

None of that was on his mind, however, when Birdie Miller figured out at last that he had not been going to school. Maybe she had been too busy to notice. Maybe she knew all along. Maybe she decided to herself that her sheltered son needed to experience a life he had never known in the mountains, away from the burdens he carried there, away from the expectations. Miller will never know, but he does remember the day she asked him about his report card.

"That's how she figured it out, the fact that she hadn't been seeing any report cards," he says. "But I also think she was just letting me go. I was so uncontrollable."

Something was different that next school year. He was at Luckie Street Elementary School. He went to school and his grades were good. Many of the students lived in the Techwood-Clark Howell Homes, a public housing project that was on Techwood Drive near Grant Field. Techwood was the nation's first attempt at public housing. President Franklin D. Roosevelt had come to Atlanta to make the dedicatory address. Miller didn't know the history. All he knew was that he liked the boys he met there. They shared a love of baseball too. Since they liked to play so much, Miller urged them to start a team and he became the manager. The caps they bought were red, so they became The Red Caps. That scrappy team went on to win the championship of the fourteen-and-under city recreation league.

An eleven-year-old kid in 1943 knew nothing about public assistance. He wouldn't have understood too much about what it meant to live in a housing project. Certainly there was no stigma attached to the kids who lived in Techwood.

Miller, in fact, wanted to move there. "It was brick. You had your *own* bathroom. I'd go into a friend's apartment and I'd think it was the greatest place I'd ever seen. I wished we could live there.

I don't know why we didn't. Maybe it was the fact that two members of our family were working. All I knew was that it was a great place to live," he says.

Only now, after nearly three years in Atlanta, it was time to go home. Though they had adjusted to the new surroundings, the Millers always knew where home was. They had gone to Young Harris for each of the Christmases they had been in Atlanta, keeping a family tradition that has never ended. Jane Miller wouldn't be going back with them, though. She was enrolling at LaGrange College, where their Aunt Verdie had been teaching since leaving Young Harris College.

When Uncle Fletcher came to pick them up and move them home, he had a load. Their possessions were in cardboard boxes that were tied to the chairs with rope. Joining them was a pet chicken named Winston and a green snake that had no name. When the pickup was filled with their belongings, it looked like the Joads in *Grapes of Wrath,* loading up a beat-up old truck to leave Oklahoma for California.

Back home, it was as if they had never been away. Miller picked up with his friends, going to the creek, swimming, fishing—whatever mountain kids did. As the war came to a close and the veterans started returning, Arnold Keys reappeared. He decided to start a baseball team for the boys under age fourteen. There had always been a hard-nosed town team, but that was for the men. When Keys got the other boys together, they soon found that the tentative baseball player that had gone to Atlanta had returned a confident ball player. But it was more than just a knowledge of a boy's game that was different. He had seen a part of the world they had never seen, indeed didn't know existed. He was stronger, tougher and street smart. "All of that was good for me," said Miller.

Birdie Miller returned to Young Harris with a dream to build a basement on that house she had never completed. Pretty soon she and Verdie Shook, an eighty-five pound neighbor woman, were digging and hauling dirt from under the house. There was another piece of business weighing on Birdie's mind. "I can remember long before we went to Atlanta going with her to the bank to borrow money. I guess they trusted her or maybe they felt sorry for her," Miller says. "After we got home from living in Atlanta ... after she went to the bank and paid off that note ... she was proud. 'Now,' she said, 'I can dig where I want to.'" Zell Miller didn't know it, but he was about to learn that he could also dig where he wanted to dig.

4

EDNA FINDS A HOME

Edna Herren arrived with a flower in her hair. There was something about her. The way she looked with that pile of dark hair. The way she presented herself. The burning respect she had for words and how they were used. The passion she delivered for putting every comma in its God-given position, a passion that was somewhere between a zealot and a terrorist: the demand for perfection—for her students and herself; the mystery and the legend that went with the flower; the aroma of her intoxicating perfume that arrived in class before she did and stayed after she was gone.

For Zell Miller, an awkward adolescent boy who looked at life as a nine-inning game, Edna Herren was a discovery. "There was an electricity about her. I smelled that scent and I had to know what it was," he says. "It was White Shoulders. I was smitten."

She came to Young Harris in 1948, to teach English and speech. Unmarried, she lived in an apartment on campus and soon became one of the busiest people on the faculty. She directed plays. She worked on debates and she was the faculty advisor to both the school newspaper and the annual. She was the sponsor of the Phi Chi Debating Society. All of this in addition to a full teaching load.

She worked, and she expected her students to work. A student had never been graded on a theme or a paper until one was marked by Herren. Sometimes after she was through, there would be more of her ink on the page than the student's. She was also intimidating. Shirley Carver—now Mrs. Zell Miller—remembers being summoned to Herren's office and how she stood in front of her trembling. That Zell was her "pet" was well known on campus, a fact that some students resented—particularly those who had to follow him in various assignments.

Much has been said by Zell Miller and others about what Herren meant to the students at Young Harris, but Hilda Dyches, one of her oldest friends, says few knew what that short five-year stay meant to Edna Herren. A native of Rutledge, Georgia, Herren was orphaned at an early age and was reared by her grandmother and her aunts. Her childhood was an emotional struggle. Even her own cousins would often remind her that they had a mother and father—she didn't.

"She longed for parents," Dyches says. "That's why she set such difficult tasks for her students and for herself. She was a stickler, so very structured. A little violation or deviation was a venial sin to her."

Her childhood reminded her of Zell Miller's. "She needed to be needed," says Dyches, the retired head of the speech and drama department at Georgia State University. "Young Harris was the closest thing to home she ever had. It was the most rewarding experience of her life and career. There's something about your first group as a teacher. You bond with those students. You remember them. Edna had all of those experiences at Young Harris."

The teenager who was so smitten with her wouldn't have asked about those things nor would Herren have realized how special those moments would become. What they would have agreed on was that the first few years after Miller came home from Atlanta were undistinguished at best. For the first two years he was in high school, he was too timid to even have his picture taken for the yearbook. He had no direction or goals—only baseball. Everywhere he went, he carried his baseball glove. "I didn't care about school or girls," he says. "Or smoking tobacco. All I cared about was baseball."

He was floundering. His Aunt Verdie sensed his insecurities, and even after she became Dean of Women at LaGrange College she continued to encourage him by long distance, sending books and even signing him up for a correspondence course. "She was a combination father-figure, friend, confidante, idol and awesome taskmaster who could be as gentle as an angel and as stern as a judge. She was more than an aunt, and I loved her more than anyone else except my mother," Miller once said of Aunt Verdie who died in 1970.

For an adolescent boy with confidence, even the heroic aunt who used to haul him all over the mountains in her car could be a problem. People at school and in town were forever asking about Aunt Verdie, just like they reminded him how they remembered Professor Miller. There was no escape.

Into that breech came Edna Herren. Giving in to pressure and tradition, in his third year of high school Miller joined the Phi Chi Debating Society—just like his father . "It was expected of me," he says. Even with the expectations, his reason for signing up was not entirely admirable. In addition to debates, the Phi Chis and the Young Harris Debating Society competed in football, basketball and baseball. If he wanted to play, he had to join.

He did not go to society meetings very often, knowing that every week someone gave a speech and participated in a debate. Worse than that, after the speaker had finished, the other members critiqued. As fragile as Zell was, he couldn't imagine sitting there for anything like that. Someone—it could have been Herren— noticed that skinny Miller kid hadn't participated in a debate, so he was told to prepare a debate on inflation. He had two weeks. For him, it was either the shortest or longest two weeks he had ever spent.

Some of the pressures Miller felt were not imagined. Debating had been an integral part of Young Harris life since 1887, the second year of the school. So was public speaking. The Young Harris Society was founded that year and the annual championship debate began soon afterward. In 1890, following a dispute over the previous year's winner, the Phi Chi Society was chartered. The new group won the championship its very first year. As the years passed and rivalries grew, there were always arguments over which society had won the most often. Among the Phi Chi champions had been Grady Miller, Class of 1912.

Young Harris took pride in preparing ministers and teachers, and it was believed that elocution and forensics would be a benefit to both professions. But before long, it didn't matter how well you spoke or how strong your case was. It was all about winning and losing. "It was like the Tech-Georgia game," Zell Miller says.

The championship debate was the culmination of a year of competition. It was traditionally a part of graduation week. In the early years of the school people would come by covered wagon and camp out on the school grounds until the day of the graduation ceremony. Each society had its following, and allegiances were so strong that fist-fights would break out in the hallway before and after the events. The debaters were aware of the atmosphere. To avoid the friction, some would climb up into the hills to rehearse their presentations. The echoes of their voices could be heard in the valley as they practiced their inflections.

Even before he was a teen-ager, Miller knew more than most about these things. For him, it was family lore as well as school tradition. He had heard the legends and the stories. He remembered how a local man had called long distance from overseas during World War II to find out who had won the debate.

As a young boy, he had seen it for himself. "I remember as a child that chapel was always packed full," he says. "There were people standing outside listening, sitting in the windows, standing in the back. It was a huge, huge thing."

During that two-week wait before his own debut as a debater Miller couldn't help but think about what this simple speech meant to him, to Birdie, to the memory of his father, and to Edna Herren, who was quietly telling him that he could be more than he thought he could be. "She was regal, eloquent," says Jack Brinkley, a Phi Chi champion in 1949 and later a United States

Congressman from Georgia. "She really wanted you to improve. She would correct our pronunciation. I would say 'gen-u-wine,' and she trained me to say genuine. She had a good heart. You couldn't see love demonstrated, but obviously it was love, a commitment to all of us." Miller adds, "When Miss Herren taught, it was like turning on a light. Without realizing it, I enjoyed the printed word, but I had never really fallen in love with literature until Edna Herren. She made it live. It was the way she read it aloud. I liked that. But I loved her."

"She was Zell's mentor," says O. V. Lewis, who still teaches accounting at Young Harris and who for years was a close friend of Herren's. "She saw what he could become." Birdie was beginning to see something in him, too. She could see he was terrified as he worked on that speech, but she could also see how hard he was working. And not on baseball. He had written and rewritten the speech and after giving it over and over in front of a mirror, his mother became his audience. He wasn't sure if he was happy, but she was. Her Zell was doing what she wanted him to do the most.

Finally, the day in January of 1948 arrived. Miller felt like he was pale, trembling and that his knees were shaking. The debate was in the Reid Building, named for the lawyer who had spoken at his father's campus memorial. Miller's goal was simple: not to embarrass either himself or his mother.

"When it was announced my side had won, all of a sudden, like the clouds parting and the sun shining through, I awoke to the exhilaration of having an audience listening to what I was saying and applauding. I must have done better than I thought because, when the champion debaters were chosen a few weeks later, I was elected an alternate," Miller said.

What he said that day wasn't important. Nor was it important that his team won, though to a competitive person like Miller winning was never something you discounted. Those inner feelings he described made that event an important intersection in his life. He liked the rush the applause gave him. Even more than that, he noticed they were listening to what he said. It followed that if people were going to listen, he better have something to say, he had better prepare. He had found a goal that now belonged to him. He also found on that stage a confidence that he did not know he had.

It was a confidence that would grow. Edna Herren would see to that. By the spring of that year, a debater left and Miller became one of the Phi Chi debaters in the championships. The topic was "Resolved: That Federal Aid to Education Should Be Adopted." Joined by a pair of college upperclassmen, Luke Dorris and Clyde Lee Jr., Miller and the Phi Chis won the spring event. It was his first of four championships.

The Young Harris Debating Society had chosen the topic so the Phi Chi team elected to take the affirmative side. In 1948, supporting federal aid to education was considered a liberal stance, something Miller would experience several times during those next four years. Ironically, sixteen years later, when Miller was a candidate for Congress, that same issue would play a vital role in the campaign.

William Henry Duckworth had grown up in Choestoe with Grady Miller, and after graduating from Young Harris he went on to become Chief Justice of the Georgia Supreme Court. Many alumni returned for the debates, and after hearing young Zell take the liberal side, he had a word of caution. "I hope you're not believing all this stuff you're saying," Duckworth warned. Miller says those debates reshaped his life. "We'd practice and practice— up at Cupid Falls, down at my house, early in the morning in the chapel before the wake-up bell rang. Miss Herren brought out the best in us."

Miller was still in high school, but he was participating in activities with the college students. Herren was the faculty advisor to *The Enotah Echoes* and he worked on the school paper every year, becoming first sports editor then editor. Herren was the advisor to the yearbook and he worked on it, also rising to editor. Herren was advisor to Phi Chi and he became active, serving as society president three times and as captain of all of its sports teams. Herren directed student plays and he starred as Mel White, a reporter in "False Colors."

Like Birdie, he never ran short of energy. If there was an office to seek, he ran. If there was a team, he played. Young people coming out of high school today see such activities as a way of impressing major universities, a way to flesh out their resume. Miller was getting his ticket punched for other reasons. In the beginning, it was to please other people; along the way he found he was pleasing himself.

Baseball was still a big part of his life. In the summers he played on the town team. As a young child, he had been the bat boy. Hoyle Bryson, his uncle, was always one of their key players and Zell worshipped the older man and dreamed that one day he would get a chance to play professional baseball. Uncle Hoyle was one of the first of many men in his life that Miller would call a surrogate father. It was a fast league with teams in Georgia, Tennessee, and North Carolina. Later he would be the manager, decide the lineup, and play second base and shortstop. He would lead off, his uncle would hit third, and his cousins Bryan and Bob Bryson were fourth and seventh. This was big stuff. A kid telling those guys who had been in World War II where they hit in the batting order was not easy. But Miller took charge. "I've been told I was always like that," Miller says.

He also continued to be a leader at the podium. In 1949 he joined two more upperclassmen, Brinkley and Guy Sharpe, as Phi Chi's championship debaters. Brinkley had come to Young Harris from Bainbridge, Georgia to play basketball and to prepare himself for Harvard Law School. All he knew about debating he had learned from reading Perry Mason novels. Sharpe, born in Florida, came to the mountains from Atlanta's Tech High School by way of Emory University, where he had trouble explaining his grades to his father.

"I started over again at Young Harris and did two years in four quarters," says Sharpe, later one of the most popular broadcasters in Atlanta television. Sharpe and Brinkley adopted the younger Miller. "Zell was the kid brother, the rising star," Brinkley says. "Everybody liked him. He was so gifted, he spoke with such passion, with all the right inflections. He could memorize anything by just reading it over and over." The three of them went to Murphy, North Carolina to be fitted for their tuxedos for, following tradition, all of the debaters were to be dressed in formal wear. Herren worked patiently with them. They worked together. It was a night each of them still remembers.

Brinkley was the first to speak. *"Mr. Chairman, honorable judges, gentlemen of the opposition and friends. The question for debate this evening is: Resolved, that government ownership of present day radio facilities would be more desirable than private ownership."* Sharpe followed. Miller gave the rebuttal.

Years later, Brinkley still has a wrinkled copy of his part. He laughs at how concerned they were that Sharpe wouldn't know his remarks, that he would try and rely on his natural glibness. "I didn't know it until forty-eight hours before the debate," Sharpe confesses. "I went up to Double Knobs and I must have stayed there eight hours. That wasn't where you went to learn a speech. That was where you sneaked away with a girl. But when I came down, I knew that speech." "He was gang-busters," Brinkley says of Sharpe, who was a Methodist minister before getting into broadcasting, first in radio, then in television. Both of them marvel at the oratory gifts of the young Miller. "I'll say this," Sharpe shares. "He's a good speaker now, but he was better back then." As for Brinkley, he says Miller's young voice was pure, "the golden voice of William Jennings Bryan."

For Miller there were many honors at Young Harris. "I just stayed around a long time," says Miller, discounting those activities. "It was one thing to do all of those things in two or three years. But I was there all through high school and two years of college. I just wouldn't go away." Staying around and not going away would later be a political lesson for him.

Brinkley, who was elected to the House of Representatives, came back home after his time in Congress and now shares a quiet Columbus, Georgia law practice with his son. He says Young Harris classmates always knew there was something special about Miller. In 1982, Brinkley—the dean of the Georgia Congressional Delegation—retired after representing the Third District for fifteen years. Two years later, he was invited to deliver the Zell Miller Lecture at Young Harris, an annual address that was begun by Edna Herren. At the time, his fellow debater was lieutenant governor.

Back on the familiar campus, Brinkley talked about the time he and Miller had spent together there. "Zell Miller has always been Mr. Young Harris to many of us. He was in high school when I was here, and on the last page of my yearbook there is a line across the page about half way down with Zell's notation: 'Reserved for Zell Miller!' The trouble is, Zell never filled it in. It is an unfinished page. There is an analogy here. Zell Miller, in my judgment, has an unfinished page in state or national government—if he chooses to pursue it," Brinkley said that day at the Susan B. Harris Chapel.

For Brinkley, those days at Young Harris College were important. "We got a participatory education," he says. "We knew our leaders and more importantly they knew us. It was a friendship. They were trying to shape us to do well in school and in life." Those years were also important for Miller. He was learning for himself the importance of education. With the people he had come into contact with as a boy around the Young Harris campus, education was taken for granted. At his home, it was also a given. There was his father, his mother and his aunt. Later there was his sister Jane. After graduating from LaGrange College and marrying William "Red" Ross, she too had become a teacher. Miller had been born into an artificial world that was an island in a section of Georgia where not everyone valued learning, but they worked hard to overcome the things they didn't know. These were differences he would balance for himself in the coming years. They were connected to the expectations that people had attached to him for as long as he could remember. Inside him, they were connected to the burning competitive spirit that was coming out as he grew. It was a spirit that was played out when he entered the college campus and continued to be a Phi Chi debater.

"I am just a very competitive person," Miller says. "When I won the first debate, I wanted the second. When I won the second one, I wanted a third. Then, when I got to the fourth one, I sure wasn't going to lose the final one. Ed Jenkins (another future Congressman) talks about not wanting to spoil Zell's perfect string. It was just plain old competition—wanting to win. I was competing against those others, but I was also competing against myself—and the ghost. For most of my early life, it was like it was written that I had to do something exceptional."

As editor of *The Enotah Echoes,* Miller wrote about those expectations in an obtrusive way. His column was called "Miller's Meddlings." When he first started to work on the paper, he often used his childhood nickname, Zip Miller, as a byline. By the fall of 1950, he was a more formal Zell Miller. Once, after failing two courses, he misused that column, questioning the emphasis Young Harris put on academics. This 1950 column was about the world's need for scholarship.

"This great day is calling for thinkers, not in one channel—but men of broad views—in fact, it wants men who know and know that they know. People who do things ... In the past, the world has been satisfied to honor the men who were willing to work for it. In the future, the crown will be placed upon the brow of the ones who will think for it, " he wrote.

Something had happened to the boy with the baseball glove. That ten-year-old who pitched pennies with The Varsity carhops was beginning to find direction. He had been haunted by expectations. Now he was finding that following in the footsteps of his late father was not so bad.

The column—written in the stilted, overcharged prose of an adolescent journalist—was a hint that the writer had found some expectations of his own. "So it is in every relation of life. Work and action ought to be planned so far as either lies within the control of the planner. Every life ought to be dominated by a general aim. Every one ought to be working for some ultimate purpose, but the ultimate purpose is accomplished and the remotest goal is reached, not by continually meditating upon them but by getting the vantage ground which comes when each day receives the deposit of all that man can give out of his conscience, his intelligence, and his character," Miller wrote.

Reading those old newspapers offers a glimpse of how Miller was dealing with his father's legacy. He wrote a story about a fund-raising campaign for the chimes at Sharp Memorial Methodist Church and, in the detached manner of a reporter, never indicated that the man they would be named for was his father. His mother was chairing the drive, and when the money had been raised and the chimes were being dedicated, he wrote another article, again as an objective observer. Only an editor's note gave away the identity of the writer.

While he was sports editor of the newspaper, Miller got involved in Coach Luke Rushton's high-powered basketball program. At times, he was a backup guard on the team. He even helped recruit talent, and the coach asked him to go to Clayton, Georgia to see a high-scoring player named Bob Short. That night, Short got forty points and after the game Miller came over to talk to him. "I knew him a little bit before that night. Even as boys, we had both played for our town baseball teams. He wanted me to come to Young Harris to play ball and to join something called the Phi Chi Debating Society. I didn't know what that was," said Short, who like Miller went on to a career in state politics and a lifelong friendship with the future governor.

Short did come to Young Harris, and became one of the school's all-time great players. "He could shoot, but I don't think he ever passed the ball in his life," Miller jokes. In addition to basketball, Short and Miller also shared a love of square dancing. Students were not allowed to have cars, so they hitch-hiked everywhere. On Friday or Saturday nights, the two of them would snag rides to nearby dances, sometimes at a high school gym, but often at a place called Club Nottley.

"That's where we were this one night and it was a ways away. Zell got to dancing with this pretty little girl and he wouldn't leave. We had to leave enough time to get a ride back to school, but he wouldn't go. It got late, but this one fellow stopped to pick us up in his truck. His family was packed into the cab, but he said the two of us could get in the back. It was full of manure," said Short, who has advised and written speeches for a long list of Georgia politicians. "I always told Zell that the smell wore off of me quicker than it did him."

In 1951, his final year of college, Miller would again be confronted by his father's memory. Hilda Dyches was a senior at the University of Georgia. Her professor had received a request from Edna Herren, the forensic director at Young Harris. She needed a judge for a speaking contest and Dyches' professor asked if she would go.

It was her first meeting with Herren. Years later, both of them would end up on the faculty at what is now Georgia State University in Atlanta. They began as part-time instructors. Herren was also a member of the faculty at Druid Hills High School in Atlanta, and Dyches was at Avondale High. In the beginning at Georgia State, they mainly taught night classes. Herren was an instructor in freshman English and Dyches was in speech and drama.

When the two young teachers were first introduced, Herren was still at Young Harris and Dyches was an unsuspecting judge for an annual speech competition which until that night had been known as the Clay Medal Speaking Contest. The Susan B. Harris Chapel was bulging with people when she arrived that evening.

"We didn't know who Zell Miller was when he came out, and I remember when he won and the whole school erupted. They were elated. It was the first year they had named the competition in honor of his father," says Dyches, now retired and living near Atlanta.

Miller wasn't scheduled to compete for that was a busy week for him. The speech competition was held during the week of commencement. Miller was graduating from the junior college that weekend, and on Friday he would be going for his fourth straight debating championship. However, the day before the Thursday competition, the Phi Chi speaker was expelled from school. His teammates did not want to relinquish their chance in the contest so Miller volunteered to step in, recycling a speech he had used in the past.

Knowing that his mother would be at the chapel that night to present the first Grady Miller Memorial loving cup, he had one stipulation: it would not be announced to the audience in the chapel that the Phi Chi's replacement speaker was the son of Stephen Grady Miller.

The program still had the name of the original speaker, and no one corrected it that night. Only afterward, when Birdie Bryan Miller came forward to make the presentation in honor of her late husband, was Zell Miller identified as her son.

Edna Herren must have been proud, O. V. Lewis said. "Over the years, I never heard her say anything critical of Zell or his family," Lewis says. "It was if she was a member of that family." Shirley Carver Miller says she was.

"Why shouldn't we? We both thought Zell Miller was the stuff. Over the years, I would write to her and keep her up to date. I'd send her newspaper clippings and later all of the children's and grand-children's pictures. She was like a member of our family," she said.

Dyches said Herren often talked about Young Harris and how she had taken Miller under her wing, encouraged him and made him believe in himself. It was the beginning of a lifelong friendship.

In 1976, when Miller wrote his first book, *The Mountains Within Me,* he had been lieutenant governor of Georgia two years. The book was a look back at his experiences in the mountains, dealing with everything from school to moonshine to politics.

At the beginning of the book were these dedications:

Birdie Bryan Miller,
who made it possible

Edna Herren,
who showed me the way

Shirley Carver Miller,
who held my hand

Family, Relatives and Friends,
who were with me in the mountains.

To introduce the new book the lieutenant governor hosted a luncheon at the Garden Room, across from the State Capitol in Atlanta. Proceeds from the book would go to the Zell Miller Lecture Series, established by his former teacher and mentor. Edna Herren was seated at the head table. Naturally there was a flower in her hair. Wherever she taught, students had for decades speculated about the story behind the flower. Her striking black hair had turned to a stately gray, but the flower remained. The legend was that she had had a lover who left for the war and she promised to wear a flower until he returned. He had been killed, so she wore the flower to remember him.

"Those stories were romantic and mysterious, but they weren't true. There were all types of mysteries about it. Edna had heard them all and we used to laugh about them. She just loved flowers. It was part of her identity," Dyches says. She wore one until she died.

Herren always despised going to doctors's offices. In the months leading up to her death, with mounting heart problems, she had been seeing more doctors than she cared to see. Her friends sensed it was serious. Across the state, Miller was concerned. He wanted to know how she was.

Steve Wrigley, the governor's chief of staff, remembers being in Miller's office for an important meeting in the summer of 1994. Miller must have noticed the time and he picked up the telephone and made a call. It was to Herren's doctor, just to find out how she was. Told that she would need someone to care for her, Miller said he would take care of the arrangements. Finally, on July 7,1994, she died in a doctor's office in St. Simons, Georgia where she had moved after leaving Atlanta and Georgia State.

During all of those years, she had remained a part of Zell Miller's family. When he was inaugurated for his first term as governor in January of 1991, he sent a plane to the Georgia Coast to bring her to Atlanta for the ceremony.

During his second campaign for governor, a very personal political ad talked about the role a teacher or mentor can play in a person's life. In this case, it was the role Edna Herren had played in the life of Zell Miller. The approach for the television advertisement was personal, not political. A camera crew was dispatched to the Georgia coast for the taping. Edna Herren never saw the finished product. As the ad ended, it noted somberly that she had died recently.

Zell Miller, the boy who once thought he would never be able to get up and make a speech, spoke at Edna Herren's memorial service at Christ Church in St. Simons. It was a honor he both dreaded and cherished. As he sat there and waited to speak, he added thoughts in the margin of the page.

"I speak today for all those students whose lives were touched by this remarkable woman.

Edna Herren was first, last and always a teacher. A teacher unrelenting in her demands, but with extraordinary magnetism—dramatic and spellbinding in the way she made the personalities in English literature come alive.

I go back and read the same passages that she once read to us, and the realism, the drama, the emotion are just not there. I read Chaucer and Beowulf and they are boring and plodding now, but, when she read them, they lived so vividly, you'd get goose bumps.

What a teacher! What a teacher! And she had the wonderful ability to make each one of us feel so very special—that we were somebody. Or could be if we'd just listen to her and work hard.

For years, I lived with the impression that she directed most of her attention to just me. In an egotistical way, I felt I was so special that she gave me all her undivided attention. I thought how fortunate I was that she had singled me out.

And then, as I met others over the years who felt the same way, I realized that was her magic: she made you feel like you were hers. You! You were so important to her.

What a gift! What a gift! And she gave it in abundance to so many, many of us. So, for all of them, for all of us, I say thank you. Our wonderful friend, you blessed our lives.

And you did especially bless mine.

I took every course you taught. I joined every organization you advised. I tried to debate because of you, although I was absolutely terrified to speak in public.

During most of my teenage years—and beyond—my goal was to please you. Later, I compared every other teacher I knew to you. I compared every woman to you. I compared my mother to you. I compared my wife to you. You were my life's yardstick. And to this very day, something deep inside me says I must measure up to your expectations.

You will be forever with me."

When Edna Herren was laid to rest in her hometown of Rutledge, Georgia, her few remaining relatives asked Zell and Shirley Miller to sit with them in an area reserved for her family.

O. V. Lewis was in Rutledge that afternoon and he marvels at how many Young Harris people were there, how well Herren was remembered after so many years. She taught at the mountain school for only five years, but for years afterward she operated the school's Atlanta office. "That day reminded me of a Young Harris Homecoming," Lewis says. "At Homecoming, if you saw a crowd, Edna was usually in the middle of it." That service was the end of her life, but not of her influence. "When we were leaving the service, " Lewis remembers, "I looked back. All I could see was Shirley and Zell and an empty tent."

After World War I, Grady Miller studied in England. (1918)

Returning to Young Harris, Grady Miller often wore his uniform to class. (1919)

When Jane Miller was born, it was front
page news in the college newspaper.

As a child in Young Harris, Zell Miller's
playground was the college campus. (1940)

Zell and Jane in front of the Georgia capital. (1943)

This is the rock house that Birdie Miller built, hauling stones from a nearby creek and then working on it for years.

Zell Miller was a big man on a small campus.

Baseball has always been one of Zell Miller's passions. (1947)

Even in school, Zell was a campus politician.

Edna Herren

Jane, Birdie and Zell pose for a rare family portrait. (1942)

When the crew was building a road to the top of Bald Mountain, Birdie joined them. (4th from right)

As an insecure youngster, Zell never liked to have his photograph taken. (1947)

Zell Miller was always a leader – even in the Boy Scouts. (1944)

This clipping of Birdie presenting Zell the Grady Miller Cup was in the Atlanta Journal. (1951)

Zell was a backup guard on the Young Harris basketball team of 1950. (Top row, 2nd from right)

In this old college-owned house, Zell Miller
was born in Young Harris, Feb. 24, 1932.

When Zell Miller was growing up, kids
could play hop-scotch on the narrow
highway through Young Harris.

For Zell Miller, the mountains of North
Georgia have always been the place where he
is most comfortable.

Shirley Carver came to Young Harris College
in 1953 to prepare for law school.

Wearing his Marine uniform, Zell holds son
Murphy in his arms.

Everything you need to know, Zell Miller
learned in the Marine Corps.

5

MAKING HISTORY COME TO LIFE

Zell Miller wept the day he graduated from Young Harris College. Those had been good years for him. He had been a big man on a small campus. Now he was packing up his diploma, his belongings, and all the expectations he had carried with him since he was born. For a young man who hadn't wandered far from that place, there were fears. This wasn't just a school he was leaving behind. It was a sanctuary. His fellow graduates had come from all over the country and were either going back home or to a college they had dreamed about. They seemed so confident. Despite a swagger that became a trademark, his confidence didn't extend beyond the Towns County line. The others were carefree. He felt the burden of living not only for himself, but for the mountain people who expected so much of him and for a father whose memory kept getting in his way. He was nineteen years old. The anxieties of that ten year old kid who had heard the city kids giggle about the way he talked had never really gone away.

Two years later, he was thrown into the drunk tank at the Gilmer County jail. It was a Saturday night. He was driving under the influence. The cell was dirty and smelly, and he came to think it was what he deserved. He was being punished, not just for a DUI, but for all the things he hadn't done. "The Big Man on

Campus had failed," Zell Miller says. "The guy that so much was expected of was a Big Failure."

There had been a partial scholarship to study political science at Emory University, a campus rich in Coca-Cola money that is surrounded by an old Atlanta neighborhood of well-established homes and trust funds. His family and friends were excited. Edna Herren sent him a season ticket to the Atlanta Symphony. His Aunt Verdie was writing encouraging letters from LaGrange College. His mother just knew he was going to do well, he always did well. Yet, from the beginning, he felt like he was a piece to a different puzzle, that he had no reason being there.

When he talks about the campus, he says it was "worldly" and "metropolitan." About the other students, he talks of their "sophist-ication." The obvious inference is how far he was from being any of those things. He had a twang in his voice that amused everyone who heard it. Other students dressed right. No matter what he wore, he was uncomfortable. Classes were hard and the students in them were articulate. The other young people had traveled, and the only travel he looked forward to was the Trailways bus that carried him back to the mountains every Friday. "A feeling of inferiority permeated my whole being," he wrote.

He wasn't failing. He was making B's and C's. There were those expectations again. Zell Miller was supposed to do better. People expect it. Elliott Levitas, an Atlantan who would go on to be a Rhodes Scholar and a United States Congressman, was also an Emory student then and Miller saw in him something he could never become. Life was fast-forwarding. He wasn't living extravagantly, but in two quarters the money he had borrowed from the Pickett-Hatchett Scholarship Fund in Columbus was already running out, he'd have to borrow more, and he felt everything was closing in him, leaving no way out.

So he quit and went home. "I dropped out and returned to my mountain home to the great disappointment of my mother and aunt and the arched brows of the town and college gentry who had wondered if the orphaned boy would be able to make it in the real world," he has written. Not even a smelly cell in Gilmer County was punishment enough, he felt. At Young Harris, he had never even tasted alcohol, not even a beer. "I don't know why, but I didn't," he says. "Maybe because I was a ball player." After he got out of Young Harris, he went to Emory, "That's when I had trouble with alcohol."

George Berry can't remember not knowing Zell Miller. An executive with Cousins Properties in Atlanta, Berry is a former director of the state's Department of Industry and Trade. He grew up in Blairsville, but two of his uncles lived in Young Harris right next to Birdie Miller's house. Berry was four years younger than Zell so he grew up knowing about the college debates, the baseball and all of Miller's other exploits as a student and an athlete. "Zell was considered set apart by everyone," Berry says. "He was a whiz, a marvel. He accomplished everything he set out to do it seemed."

So it was natural that everyone in the area noticed when Miller dropped out of Emory University. "There was a lot of clucking among the local people," Berry says. "I remember all the buzz. I was a teen-ager and it was a shock to me, too. It was so out of character for this whiz kid we all thought we knew."

Now he had the shame of quitting school and the guilt of being locked up. "That next Sunday evening, I was in a pew at Sharp Memorial Methodist Church like I was supposed to be," he says. But singing the old songs from the Cokesbury Hymnals wasn't enough. "My Methodist foresight, I guess, made me believe that unless I did something drastic, that I was destined for a life as the town bum at best or early death at the probable worst," he has written. Years later, no one hints that he was ever an alcoholic. They will roll their eyes when asked if he has ever drunk too much, but that's all. "I've been concerned about it," Shirley Miller says, "but never considered it serious."

Those close to him are very aware that Zell Miller saw it as a problem—if for no other reason than for one time in his life the person who thrives on control had lost it. In his personal recollections in *The Mountains Within Me*, Miller said he enlisted in the Marine Corps to "lick this weakness." "It was bad enough," Miller says. "For a person who hadn't drunk before and wasn't expected to, it was bad." Bad enough for him later to spend a political career trying to strengthen DUI legislation.

That long battle came to a head in 1997. In his State of the State address, he talked about how many items he had brought to the legislature from his "long life of hard knocks and experience," such as growing up in a single-parent home, and getting the special GI Bill benefits to go to college. "I also know what it's like to spend the night in jail on a drunk charge, because I've done that, too," he said, "so again, this old voice of experience, who's been there and done that says: 'Put those drunks in jail and let them see what it's like, let them discover how miserable and degrading it is, and how good that sunlight feels and how good that fresh air smells the next morning."

The 1997 legislation called for a curfew on teen driving, zero tolerance for teen drinking and driving, and changed the law so that a no-contest plea was the same as guilty. Miller, as governor, described the complexity of the law by saying, "If anyone other than a lawyer or a drunk can explain that to me, I'd like to hear it." That statement put him face to face with his longtime adversary, Speaker of the House Tom Murphy, a lawyer. But the package of bills passed the Georgia House, which elated Miller. "Today has been a long, hard struggle," he said. "Today we achieved things I've been fighting for my entire time in office."

In the summer of 1953, it was a different struggle—one serious enough for the twenty-one-year-old Miller to sign up for a three-year enlistment in the United States Marine Corps. "I was punishing myself for my transgressions. I needed discipline in my life. That, more than anything else, led me to the Marine Corps. And it worked. The Marine Corps was perfect for me," Miller says.

While it may have been alcohol that pushed him in that direction, the Marines would change him in other ways. He had been reared in a world of women, his mother, his aunts, Miss Herren. There had been no consistent male figures in his life. He had seen Uncle Hoyle, on a jump ball at the free throw line, effortlessly hang in the air and softly tap the ball in the basket. But that was fun, not authority. Charlie Jenkins could hold a broomstick in his hands and jump over it flatfooted. That was manly, but it didn't give him any rules to be a man. Arnold Keys had been important because he got the boys together and formed a baseball team, but that wasn't male discipline.

He admired men like those three, but females had dominated his life, and when he got away from them and the safety of the mountains, he didn't know what the world expected of him. Throughout Miller's life this would be a search. Men he respected would take on fatherly roles. He was almost forty when he left a position with Lt. Governor Lester Maddox, and in leaving he talked about how Maddox had been a father figure for him.

Though the Marine Corps would hardly give Miller a father figure, they did bring more male delivered discipline than the recruiting poster he had seen that proudly said "We Make Men." There were times in boot camp at Parris Island, South Carolina when he wondered if they were making men or breaking men. Birdie, a typical artist, always lived in a world without clocks. She did things when she felt like doing them, not because it was time. She just worked until she finished, whatever time it was. This had given him more freedom than most boys his age.

"My life in Young Harris, other than school, had never been regimented. There was no certain time to eat. Mama was always outside working. I either fixed something myself or ate at Aunt Phoebe's and Uncle Hoyle's. Nobody thought that was wrong. That's just the way Birdie was," he says.

Life in the Marines was regimented even when he was sleeping. "I came to love a routine and still do. There's something comforting about a routine to me. I follow them rigidly. I'm uncomfortable if I'm not on a schedule. I get up at the same time. I do the same things. I eat at the same places, and eat the same foods. I like it that way," Miller says. As lieutenant governor and governor, he has lived a detailed, to-the-minute schedule each day and each week. Others wonder how a person can enjoy the structure of having everything laid out by the minute day in and day out. Not Miller. That's him. Marti Fullerton, who has known him as student, employee and friend, says she drank coffee with cream and sugar when she met him but learned to drink it black. "Miller doesn't give you time to put in the cream and sugar," she laughs.

Blame or credit for this lies with the Marines which the subtitle of his 1997 book, *Corps Values,* spells out in a play on words in the title of Robert Fulghum's book *All I Really Need to Know I Learned in Kindergarten.* Miller's approach was "Everything You Need to Know I Learned in the Marines." The values that were pinned on him in those three years shaped his life and his politics. The unsure kid who left Macon on a hot morning in August of 1953 did not return. "The kill almost came before the cure, but it turned out to be the turning point of my life. Everything that has happened to me since has been at least an indirect product of that decision and in the twelve weeks of hell and transformation that was Marine Corps boot camp. I learned the values of achieving a successful life that have guided and sustained me on the course, which, although sometimes checkered and detoured, I have followed ever since," Miller said in his book.

That experience was something between a rebirth and a rebuilding. Out of those twelve weeks came twelve values that would not surprise anyone who has ever worked with or around him: neatness, punctuality, brotherhood, persistence, pride, respect, shame, responsibility, achievement, courage, discipline and loyalty. He also learned about hitting a target and it did not come easy. His cousin, Eric England, was a lifer and an Expert Marksman. Miller wanted to wear that coveted badge just like his cousin, a sniper in Vietnam, a member of the Marine Rifle Team and a small-town legend in the mountains. After weeks of training, he only made "Marksman," but he didn't quit. Even at Camp Lejeune, North Carolina, where he went after boot camp he worked on his own time. Nobody could understand why. They didn't know Miller. He finally came in with a score of 220 out of 250 which qualified him for the coveted badge only one of ten marines get. He didn't quit. And for a future politician who would lose two races for Congress before the age of forty, leaving him nearly bankrupt, and a race for the United States Senate before he was fifty that made him question himself, that persistence would be important.

Miller hadn't always gotten along well with firearms. When he was twenty-one his carelessness with a .22 caliber rifle cost him the index finger on his left hand and could have done more damage. He and his cousin Bryan Bryson had gone to Big Creek to shoot at tin cans and wood chips in the water. He had laid the rifle across his knees. It broke down like a shotgun with a hammer you pulled back to cock. It didn't have a safety. It was a short, little rifle they kept around for hog killings in the fall. When Miller jerked it up to shoot at a wood chip, it went off and shattered the knuckle.

"It didn't hurt or even bleed, but I knew I needed to have it seen about. I walked out of the woods to the clinic to see old Dr. Tanner," Miller says. "He proceeded to take the finger off, explaining that it would be stiff and get in the way if he didn't. It never bothered me at all. It healed rapidly. I even played baseball that summer." He was never self conscious about it since he had grown up in an area where missing fingers, thumbs and hands were common, often due to sawmill accidents. "And most folks, especially when they find out I actually worked in a sawmill, think I lost my finger there. But I didn't."

That new badge on his uniform wasn't the only change in Miller's life. Almost every day, he was writing letters to Shirley Carver, a coed who he had known casually even before she came to Young Harris in 1952 as a sixteen-year-old student with plans for law school. They had a few dates that summer before he left for the Marines and both of them began to look forward to the mailman's arrival. She was a mountain person, from Cherokee County, North Carolina, only a few minutes away from Young Harris. She came from a home where politics was always spoken. Daddy Luke, her father, worked heavy construction jobs, mostly in tunnels. He had worked for the TVA building Fontana Dam He worked mainly with dynamite. When he wasn't in construction, he worked as a deputy sheriff, police chief, and for awhile was sheriff of Cherokee County.

Her mother, Mama Bea, was a liberal Democrat who, like Birdie Miller, was involved in running elections. She was part Cherokee Indian which may explain why she was so adamant about anything that hinted of bias. The family lived in Rail Cove, an isolated hollow nestled between mountains. Her parents were involved in local politics and her mother tried to keep up with it at all levels. She listened to the news on the radio and every day she read the newspaper, the Asheville Citizen. "It came by mail and the postman couldn't come all the way up into Rail Cove. Doc Ensley's family lived at the mouth of the cove and he'd get up early every morning and go down and get the mail. He would read it first and then my mama," Shirley says.

Daddy Luke, as a lawman, went to court on a regular basis. Shirley tagged along whenever he would let her. "I was a courtroom junkie," she says. "I don't know why, but I always was. My daddy would go there on his job and I'd sit in the back. In the mountains, lawyers were usually involved in politics, so I knew them all."

She had an aunt and some older cousins who lived in Young Harris, so she had visited the town and the nearby college most of her life. Three of her cousins had even married some of Miller's relatives. She knew about Birdie and the rock house. She knew about Zell. "I knew about Zell before he knew about me," she says. "He had graduated before I got to Young Harris, but I'd see him sometimes. I had dated one of his friends."

While Miller talks about his timidity, Shirley doesn't. "I found him pushy. He was never shy with me. He's just a very strong personality. We had gone out a few times and we were writing to each other after he was in the Marines. It was only when we started writing that I began to think there was some depth to this guy," she says.

Miller was out of boot camp and stationed at Camp Lejeune when he came home for a weekend in early 1954. He asked Shirley to marry him and they eloped to Walhalla, South Carolina for a quiet and quick ceremony. Together they told her parents the next day after spending their first night of marriage at the rock house.

That he would marry a Young Harris girl was not unusual. That practice began long before Zell and Shirley. Dr. Charles Clegg, a former president of the school, said Young Harris College "is like a shoe factory. They come out of here in pairs."

Shirley soon joined him at LeJeune and Miller became a "brown bagger," an affectionate term for married Marines. They moved into a cramped eight-foot trailer at the Camp Geiger Trailer Park. In the industry today, the preferred term is mobile home. But theirs was a trailer.

Miller rapidly rose to the rank of sergeant. He served in an artillery regiment and was the editor of the Tenth Marine regimental newspaper, "The Cannoneer." He was still a Marine on June 25, 1955 when their first son, Murphy Carver, was born. In August of 1956, his three-year duty was over and he headed to Athens, Georgia. He was going to be a student again.

This time, the feelings were different. He was a Marine. He had the GI Bill. He could do anything and he planned to get an undergraduate degree at the University of Georgia and go on to law school. Within the first quarter when he was back in class, those plans changed. He shifted his major to history. Again, it was because of a teacher. Sitting in the classroom with Dr. Merton Coulter, he began to see why his father had apparently been so fascinated with history. Coulter was one of the South's premier historians and his classrooms reflected that knowledge and experience. Miller tried to take every course Coulter taught, not just because of the subject but because of the teacher. For the first time in his life, he began to think about being a teacher himself.

While they were in Athens, their second son was born. Matthew Stephen was premature, and taking care of him was a major responsibility. Shirley took care of the two babies in their apartment in the campus married housing area. She wasn't alone. There were many other couples there. It was just after the Korean War and not that long after World War II. Other young men were taking advantage of the GI Bill. But even with the money that Miller now calls "a special scholarship," they had to watch their money. Shirley did typing at home and Zell had a variety of jobs.

He was a tutor for Georgia football players. He flipped hamburgers for $7 a night at Allen's, a popular student hangout on Prince Street. While he studied for his Master's Degree, he was a graduate teacher in the history department.

Selby McCash is press secretary for Georgia Congressman Sanford Bishop. In the past, he was political editor for both *The Macon Telegraph* and *The Atlanta Journal* so he has known Miller for decades. Before he knew him as a politician he knew of him as a student and a teacher. "My late brother, Bart, was also a graduate student in history with Miller. Zell was respected, and they liked him, but behind his back they kind of laughed at him. He was so intense. Bart could remember Zell saying to them that he would be governor one day," McCash says.

Politics had to wait. With two small boys, he was thinking more about making a living. Neither Zell nor Shirley remembers a conscious decision that they would one day return to the mountains. It was just assumed. When an opening in the history and political science department at Young Harris came in the fall of 1959, he became a teacher at their alma mater. Like Grady and Birdie had done thirty-seven years before, they moved into a house the college owned. Zell and Shirley were home. Being back there seemed natural, but there was also something portentous about teaching in the same building where his father had taught. He was on a faculty where many of the people knew his father and even more of them had known him as a student. He knew instinctively that he needed to become Zell Miller and he needed to be known as a teacher.

For the Millers and their two boys, this was their first true home. It was large and there was a yard so the children could run and fall down. Miller was making $400 a month. He was the faculty advisor to *The Enotah Echoes* where he had been editor. He was coaching the school baseball team. Don Harp arrived the year afterward and played on one of Miller's baseball teams. He said the coach seemed almost like a member of the team since he was not that much older than either his players or his students. "He was an outstanding teacher, one of the most popular on campus," says

Harp, now the pastor of Peachtree Road United Methodist Church in Atlanta. "He was not easy. He graded tough, but he brought the subject to life. He talked about current events—not just things from the past."

Hank Huckaby was a city boy from Hapeville, Georgia. He was a freshman in 1960 and during his first quarter took American Government 101, a course that could be dry and lifeless for a kid just out of high school. "He had a style about him," says Huckaby, now an administrator at Georgia State University. "He'd come into the classroom five minutes before it started and he would outline his lecture on the blackboard. He never used a note. He would take the roll, start lecturing, and cover everything that was on that board. He was demanding. But you could do well—if you studied."

Marti Fullerton didn't arrive until 1962. She remembers registration day when the student union was full of tables with teachers sitting all around the room. When the students came into the hall, they went to the teacher they wanted. "When the doors opened, all of them would line up at Miller's table to sign up for his courses," she says. "Everybody at Young Harris wanted to take whatever he was teaching—whether they needed them or not. I took every one of them."

She says he was not one to increase the sale of textbooks. "In American History, he told us, 'Don't buy the textbook. We're gonna handle this differently. He said the same thing in Political Science. You won't learn anything from that book. I'm going to tell you what it's like in the real world. And he did. He would tell you the little things that weren't in the history books, things he had read about. He was spellbinding."

"He impressed us as a man," says Chip Conyers, a member of the Class of 1964. "Although he was one of the two or three most outstanding professors of my college career, he wasn't the kind of man I thought of in terms of Professor Miller."

"This man lived his teaching and relived what he taught in both history and political science. He could make you feel like you were living during the time he was teaching about," says Mack Poss, another former student.

Huckaby, like Fullerton, went on to work for Miller in a variety of jobs—some for free, some with a paycheck. All of them have been friends all of these years and it began in a classroom. Fullerton came to Young Harris with an interest in politics and Miller cemented that interest. Huckaby looks back on those classes under Miller as landmarks in his life and his career. More than three decades later, he remembers the challenge Miller issued for students to be citizens.

Says Huckaby: "He wanted to know if we were registered to vote. He asked about our local governments and how they worked, who our legislators were, did we know anything about them, about Georgia's Congressional Delegation and how it affected us. He didn't just teach from a strict academic standpoint. He wanted to inspire us, to link what we were talking about in the classroom to citizenship. He understood then and he understands now what an impact a good teacher can have on a person. For me, he was one of those teachers."

Says Fullerton: "He would come into class with a little scrap of paper and write ten things on the board. He never had to turn around again and he would cover each one of those points. In political science, he would read to us about how a bill became a law. Then, he'd say, 'Now I'm gonna tell you how a bill REALLY becomes law." He was about to find out for himself.

6

BATTLING FOR THE 'GETTABLES'

Morning comes early in winter, and it was dark and cold. A frost layered the ground and a mist was wedged between the ground and the horizon. Zell Miller dressed quietly. The boys were asleep and he didn't want to wake them. He wanted to be in Owl Creek, Scataway, Bugscuffle, or Bearmeat before the coffee was brewing.

By the time the sun had opened its eyes, he would be asking for votes. "Getting a person out of bed to ask for their vote was considered a compliment. I remember those frosty mornings, knocking on a door before the lights had been turned on. I could hear them shuffle to the door and flick on the light. They'd open the door and there I'd be. They'd invite me in. I'd have a cup of coffee with the man while his wife cooked breakfast. Then I'd ask them for their vote. The earlier the better. That was a compliment. Late at night also worked," he adds.

Zell Miller was running for the Georgia State Senate. It was 1960. At the age of twenty-eight, he was an idealistic political science professor who thought voters deserved a choice. No one had done it this way before, but he was taking his unlikely campaign to people's kitchens.

Especially the gettables. His main advisors, Guy Puett, Ed Heddon, and J. William Denton, knew everybody in the county.

They would run down the voter list and say a name. If they didn't like his opponent, Zell would put down a plus sign. If they liked him, we put down a minus sign. The few we didn't know he put down a zero." We were looking for the gettables," Miller recalls. It was his opponent who inspired the young college professor to get into the race. W. K. "Kiser" Dean was the county's political boss. He had served in both the state House and the Senate. That was not unusual in those days, for the Senate, because of the rotation policy, had very little power. Consequently, former House members would often spend a term in the other chamber until they could return to the House.

Dean was also chairman of the Towns County Democratic Party. He controlled the patronage, which meant in that small, rural county that he had the say-so in who was hired by the Highway Department, the Revenue Department and the Game & Fish Department. At one level, that was one of the definitions of power. Everybody knew that if you wanted to get something done in Towns County, you came calling on Kiser Dean. "You can imagine that as a young political science professor I thought all of that was wrong," Miller says." "What really bothered me was that Dean had no opposition."

First he talked it over with Shirley. She understood politics so to her it seemed to be the thing to do. She says, "Politics was part of my growing up. My family always had their candidates. Some of them won and some didn't."

Then Miller went to see Dr. Charles Clegg, the Young Harris president. Thirty years before, Grady Miller had paid a similar visit to Dr. Joseph A. Sharp, asking that president of another era if he could run for that same political body. None of that was lost on Clegg, who had been a student of the elder Miller when he was a state senator. Miller had a proposition. If Clegg allowed him to run and if he won, he would teach four classes in the fall and spring and take the winter off for the forty days of the General Assembly. Then he would teach during the summer session.

To the young professor's surprise, Clegg said yes. "I think he wanted me to get this out of my system. He also may have seen some of my father in me. More than anything, he didn't look down at politics or politicians. He didn't think it was dirty," Miller says.

While some of his colleagues in education might have thought politics was a low calling, folks around Young Harris had always been involved in the game of politics. It was part of life, giving the fellows who met around the "loafer's bench" in town something to gripe about. But politics in the highlands was played by a different set of rules. For one thing, while the rest of the state believed you were born a Yellow Dog Democrat, people in north Georgia could dance at either party. The term "Yellow Dog Democrat" was born out of the idea that Georgians would vote Democrat even if the party put an old yellow dog on the ballot. And most of them would. It wasn't that way in the mountains. Politics was a two-party passion. It divided families. It meant that Democrats didn't buy a loaf of bread at the Republican market and even if you were running out of gas you didn't fill up the tank at a service station run by a member of the opposing party.

Mountain counties had been bipartisan since before the Civil War. Settlers had brought with them a brand of Jacksonian democracy and the beliefs of Andrew Jackson immediately clashed with the ideology of the traditional Southerners. Bitter divisions were formed—even within families. In Miller's own family there had been breaks along party lines. They were so divided that his grandmother, Jane Collins, a staunch Democrat, refused to vote for her Republican brother Bud when he was running for the Georgia General Assembly. He won anyway. In the Collins clan, that was not unusual. The story is told of how Neal Collins, a Democrat, defeated Gene Collins, a Republican, by a few votes after Gene Collins had defeated Democrat Wayne Collins by a single vote. Among the Collinses, that had been the case since the Civil War. Miller laughs about his Collins ancestors: "Someone once said that it was the Democratic side of the family who first learned to read and write."

Old-timers could identify party affiliation by a person's last name. The Taylors were Democrats. Shooks were Republicans. The

Brysons, Dentons and Plotts were Democrats and the Corns, Garretts and Woods voted the other way. Several of the local Republicans were neighbors of the Millers.

While he was going back and forth to Athens for graduate school at the University of Georgia, Miller had begun to get involved in local politics—the longtime domain of his mother. Birdie Miller was a member of the Young Harris City Council for more than twenty-five years—usually without opposition, which was all but unheard of in that community. Twice in the 1950s she was mayor, one of the few female mayors in the state. Usually, she was treasurer or the clerk and with those jobs came the job of collecting taxes, and later, when the town got a water system, the collection of water bills. There was a certain day people were supposed to pay those bills and taxes at the "Law House," a tiny, frame building in town that passed as a city hall. Most people just came by Birdie's house to drop off their payments. Often, her little boy would hear them deliver not only their money, but also a strong opinion about how high taxes were getting and how their tax money was being spent. Years later, when he was an office holder himself and the question of taxes would come up, he would remember those living room lessons.

Because she was apolitical and not a diehard loyalist of either party—and because folks knew she needed the meager money— Birdie was usually hired to work at the polls on election day. The election was held at the "Law House," and with the voters came the hard core political watchers with their unshaven faces and their overalls. Between voters, they passed around some locally produced whiskey and by nightfall, their eyes were red and their tongues were uninhibited.

As a child, Miller sat meekly in the corner and watched as the votes were gathered and his mama conducted the "count out," calling out a "tally" whenever another five votes were recorded for a candidate. Birdie was the only woman in the room, but despite the clashes between party people and several hits of the moonshine, she was treated with respect. It was part of the code.

Soon after he was discharged from the Marine Corps in 1956, Miller had taken part in his first election. He was a Democratic "marker" at a local election. That was the person who assisted the elderly, the blind, the disabled or the illiterate when they came to vote. A motivated "marker" could make a difference in a close election. Such jobs were understood to be part of the local process. Zell Miller was never that interested in being personally involved in those local shenanigans. But on a fall Saturday in 1959, after arriving home from Sanford Stadium and a University of Georgia football game, there was a knock at his door and a neighbor was waiting to congratulate him.

To Miller's surprise, in his absence he had been elected the new mayor of Young Harris. His mother had voluntarily gone off the city council so there would be room for "another Miller" and to make way for some "young blood." He received sixty-six of eighty votes. That December, a short article in the state edition of *The Atlanta Journal* noted Zell Miller's election and said he was the youngest mayor in the town's history. He was twenty-seven years old.

There were no speeches or ceremonies. Miller just got the city seal, city records—along with a .38 special and a blackjack. Young Harris had no police force so the mayor was effectively the public safety director. He still enjoys telling the story of a speeding driver that he had to apprehend. The mayor had tried to catch the person before. Then one day, while Miller was in his yard playing pitch, the driver did a "wheelie" and started to speed away. The old baseball player threw the baseball through the car window. "I took the law into my own hands," he laughs.

Not surprisingly, Miller was an active mayor. It had been fifty years since the town had adopted a new charter. He soon wrote one. Miller instituted a road-paving program and conducted regular meetings of the town council. Previous councils had operated whenever and wherever they pleased and had followed a haphazard schedule. The new mayor changed all of that, so the meetings could be open to the public.

In 1958, he had campaigned for his first elected office. He had stood all day outside the "Law House" and asked people to support him for the Democratic Executive Committee. That fifteen member board was powerful, since it nominated candidates rather than have Democrats run against one another in an expensive primary. Miller was elected and was immediately pushed as a candidate for the Georgia House. But, according to party rules, the old committee selected the candidates, not the newly-elected group. Miller lost by a single vote.

In 1960, under an unusual rotation system that existed at the time because of Georgia's County Unit System, it was Towns County's turn to elect a state senator. Neither Kiser Dean nor the executive committee would decide who that senator would be. The voters would. That is, if Miller could figure a way to get his name on the ballot. Candidates had to qualify with the chairman of the local party. That was Dean, and neither the chairman nor the party secretary wanted to let Miller qualify. They avoided him for days. "I finally went to the secretary's house real early in the morning. He wasn't up yet and when he came to the door, I just dropped the $150 check on the floor and left," Miller remembers.

Miller's campaign strategy sounds routine, but in Towns County in 1960, it was unorthodox. Candidates had knocked on people's doors before but not like Miller did. He didn't miss a house. Usually, candidates only had to call on the local ward bosses since they controlled the votes. Not Miller. He went everywhere— to Brasstown, to Hiawassee, to Lower and Upper Hightower. Even to Tate City and its fourteen votes. He would carry Tate City, eight to six.

Miller was typically busy. He bought time on a Murphy, North Carolina, radio station that beamed into the area. He made a speech and took along Mr. Lee Kirby, his fiddle-playing friend. "We bought newspaper ads. We gave away peanuts outside the courthouse in Hiawassee. Nobody had ever done that kind of retail politics before," he says. Later on, in a campaign style that would follow him, Miller got the Kirbys—Mr. Lee and Robert, his guitar playing son—to join him outside the courthouse at lunch when court was in session and their lively music drew a quick crowd before the candidate got up on a stone pillar and gave a campaign speech.

For Towns County it was a calm and uneventful campaign. There were no fist-fights and no real arguments, although people voted in unusual places. One polling place held its election on the back of a truck. When a fight would break out, they just started up the truck and moved on down the road. Sometimes in that precinct, the truck would end up a mile from where it had been when the polls opened.

Not that it was easy in 1960. Agricultural Commissioner Tommy Irvin has been in office longer than any other statewide elected official in Georgia. A native of Habersham County, he is well versed in mountain politics. He was also a long-time member of the Georgia House, and he remembers the night of Miller's first election.

"North Georgia politics is different than anything I've ever seen. Remember, Zell lives on one side of the mountain and I live on the other. I'd never been across the mountain when there was an election taking place, but I made it my business to go over to Hiawassee that night. Our results were in and I went over there to the courthouse. I heard them challenge every vote as soon as they were counted. It didn't make any difference which way the vote went. It was challenged," Irvin says.

A year later, in a special election for that same Senate seat, Miller would defeat the agriculture commissioner's uncle, Bob Irvin, in an election that lived up to mountain partisanship. Seven years later, Irvin would recommend Miller for a key position with Lester Maddox that gave him a unique opportunity for on-the-job training to be governor.

Miller's first campaign for the Senate had been unusual, but to some grizzled voters his uptown tactics meant nothing. "You'll never get elected to anything, son," the local banker told him. "Not with your hair like that." Crew-cut or not, he won by 151 votes. When all the votes had been counted late that night, the bossy reign of Kiser Dean was over. The upstart professor with the

Marine haircut and horn-rimmed glasses had surprised folks. After the back–slapping was over, Miller left the raucous traditions of the Hiawassee courthouse and headed home.

Shirley was still up. So were the boys, Matthew and Murphy, who were not yet old enough for school. A larger crowd of his hopeful college students and most of the members of the Young Harris baseball team he coached were there. It wasn't unusual for students to be around. Shirley Miller treated them like they were part of the family. She even washed the uniforms for the baseball team. Don Harp was a member of that team and one of Miller's students. He had gone to Young Harris to prepare for the ministry. He has been a Methodist pastor throughout Georgia for more than thirty years.

With the ball players, the coach had talked about his own plans. "One day," he told us, 'I want to be governor'—and he was serious. We didn't laugh. We were pulling for him," says Harp, who has offered a prayer at each of his former coach's inaugurations—for lieutenant governor and governor.

His students and players also had been pulling for him in that senate race. That's why they had all gathered at the Miller house on election night to celebrate with their professor. When he drove up, he was serenaded with a rousing chorus of "For He's a Jolly Good Fellow."

Zell Miller, like his father, was now a state senator. But like the naive students who were singing, all the twenty-eight-year-old college professor really knew about practicing politics were the theories you learn in a textbook. And the Georgia Senate that awaited him was anything but a classroom.

7

FIGHTING FOR EDUCATION

Friday. January 6, 1961.

Atlanta. The boys were back in town. For forty days they would make the laws. Forty nights they would make the bars. Never mind that the first gavel of the General Assembly wasn't until Monday. The lobby of the Henry Grady Hotel was already filled with a swarm of Georgia legislators who were as giddy as hormone-ravaged teenaged boys whose parents have just left them alone for the weekend. Upstairs, the parties had begun. So had the boozing a few blocks away in the Georgia Hotel, where other legislators stayed. In Parlor A, someone had ripped a deck of Bicycle playing cards in half and was selling one-dollar chances for Sunday's raffle—the lucky winner getting a night with the hooker who pulled his card out of the hat.

Macon. At three o'clock in the afternoon, at the dignified federal building, a law clerk in the United States District Court released a twenty-eight page judicial order. It said, in stern legal language, that Charlayne Hunter and Hamilton Holmes were qualified students and that they were being deprived of their Constitutional rights by being denied admission to the University of Georgia. A Republican jurist, Judge William A. Bootle, ruled that the two plaintiffs "would already have been admitted had it not been for their race and color." It further stated that Monday, at nine AM, when the new term began, the two students were to be part of the school's student body. With that order, 175 years of segregated education came to an end at the University of Georgia.

Athens. The University of Georgia's O. C. Aderhold was not a happy president that afternoon. The Bulldogs didn't have a football coach. A plan to allow Wally Butts to retire and to announce a University of Florida assistant coach as his successor in one neat media package, had been blown by a report out of Columbus that Butts had been forced out. By early that evening, there were problems much more serious than football. Word of what that meddling federal judge in Macon had done had spread through the campus, and students had gathered. They were shouting taunts and singing "Glory, Glory to Old Georgia," over and over again. Someone had strung up a black-faced dummy, but Bill Tate, the school's beloved dean of students, climbed up and courageously cut it down.

Monday would be a historic day. The application of Horace Ward, later a state senator and federal judge, had been turned down by the University of Georgia in 1953, and until 1960 the university had received no other black applicants. Hunter and Holmes were ideal choices. Both were honor graduates of Archer High School in Atlanta. Holmes, who died in 1996, was from a family of physicians, wanted to study medicine, and would become a surgeon. Hunter planned to study journalism, and is now a reporter and anchor person for National Public Television.

That Monday morning, the two students went from unknown litigants in a court case to partners in history, a history that until that moment had been circling on a lazy merry-go-round. Now it was on a runaway roller coaster. The ride was coming to an end in Georgia that January, and it was converging on the 1961 General Assembly. Ahead was a series of historic changes that would extend beyond those forty days of legislation and beyond the events that were taking place in either Macon or Athens.

Most of those changes revolved around segregation.

• 1945—The Federal District Court threw out the state's all-white and virtually all-Democratic primary as unconstitutional after it was challenged by the Reverend Primus King, a Columbus barber.

• 1954—The United States Supreme Court outlawed segregated schools in its decision on *Brown versus the Board of Education,* ending the proposition of "separate but equal" schools.

• 1955—The United Supreme Court said schools must be desegregated with "all deliberate speed."

• 1955—The Georgia General Assembly voted to cut off funding to any Georgia school that is integrated.

• 1955—The Georgia Board of Regents voted 14-1 to overrule Gov. Marvin Griffin's decision and allowed Georgia Tech to play in the Sugar Bowl against the University of Pittsburgh despite the fact that Panther fullback Bob Grier was black.

• 1956—The Georgia General Assembly voted to change the historical state flag "to honor the memory of our ancestors on the eve of the Civil War."

• 1958—Ernest Vandiver was elected governor of Georgia with the promise of school segregation and a slogan of "No, Not One." He carried 156 of the state's 159 counties.

• 1958—The Atlanta Jewish Temple was bombed and a column by Constitution editor Ralph McGill that called the act "the harvest of defiance" won the Pulitzer Prize for journalism.

• 1959—A federal judge ordered the Atlanta School system to formulate a plan to desegregate its schools, then allowed the city a one-year period of grace.

• 1960—The Reverend Martin Luther King Jr. moved back home to serve under his father as associate pastor at Atlanta's Ebenezer Baptist Church.

• 1960—A federal judge warned the Georgia Legislature to repeal laws forbidding integration.

• 1960—The Sibley Commission—composed of nineteen white males—chaired by Atlanta banker John Sibley, was appointed by Gov. Ernest Vandiver. After a series of statewide hearings, the commission reported that Georgia residents wanted to keep their public schools open at all cost.

• 1960—Atlanta lunch counters are integrated and, in response, the Ku Klux Klan stages a protest on the roof of the city's Dinkler Plaza Hotel.

During the decade of the fifties, Georgia and the South had been able to stall and deny. It was as though people figured if the problem were ignored, it would go away. The events of 1960 had taken the focus from the courtroom to the street corner, but when the new year began, the issue was in court in Macon.

William Augustus Bootle was an unlikely jurist to be hearing such a case. He had been a Mercer University classmate of Carl Vinson, a staunch Democrat. But it was the powerful congressman from Milledgeville who secured Bootle's appointment to the bench, even though the Macon attorney had been a Republican since the days of Herbert Hoover. At one time, Bootle was the dean of the law school at Mercer —a law school named for United States Sen. Walter F. George, a traditional hard-core Southern segregationist. Even though the two would-be students were residents of Atlanta, the case was filed in Bootle's court because Athens was part of the Middle Georgia District.

Many years later, Bootle explained his feelings on the case. "I was a judge of the United States," he said, "solemnly sworn not to flinch from any duty that came my way. There were never two sides to the issue. Absolutely! It was absolutely clear to me from the outset that the two young people must be admitted. It was the law! Judges do not make law. It is their task, brooding though it may sometimes be, to say to the citizenry, 'Here is the what the law says.' And there is a penalty if you are found in violation."

And on January 6, 1961, when that law clerk in Macon delivered Judge Bootle's decision, the past was about to converge on the unlikely shoulders of the Georgia Legislature. It was a body that was changing as slow as Steinbeck's turtle crossing the highway, but it was changing. Among the first order of business when the legislature was called to order would be the seating of a record eighty-four man freshman class. Among those freshmen was State Senator Zell Miller. "It was a fascinating time to be in politics,"

Miller says, remembering that stressful year. "Those were some of the Georgia Legislature's finest hours."

No one could know that as the session began, but the Atlanta Constitution's veteran political watcher Celestine Sibley did note that this group of newcomers was a "New breed, unfettered . . . Their mouths no longer slobber like Pavlov's dog at the mention of the County Unit System."

The state was becoming more urban. It was part of a region that was emerging from a cocoon that had strangled it for generations. World War II had opened the gates, and the industry that came South brought new ideas and new dreams. While the old leadership had done nothing to deal with these changes but posture and pontificate, some people were now questioning the price of maintaining two separate—and legal—cultures. Racial separation was slowly seen as not only a social issue but an economic issue. A New Georgia was emerging.

But Old Georgia was carrying baggage. The typical Georgian of 1960 had nine years of school and lived in the city rather than on the farm. The ones left behind on the farm were racked with poverty, and rural counties were beginning to choke on their own soil. Industry had not progressed for decades, and sixty-five percent of the industrial workers in the state were employed at low-paying textile mills. And while it was true that over a million Georgians were in school—47,450 in higher education— 288,585 people in the state had not gone beyond the fourth grade and a tragic 66,668 residents over the age of twenty-five had not even completed a single year of school.

A single year of school.

Black Georgians were ever farther down that economic and social food chain, so the impetus for the push for change is evident. Appealing to the conscience had not worked. Appealing to the pocket book might.

That all of this would be left outside the historic chambers of the Georgia General Assembly is ironic. This was a group that was all white and had been so since Reconstruction. It was all male and reveled in its manliness. It was all Democrat, though at the time the sounds of Goldwater Republicanism could almost be heard. It was dominated by rural legislators and it was ruled by an old guard that tried to run Georgia politics like Kiser Dean ran Towns County.

Blame for these things could be placed on the County Unit System, an electoral plan that had been a millstone around the neck of Georgia since a legislator from Columbus turned it into law in 1917. It specified that each county in the state should have no fewer than two and no more than six representatives. Eight of the largest counties had six. The next thirty counties had four and 121 had two each. It was a unique system whose legacy was passed down from the method of representation during Colonial America, when states were dominated by rural voters. In elections for state offices, the popular vote was secondary so candidates played to the rural audience. To be elected, you had to accumulate county units, and since they were concentrated in rural Georgia that was the audience to which candidates had to appeal.

By 1961, more Georgians were living in urban counties such as Fulton, DeKalb, Muscogee, Bibb, Richmond and Chatham than were living in the rest of the state. Urban voters in those areas were effectively disinfranchised. The popular formula at the time was to consider that in Echols County, the 159th smallest in the state, one vote equaled ninety-nine in Fulton County, the largest county.

For most of the century, rural-dominated government had ruled the state. Firmly in place was a network of wool-hatted politicians that was commonly called "the courthouse crowd." Historically composed of planter aristocrats who were comfortable with keeping Georgia the way it was, it had fostered a number of elected leaders but most of its interest and influence had centered around Eugene Talmadge. Aptly labeled "The Wild Man from Sugar Creek," Talmadge was governor from 1933 to 1937 and 1941 to 1943. He was elected again in 1946, but died before taking office.

Liberal critics described him as "Georgia's Demagogue" or a "Wool Hat Dictator." Call him what you like, he was the most dynamic force in state government in this century. He won seven out of ten statewide campaigns—four as chief executive, a feat equaled by only one other governor in Georgia history. But his power went beyond the number of times he held office. For decades, you were either for him or against him. With that came a generation of Talmadge people who controlled Georgia politics and politicians. His web of power was inherited by his son, Herman Talmadge, who was governor from 1948 to 1955 and United States Senator from 1956 to 1980. Though there were accomplishments under Talmadge rule, the philosophy that you didn't need votes in any county that had a streetcar did nothing to encourage the growing influence of urban Georgia.

That rural philosophy was crumbling in 1961. Litigation was already pending that would eliminate the County Unit System a year later. With that in mind, eighteen pieces of apportionment legislation were introduced as the bell rang on the new session that Monday morning in January of 1961. "The legislature was changing, but we knew it wasn't going to be easy and it wasn't," says Hamilton McWhorter. In 1961 he was a senator from Clarke County, but he is better known for his long tenure as Secretary of the Senate.

As the session began, Lt. Governor Garland Byrd of Butler told reporters that he was planning an attempt "to save the County Unit System from destruction at the hands of the courts." Byrd, who was to be a candidate for governor in 1962, said he would introduce a plan that year that would strengthen the metropolitan counties. "And," he added, "Herman Talmadge will not oppose it."

As legislators gathered at the State Capitol that week, they were bombarded with advice from all sectors of the state. Phones were buzzing and mailmen were delivering letters by the bag full. The state's newspapers were also busy that week. *The Macon Telegraph* ran an editorial calling for statesmanship. *The Atlanta Constitution* said don't abandon public education.

"Georgia is at a point in her history when true statesmanship, courage and a willingness to face facts are needed as never before. What is said and done this epochal legislative session will decide whether our state leads with reality maturely and wisely, or whether it follows the rocky, futile paths that some other states have followed, only to have to retrace their footsteps," the Macon editorialist wrote.

"(Vandiver) asked the Legislature not to abandon public schools. The people are behind the governor on that, and they are looking to the Legislature for strong men to do the job," the Atlanta editorialist wrote.

Few people had ever looked at the Georgia legislators as statesmen or as strong men who came to the capital city to do a job. It was generally seen as a body without decorum, with no sense of purpose, and as a bunch of unruly men who came to Atlanta with attitudes similar to Shriners going to a convention—to have fun and ride around in funny little cars. Legislators didn't even take themselves seriously.

Tommy Irvin, was a longtime state representative from Habersham County. He remembers the attitude when he came to the House in 1956.

"There was a Republican from Fannin County, the only Republican in either the House or Senate. He was a nice fellow, but he only came to the session one or two times a week. He was a traveling salesman, I came to find out. He had been a there a couple of years and I finally asked him how he got elected. It's easy, he told me. Nobody up home knows we have this office," Irvin says.

This was long before Georgia Public Television began putting legislative sessions on the TV screen every night and before television news coverage had become so dominant. Without a stage full of cameras in the hall to record their frivolity, the atmosphere was often chaotic. Peanut shells were tossed on the floor. Someone would send an aide to The Varsity for dinner and pretty soon the chamber was filled with the smell of fresh onions and littered with red take-out boxes. Invariably, some comedic legislator would put on one of the red paper hats the countermen at the Atlanta restaurant wore and prance around the floor.

Veteran political columnist Bill Shipp spent many years covering the capitol for *The Atlanta Constitution* when as much business was being done at the Henry Grady Hotel as at the capitol. The hotel was on Peachtree Street, at the site of the one-time governor's mansion. The state continued to own the property for years afterward and leased it to the hotel's owners. Every January, when the politicians hit town, the Henry Grady came alive. Deals were cut and careers were born—and ended—in the halls of that hotel for more than forty years. Later, it was torn down to make way for the impressive spiral of the Peachtree Plaza Hotel.

Shipp remembers well those years when reporters considered what went on at the Henry Grady Hotel as off limits and took a boys-will-be boys attitude about activities on the floors of the House and Senate. There were frequent published stories about their high-jinks, but the tone of the articles was always in fun. The Senate in 1961 was known as "The Drunk Senate" and Shipp says that the term was well earned.

Sam Hopkins, a morning reporter for *The Atlanta Constitution,* was assigned to cover the committee on alcohol and temperance. "Some came back after lunch drunk as a skunk," says Hopkins, now retired in Atlanta. During one session, the Atlanta newspapers had assigned a reporter to the team of news people assigned to the session. One of his jobs was to keep up with the status of each bill and to file a report each day. As usual, the final day was madness with bills being passed back and forth between chambers. Late in the day, Shipp checked with the newsroom to see how much the new reporter had sent in. The fellow on the desk said they hadn't heard from him. Rushing around the capitol halls, Shipp finally found the missing reporter—drunk in the private quarters of Milledgeville's Culver Kidd—an office in the capitol where every evening lies were told and drinks were poured. It was a daily tradition that continued until the irrepressible senator's death.

"Why haven't you filed your summary?" Shipp asked the wobbling reporter. " 'Cause Culver told me that's all you white boys want to do is work, work, work," he said. Not that the other reporters in the press gallery were always sober. Like the legislators, they operated on a good old boy system. They drank out of the bottles the lobbyists had bought, and laughed at the same jokes as the legislators. It was a time when if you reached into a newsman's desk drawer, you would probably find an open bottle of liquor right next to his spare notebooks.

Billy Winn, now the editorial page editor of *The Columbus Ledger-Enquirer,* was a political reporter for *The Atlanta Journal* in the mid-to-late 1960s. He remembers a session that went *sine die* as one of his Journal colleagues went to the well of the Senate with a pitcher of beer in each hand and made a colorful speech that called for Winn's impeachment. No one cared, for most of the people in the chamber were just as drunk as that reporter.

Meanwhile, on the floor of both houses, there would be a chronic number of passionate speeches about the evil of alcohol. It was a sin! A blight. An abomination! It must be eradicated! Rep. Dorsey Matthews of Moultrie was among the most strident voices about alcohol. He had only one arm, and when he got on an evangelical roll about "al-key-hawl," he would beat that stump on the podium as if he were trying to drive a nail into the mahogany.

Usually, nobody was listening. "You could walk into the General Assembly and somebody like Dorsey would be up there making a speech and other fellows would be reading the newspaper, talking, sleeping, walking around and not paying a bit of attention to whoever was up there pouring out their heart. There was no decorum at all. Television did kind of straighten that out," Shipp says. Perhaps former Gov. Marvin Griffin had the best description of legislative decorum: "It's like three truckloads of bean pickers in the field without a foreman."

Neither the Speaker of the House nor the Lieutenant Governor, who presided over the Senate, were that interested in changing this undignified atmosphere. They were more interested in how the legislators voted than in how they behaved—during the workday or after hours.

A Speaker of the House during that time was asked how many votes he needed to be reelected to that position and he said one— the governor's. The governor was such a powerful figure that on the House speaker's podium there was a telephone with a direct line to the chief executive. It was there so the governor could always reach the speaker, not the other way around. Members of the Senate were almost second—class citizens in a capitol society where longevity prevailed. Because of the County Unit System, senators rotated in and out of office so often that few had a chance to build a power base or to accumulate seniority. Only senators from Fulton County could succeed themselves in that system, so in effect individual senators were lame-ducks on the day they took the oath of office. This made the lieutenant governor even more influential, since he was the constant force who guided and nurtured the ever-present newcomers.

"We were novices," says Robert Smalley of Griffin, a state senator for sixteen years and a freshman in 1961. "There was no institutional memory at all, almost no resistance to the influence of the governor. How could you build up any influence when the fellow sitting next to you wasn't going to be there the next session and neither were you?"

That was why Senator Carl Sanders of Augusta was such a focal point as the session began in 1961. He had represented Richmond County for one term but Jefferson County gave up its turn and allowed him to serve a second two-year term. With that kind of staying power came influence, and he was elected president pro-tem of the senate. It would be Glascock County's time to elect a senator in 1960, so Sanders was considering a run for the Georgia House. But in deference to Sanders and after some hard-nosed political maneuvering, Glascock stepped aside and enabled him to return to the senate. Sanders, an urbane and ambitious attorney, was also considered a possibility for higher office—lieutenant governor, everyone assumed.

Before that session had begun, Sanders was part of the Georgia Chamber of Commerce's annual Pre-Legislative Forum, a tour that takes political leaders to selected Georgia cities. The tour stopped in thirteen communities that year, ending in Sanders' hometown of Augusta. That morning at breakfast, a questioner from the floor asked Sanders if he would favor token school integration. "I don't favor any kind of integration," Sanders said. "I favor public schools."

And, as Zell Miller soon learned, it was public education that was at stake as the gavel sounded in 1961.

8

AN INDEPENDENT VOICE

His black-rimmed glasses made him look like a teacher, which he was. His well-trimmed crew cut made him look young, which he also was. His rough-edged mountain accent might have made some people conclude he was thinking as slow as he talked, which he wasn't. Appearances were deceiving, and Zell Miller soon let his colleagues in the Georgia Senate know that the gentleman from the 40th District was not going to be a freshman who stayed in his seat and kept his mouth shut. That was apparent the first week of the session, and it soon put him at odds with the man who sat in the Big Office downstairs. Senate Floor Leader Gordon Knox had presented a bill that would allow any Georgia student to forego school if Negroes were enrolled. It passed, twenty-nine to fourteen, and four senators spoke in opposition: Charlie Brown of Atlanta, Hugh McWhorter of Decatur, Erwin Mitchell of Dalton and the freshman from Young Harris, Mr. Miller.

McWhorter reminded senators that thousands of children would not get an education if this occurred, and recalled the past. "If they had compulsory education 100 years ago, the South wouldn't be in the shape it is," he said. Senator Dan Hart of Quitman, the co-author of the legislation, naturally spoke in favor of it, and added a word of caution to those who might not be aware that Gov. Ernest Vandiver had seen the bill. "He knows all about it," Hart said, which in legislative code meant the train was leaving the station and you'd better get aboard. Senator Carl Sanders, the president pro tem, said he was for compulsory education but was against integration. He voted for the bill.

Miller did not. And when the enabling education bill passed on a simple show of hands—a tactic that would mask the way an individual legislator voted—the freshman senator rose and asked that his "no" vote be recorded. First Mitchell, then Brown, rose with the same request. If there was any doubt that Miller was going to be an independent voice, it was erased when he led a fight for repealing a limit on the age of college applicants. "Some of my best students were the oldest ones," he said. This also put him at odds with Vandiver, who in 1960 had vetoed an identical bill. When the governor's veto was pointed out to him, Miller fired back that the only reason Vandiver did so was because at the time a twenty-three-year-old Negro was trying to get into Armstrong Junior College in Savannah. "And I understand he isn't even trying now," Miller answered.

The session was consumed by legislation dealing with schools and school integration, and so were the members of the General Assembly. Before it was over, there would even be a bill that suggested Georgia seced from the Union. From the beginning, Zell Miller and a small group of his colleagues were consumed with keeping schools open. For Miller to be so involved in that issue is not surprising. Education had been an obsession in his home for as long as he could remember. He was reared in a culture where learning was expected and education was demanded. Just three years before he came into the Senate, he had been a graduate student at the very university that was under siege. Students he had tutored were still there. So were the faculty friends he had made and admired. He had left a classroom to make the trip to the Legislature. So when Miller said Georgians had a stake in what the politicians were doing, he felt he was one of those Georgians.

Sanders remembers the pressures of that session. "It was a difficult time to speak up, because if you spoke up people thought it indicated you were not totally committed to segregation in every instance. In those days, if that happened, you might as well go back home and fold your tent and not expect to come back to the General Assembly of Georgia. Zell Miller was always an advocate of public schools and was firmly on the side of protecting the public school system at a time when there weren't many people who were thinking in that direction," says Sanders, now an Atlanta attorney.

Miller's first week as a senator was a volatile one. Appeals of Judge William Bootle's decision to break the racial barrier at the University of Georgia were being filed every day, and the courts were promptly issuing new orders. Angry students were marching and screaming racial epithets all over the campus in Athens. Picketers from both sides were outside the capitol every morning when the legislators came to work. The governor received 318 pieces of mail on the issue; 314 said don't close the university. One of the four that said shut the doors was from Lester Maddox, who at the time was still frying chicken in his Atlanta restaurant.

It was a serious time, and legislators were also serious. "Gone was the ribald, carnival air of the old political hustings," wrote Celestine Sibley in *The Atlanta Constitution*. "Gone were the jokes and hearty back-slapping reunions. No high school bands played. No carefree heaps of peanut shells littered the aisles." "Sometimes before you can build a bridge, you have to blow one up," Miller says. "There is a time for political rhetoric and a time for playing political games. Sometimes, when things are serious, you push aside those things, and 1961 was one of those times."

The events in Athens were too tense to be playing. The session had opened on Monday. Wednesday night there was a basketball game between Georgia Tech and Georgia at old Woodruff Hall, a gym so small that fans could almost shake hands with players as they ran down the court. Tech featured the school's first All-American player, Roger Kaiser. But the outmanned Bulldogs threw a defensive blanket over Kaiser that night and seemed to be on their way to an upset victory. Tech fought back, however, and as time was running out, Kaiser got loose from his defender and from

113

forty-five feet out hit a controversial basket to tie the game and force it into overtime. In the extra period, the Yellow Jackets took control and went on to win, 89-80. Georgia fans were not happy.

On their way back to their dormitories that night, Georgia students who had elbowed their way into the bandbox gym met up with others, and the growing crowd decided to go to the girl's dorm where Charlayne Hunter lived. What followed was nasty. Someone threw a bound stack of KKK newspapers from a car. There were constant cries of "Nigger, go home" ringing through the winter night. Hunter was rushed away and taken back to Atlanta with the ever-present Dean Bill Tate at her side. But before the car pulled out, a news photographer captured her weeping in the back seat. That photograph turned the hearts of many Georgians who, though they resented the two students being there, were embarrassed by that scene. That's not Georgia, they thought. Things like that just didn't happen in their state.

Harley Bowers, a sports columnist in Macon, however, did not see it just that way. Like many people in the state, especially Georgia graduates, he was looking for a defense for some of the events that were taking place in Athens. In a column that followed that week, he blamed Kaiser for what happened. "News analysts have not given Kaiser proper credit for his part in the post-game activities. There is every reason to believe the students attending the game would have gone home without a thought of Charlayne were it not for Kaiser's shot," Bowers wrote.

No one at the state capitol was accusing Kaiser, now the successful basketball coach at Life College in Atlanta. They knew better. They sensed that they shared the blame for what transpired that night, along with everyone else in the state.

With Miller and a small group of legislators leading the way, the tide was turning. Early in the session, Miller stepped out. An Atlanta newsman asked the unknown senator where Miller stood on the integration issue. He said, "Integration is not the worst thing that could happen. The worst thing is locking the doors to the university."

Hamilton McWhorter had the toughest task of any senator that year. He represented Clarke County, the home of the university. He was on the spot when he went home and when he took his seat in the Georgia Senate. "I was the guy who had to face the music," McWhorter says. "When I said we had to keep the school open, it wasn't popular, but I was doing what I had to do. Zell didn't have to do that, but he was willing to face it head-on."

Ernest Vandiver had come into that year's General Assembly as a crippled governor. The week before the session, *The Atlanta Constitution* had reported—emphatically, with no room to waver—that Vandiver would be President John F. Kennedy's new secretary of the Army and that Lt. Governor Garland Byrd would take over as governor. The paper cited "high-level sources" and even had a confirmation from United States Rep. Carl Vinson of Milledgeville, who chaired the influential House Armed Services Committee.

For several days, newspapers around the state ran the story. Byrd was already accepting congratulations, and editorial writers were speculating what the move would mean to Georgia. Then, just as suddenly as the story had broken on January 2, the White House issued a statement that Kennedy was now saying no, that Vandiver would not be joining his cabinet. The president complained that he had received too much pressure. Speculation at the time was that JFK's statement referred to Vinson and United States Sen. Richard B. Russell of Georgia since both had openly supported Vandiver for the post.

But in his book *Atlanta Rising*, Frederick Allen said the newspaper's "high-level source" for the original report was Vandiver himself and that Constitution publisher Ralph McGill had joined in lobbying with Kennedy. Allen said Vandiver felt hemmed in by his statements in the 1958 gubernatorial campaign, and didn't see how he could back down. Since he had experience as Georgia's Adjutant General, he thought the job in Washington would be an honorable escape.

The statement he had made was "No, not one." Three words that wouldn't go away. With Vandiver weakened by the stories from the previous week and with the governor locked into his pledge of the past, he appeared to be invisible as the session began. Even his good friends were teasing him and saying he had pledged, "No, not one" and not "No, not two."

What ultimately saved Vandiver was the Sibley Commission that he had appointed the previous summer. Smalley said that plan had evolved on a hunting trip in Albany and that during the weekend George Busbee, an obscure member of the House from Albany, was asked to introduce the measure in the Legislature. The idea for the commission had been born with Coca-Cola chairman Robert Woodruff, and with the counsel of Vandiver's unofficial chief of staff, Griffin Bell. Like other business leaders in the state, Woodruff, even in 1959, was looking for a calm way for Georgia to deal with the school integration question.

When Vandiver emerged and came before a joint session of the General Assembly, he was brilliant. "We must meet together to proclaim to the whole world that public education will be preserved," he said. He called the issue a cancerous growth. "It will devour progress—consuming all in its path—pitting friend against friend, demoralizing all that is good, stifling the economic growth of our state."

What had seemed like disaster became a solution. The Sibley Commission had reported that Georgians wanted to keep schools open at all costs. Legislators could then say that the people of the state had spoken and they were just going along. A solution was there, but for the diehards it was still hard to swallow. "I saw arch segregationists—faced with all that rhetoric they had espoused—come to grips with reality. Those rural, wool-hat conservatives said yes, we'll go along. They reluctantly did what the courts said we had to do. Since then, when the shoe has been on the other foot with liberals, they wouldn't face up. They would have said yes in 1961, but now they say no. I've seen it go full circle. It's interesting to have stayed around that long," Miller says, referring to recent struggles over congressional reapportionment.

Ultimately the Georgia Legislature did what it had to do to preserve Georgia's public school system in what Miller says were some of that body's finest hours. Hunter and Holmes became part of the student body and eventually graduated from the University of Georgia. In recent years, each was honored by the same institution that once did everything in its power to block their admission.

Miller can look back and know that he was part of the small group that stubbornly fought for public education in an atmosphere that Sanders says was total polarization. "That's just Zell's characteristics," Smalley says. "He has an independent mind and he has strong convictions."

Hamilton McWhorter notes that even then people thought Miller had political potential. "He took things so serious, but he was marked for the future. That's easy to say now, but I knew it then. He was going to do well—in politics or in education," says McWhorter, now retired in Atlanta. Through all the acrimony on the floor, the senators of that era were able to separate personalities from issues.

In today's political climate, that often isn't the case. For people such as Miller, that isn't a change for the better. "Politics itself just isn't as much fun. There's too much tension. Among Atlanta and rural legislators. Along racial lines. Between Democrats and Republicans. There is a hardness that didn't used to be here. Used to be legislators could have a knock-down drag-out on a bill, almost come to blows, then that night go out to dinner together and the next day work side-by-side on another bill. The camaraderie, the sense of being a family, the civility is just about lost. I miss it," Miller says.

Sanders says although it wasn't harmonious that year, it did not get physical. "We had some serious discussions and debates, but we got along all right. We accomplished a lot. We passed some good laws and I guess we passed some bad ones. We were cordial, but we were also divided on that one issue," he says. Smalley remembers that in the years that followed, senators evolved into cliques. "In the beginning, we might not agree politically, but we still had respect for each other's rights. That was lost when Lester Maddox came in as lieutenant governor and completely divided the Senate. That's a loss," he says.

McWhorter says those early clashes made Zell Miller a force. "Senators knew where he stood," he said. "You had Zell, Smalley, Sanders and some others. They were willing to take unpopular stands. You could cut the atmosphere in the chambers with a blade when we were debating over the school thing. But we didn't take it personal and it probably brought us closer together. As for Zell, it wasn't popular to believe the way he did, but he never did take on popular issues, did he? You might say he wasn't a good politician, but Zell Miller always voted the way he thought."

The 1961 session was the first for both Smalley and Miller, and when the stately lawyer got home to Griffin in March of that year, he wrote his new friend a letter that Miller still has. "I think if there is one Senator who has been right on every issue that came before us and who has expressed himself fearlessly without condescension, you are certainly that man," wrote Smalley, who left the Senate in 1974, before Miller became its presiding officer.

The year after the Senate dealt with the school crisis, it had to face the prickly issue of one man, one vote, reapportionment and ultimately the demise of the County Unit System. Like so many others, Miller introduced his own plan to apportion the districts. His plan was not adopted, but that didn't stop him from introducing numerous other bills that year. When the 1962 session was over, he was the second busiest senator behind Floor Leader Gordon Knox. There was little rhyme or reason to his proposals, which included bills :

• To require seat belts in all new cars sold in Georgia.

• To require local school superintendents to have professional qualifications.

• To halt tree poaching.

• To create a department of juvenile justice.

• A prohibition bill.

• To allow lawmen to deliver to schools any sugar confiscated from an illegal still.

• To provide grants for needy and qualified students to attend private colleges.

• To ban plastic wrappers on dry cleaning.

• To open a road from the top of Brasstown Bald to Young Harris.

• To provide new governors with proper information after their election.

• To relocate loan offices.

• To authorize state fire marshals to make arrests and carry weapons.

Six became law. "I've always been in a hurry," Miller says. "That's the nature of the beast in me." *The Atlanta Journal* cited the second year legislator as one of the leaders of the Senate in 1962. But *The Augusta Herald* and one of his colleagues had fun with a Miller bill that would change Georgia from the Peach State to the Poultry State. "Georgia might as well admit that South Carolina is now the Number One peach-growing state," Miller told the Senate Rules Committee. Then he cited figures that showed Georgia's income from poultry was twenty-seven times that of the peach crop and represented thirty-two percent of the state's farm income.

When Miller was through, Senator Julian Webb of Donalsonville observed "Will the Senator from the 40th agree that we've got some girls in this state who are peaches?" "Yes, we do," Miller said. "But we have some chicks, too." When the Augusta newspaper decided to take a stand on the peach versus poultry question, its editorial had "beak in cheek" as it commented on Miller's figures and on his estimation that Georgia's broiler production would stretch around the world two-and-a-half times. "The Noble Hen has suffered from the effects of a public image which is somewhat less than inspiring. Such phrases as 'to chicken out' and 'reduced to the state of a plucked chicken' have turned the major part of the poultry world into an unfruitful field for heroic symbols . . . As for placing them around the world, he may have to place them in just such a spectacular formation to overcome the reluctance of Georgians who like their chicken on their dinner plates—not their license plates," the Herald wrote.

The bill never made it to the floor, but Miller was appointed to a study committee. After toying with a run for the House, Miller decided on another run for the Senate. He went back to campaigning in October of 1962, in a special election necessitated by the creation of new districts statewide. In the Democratic Primary, he faced four opponents in a newly drawn district—including Lee Irvin of Cornelia. Irvin forced it into a runoff even though he carried only Habersham, and Miller took seven counties. Only eighty-one votes separated the two.

Before the runoff, Miller sought and received support from the three defeated candidates. He defeated Irvin in the runoff by 553 votes. But this time, he would face opposition in the General Election from a Republican, Dr. C. J. Roper, a Jasper physician. This taught Miller a lesson that was valuable then and continues to be valuable today as the number of Republicans continues to grow in state government.

"In the primary, you have to beat your fellow Democrat. You have beaten each other up real bad, but the next day you have to go out and get his support and the support of his people in order to beat the Republican. It was an amazing lesson. It told me that a fight in politics is only temporary. You have to put it back together to win, and you have to put it back together to govern," Miller says. He defeated Roper with sixty-two percent of the vote.

When the 1962 session was over, Carl Sanders wrote a letter to Miller. "As I have stated on the floor of the Senate," he wrote, "I hope our paths will cross many times in the coming years and that the friendship we have developed will remain as strong as it is today."

Their paths did cross. After the 1962 session, Sanders decided not to run for lieutenant governor and instead entered the race for governor. Former Governor Marvin Griffin was in the race and so was Byrd, who was considered the early favorite. The former lieutenant governor, however, claiming a heart attack, dropped out of the race although to this day many people think Byrd's departure was political, not medical. Ultimately, the race came down to symbols. Griffin represented the old. He campaigned the traditional way, serving barbeque and speeches all over the state. Sanders symbolized the new. He used modern techniques, including television.

When it was over, Griffin said it was apparent that a lot of people who ate his barbeque didn't vote for him. Sanders became the first governor this century to be elected on a popular vote. Sanders, however, is still proud of the fact that he would also have been elected under the old County Unit System. Taking a chance, Miller used a photograph of him and Sanders on his campaign literature in his Senate race against Irvin and Roper. Sanders even endorsed him in that race, and Miller returned the favor in Sanders' campaign against Griffin. They both won, of course.

The General Assembly they would greet that next January was truly changed. The end of the County Unit System meant a new generation of Georgians were now able to be involved. Of the old Senate, only five returned: Miller, Smalley, Charlie Brown of Atlanta, Harry Jackson of Columbus, and Erwin Owens of Dahlonega. Among the promising freshman class was LeRoy Johnson of Atlanta, the first black to serve in the Georgia Senate and the first to serve in a deep South Legislature since Reconstruction. Included in that new group was a former school board member from Plains, Jimmy Carter. Carter was seated after the courts found vote tampering in Georgetown and called for a second election. Like Miller, Carter took his duties seriously, and the two began a friendship that would later affect both of their political careers.

It was a period in Miller's career that he relished. "I just loved the legislative process," he said. "I tell freshman legislators now that none of them look forward to the first buzzer of a legislative session more than I do. I loved it then and I love it now."

9

ZELL AND THE 'KIDS'

The trip was decorated with presidential show biz. Lyndon B. Johnson was coming. Too bad Lady Bird couldn't make it, but she would come to Georgia in a few days. Every seat on the plane had a politician and a purpose. The governor would be there in Atlanta to meet him, with his wife of course. There would be high school bands. There were adoring Democrats to fawn over the big-boned Texan and reporters to record his every move.

Up in Gainesville, his staff arranged for him to meet some poor people. In a nice theatrical touch, he would be speaking at Roosevelt Square, near the very spot where Franklin Delano Roosevelt spoke twenty-six years before. Then it was on to the mountains, where the president could dramatize his war on Appalachian poverty. Carl Sanders, the governor of Georgia, received the unexpected call just days before Lyndon Baines Johnson's arrival on May 7, 1964. It was a whirlwind week for Sanders since Senator Edward Kennedy of Massachusetts had just passed through town on his way to a speech at the University of Georgia and had stopped off at the Governor's Mansion.

Not surprisingly, there was a hot political summer ahead. Senator Barry Goldwater of Arizona, working hard for the GOP presidential nomination, had just been in the state for the annual meeting of Georgia Republicans and had made enthusiastic speeches in Atlanta and Columbus. By the time folks at the state's new governor's mansion could change the sheets from Kennedy's visit, Lady Bird Johnson would be checking in. Not that Sanders would tell the White House how busy it was down in Georgia, for in 1964 visits from presidents were special occasions, especially in the South, a region the Democrats and the Republicans had taken for granted too long.

Lyndon Baines Johnson was coming through Georgia as part of a tour to collect votes and to sell his $228 million emergency relief program for the people of Appalachia. "Progress has passed this region by," he said. It was appropriate for him to stop in the state since 675,000 Georgians lived in the affected area with a per capita income of $1,169 a year.

Phil Landrum would be traveling with the president. Nothing unusual about that. So would two other ranking Democrats, Senator Herman Talmadge and Representative Carl Vinson. Presidents like to surround themselves with home folks. Democrats like to travel with Democrats, and incumbents enjoy being around incumbents. Besides, Johnson's primary speech on the trip would be in Gainesville, one of the major towns in Landrum's Ninth Congressional District. It was natural that Landrum and his wife have seats on Air Force One. What made this unusual was that Landrum for the first time in five terms had some pesky opposition that year in a former state senator from Young Harris, Zell Miller. He was also a Democrat, so the president would never get involved in a family political squabble, would he?

A reporter in Atlanta asked the president about the politics of his trip when he arrived. "This is the politics of trying to get an Appalachia bill passed," Johnson said. "But as for partisan politics, no." The arrival of President Johnson late on the night of May 7th made the front page of the next morning's Atlanta Constitution. It was after ten PM when he arrived and the deadline clock was ticking, but that didn't stop the newspaper. It covered every aspect of his visit, from the giddy women who got to shake his hand outside the Dinkler Plaza Hotel to the hotel staff that prepared his room. The fact that Lynda Bird Johnson, his college-age daughter was along drew another article.

Reading the paper, one learned that Johnson was the first sitting president to spend the night in Atlanta since William McKinley in 1898. The Democratic Party scrapbooks would be filled with articles and, more importantly, with that kind of coverage and some good weather, there probably would be a large crowd, and there was. Officials estimated 500,000 people turned out along the way. Someone asked Herman Talmadge how many he thought were there and the senator wouldn't venture a guess. "I've never seen such a crowd," Talmadge said. Johnson's schedule worked to perfection. When he went to the microphone in a festive Gainesville it was on a podium a local woodworker had made for Franklin Delano Roosevelt when he came to Hall County to view the damage left behind by the Tornado of 1938.

As advertised, Johnson talked about the plight of the Appalachian poor and how his plan would put food on their table and money in their pocket. The next day's *Constitution* draped an eight-column photograph across the page depicting a panoramic view of the scene at the Gainesville square. There were stories from all the paper's star reporters with political editor Reg Murphy's main story nestled under a headline that an old school newspaperman would say they had been saving for the Second Coming.

Nudged in under the lead story about the day was a one-column headline above the fold that gave Phil Landrum a page one push he could not have bought in the state's largest daily newspaper. The headline told even those who were not there that the President had endorsed Landrum.

Lyndon Baines Johnson was as direct as the headline writer. He said the Georgian was one of the leading congressmen in the country and that his administration needed leadership that only Phil Landrum could offer. Then, in one breath, he linked Landrum to the most holy name in Democratic party politics. "I want you to get a monument to Phil Landrum that you can put over there beside the one of Franklin D. Roosevelt," Johnson said. Zell Miller stood there in that mob of cheering people and was devastated. So were the college kids who made up his campaign staff. More than three decades later, and with Lyndon Johnson long since dead, Phil Gailey can still get angry about Johnson's use of the presidential pulpit. "I still hold a grudge against old Lyndon," Gailey says. That morning, all he could do was listen.

"It was the only experience I've ever had with politics outside journalism and it was enough to convince me that I wanted to pursue journalism. We were under-funded. We had no money. Zell was up against one of the most entrenched members of Congress. Then Lyndon Johnson, President Lyndon Johnson, comes down to campaign for Landrum who had everything going for him—money, name recognition, the powers of the incumbency. I resented the fact that he also had the President of the United States up there, who should have been impartial or neutral. I still hold that grudge," Gailey says.

As Johnson spoke, some of Miller's young lieutenants pulled a 'Zell Miller for Congress' sign around as close as the Secret Service and police would let them. As they did, they heard taunts and jeers. Mainly, they were ignored. "We tried to work the perimeter. It was primitive. But you work with what you have and all we had were volunteers, ideas, energy, a trailer and a sign," Gailey says. Marti Fullerton and Hank Huckaby were there with Gailey. All were college students at the time. Gailey came from the University of Georgia. His interest in the campaign was kindled after reading about Miller's candidacy and hearing first-hand information about him from some family friends in Homer, Georgia. He wrote Miller a letter, asking idealistic questions about where the candidate stood on all of the issues of the day. At the bottom of the letter was a PS. "No hedging please."

Miller might have sent some kind of political brochure, but instead he wrote out detailed answers to Gailey's questions. It impressed Gailey so much that he gave up his quest for a newspaper internship that summer and joined Miller's campaign.

On the square that morning with Johnson on the podium, Zell and Shirley Miller tried not to show their emotions. It was the first time either of them had ever seen a President of the United States, only they could not appreciate the aura of the man or the office. They knew LBJ didn't know Zell Miller, that it was politics—good politics, the candidate had to admit—but it still stung. "I was shocked," Miller said. "I considered myself much closer to Johnson's Appalachian programs philosophically than Landrum. It was a brilliant move on LBJ's part. But once the shock subsided, I was the rabbit in the briar patch. It attracted attention. I became even more the underdog. I was suddenly in the majors hitting against the hardest throwers of them all." "Within twenty-four hours, Zell said we had a bumper sticker: 'Think for Yourself,' and we were off and running against LBJ *and* Landrum," Shirley Miller remembers.

Three days later, with the president back in Washington, Miller took the Georgia Senate floor on a point of personal privilege, and criticized Landrum and—indirectly—the president of the United States. Miller said the president's advisors either had not done their homework or, perhaps, they had and learned the congressman was in serious trouble with the homefolks. "I'm not here to yelp like a beagle hound held up by the ears but I know how he feels," he said, referring to some legendary flak LBJ had received for holding up some White House dogs by their ears. Nor was Miller there to "suggest that an Association for the Prevention of Cruelty to Congressional candidates be established."

Even then he had a gift for turning biting phrases that media folks love to quote. But once the sarcasm was over, Miller ran down a list of political questions Landrum should answer, centering around the Ninth District Congressman's opposition to federal aid for education. "The school teachers and school children want to know why," he said. Miller also took on Johnson. "It was a question of the right of the people of the 9th District to choose their own congressman without dictation from the federal government," he said. "I believe the people of the 9th District want to retain this one right they still have, because if we didn't, we would be saying in effect,' Mr. LBJ, this is your congressman, not ours.' "

J. K. Hutchings wrote a folksy column called "Tootin' In Towns." Not long after the Johnson visit, he wrote a piece that reminded readers of another president who had inserted himself into Georgia politics. Before he got to Johnson, using language that would expand the definition of hyperbole, he talked about Miller's heritage, remembering both Grady and Birdie, saying that Miller "grew up in the sunlight of inspiration" and that it was "woven into his life, like the fiber of a hickory tree." As for the candidate's wife, he wrote that "It is pretty hard for any force in this world to stop or defeat in any way a couple like Zell and Shirley."

Back to Johnson, he talked about what happened in Gainesville, how the President of the United States had called Landrum to the platform and praised him and told the people of the district to vote for him. Hutchings didn't think they would. "The people of Georgia, and especially the mountain people, are sort of mule-headed," he wrote, remembering 1938 when FDR came to Georgia and asked folks to vote for an obscure attorney named Lawrence Camp instead of Walter F. George, the incumbent United States Senator. "The people voted for George," wrote Hutchings. "Let us all work together to build a monument for Zell Miller—with piles and piles of votes."

Even with overly fervent supporters such as that columnist, running against Landrum had not been an easy decision. Miller could have stayed in the Georgia Senate. He was building a base of support and seemed to have found a niche there. He was part of the governor's legislative team and he was learning more every day about the inner workings of the legislature. But to a politician or a political scientist, Washington was the pinnacle. "Washington was where it was happening. A revolution was going on with all of Johnson's initiatives. Besides, it was a higher office," Miller says, explaining his reasoning for opposing Landrum.

A few weeks before Johnson came, Miller had led a caravan of buses filled with young people to the capitol. Most of them were Young Harris students, but his campaign claimed all twenty-two counties in the district were represented. Harold Cunningham, the chairman of the Towns County Democratic Party, presented the

$750 qualifying fee, and after the money had changed hands Zell, Shirley, their two boys and Miss Birdie joined the college students for a picnic on the state capitol lawn.

By then, Fullerton and Huckaby had moved into the rock house with the Millers and were busy on the campaign. They had quit their jobs in Atlanta and moved back to Young Harris. Not for the money, either. Both were essentially unpaid, though they got room, board and a free education on gut-level politics. They knew then and they know now that it was because of Miller, their favorite professor and later a politician they both would work for many different times. "I had bought the first car I ever had and Zell paid my car payment for those three or four months. It was $71 a month," Huckaby says.

Fullerton still laughs about the Big Fish. Landrum had voted for financial aid to a national aquarium in Washington but had not supported federal aid to education. Miller wanted to use that in the campaign in a way that folks could understand so he had an idea. "He had some mountaineer in Young Harris build this huge wooden fish that he had mounted on wheels," Fullerton says. "Miller had a huge Plymouth station wagon that probably had 200,000 miles on it when we started going over the district. We called it 'Leapin' Lena.' We'd go through little towns, pulling that fish and talking about Phil Landrum over the loud speakers that were on top of the car. You don't think that wasn't a conversation piece."

Miller was frying the fish himself. "Phil Landrum voted to build a $10 million aquarium in Washington, but voted against a school construction bill that would have saved Georgia $180 million," Miller told the Gainesville Optimist Club that August. "I think our school children are more important than fish." As Landrum tried to redefine himself, Miller hammered at who he was. "This is no new model Zell Miller. This is the same highly–respected educator who has ably represented his fellow citizens in the Georgia State Senate. His support is from the people—and not from special interests," one of his campaign cards said.

Gailey is now the editor of editorials for *The St. Petersburg Times.* His newspaper resumé includes *The Atlanta Constitution, The Washington Star,* and *The New York Times.* In the summer of 1964, he was talking to the folks in Northeast Georgia over a speaker system in a station wagon that was pulling a big fish. And he was also quoting an unlikely figure in some of Miller's paid political ads. "They let me tape a few radio spots and being young and foolish from the forests of Homer, Georgia in one or two of them I quoted Shakespeare. You can imagine how that went over in Blairsville or Hiawassee. I can imagine people saying who's that idiot on the radio quoting Shakespeare and asking us to vote for Zell Miller. I said Landrum reminded me of something from King Lear: 'I shall do great things. What they are yet I know not, but they shall be the wonders of the earth.' I followed that by saying as far as we can tell, he hasn't done much of anything except serve special interests. It was fun and I guess it was harmless," Gailey says.

Most people don't remember that Landrum and Miller were not the only names on the Democratic ballot in 1964. The third candidate was Franklin Stone "Buckeye" Uhl Sr. His name was so long it took up two lines on the ballots. At that time in the Ninth District, voters were supposed to strike out all the names except for the candidate they were voting for. Only one name was supposed to be showing. Careless voters either ignored Uhl completely or left one line of his name visible. Those ballots weren't counted. Such ballots could cost either Landrum or Miller. "Nobody had ever seen him before or since. He never campaigned a day. He had no posters, no campaign literature. He was just on the ballot," Miller says. "I knew who he was, but most folks didn't. He was just on the ballot."

When the votes were counted that September, Phil Landrum was reelected. He polled 51.8 percent of the votes to the upstart Miller's 45.2 percent, and Uhl received three percent. Only 6,000 votes separated the two, nearly 7,500 votes were thrown out because of mismarked ballots. "But you don't dwell on those things," Miller says. "You move on." Huckaby says the young people remained optimistic until the end, but he now thinks Miller knew in those final weeks they were not going to win. "Given everything we had overcome, we came awfully close," he says. "I realize that more later, looking back on those events."

Today, Miller is just as proud of his college kids as he was then. "They were exceptional, very smart, very dedicated. It was exciting. David was fighting Goliath. It was new against old. I learned—and I understood this very well before I got into the race—that one can lose and still win. A basic lesson in politics is that sometimes you give ground to gain ground. I became the young "nobody" who almost beat the Dean of Georgia's Congressional Delegation *and* President Johnson *combined.* I was thirty-two years old with a good sized notch on my gun and knowing that Disraeli was right: 'Finality is not the language of politics'."

While the young people who worked for him were smart and talented, it was Zell Miller who made the decisions. He was both candidate, campaign manager, press secretary and envelope stuffer. For Miller, this would be a pattern that followed him for decades. It would become both a blessing and a curse as he would learn when he went after another position in Washington. For all of them, it was an exercise in basic political campaigning.

Miller believes Landrum was caught napping in 1964. "The first time, I slipped up on him, caught him unaware," he says. That isn't borne out by Landrum's actions. How could it be that he overlooked Miller and his campaign kids when an established congressman, the senior member of the state delegation with a political war chest of funds, invited the White House into his district to help him? He also regularly came out of his office in Washington, something he did not do that often. Someone in the Landrum camp and the Democratic Party mainstream was taking the challenge very seriously.

Two years later, when Miller again jumped into the race, the incumbent veteran certainly acknowledged his opponent's presence. "Landrum was ready. He had two years to patch up his organization. Also, with the Appalachian Poverty bill came grants by the dozens," he says. "Everybody was getting courthouses, sewer systems and water systems." Years later, opponents in campaign after campaign would study those two races and, despite that notch on his gun, use them against Miller.

It was noticed even then by Art Pine, an *Atlanta Constitution* political reporter who in 1966 wrote an analysis that compared the two congressional races. In 1964, Miller was seen to the political left of Landrum. In 1966, it seemed he moved to Landrum's right. *The Gainesville Tribune* responded in an editorial: "Pine wondered if Miller had changed in these two years from a liberal to a conservative. It is a logical enough question to ask of any candidate for such office. Another equally logical question, yet unasked by those who are analyzing this particular race and its candidates, is whether maybe Miller has stood firm and Landrum has moved from center to left."

Writing in *The Atlanta Constitution* that March, Reg Murphy wrote a column that asked if Landrum was moderate—which he said would be a key question among mountain voters. "What the race really boils down to is whether Landrum's moderation of his view in the last few years has moved him abreast of his constituents," Murphy wrote. "He did have, after voting against minimum wage increases and federal aid to education, the image of a mountain conservative. Miller is betting that the image remains and that the labor-teacher-moderate coalition he figures to put together will beat Landrum."

In August of 1964, speaking at the Gwinnett County Courthouse, Miller promised to give half of his congressional salary—$15,000—as a reward for solving the murder of three Gwinnett lawmen four months before. Before moving into a lengthy attack of Landrum's record on education, he talked about the FBI's interest in solving the cases of dead civil rights workers in Mississippi. "Why haven't we seen that same kind of diligence and money spent in Gwinnett County?" he asked. Miller then added that the Civil Rights Act was "neither constitutionally acceptable nor fundamentally proper," and said money appropriated to implement the bill "could be better spent with a thorough and complete investigation of Communist infiltration in the civil rights movement."

Gailey remembers an uneasiness on his part in 1964 when he realized that Miller had come out against the 1964 Civil Rights Bill—a stance that was hardly unusual among politicians of that era. "I understand why. It would have been an act of political suicide to have embraced it, but it still was the right thing to do. One of the things I did was to go to the small towns and meet with black ministers. I'd tell them that both of the guys were opposed to the bill, but they should consider which one of them would do the best job of representing their interests. As I recall, many of them understood why Zell had taken that position," he says.

Speaking to the Canton Kiwanis Club, Miller identified Landrum as a tool of President Johnson. Of LBJ's anti-poverty act, he said it was "laid by Lyndon Johnson and hatched by Phil Landrum." He said this act would go down in history as one of most wasteful uses of taxpayer money conceived by man. He charged that it was being used to rent tuxedos for senior proms, to fly youngsters to big league baseball games and to bail them out of jail when they got drunk."

Attacking Landrum's absenteeism in congress, a Miller ad in the paper said the incumbent "was not even present to vote on the National Defense Appropriation during the height of the fighting in Vietnam. How can he say he supports our boys in Vietnam when he isn't even present to vote for supplies and ammunition for them?" Miller followed that with a list of bills Landrum was present to vote on.

In what sounded like excerpts from a speech, an article in the campaign paper explained how Miller and Landrum differed on major issues:

> "His is the something for nothing philosophy while I was
> always taught that when someone gets
> something–for–nothing then someone else must earn
> something without getting it.

"On many pieces of legislation that have come before Congress in the last few years, my position would have been much different.

"For instance—I would not have voted to pack the House Rules committee with liberal Congressmen to make it easier to get Civil Rights legislation through Congress. Mr. Landrum did.

"I would not have voted for the Rent Subsidy Bill which uses your tax money to pay other people's rent. Mr. Landrum did.

"I would not have voted for these things, however, there are some things I would have voted for that he voted against.

"I would have voted with those who were trying to cut off trade with countries supporting North Vietnam. Mr. Landrum did not.

"I would have voted with those who were attempting to cut off foreign aid to wealthy Egypt at the very time Egyptian President Nasser was making violent anti-American speeches. Mr. Landrum did not.

"Is this the representative you want to keep 'working' for you?"

It was a race and a time when candidates were so slippery that it is difficult to label either one of them. Reading their rhetoric and examining the issues is difficult using modern standards. The bottom line is that Miller went back and forth between the two campaigns but so did Landrum. So did many candidates of that era. Expediency was a reality. Both Miller and Landrum were more interested in votes than in principle. Whether he is classified liberal, moderate or conservative, Landrum won by a greater margin the second time.

With the help of party regulars, Phil Landrum ran a methodical campaign that left very little undone. Money was always scarce. For the first—and only time—Miller was using borrowed money in the race. It was a mistake that he warns young candidates about today for it was a desperate decision that later threatened to personally bankrupt him. On a Saturday in September, just eleven days before the primary, he hired country music star Bill Anderson to spend the day in the Ninth District, picking, singing and politicking. It was a tactic that though used by Southern politicians for decades, would become a trademark of Miller's as the years went by.

Miller paid Anderson $1,000 to tour the district and the size of the crowds indicated it was money well spent. Wherever they went—Buford, Cumming, Canton, Toccoa, Commerce, Carnesville, Commerce, and Gainesville—the people were enthusiastic. Miller would learn that people will listen to your hired music just like Marvin Griffin's people ate his pork barbeque, but they may not vote for you. Anderson remembers the day and the tiny planes. "Zell chartered a bunch of little planes, and country singers have never got along very well with little planes," says Anderson, still a friend of Miller after more than three decades. "We flew all over, picking, singing and drawing a crowd."

Country musicians had been part of the political stump in the South for decades. Gene Talmadge used Fiddlin' John Carson. George Wallace in Alabama had a band that would take off their hats and do a sacred number—"The governor's favorite," they always said—just before Wallace hit the stage. If it wasn't a country singer, it was a gospel group. The Statesmen Quartet used to sing for Herman Talmadge whenever he called. Gospel singer/songwriter Lee Roy Abernathy even ran for governor of Georgia, just like in Tennessee where Roy Acuff ran for governor and Tex Ritter ran for the United States Senate.

No political figure would ever be more identified with music than Miller, however. He listened and studied it and from the beginning he used it as part of his politics. While Miller had used Lee Kirby, his fiddle-playing friend, in his 1960 State Senate campaign, it really began with Anderson, who explains why music is useful. "You can get a little old courthouse square where nothing else happens and when you start making music people just naturally come," says Anderson, who that day in 1966 brought along his band, "The Po-Boys."

Along the way that afternoon, Anderson talked to the crowd about politics. "I used to live in Commerce—in the Ninth District—and if I lived here now I know how I would vote September 14th. I would vote for Zell Miller for Congress—because he's our kind of people," said Anderson, who lived most of his early life in the comfortable Atlanta suburb of Avondale Estates.

Then Anderson would bring on the candidate. "I want to thank Bill Anderson, my college classmate at the University of Georgia, for coming down here and helping me campaign all over the Ninth District. I do not have unlimited campaign funds as my opponent does, and I have to rely on the hard work of my supporters throughout the district and friends like Bill and his boys to get my message to the people," Miller told the crowds. Anderson and his boys came to help and to pick up that thousand dollars. But they also planned to be back in Nashville in time for that night's performance of the Grand Ole Opry. Between the crowds and those little airplanes, they soon were running behind. At first it was minutes. Finally, they were two hours off schedule. The decision was made to skip Blairsville and go straight to Toccoa where they would end the hectic tour before heading for Nashville. "I remember flying right over Blairsville," Anderson says.

And Blairsville was unforgiving. "At church the next day, I ran into a firestorm," Miller remembers. "People in Blairsville were mad as hell. Not because they wanted to see me. They wanted Bill. Some folks were saying the whole bunch must have gotten drunk. I knew I had to do something." Anderson's schedule wouldn't allow him to come back before the primary, but he recommended a female singer he thought folks in the area might like. Nobody had heard of her at the time, but Anderson assured Miller that she had a great voice. Her name was Tammy Wynette.

"It was just a month before 'Apartment Number Nine' would become a big hit for Tammy. I paid her with a check for $150, drawn on the Bank of Hiawassee," Miller says. Once Tammy had finished singing for the people in Blairsville, she packed up and was heading in to Lavonia where she had a show that night. Maybe she sensed how broke Miller and his campaign were or maybe she had just worked for politicians before. Whatever the reason, she and her band pulled off the highway and she went into the Bank of Hiawassee. Tammy presented the check to a teller. "Could you cash this check?" the singer asked, laying it on the counter. "It's on a local politician and I wanted to cash it before I left town." The teller was Shirley Miller.

10

BACK TO THE ARENA

Zell Miller was making money for the first time in his forty-one years. The timing could not have been better, for two races for Congress had left his family with a second mortgage on their home in Young Harris and had drained their personal bank account. Out of politics, he had been a teacher and to supplement that he had tried the newspaper business and sold mobile homes. None of these paid that many bills. The family didn't even own a color TV, watching an eleven-inch portable and a second-hand model he had bought for $35. There was $2,418.18 in the bank, but the two boys were both headed for college. Shirley was still working at the bank. Finally, her husband was pulling his weight on payday. But Zell Miller was bored.

Governor Jimmy Carter had appointed him to the Georgia Pardons and Paroles Board, one of the safest and most sought after jobs in the state government. It carried a seven-year term, so even when Carter left office Miller would still have his job. The job paid a healthy $30,000 a year, and in July of 1974 it would bump up to $32,500. Those benefits should have been attractive to Miller and they were, because the years leading up to Pardons and Paroles had not been rewarding emotionally or financially. In some people's eyes, he was becoming a political hack. The jobs he had held were meaningful, but they were political patronage appointments, based on friendship and not necessarily ability. He was in danger of being seen as one of those people who at every meal line up at the public trough.

Carl Sanders had appointed him state director of probation. He had been the personnel officer and assistant director of the Board of Corrections. He had been executive secretary to Lester Maddox in both the governor's and lieutenant governor's office. He had been executive director of the Georgia Democratic Party. Now he was one of five people who served on the state Pardons and Paroles Board. Years down the road, he would see those jobs had served a purpose, but to an ambitious person who could still remember the ideals and challenges that brought him to the state capitol, they were mundane and boring.

Shirley Miller had not agreed with her husband's plan to run that second congressional race against Phil Landrum, but she agreed with him when he began to talk to her about running for lieutenant governor. Miller has always thought in a political vein. "I didn't need a pollster to tell me I could get into a runoff for lieutenant governor," he says. His wife was more pragmatic. "I wanted him to do this so in later years he wouldn't look back and wonder what would have happened if he had not run in 1974," she said.

Because of his job, Miller hadn't been able to talk to many people. "It was an awkward situation. I felt that I couldn't ethically talk with anybody else about my chances or my finances or anything while I was still serving on that very sensitive board. So I talked it over with Shirley and the boys since they stood to have more to lose than anybody. We discussed it for a long time," he said.

For most people, being lieutenant governor was not a political dream in 1974. Lester Maddox had turned the office into a sideshow by four years of constant public bickering with Jimmy Carter. Maddox looked at the job as only a rest stop between gubernatorial terms, and he treated it as only a platform to needle the governor and other adversaries. The state constitution and its one-term limit forced him out of office in 1970, but in 1974, he planned to move back downstairs to the big office—which at the time everyone assumed he would.

Internally, Maddox had paid little attention to senate business and it had turned into struggles that pitted senator against senator. Maddox's cronies were in control, and only a few so-called "super senators" wielded much power during the session. Politically, the office had not been a good stepping stone. Among recent office-holders, neither Garland Byrd, Peter Zack Geer nor George T. Smith had been able to build a political foundation there. Geer and Smith had not even been able to get re-elected lieutenant governor. In many people's eyes, when the General Assembly wasn't in session it was little more than a honorary position that had few duties and no power. Yet when Georgians voted in 1974, twelve people would be on the ballot. A closer look at the twelve candidates is revealing. Only two—Zell Miller and Max Cleland—have ever been heard from again politically. Most people were staying away from the race. It wasn't called "Light Governor" for nothing.

The other Democrats who eventually mounted campaigns were former Jesup Mayor Mary Hitt, professional racist and perennial candidate J.B. Stoner of Marietta, former legislators Lamar Northcutt of College Park, Frank Coggin of Hapeville, Bill Salem of Lyons and Bill Laite of Macon, along with lobbyist R.C. Mitcham of Warm Springs and Decatur physician J. D. Jackson. The Republicans were John Savage, an Atlanta dentist and a well-liked member of the Georgia House, opposed by Windell Whitmore, a Rockdale County barber. Not one of them turned into a household word.

To show how lightly the office was regarded at that time, a major part of Savage's platform was a proposal to abolish the office altogether, an idea that people around the state began to discuss thoughtfully. The Republican candidate was not alone in his thinking. Even Governor Jimmy Carter agreed with him.

Nor was Miller well known among rank-and-file Georgia voters. Within the Democratic Party, he was a familiar face. On the street, no one recognized him. He was known in north Georgia, but that part of the state was not powerful politically. Insiders saw the offices of governor and lieutenant governor as being controlled by gnat line Democrats. "Check the records, friends," Hal Gulliver wrote in the Constitution. Those north Georgians don't know much about politics. Oh, they pretend they do, and they fuss a lot with each other. But when have they ever gotten state office?"

Even close to home, his friends and neighbors in North Georgia assumed that Miller was waiting for Phil Landrum's retirement, and in 1973 there was a hot rumor floating around the state that the dean of the Georgia Delegation was about to do just that. Miller didn't wait for Landrum or his decision. On December 17 he held a press conference and announced that on the last day of 1973 he was resigning from the Pardons and Paroles Board and would become a candidate for lieutenant governor. Just after midnight, minutes after the New Year began, Zell and Shirley Miller were in Underground Atlanta handing out campaign literature to the partying crowds. They worked until two A.M.

The Georgia media knew Miller from his work with the Maddox Administration and with the state Democratic Party, and immediately labeled him the frontrunner. Ted Oglesby of *The Gainesville Times* even suggested that Miller remember what Carl Sanders had done in 1962, and instead of going after the state's No. 2 job set his sights on the governor's office. It may have been the first time that anyone had put into print the idea that Miller might one day be governor. "He has solid connections with all three elements of the party—the Carter Alliance, the Maddox Alliance and the group that likes neither," Oglesby wrote. "He is conservative but progressive. Right now, Zell Miller would be the hardest Democratic hopeful for the Republicans to beat."

Gulliver said his performance as party secretary ought to be remembered. "It is not necessarily on record, not in any one place at least, but Miller somehow functioned incredibly in that tough year in that tough job in a way that won respect from the supporters of George McGovern and the Democrats who just couldn't go that route at all. Indeed, Miller might be the only statewide candidate who might well draw the votes of both Governor Jimmy Carter and Lt. Governor Lester Maddox," wrote Gulliver.

Miller's experience around the capitol would prove invaluable and it began with Maddox. Miller had been working with the Department of Corrections when the job as the governor's executive secretary, came open late in 1968. The capitol was shocked when Agriculture Commissioner Phil Campbell and Insurance Commissioner Jimmy Bentley, two old-line Democrats, were among a number of state officials who joined the Republican Party. Campbell was not only changing parties, he was moving to Washington to become under-secretary of agriculture in the Nixon Administration. Maddox was going to appoint Irvin to Campbell's old agriculture job, leaving a key opening in his own office.

Maddox knew his way around a restaurant kitchen, but he knew very little about the inner-workings of the legislature so replacing Irvin was important. His advisors insisted that he needed a former member of the General Assembly and both Irvin, press secretary Bob Short and Walter O. Brooks—all of whom knew Miller from the mountains—began pushing the former Young Harris senator.

The governor hardly knew Miller. They had met only briefly during the 1966 campaign at a stop in Cherokee County, but with Irvin and Short's support, Maddox had appointed him to the personnel job in corrections. There Miller had soon made a mark for himself, helping raise standards for prison guards, requiring a high school education and for them to pass the State Merit exam.

When Miller joined the governor's staff, the plan was for the appointment to be temporary. Popular legislator Mac Barber of Commerce was to move into the job following the General Assembly, and Miller would go back to Corrections. That never happened, and Miller stayed with Maddox for his last two years in the governor's office.

Miller's personal and political allies were surprised. He had been seen as a progressive legislator and not even his opposition to the Civil Rights Act during his campaign against Landrum had changed that perception. For him to be connected to the axe-handle reputation of Maddox, who had openly defied the federal and state courts as a businessman, seemed incongruous.

Observers such as newsman Bill Shipp offer another theory. "A lot of people don't know this but you had a lot of Carl Sanders' influence over Maddox and his staff. Look at what he did as governor. What he did and what he had said were two entirely different things. My suggestion is that some of the wiser heads prevailed on Lester to take on people who knew their way around," Shipp says. To Shipp, the genesis of the conflicts between Miller and Tom Murphy began in the Maddox years. Murphy, who was a member of the House, had cast the symbolic vote in the Georgia House that elected Maddox over Bo Callaway in 1966. He served as Maddox's floor leader.

Shipp says the presence of both figures on the Maddox team is symbolic. "It was almost as if there was a good Lester and a bad Lester. He made great leaps in integrating state employees. He appointed the first black ever named to the State Board of Corrections. His appointments to the bench were as good as any ever made. He was a very compassionate governor and, all things considered, a good governor. And the bad Lester was epitomized by Murphy in some ways. He could be very conservative, very sensitive, very erratic. People like Miller butted heads with the other crowd all the time," he says.

Miller often blocked the way into the governor's office. "Lester Maddox was, and is, basically an honest and kind person. He was easy to work for because he delegated so much to you. His heart and instincts were largely in the right place. We just refortified them and kept some of the wrong-headed folks away," he says.

At the time, Miller operated out of a small office just off the main lobby of the governor's office. Maddox gave him free rein in many areas and Miller soon became known in many circles as "the assistant governor." In the vernacular of the capitol, he was the governor's "tail-twister" and "head counter." It was a job that expanded his view of state government dramatically, giving him experience in both politics and personalities.

Maddox was pleased, especially impressed with his young aide's energy, and often told people how much work Miller could get done. "I can't overload him," Maddox said. In 1971, Maddox talked about Miller's political potential. "He has a remarkable capacity for saying no to people without making them mad. I want to keep him as long as I can. But someday, he ought to run for some office," Maddox said.

As for Miller, he learned how the executive branch worked. He was at its center. Maddox gave him unprecedented authority and responsibility. Miller also made great contacts in every county in Georgia, and through that job the press came to regard him favorably. With that kind of authority comes friction. After Maddox was ending his term as governor and on his way up the steps of the capitol to the lieutenant governor's office Miller began to sense that more and more of those "wrong-headed" people had his boss' ear. That became more acute after Jimmy Carter was governor and he and Maddox were fighting their undeclared war. Mike Padgett of Augusta, Stanley Smith of Perry and others were spending time with the new lieutenant governor and they were hardly temperate in the way they advised Maddox on his dealings with Carter.

Looking back at those two years, Miller has no regrets. He points with pride to the Maddox Administration's appointments, how it broke the racial barrier on state boards, county welfare boards and the Georgia State Patrol. More than anything, he says his departure was inevitable once Maddox took his new job. "I left because it was much different being an advisor to a *lieutenant* governor and a *governor*. All the difference in the world," says Miller who at the time said there just wasn't that much to do. "Also, many of the senators were beginning to get to him in a way that disturbed me, too much fighting between him and Carter."

Those things weren't mentioned in 1970 when he left an office he called a family. "I look upon our relationship as that of a father and son, because you have had a father's influence upon my life. Having lost my own as an infant, I have found out now what it means to have someone you love, respect and look up to and to play a father's role in my life," Miller said in his letter of resignation to Maddox.

But the father was not pleased with the son's new job. When Zell Miller was introduced as the new executive director of the

Georgia Democratic Party, nothing registered with Maddox except for the fact that the person making the announcement was Governor Jimmy Carter. The name said it all. To Maddox, it was one of his people going over the wall to the other side. "Industrial piracy," Maddox said, attacking the governor for taking his valued aide.

Maddox has never forgiven Carter for hiring Miller away, or for anything else. But he has forgiven Miller, who looks back on his time with Maddox and his job with the Democratic Party as the foundation for what was ahead. In 1994, when Miller was watching election returns in a suite at the Colony Square Hotel, Maddox dropped by for a visit. Later, in the lobby outside the ballroom, he entertained anyone who reached out their hand with his lively chatter or by jauntily bouncing over to touch his toes. That night, his one-time assistant was on his way to being elected to a second term as governor of Georgia. "He should be a good governor," Maddox said. "I taught him. He's the only governor we've ever had who had on-the-job training."

But in 1971, when Miller moved into the party job, there were many times ahead when he would go toe-to-toe with his former boss. Even then, Maddox and others were at odds with state Democrats over their support of the national party, and with the 1972 presidential season on the horizon that conflict was already simmering.

Miller had applied for the party job, and Carter confidante Charles Kirbo came to Crawford Long Hospital in Atlanta to offer it to him. Shirley Miller was convalescing from surgery, and before the Atlanta attorney left that evening Miller had accepted the job. He had been considered for a job with the Public Service Commission and had interviewed for a position at North Georgia College in Dahlonega. But to Miller, the party position was a natural—even though it paid only $17,000 a year.

One thing that must have appealed to Miller was the competitive challenges. "It was just a mountain that was there," he says. Bert Lance was Carter's highway director and had known of Miller since childhood. Lance said Carter and Kirbo were impressed with

Miller's Democratic Party legacy. "He knew the process, but in 1971 party loyalty was what was important to them," Lance says.

Loyalty was important because the first mountain Miller would have to climb was party unification. The 1968 Democratic National Convention in Chicago had been a tragedy that poured onto the streets of Chicago. The credential questions surrounding the Georgia Delegation was only one of the party's problems. Afterward, there was high-level pressure to open up Georgia's delegate selection process so that ordinary people, blacks and women could have an opportunity to be part of the nominating system.

In Chicago, Georgia had ended up with two delegations. Maddox had allowed party chairman James Gray of Albany to handpick the delegates that year, and its makeup was successfully challenged on the convention floor by Atlanta Civil Rights leaders Julian Bond and Ben Brown who headed the alternative delegation. It had been embarrassing to the state as well as a political dilemma, so Kirbo and Carter were committed to democratization. That would be Miller's mountain.

Reg Murphy, who had become editor of *The Atlanta Constitution,* wrote a column on the editorial page about Miller's appointment to the party job. Murphy had been the paper's lead reporter in May of 1964 when President Lyndon Johnson came to Georgia to endorse Phil Landrum over Miller and he remembered well how the young challenger had handled the events of that day. "Unlike everyone else in the crowd," he wrote, "Miller's world blew up."

Murphy described Miller as a person who had a resilient talent for absorbing punishment, and his new assignment of having a single Georgia Delegation at the 1972 Democratic Convention "couldn't be any harder than running against both Landrum and Johnson in 1964."

Miller's first public confrontation was with his former boss. Maddox suggested that a series of statewide primaries be held to select the convention delegates—an idea that Miller said was "prohibitive, unwise, preposterous and so much eyewash." Miller said such a plan would cost $600,000. "Really, I think the Presidential

Primary has turned into a preposterous way of choosing delegates. The first primary ever held in the nation was in Georgia in 1898. After the flood of primaries reached its height in 1916, it became evident that it was an awkward and expensive method which more often than not proved absolutely nothing," Miller said.

The plan that finally emerged called for a party caucus in each of the state's ten congressional districts. At those gatherings, each district would select delegates. Even then there were disputes all over the state. At the Third Congressional District caucus in Americus, a group of Columbus College students packed the hall in support of fellow student Mike Blackwell, who was blatantly running against Carter. Blackwell's race was supported by Columbus insurance magnate John B. Amos, a powerful national Democrat and one of the founders of AFLAC Inc., who wanted to embarrass the governor. After a heated compromise, Carter was finally elected.

As Senator George McGovern of South Dakota began to emerge as the party's frontrunner, there were even greater splits in the state party. Adding to the problem was the presence of Alabama Gov. George Wallace who was running a strong third party campaign and was very popular in Georgia—especially with the lieutenant governor, who had invited Wallace to the state when he was governor.

Miller says the party was in no more turmoil than usual when he took over. "The McGovernites and the delegate selection were to throw it into turmoil," he says. For many years, each day's front page of *The Atlanta Journal* included a brief "message" to the editor from Piney Woods Pete, a fictional character who usually offered sage comment on events of the day. No one ever identified the author, but many assumed it was written by longtime Atlanta newspaper executive Jack Tarver, who in earlier years had wriitten a witty column in both Macon and Atlanta. In March of 1972, the outspoken Pete wrote about the selection of delegates.

Dear Mister Editor:
Zell Miller has a tough time of it as he has been trying to hold together a wide assortment of characters and

viewpoints and call them Democrats. This is doubled by the fact that few people would recognize a bona fide Democrat if they met one in the middle of the road.

Miller admitted there's a lot of differences of opinion, but once the smoke clears we're going to have a stronger Democratic Party.

Such statements are beautiful, because no one will ever be able to stamp right or wrong on them. We have to wait until the smoke clears to know. And I don't ever remember when it ever cleared before.

Yours truly,

Piney Woods Pete.

Miller's plan prevailed, and the Georgia delegation was at the 1972 Democratic Convention in Miami. Miller and Julian Bond made short speeches and Carter made a nominating speech for Sen. Henry "Scoop" Jackson of Washington, who lost the nomination to McGovern. It went so well that at the convention there was even talk that Carter should be considered as a vice presidential candidate. Miller was a member of the platform committee and went to the convention as a committed delegate, but supported McGovern when he got the nomination. After the convention he even matched headlines with Harry Dent, a spokesman for Richard Nixon. Dent had roundly criticized Carter for making a statement against Nixon's anti-busing stance. Miller called Dent "Nixon's hired mouthpiece."

The Democrats, like the Republicans, were beginning to pay attention to the South again. No longer could the Democrats assume support from either Georgia or the South. Both Eisenhower and Goldwater had proven that at the national level Georgia was becoming a two-party state. "They're not writing off Georgia anymore," Miller said at the time. For Miller, each of those positions was much more than lines on his resume. As he had with Maddox, he was adding names and contacts to his Rolodex. Around the state, he was being seen as part of the party team. His circle was expanding far from the mountains. "This was where I cemented my friendship with John Lewis, a friendship that has lasted more than a quarter of a century. This was where I got to know Julian Bond, Vernon Jordan, C. B. King, Ben Brown, and many others," Miller says.

It was a critical year for Georgia Democrats. Richard Russell had died in 1971 after serving in the United States Senate for thirty-eight years. Carter had appointed Atlanta lawyer David Gambrell to the seat, and privately had set his own sights on a race for the seat in 1972. That did not materialize and a number of candidates were challenging Gambrell, including former Gov. Ernest Vandiver, who claimed Carter had promised him the job held by his wife's late uncle. Also in the race was an obscure member of the Georgia House, Sam Nunn of Perry.

Miller was faced not only with being a statesman during the primary season, but he knew that in the general election there would a strong Republican challenge. This was only six years after Republican Howard "Bo" Callaway had received more votes than anyone on the ballot for governor. Though Callaway never held office, two Republican congressmen were elected from Atlanta in 1966. This was just four years after those five state officials had switched to the GOP, so there seemed to be a growing Republican movement in the state. For Russell's old seat the GOP was running Fletcher Thompson, a popular member of Congress from South Atlanta. Given his ultra-liberal platform, the fact that McGovern led the Democratic ticket would probably be another plus for the opposing party.

Which it most definitely was. In 1972, Richard Nixon collected 75 percent of the vote in Georgia, leaving McGovern in his wake. Despite those numbers, the thirty-four-year-old Nunn ran away with the Senate race and in Atlanta Democrat Andrew Young became the first black elected to Congress in the Deep South, outpolling McGovern in every precinct in the predominantly white district.

Miller is justifiably proud of those things. "The amazing thing was that we were able to carry Georgia for Sam Nunn over a popular Republican congressman while McGovern was getting only 25 percent of the vote. Nunn will tell you that was quite an achievement," Miller said. It was a job that opened new doors for the former history professor. "It gave me a whole new league to play in," he says. "I saw it as a great opportunity to learn a new pitch and to become a more complete player."

When Miller announced his candidacy for lieutenant governor, not all of the responses were positive. Maddox wanted to handpick his successor so that as governor he would have an ally controlling the senate. He was going with Coggin, who had years of experience in that chamber. Maddox had another motivation, as he described in a speech in Gainesville. It was obvious he had not forgotten that Miller had deserted him for the party job. He called Miller a traitor.

More than Maddox, Miller had to deal with the idea that lieutenant governor was a toothless job. He began to redefine the position, telling voters they should be interested in who holds that spot and in the job itself. "Add duties, not power," he suggested, and all over the state he began to talk about what those duties should be.

On crime: "There is a direct correlation between crime and education. I'm the only Georgian who has ever served in all three areas of criminal rehabilitation: probation, corrections and parole."

On education: "Every child in Georgia needs the opportunity to go to kindergarten."

On attracting new industry: "The governor doesn't have time for all those trips. Send me."

On women in politics: "Women bring something to it that men lack—compassion, for example. I support the ERA."

On political education: "This office should educate young people on government. I will be in schools once a week and I will open the lieutenant governor's office in the evenings and on weekends."

On administrative changes in the Senate: "I want to show good faith. To show that I am willing to give up some power, hoping they are also willing to give a little. I believe the powers of the lieutenant governor should be diluted and that the leadership of the Senate should be broadened."

More than anything Georgians wanted to be proud of their government. The shenanigans of Maddox as governor were bad enough. He carried that reputation with him to the lieutenant governor's office. But more important than clowning for a photographer and riding a bicycle backwards was the behavior of Carter and Maddox—the state's two most visible elected officials. Carter pointed at Maddox and the senate. "One of the truisms about the politicial situation in Georgia is that candidates are finding out that the worse cancer in state government has been the state senate. It has been a disgrace to this state. The committee system—controlled by a few influential senators—is a disgrace," Carter said as his four-year term came to a close.

Miller said Georgia people were not pointing fingers of blame. "People want the squabbling to stop," Miller said. "Some blame one. Some blame the other. Many blame both. The point is, they don't like it. To symbolize that he could work in harmony, he brought an ox yoke to the capitol the day he qualified and stuck his head through it. Noting his message, as Miller knew they would, a *Constitution* editorial said the state needed a two-yoke team.

Judged by the calendar, 1974 was not that many years ago. Judged by the changes that have come in running a political campaign, it belongs in another century. The Miller campaign needed little more than $150,000 to run a statewide race and its chain of command consisted of the candidate and a host of young volunteers. There was no doubt who was in charge. "Miller wanted to be the candidate and he also wanted to be the campaign manager," says Ed Johnson, who was a campaign volunteer that summer. "He was a hard person to convince of the wisdom of letting other people, who could be more objective and more detached from the campaign, make decisions about where he ought to be going, who he should talk to and how to schedule his day."

It was also low-budget politics. "In those years, you could run a race on a small budget. We didn't worry about TV. We did lots of radio, and a lot of that was free because you would just go into a small town, look for an antenna, drop by the radio station and they would stop everything and put you on the air," Johnson says.

Johnson now sits on the Georgia Court of Appeals, after serving as a Superior Court judge and a former member of the Georgia Senate. He laughs at the simplicity of Miller's 1974 campaign, which he joined right after graduating from law school. "It was 'Ed, can you go to Marietta on the Fourth of July?' Miller would ask and I would say yes. That's the way we scheduled things and a lot of times I wouldn't know until the day before where I was going. I was young. Prior to the campaign, we had met a few times, but he gave me serious responsibilities. We now know that was common for him. He identifies a person, makes a judgement that he's good, that he's safe, that he's qualified. He thinks of himself as a talent scout."

Keith Mason was another of those young talents who through the years have gravitated to Miller. His family was involved in Gwinnett County, and he met him during that first race when he was a middle school student. Their relationship extended all the way to the lieutenant governor's and governor's offices, with Mason serving as his campaign manager in 1990 and later as his executive secretary in the governor's office.

Mason says the use of young people is an extension of Zell Miller the teacher. "Using students is not unique to him. A lot of political candidates do that, because of their energy and their curiousity and because they have time. But in the mid 1970s it was not so common, and he was an exception. I think it reflects his experience as a college professor. He was exposed to people at that level, and he has always wanted to get young people involved in politics," says Mason, now a senior vice president with Public Strategies Inc.'s Atlanta office.

Another key volunteer in the Miller camp was former Atlanta Braves pitcher Pat Jarvis. Miller's interest in baseball led to a frienship with Jarvis who had recently retired from major league baseball. Jarvis became his driver and traveling companion. Even if a town didn't care much for the political candidate, they would like to talk baseball with Jarvis. Looking at newspapers around the state during that summer, there were as many photographs published of Jarvis as there were of the would-be lieutenant governor. "Sometimes I had to remind folks I was the one running—not him," Miller laughs.

The race in 1974 was grassroots, hands-on politics. Johnson experienced it up close and he still marvels at how many people Miller knew in every community they visited. He didn't just know them. He called them by their first name and asked about their kids. Not that these skills began with Miller. He was following a tradition of Georgia politics. It was a style that was warm and personal, before television turned candidates into one-dimensional figures on a screen. It was the politics Miller had been reared on, a politics where you rely on instincts, not polls, one where you sit on the town square and ask a person what you can do to make their life better.

The only constants in the organization were Zell and Shirley, but she was still working for C&S Bank and would until the second year of his term as lieutenant governor. So often it was only Zell. Critics would say this single-headed chain of command created a bunker mentality where it was Miller against the political world. But this was the only way he knew to operate. It was a tradition and a habit that would be hard to break. He would run his campaigns himself, the way he wanted them to be run, until something or someone made him change. That day would come, but in 1974—and again in 1978—he was riding high on the ballot.

As that first race evolved, it soon narrowed down to three candidates—Miller, Cleland, and Hitt. With ten candidates on the ballot it seemed likely there would be a runoff and most observers predicted that Miller would be one of the two. Trying to break out of the pack, he became the candidate who offered a money-back guarantee. "I am the only candidate with a warranty," he said. "I promise my supporters their money back if they're not satisfied." Each contributor was given one of these certificates, but no one ever redeemed one.

Others were also trying to find an identity; Bill Laite, a former legislator from Macon, was pushing hard for law and order. At the Georgia Jaycees convention on Jekyll Island, he made a strong push against crime and since they were speaking in alphabetical order Miller followed. "The fellow who just made the law and order speech is the same fellow who just ran over my signs on the causeway," Miller charged.

After the speeches, with anger in the air, reporters gathered around the two of them with questions. Neither of the candidates disappointed them. "Miller has threatened to whip my ass," Laite said. Miller did not deny it. "I did say I'd whip his ass if he tears down any more of my signs." Even the candidates knew they were groping. On a campaign stop in Gwinnett County, where he lived, one of the popular issues was the construction of a two-year college in the rapidly-growing county. When Miller came to the microphone at the forum, he said someone had told him that the only reason he was for building that school was so he would have a place to teach if he lost this race.

As the weather and the race grew hotter, Cleland became agressive, saying Miller was a product of "backroom politics." He talked about Miller's connections to the state party and cited his changing platforms in the races against Landrum. Hitt, who was the most conservative of the front-runners, also started attacking Miller's "liberalism." He did openly court black votes—the first statewide candidate to do so personally. He went door-to-door on Auburn Avenue, in the heart of Atlanta's black business district with John Lewis, Julian Bond in Macon he went with civil rights pioneer Bill Randall, Sr. and Rev. Julius C. Hope and in Thomasville with Elijah Hill.

At every opportunity, Hitt invoked the names of Bond and McGovern. "A leopard doesn't change its spots. Zell Miller is a liberal professional. He has received endorsements from Atlantans such as Julian Bond and he campaigned all over the state of Georgia for George McGovern," a Hitt news release said. Hitt needed to grab headlines. Newspapers all over the state were endorsing Miller's candidacy. He got support from both daily newspapers in Atlanta, Columbus, Macon, Augusta and Savannah as well as a number of the state's smaller dailies. When election night came, two runoffs were required—for governor and for lieutenant governor.

In the governor's race Maddox led as expected. However, the margin was alarmingly small as three of five Georgia Democrats went for one of the other candidates. Trailing Maddox that night was Albany legislator George Busbee, who had become a key part of the House leadership. It brought back memories of 1966 when Sanders, the favorite, found himself in a runoff against Carter, who dominated the runoff. In the race for lieutenant governor, Miller collected 31 percent followed by Hitt at 18.6 percent and Cleland just behind at 17.2 percent. To everyone's surprise, Stoner was fourth at 9.3 percent.

As the runoff campaign began, Miller was again seen as the heavy favorite, but Hitt was a hardnosed campaigner and she carried the fight to the more established Democrat, increasing the volume of her charges of liberalism. "In south Georgia, Miller puts on his cowboy boots and talks about when he was Lester Maddox's executive secretary. Then he comes to Atlanta, puts on a chic suit and has cocktails with Julian Bond," she told voters all over the state.

At one stop, someone asked Hitt if she would hire Miller to join her staff as lieutenant governor. She thought for a moment and said she would, that "he would be a good behind-the-scenes man." The reporter asked Miller the same question and he didn't think at all. "No, I wouldn't hire her, and I'm surprised she would want a *liberal* like me on her staff," Miller said with sarcasm.

Miller defeated Hitt in the runoff and easily outdistanced Savage in the general election. Busbee also prevailed, effectively ending Maddox's eight unlikely years of statewide influence. On election night at the Royal Coach Hotel, the Democrats celebrated. Raising their hands high were Busbee and Miller, joined by Herman Talmadge who, in his usually invincible manner, had been elected to his fourth term in the United States Senate. For the Democrats, it was a night to be family.

If a lengthy campaign can be capsulized by a single episode, that one would come down to the night of a one-on-one debate between Miller and Hitt in the studio of an Albany television station. After the usual discussions, the two campaigns ironed out a series of typical rules. Reporters would ask each candidate questions. There was a specified time for them to answer. There was time for followup. Then, at the end of the night, there would be an opportunity for each candidate to ask the other a question of their choice.

On the air that night, the questions were predictable, and so were the answers. By that point in the campaign, Miller knew Hitt's platform and she could have answered questions for him. They had been together that often. Time came for Miller to ask his question. "Can you tell me, Mrs. Hitt, what is the state budget of Georgia?" "I'm not here to answer questions for you like a school girl," she snapped. Mary Hitt was on the ropes. She was struggling. "Mrs. Hitt," he said again. "What is the state budget, within a billion dollars?" She was talking, but she wasn't answering.

Zell Miller knew she was through when he confidently looked into the camera and gave the state budget down to the very penny. A message had been delivered to the voters and to Mary Hitt. Under the heat of those studio lights, Mary Hitt learned a lesson from a teacher who knew how to play the game. For Zell Miller, there would be another night and another debate against a teacher from another generation. And that one would threaten him in ways that transcended the game of politics.

Like his father, Zell Milller taught history at
Young Harris College (1959).

Coach Zell Miller, far left, poses for a yearbook photo
with his Young Harris College baseball team. The house
in the background is the house in which Zell was born.

Birdie stayed home to build this sign in her front yard instead of going to the press conference announcing her son's race for lieutenant governor in 1974. She was 81.

When Zell went to the Georgia Senate, he was a college professor with a flat-top haircut.

1962 Senate Campaign Card

Joining an entourage of his students, Shirley
looked over the shoulders of Murphy and
Matt when Zell came to Atlanta to qualify
for Congress in 1964.

LET **ZELL MILLER** *YOU!*

REPRESENT

IN CONGRESS

President Lyndon Johnson campaigned for Phil Landrum when Zell challenged the veteran congressman. This was 1966.

College students Phil Gailey, Marti Fullerton and Hank Huckaby composed Zell's congressional campaign staff in 1964.

On the campaign trail, a busy candidate
learns to eat his fried chicken when he can.

Gov. Lester Maddox gives Zell the oath of
office as his Executive Secretary.

Shirley traveled Georgia in the Zell Mobile,
joined by Walt Bellamy, Keith Mason,
Murphy and Matt Miller, Dan and Sarah
Eby-Ebersole, Paula Taylor and Carl
Hartmarph. They helped elect Miller
Lieutenant governor.

For most of his adult life, Zell has been at
home behind a podium.

The Little Generals from Kennesaw were
dancing on the Grand Ole Opry and Roy
Acuff asked Zell to introduce them.

Georgians Bill Anderson and Little Richard
do the singing – Zell does the listening.

Zell is joined by singing stars Bertie Higgins, Billy Joe Royal, Alan Jackson and Jan Howard.

Johnny Cash visited Zell when he was lieutenant governor.

Zell couldn't resist throwing his hat into the
ring while Roni Stoneman picked her banjo.

Georgia has always been on the mind of
both Ray Charles and Zell Miller.

Shirley and Zell have always looked at home in the mountains of Towns County.

George and Mary Beth Busbee joined Zell at one of his annual birthday parties.

When old friend Ed Johnson gave Zell the oath in 1982, Zell became the longest-serving lieutenant governor in Georgia history.

Zell Miller strikes a pensive pose for a newspaper photographer.

People on the streets of Savannah were celebrating St. Patrick's Day in 1974, Zell was running for lieutenant governor.

Even after living in Atlanta for years, Zell sometimes felt on the inside looking out.

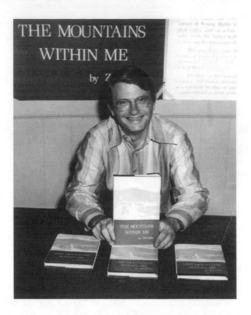

Zell's first book was dedicated to his mother, his favorite teacher and his wife.

Wearing an informal plaid shirt, Zell greets guests at one of his traditional birthday parties.

When Miller was presiding in the Senate,
there was no doubt who was in charge.

Many times over the past four decades,
Shirley Miller's outfit has included one of her
husband's campaign button.

Shirley Miller says her husband is never more at home than when he's talking with students.

With a watermelon resting on his windshield, Zell rides in another campaign parade.

While Zell was in politics, Shirley Miller
found a rewarding career as a banker.

Young Harris: This was where Zell life began
and this is where he says it will end. Sharp
Memorial United Methodist Church in
background.

Tom Murphy has stood at that podium longer than any other Speaker of the Georgia House.

Birdie Miller clutches her pocketbook in her hands as she joins her son at his first inaugural ceremony, in 1975, when George Busbee became governor.

Promising to work as a team with the
governor, Zell brought a yoke to his
announcement for lieutenant governor in
1974.

With his gavel in the air, Zell closes his final session as
lieutenant governor in 1990 as Bill Stephens, Steve
Wrigley and Joe Kennedy look on.

Zell has taken the oath of office more times than any person who has served in the executive branch.

The Lord is always in his temple, and when running for office so are Georgia politicians.

Realizing a life-long dream, Zell gets to put on a Braves uniform.

11

A SIBLING RIVALRY

Their labels are pinned on like battlefield commissions. Zell Miller, the professor, with cowboy boots worn for symbol as well as comfort. A hawkish nose separates eyes that one minute dance a jig and the next have an edge that could peel an apple. He can talk the language of the filling station or he can converse with the thinkers he calls "Propeller Heads". He can play you the new bluegrass CD in his machine or offer a review of the latest how-to-do-it text on management. He is so orderly and organized that he has planned his own funeral down to what song and what verse.

Tom Murphy, with the face of an Irish cop, a face only an editorial cartoonist could love. An LBJ Stetson on his head. An unlit cigar in his mouth, or on its way, the ring still wrapped around it. Suits that are bought, not tailored. Eyes that droop with the sadness of a front porch hound. His progeny, a small town mafioso, trails him as if they are attached. Around the capitol, he's known by title more than name. Just *The Speaker*.

For a quarter of a century they've been fussing, right out where Georgia can see them. They've called each other names on the 6 o'clock news, in press conferences with cameras rolling, from the stately wooden wells of their respective chambers, in their offices, throwing out spicy allegations that send reporters from one floor of the capitol to the other on a mission of you-said-he-said. Dick Pettys of the Associated Press, dean of capitol reporters, says they are street-fighters. "They grew up fighting for everything they got. They know how to protect their turf and the only way they know how to fight is to go for the jugular."

For almost a quarter of a century, they have dominated the headlines. Busbee, Griffin, Maddox, Harris, the rest of them, have come and gone, but Miller and Murphy, these sometimes blustery giants, have survived. If folks talked politics, it was Miller-Murphy, the yin and the yang. They have been such perfect foils for one another that if Murphy hadn't existed, Miller would have invented him.

Veteran capitol observer Bill Shipp says the conflict goes back to their earliest relationships. "They've had so many wars that you can't count them. Generally, if Murphy has wanted something, Zell was against it, and if Zell wanted it, Murphy was against it." Often they have been portrayed by reporters as Mr. good and Mr. evil. Zell Miller the progressive. Tom Murphy the throwback. Miller the intellectual, the leader. Murphy the dominator, who speaks loudly and carries a big gavel. It is not so simple.

Former *Atlanta Constitution* political editor Frederick Allen confesses to such analyses and still believes they were a great morality tale. After fourteen sessions, his observations have expanded. "A lot of times, I have to admit what they were doing wasn't always that important. Oh, it was important, but not earth shattering. So they just messed with each other. Like in campus politics. It was vicious because they weren't fighting over very much. They had intramural squabbles and the moral posturing was part of the fight. I'm not sure there were any moral issues at work at that point."

Peel away the facades and in many ways they are the same product in different packaging. Both are stubborn and bullheaded. Both can be hard. Both like to win. Both explode, then deal with it later. Both lead, only one makes more noise at it. Both have simple rural backgrounds that have shaped their personalities and their politics. Both are Democrat to the bone but one is more tolerant of those wayward people who sit on the other side of the chamber.

Larry Walker of Perry, House Majority Leader, is considered the heir to the gavel when the day comes that Murphy decides to step aside. More than that, he is one of the Bremen legislator's closest confidantes. He says the difference is style. "Miller is from the Old School polished up. Murphy's from the Old School."

A political scientist might look at their conflicts and explain it as institutional, a natural extension of the competition between Senate and House. Such schisms occur in state houses around the country as the two bodies fight for dominance. Historically that was not the case in Georgia since the sun didn't set it in the West, it set in the House. The rotation system in the Senate that was created by the County Unit System neutered its influence. The fact that the House effectively handled the state budget gave it enormous power.

Since 1963, when the one-man, one-vote concept was installed, the competition between the two chambers has intensified. In some ways, it peaked when Jimmy Carter was governor. Lester Maddox, coming directly out of the governor's office, was lieutenant governor, and first George L. Smith, then Murphy, was Speaker of the House. Ironically, it was that conflict with Carter that helped Zell Miller decide the time had come for him to leave Maddox's staff.

When Miller was elected lieutenant governor and took over the Senate in 1975, Murphy had been speaker for a year. Both of the bodies they served were vastly different than they are today. The Senate leadership was older and more established. The House was beginning to turn over much of its leadership to a younger generation. Unlike other states, in Georgia the Senate was considered to be the more liberal body in many respects. And while Miller got along with newly-elected Gov. George Busbee much better than Maddox had with Carter, the difficulties with Murphy and the House began almost immediately.

Some of it was style. Murphy saw Miller's democratization of the Senate as weak. Miller planned to give up some of his influence in the appointment of chairmen. Such a notion was foreign to Murphy, who embraced power like a new mother in the maternity ward holds on to her baby. Murphy freely admits that he is in charge of the House. "What people need to understand—but I don't know that they ever will—is that I have 179 strong-willed people out in front of me with a certain amount of egotism or they wouldn't be in public life. Somebody has to hold them in reign or there would be chaos. You have to run the place, but you have to treat your worst enemy like your best friend. You have to be fair," Murphy says, emphasizing fair—a word that he is proud of.

In 1975, Miller arrived in the lieutenant governor's office with a flourish. Since his election the previous fall, he had guided the senate through its most wide-ranging reform in recent history, except for the new Georgia Constitution in 1945 and reapportionment. Historically, lieutenant governors had not been a major part of inaugurations, but Miller was added to the program that year. After Busbee had been sworn in and made his address, Miller took the oath from Judge Charles Pannell of the Georgia Court of Appeals. The speech that followed was a preview of his terms as lieutenant governor and of the issues he would carry with him.

Acknowledging the conflicts of the past four years, he talked about sitting on a conspicuous stage where people within the borders of Georgia "will mark our demeanor." He chronicled the problems the state was facing—inadequate schools, an inadequate tax structure, a rising crime rate, racial prejudice and a distrust of political leadership.

After citing the problems Miller said he would face them "in a spirit of harmony with the Chief Executive, working not only with him, but for him when requested . . . bearing in mind that no two men will ever agree on every issue, but also fully understanding that the problems of this time are so many and so complex that teamwork is not only needed but is absolutely necessary."

Remembering what he had said in his lengthy campaign, after every one he said "I will keep that promise." Included in his litany of promises were the operational changes in the Senate, some of which had been dealt with during the pre-legislative meeting on rules. One of them was a conviction that senate meetings should be open under the Georgia Sunshine Law.

"Yes, I have promises to keep, and one is to improve the operations of the Georgia Senate and to preside over this legislative body with fairness, with dignity . . . and with openness. The veil of secrecy must be removed from all legislative deliberations concerning public policy, because you cannot limit the right to know without limiting democracy itself. I will keep that promise," Miller said to an audience that included the leadership of the House—a group that was listening closely.

There would be conflict over that suggestion, but there was also conflict not over what Miller had said but how he had delivered those words. Busbee had come first, and their abilities at the podium were several leagues apart.

Norman Underwood, now an Atlanta attorney, was Busbee's executive secretary; he remembers discussions in the governor's office that followed the speech. "George Busbee always had an ego which was well in line. But I remember a couple of people around him saying that for Zell to make that speech with so much emotional content at the inauguration was something of an upstaging of Busbee," Underwood says.

Murphy certainly listened to the speech. Though he may have appreciated the art of political speaking, he was more interested in what the new lieutenant governor had to say about his belief that legislative meetings should be open. Miller had been pushing for such things since he was the mayor of Young Harris. But Tom Murphy's "home" wasn't Young Harris; his "home" is the Georgia House, and he saw no reason to open up committee meetings—especially conference committee meetings where individuals appointed by both bodies come together to iron out their differences on particular pieces of legislation. Sides were being chosen for their first clash—and neither body had even had their first meeting of the new session.

Murphy's response was a lecture to the former teacher.

"I was very sorry to hear that the lieutenant governor—who is a fine man and an old friend of mine who came to the Senate the same year I came to the House—said that he would not appoint a conference committee unless they were pledged to have open committee meetings ... I think the presiding officer is carrying it entirely too far when he's going to appoint conference committee members and tell them what to do. That's carrying it too far," he said.

"But maybe Miller is just inexperienced. I doubt that the lieutenant governor—and he's a distinguished gentleman and a very intelligent gentleman—I doubt that he has ever served on a conference committee on the budget." At first the courts ruled that the General Assembly didn't have to follow the state's Open Meeting's Law. "That doesn't make me any less determined. I don't think you can limit the right to know without limiting democracy," Miller said, accusing the speaker of meddling in the Senate by drumming opposition to open sessions.

Miller eventually prevailed. Taking note of the newcomer's reform plans, former *Atlanta Journal* political columnist David Nordan likened the lieutenant governor to a new face at the neighborhood tavern. "The soft-spoken college teacher from Young Harris is beginning to look more and more like he's going to be the kind of new guy in town who walks into the saloon and takes on the biggest bully at the bar before he unsaddles his horse," Nordan wrote.

The analogies in that early analysis quickly set a tone. Miller is the soft-spoken professor. Murphy was depicted as the barroom bully. It was a theme that columnists and editorial writers would use often in the years and feuds that would follow.

The antagonism between the two officials has been compared to something as regional as Tech versus Georgia or as global as the generational struggle between Arab and Israeli. But as often as not, the tiffs between Zell and Tom have been little more than siblings quarreling at the dinner table, each wanting to be heard, each wanting his own way. Never mind that the mashed potatoes are getting cold. Nothing is as important as the last word.

Murphy says their quarrels usually involved money. "I'm a fiscal conservative. Everybody knows that. And most of our fusses have been over dollars and cents. I guess I'm partially at fault because I am so conservative. I just believe you ought to live within your means. I believe that personally and as a member of the state legislature. Those kinds of things are what make it work. They make you get together and mediate your differences, to find what's best for the people. We don't disagree on everything and that's where the budget gets pared down to a size everybody can live with," Murphy says.

But Murphy in recent years has been the defender of the old 'New Deal' order of high taxes and government jobs. Miller has modified and modernized his views while the Speaker has clung to a Democratic philosophy rejected by the voters.

For many years that philosophical difference was played out over a sales tax on groceries. Miller wanted it eliminated. Murphy resisted. "I knew we couldn't afford it," the speaker says. "I blocked it ten, maybe twelve times through the years. It finally got to where I got tired of fighting the world by myself. I still think it was fiscally irresponsible to take it off because nobody even knows they got it. First of all, we took it off so gradually that nobody notices. Second, grocery stores have raised their prices to what they were with the sales tax. He was much more liberal on finances then than he is as governor. I guess it was because before he wasn't responsible for the money," Murphy says.

Murphy proudly wears the label of a fiscal conservative, yet it was the speaker who helped spearhead legislation for the World Congress Center, MARTA and the Georgia Dome. It was also Murphy who in 1987 led the fight for the $12.7 million Northwest Georgia Convention and Trade Center in Dalton, an action the then-lieutenant governor called "irresponsible." Sending a message by media, Miller said he was reluctant to bring it up "because it puts me on opposite sides of my friend, the Speaker."

Writing in *The Atlanta Constitution,* Duane Riner—a former press secretary for Busbee—accused Miller of using the Dalton issue to kick off his 1990 gubernatorial campaign, a conclusion that riled Miller. "If I am, it's the worst politics in the world to get these people in Dalton mad at me," he said. "The way I see it, you've got two presiding officers, both pretty secure in their positions, and I'm going to do what is right regardless of the consequences." Not to be outdone, Murphy told Bill Shipp that if Miller wanted trouble, then trouble he was going to get. Shipp said friends of the Speaker's believed the lieutenant governor was getting too big for his britches.

Finally, the issue came down to the Dalton proposal being held hostage so the Senate could push through its alternative amendment to a gas tax. "It's a petty move, but it's an answer to a petty move," Miller said. Pettys remembers the arguments that year. "It was huge. It went on into the night and Murphy won," he says. "It was huge at the time, but at no point was the government really at risk."

The Northwest Georgia Convention and Trade Center was finally added to the state budget. And in 1988 the two adversaries shared a shovel as ground was broken for the Dalton facility. As of 1997, it had not yet turned a profit.

Walker said though both of them claim to be fiscally conservative, they also share a populist streak. "Though as governor Miller's may not be as wide as it used to be. Being governor may do that to you," Walker says. "The governor has to present a budget every year. Ninety percent of it he writes, and the Legislature fusses over about ten percent of it. And a lot of their conflicts started with that ten percent."

Over the sixteen years the two of them presided over the competing bodies, squabbles over money did set off many altercations. A round-by-round, blow-by-blow of their past would include:

1978—Murphy contradicted Miller on a TV show and disputed his statement that senators Talmadge and Nunn supported a constitutional amendment to give congressional representation to the District of Columbia. "It was not the kind of statement a political friend would make to another," the Speaker said.

1979—At the Lowndes County Bird Supper, Murphy referred to Miller as "the extinguished lieutenant governor."

1979—Miller had commented on the Speaker's "decorum" and Murphy replied, "I love to have people admire my decorum."

1979—Visiting the capitol where he once was governor, President Carter commented on the Miller-Murphy feud. "I am glad to see the same degree of cooperation exists today as did between the Speaker, Lt. Gov. Maddox and myself."

1979—Miller called Murphy a liar and two days later apologized. Busbee got them together, but only to pose for a gag photograph of them smoking a peace pipe. Each promised to be more sensitive.

1979—At Miller's birthday, senators gave him a horse trailer and the irrepressible Sen. Culver Kidd suggested it "would be suitable for hauling a pair of jackasses, which Miller and Murphy have resembled at times during the session."

1980—Murphy said "it would be accurate to say that the lieutenant governor and I haven't been close."

1982—The two leaders said they had buried the hatchet and a columnist predicted they would work together like two peas in a pod that session.

1984—Miller's and Murphy's leadership in the General Assembly is like "two tinhorn tyrants parading around trying to prove how important they are," a columnist wrote.

1984—Miller said of Murphy: "We haven't always agreed in our political careers, but we have a personal friendship and a great deal of respect for each other."

1986—Miller and Murphy "behaved like feuding siblings."

1986—Appearing together at a forum, the two of them agreed they didn't see eye to eye on many issues. "I ain't near as happy to be here as Zell is. He's smarter than I am and there are very few things he's said that I agree with."

1987—In an analysis of the upcoming session, a columnist said: "Take a lieutenant governor who has an eye on the state's top job ... add a House Speaker who is at the peak of his power. Each will be trying to thwart the other."

1987—As Murphy introduced Miller at his inauguration, he drew a laugh when he presented him as "the past, present and future lieutenant governor of Georgia."

1987—Looking at that year's squabble, an editorial writer said, "The problem is not one of personalities. It's not a question of whether or not Tom Murphy is a fine gentleman or a stubborn old goat, or whether Zell Miller is a selfless statesman or a zigzagging opportunist. The problem is that an unelected post shouldn't have the power of the Speaker of the House."

1988—Going full circle from the squabble of their opening session, Miller and Murphy clashed over open meeting legislation but the rift stopped short of name-calling or headlines.

1988—Months after that year's session, with a struggle over appointments to the Department of Transportation board raging with the speaker, Miller said he wanted peace, but "When somebody shoots at you, you are either going to duck or shoot back."

1990—Miller, in an Eggs and Issues speech during the session, referred to the House as "Murphy's Mausoleum."

Over and over, they took the pledge. They're going to be more thoughtful. They're going to be sensitive. They're going to be easier to get along with. Third parties sometimes tried to intervene and to suggest that the two of them just sit down and talk things out. Murphy says that over the years he listened to only one person— Shirley Miller. "Miss Shirley was always there to get us back together when we got too far apart," says Murphy—never calling her Shirley, always an affectionate and courtly "Miss Shirley."

He never knew her until Zell Miller was elected lieutenant governor. "Miss Shirley is one of the greatest ladies I've ever known, a fine, fine lady. She'd ease both of us down some. Of course, she did most of her talking to her husband. Her being there kept me from doing and saying some of the things I might have done or said. I just have so much respect for her," Murphy says.

Zell Miller said he did not realize how much influence she carried, but he said he knew that the speaker admired her and that she felt close to him. "The Speaker reminds her of her daddy and I can see that, too," he says. Murphy said her influence wasn't political. "She's just a nice, sweet lady. You can't help but love her. She's worked hard for the underprivileged and undereducated since I've known her."

Shirley Miller agrees with her husband. The Speaker does look like Luke Carver. "He reminds me of my daddy in many ways. To him, there's no place like Harrelson County, Georgia. No football or baseball team is as good as those kids over there. My daddy was like that. They loved their homes," she says.

Like Murphy, she sees their friendship beyond politics. She was fond of his late wife, remembering how she was a down-to-earth person and how warm her personality was. She has seen his daughters grow up. "I see Tom Murphy beyond the Speaker of the Georgia House," she says.

Like others who have been part of public service, she knows that things are never black and white. "There's lots of gray," she said. "You can disagree. If you agree with someone 100 percent, you ought to be elected to that job yourself. You can disagree, you can feel strongly about something, but you don't have to be disagreeable. You have to find common ground and you can't do that if you have animosity."

As the 1997 session began, the Millers were hosts for the annual Legislative Dinner, a formal affair at the Governor's Mansion. As hosts, the governor and the first lady greet their guests near the main door. Shirley Miller remembers Murphy's arrival well. "They had been bickering over that DUI bill. When The Speaker came in the door, I smiled and said, 'I think I'm going to have to get you two together on this one.' He just laughed and laughed," she said.

Miller and Murphy have over their years at the capitol shared that common respect for Shirley Miller, but that has never stopped them from putting on the gloves and coming out fighting. Much of it erupted from two explosive personalities. But some of it was a result of the natural friction between two competing legislative bodies. Frank Eldridge was a senator from Waycross and now serves as Secretary of the Senate. He said that competition will always be there.

"It is not unique and it is not indicative of just the Georgia Legislature," Eldridge says. "That is true throughout this nation. You have two bodies of very strong-willed people, presided over by two people with very strong wills. There are forces at work that are to be there no matter who is charge—whether it is Miller and Murphy or Pierre Howard and Murphy. It was the same way years ago when George L. Smith was the speaker. You're just going to have these kinds of feelings. It is a competition of ideas and opinions and this isn't bad. Because what is a legislature? It is a filtering process of ideas, a common marketplace for ideas. So it's not all bad. As long as the conflict is resolved in a positive manner," Eldridge says.

Positive or not, both Miller and Murphy knew how to push the other's buttons. It wasn't hard. They wore their issues on their sleeves in those years. Steve Wrigley was a member of the lieutenant governor's staff and is now chief of staff to the governor. He confesses that at times Miller's people used the volatility of the Speaker as part of the strategy to pass a particular piece of legislation. "Sometimes we used the conflict to help a bill," Wrigley says. He agreed that the arguments between the two officials didn't hurt their programs. "Usually, they would be fighting over a single bill. Sometimes other things would get wrapped up in it, but not often."

In 1990, in Miller's final session as lieutenant governor, the campaign for governor already was taking shape. Everyone on his staff was well aware that the lottery was going to be a major issue. Murphy was strongly against the lottery politically, and as is often the case with the Speaker, his personal emotions had become part of his opposition.

On the political side, his protégé in the governor's race—State Rep. Lauren "Bubba" McDonald—had spoken out against Miller's suggestion of a lottery while still a member of the House. Playing the subtle role of kingmaker had become important to Murphy. He played a part in Busbee's election in 1974, supported efforts to allow the former House member a second term in 1978, then played a major role in the election of Joe Frank Harris in 1982 and

1986. With the 1990 race shaping up, Murphy definitely hoped to add McDonald to his trophy case. Add those considerations to his personal convictions, and Murphy was determined not to let the enabling legislation for the lottery get through *his* chamber.

The Senate passed a measure which simply would allow Georgia voters to decide if they wanted a lottery in the state. Knowing what Murphy's reaction would be was part of the strategy in the Miller camp. "We made him defeat a piece of legislation," Wrigley confesses. "We got the attention to the issue we wanted and we could remind voters that it had been left in a House committee, knowing that the people favored it. We knew the Speaker would oppose it."

Walker's view comes from the other side of the rotunda, since he was born and raised in the House of Murphy. Looking at it through a partisan lens, he says the conflicts were more intense when the only feud was between House and Senate, when there were no Republicans. "I tell people coming into the House today that we ought to spend our time countering the opposition party when we're right or think we're right, instead of fussing with the Senate," he says.

In twenty-five years at the capitol, Walker calculates a crisis a day. "Most work themselves out," he says. "In fact all of them do. Not always the way you want them to, but they do work out. I just try to make sure I can go home at night and forget it. When we were working around spats between the speaker and Miller, I don't think we were affected too much. We operated about the same. Of course we laughed and joked about it at times. When there was tension, sometimes I hated to go over there. At those times, we would laugh and say that in wartime it was the soldiers who got killed. The generals were up on top of the hill. We'd laugh and say we were the ones getting hurt."

Many legislators from that time say the quality of the legislation that evolved from both chambers may have been better because of the conflicts. Walker said there is a natural tendency to look much closer at what your adversaries are doing than what your allies are doing.

Pettys said the rifts only slowed down controversial issues. "Nothing important has been halted," he says. Bill Shipp is one who thinks the legislation might have been improved. "It made lawmakers take sides instead of straddling the fence, instead of sitting back and saying they didn't want to rock the boat. It made them stand up and say, 'This is what I stand for. This is what is good for Georgia.' Whether it was Murphy fighting for the gasoline tax or Miller fighting to take the sales tax off food, or whether it was one of their fights over open meetings, their arguments made other people think," Shipp says.

Now, since Miller moved into the governor's office, they sound like a pair of aging fighters who only talk about how hard they used to punch. They would like people to think they have retired to their respective corners. They throw a light jab only now and then. It was a movement that had its genesis after the 1990 Democratic Primary when Miller was preparing to face Republican Johnny Isakson. Murphy had supported McDonald, but he was not a factor in that summer's race. As his protégé faded, and with the Republican Party as his only other choice, Murphy began to move toward Miller. He truly reached out once Zell Miller was the duly-elected governor.

Now both sound mellow. Says Miller: "We were never enemies. Most of our conflicts came more from being leaders of the two houses. That's the nature of things. We just had more longevity than most."

Says Murphy: "We've always been fairly good friends. It was always a difference in mine and his philosophy. I found out a long time ago that the Speaker is a good whippin' boy. He's out there. He's not elected by all the people. He was just elected by the House members so he's a good whippin' boy."

Pressed, the two of them concede that they share a kinship in ways they don't like to admit. At the personal level, they're both rural, they both enjoy country music, and they share a deep love for baseball. At a deeper level, it is similarities in their personalities that have led to many of their differences. Not that these are two men who enjoy picking up a six-pack and watching a ball game together, but neither are they the bitter enemies they would have their constituents believe them to be.

Walker says if you really want a study in contrast, look at Murphy and current Lt. Governor Pierre Howard. "They are much more different than Miller and Murphy ever were," he says. "Murphy and Miller are determined, hardheaded, and have strong ideas and strong beliefs. Both came from humble beginnings. They're both survivors. All of that they have in common—only Miller has more sophistication. They're from the old school. Reward your friends, or make that, don't reward your enemies. They have a love-hate relationship. They are antagonists at times and allies at times."

Shipp looks beyond the stereotypes. "They're almost out of the same cloth," he says. "That's why they have so much conflict. Georgia has the most liberal abortion laws in the country. Who's responsible? Tom Murphy. If you get past the stereotype of Murphy's white Stetson and cigar and look at what he has stood for over the years, they are very much alike."

Pettys believes their rural upbringing was often at the core of their disputes. "Both of them always want the last word or the final funny insult," he says. "Maybe it's a rural thing. You'll see old fellows on the bench outside the courthouse staying there for hours trying to get that final word. They're both that way."

Pettys is fond of sharing a funny episode that occurred after Miller was in the governor's office. He was part of the story, but it also involved Shipp, a frequent target of Miller barbs. Sometimes they are trusted colleagues, as close to friends as a politician or a reporter will allow it to be. Other times they aren't speaking and Miller—who always wants to be in control—doesn't want his staff even to take a phone call from Shipp. This was one of those times when Zell Miller wanted the last word.

A few years ago, Shipp reported in his monthly political newsletter that Miller was secretly ill, that he may have been suffering from prostate cancer. Fortunately it was not that serious, but the Associated Press was compelled to follow up on any report on a governor's health, which Pettys did, making a phone call to press secretary Rick Dent.

A few mornings later, on his way to the press office, Pettys was coming toward the Mitchell Street doorway. Next to that door is the governor's parking place. Miller was just arriving, and hailed the AP reporter. "Hear you've been asking about my health?" he said. Pettys said he had, and the governor said for him to hold out his hand while he fished around in his pocket for something. Into Pettys' outstretched hand, Miller put a rubber surgical glove. "You can either ask my doctor or you can test me for yourself."

Miller admits that was an effort for the final word. "You don't know how many days I carried that glove around with me," he says. Once Miller was governor, Murphy did not seek that final word as often. Much of their stormy past was over. That new relationship began with Murphy. No one had to ask. Understanding that he was the speaker and Miller was the governor, it was his place. "He called the governor," Wrigley says. "He said he wanted to help. You have to understand, no one respects the office of governor more than the Speaker. He observes the proper protocol and courtesy. And, almost unspoken, they each knew that they needed to work together."

Finally Miller went to Murphy's office, with dozens of framed photographs of political figures posing next to The Speaker. In a building that thrives on symbols, you must go through two outer rooms before you get your audience. "Mr. Speaker," Miller said. "I might get elected without your help, but I can't run the state without you."

Stubbornness brought them there. Miller had been elected, and Murphy respected that. He also knew that Miller had carried his own county. And he also knew, that if he wanted legislation that he or the House he controlled wanted to become law, he would need the official seal and signature of Gov. Zell Miller.

No one ever said either of those men weren't smart. They needed no one to read the writing on that wall. So from the earliest days of the Miller administration, Murphy was an ally. Most of his support was private, but their new and improved relationship became more apparent six months into Miller's first term, when Miller wanted to make changes in the always testy Department of Transportation. Highway building has traditionally been a political land-mine in Georgia. According to legislative math, roads equaled votes.

Other governors had learned that lesson the hard way. One of them was Miller's predecessor, Joe Frank Harris, a crafty veteran of capitol politics who went into office with the ear of Speaker Murphy. Early on his watch, Harris had wanted to oust Tom Moreland as the DOT commissioner. He called what he thought would be a private meeting of the DOT board at an unobtrusive Holiday Inn off Interstate 20, near Six Flags Over Georgia.

The meeting was private only until the late Frank Morast was called about the meeting over that weekend. Morast, who represented the Third Congressional District on the board, called Glenn Vaughn, the publisher of his hometown *Columbus Ledger-Enquirer,* and told him what the governor was planning to do. On Monday morning, Harris found that there was room at the Holiday Inn for a reporter and a photographer. Photographer Lawrence Smith snapped a telling photograph of Harris and his press secretary, Barbara Morgan, conferring over the presence of a reporter as the governor entered the hotel.

Moreland wasn't fired that day, and Harris was splattered with DOT asphalt. Well aware of this gubernatorial history, Miller was determined that he would not fail. He wanted to replace Commissioner Hal Rives. The DOT board, determined to show its independence, did not. If Miller was going to prevail, he would need help that would have to include the Speaker of the Georgia House.

In a January 1992 article in *Atlanta Magazine,* writer R. Robin McDonald wrote about this situation in detail. She said it was an example of Miller showing others that he knew how to use his power as governor. A turning point, she wrote. If friend and foe were afraid of him, Miller didn't care. The episode occurred during lunch at the Governor's Mansion and by the time all of the courses had been served and the table cleared, Miller had a newfound influence—and it was no coincidence that Tom Murphy was at his side.

McDonald, now a reporter at *The Atlanta Journal-Constitution,* carefully described how lunch began. Miller, Murphy and Lt. Governor Pierre Howard rode together from the capitol, a symbol of solidarity. They were together when the DOT board arrived, just after a morning meeting where they voted in support of Rives. Inside the stuffy dining room, the governor sat at the head of the table, with Howard at one arm and Murphy at the other. Miller's closest aide, Keith Mason, sat next to the Speaker. This wasn't protocol. This was politics.

Playing the game of political symbolism, Morast—by now the board chairman—sat in front of Miller, at the other end of the table. Eight board members sat between them, as if they might need someone to keep them apart. Miller is a person who enjoys a good meal and puts off business until after the dishes are cleared. He invited the group to enjoy lunch, but everyone knew what was coming.

Salads were served, then grilled steaks, baked potatoes and steamed asparagus. Then came strawberry shortcake and cups of hot coffee. Finally, on cue, Miller pushed back his chair. "Gentlemen, we have some business to discuss."

McDonald paints a vivid picture as she describes the formal, austere setting. She also describes so very well how Miller delivered the message that he not only wanted Rives replaced, he wanted him to be replaced by Wayne Shackelford, former executive assistant to the Gwinnett County Commission. A real estate developer, Shackelford had a fortunate line on his resume that said his first job as a University of Georgia Extension Agent was in Murphy's home county. Miller was clear that he did not want Rives replaced with a department regular. Neither did Murphy. Neither did Howard.

Morast, a large hulking man who by then had lost a leg to diabetes, also stood. He explained that the board really didn't know Mr. Shackelford very well, that there was no way they could do anything right then anyway. Miller didn't flinch and said reporters were waiting for him and that he wasn't going to talk to them until he could announce a change in commissioners.

If the members of the DOT had not experienced the Miller temper before, they did that afternoon. He told them that while they might not know Shackelford they should get to know Zell Miller.

"You know, I'm a little crazy. If you think that I'm going to destroy my administration, then you're dead wrong. I've got some tools at my disposal to prevent you from doing that," he reminded the board. Spelling it out, there was the matter of a $500 million state allotment that was earmarked for the DOT. "I start the budget," he snapped. "It begins with me and it ends with me."

Besides, he reminded them, as governor he had the power to create new boards. And if there was a parallel board to this one, the new DOT would be the ones to receive the dedicated funds. The men around the table knew that their power came from the budget they handed out. Miller continued, again reminding them that Murphy and Howard were in his corner. Finally, in this atmosphere one could cut with a knife, the Lt. Governor spoke up. "Why don't you step out of the room and let me and the Speaker talk to them," Howard suggested. Following the prepared script, Miller left the dining room with Mason at his heels.

Legend and headline have described the explosive temper of Tom Murphy, but it was the aging Irishman who tried to calm the temper and tension that still hung over the room, after Miller had made his exit stage right. "We told them what the situation was," Murphy said, "that we wanted Mr. Rives to retire with dignity, and that they ought to understand what was facing them if they bucked all three of us."

After Murphy offered his explanation, he and Howard were asked to leave so the board could talk in private. In fifteen minutes, the governor, lieutenant governor and speaker were invited back in and told that Mr. Rives would be asked to retire, and they agreed that his successor would not come from within the department. Certainly, they would interview Shackelford for the board and no, they would not be promoting an increase in the state's motor fuel tax.

That drama was played out on West Paces Ferry Road, but the stage where both Miller and Murphy are most comfortable is under the gold dome. Even there, they prefer the spotlight be kept off them except when it is under their control.

Murphy, a master thespian as well as a crafty country lawyer, loves to give up the gavel to a colleague and take a point of personal privilege, going to the well of the House to speak on a particular bill. Usually, it is a piece of legislation that he takes very personally. Often he cries. He is comfortable if that is reported. If the emotions are more private, he balks. "I remember once describing him in a column as being mawkish," Frederick Allen says. "He came screaming out of the well of the House demanding to know what in the hell that word meant. I said it meant given to bouts of simple sentimentality. Mr. Speaker, it means you're very emotional, and you don't want people to know that. 'Oh, well, I guess that's right.' And he went away."

For the first seven years Miller has been Georgia's chief executive, the two had held back the storm. But the 1997 session of the General Assembly was a throwback to their earlier squabbles. It started over Miller's package of DUI legislation and continued over welfare reform, but it was an innocent bill that dealt with Medicaid fraud that first sent them to their neutral corners. The bill itself appeared to be routine. It had come through the House Rules Committee without incident. Murphy had said nothing and neither had his closest allies on the committee. Federal authorities had the ability to seize property involved in drug cases, but their counterparts at the state level did not. Under this legislation, the state would now have that right. No one had said a word about the bill and it finally came to the House calendar.

That afternoon, Murphy gave up the gavel, left the podium, and under parliamentary procedure was recognized by the new chair. Only then, could the gentleman from the 18th District enter the well of the House and speak on a bill. That act is always a signal to the membership that The Speaker has an interest in whatever legislation is on the floor. They listened. They always listen to him. In the halls outside the House chamber, the usual gabfests ended. Around the television monitors were gathered lobbyists who sensed something was brewing. Like the House members, they were listening. Down in the lower levels of the capitol, where Zell Miller's key staff members work, most of them had left their individual offices and were huddled around an audio box in Steve Wrigley's office. They also listened.

Murphy was angry and he was on stage. It was his stage, one he had acted on so many times. It was a familiar role, one he plays as well as anyone. Tightly rolled up in his oversized hand was a letter that dealt with that Medicaid bill. It was from Zell Miller. His friend, Zell Miller. Murphy balled his hand into a fist around the sheet of paper. He waved it next to his right ear as he spoke. His voice started softly, then roared. It was vintage Murphy.

"I don't like Mike Bowers," he said, stating an established fact about the Democrat-turned-Republican who at the time was Georgia's attorney general. "He doesn't like me. We make no bones about that. But this letter from my friend, the governor. When it says I consort with thieves, my friends, that hurts … "

The rift between the governor and the House leadership continued throughout the 1997 session. It intensified when Miller concluded that Murphy's forces were threatening the six percent teacher pay raise. Miller fought back as he always did, and the results came, but not without wounds. Near the end of the session, Murphy bitterly attacked Miller then came back and issued an emotional, public apology. The days of Murphy's total domination were slowly coming to an end. The chamber he looked upon from that tall podium was changing with every election. Months after the end of the session, there were rumbles that the Democratic leadership was whispering to Murphy that he ought to begin the transition of power. As the 1997 session ended, Murphy seemed tired. The flame was flickering. Miller must have sensed what that meant to his old adversary, and he called The Speaker that evening to acknowledge the remarks. Arriving at the capitol early the next morning, he went straight to Murphy's office, just to talk, just to visit. For Miller, the exercise was more personal than political. He's always operated on the theory that an aggressive fight with a strong enemy builds a political base—if you're patient enough. He was never one of the people Teddy Roosevelt talked about in a quote Miller fondly cites: "Dare greatly, don't be one of those cold and timid souls."

By this time, Miller was sixty-five years old. The events of the Legislature had showed that he could still get a rage-on, that he still wore a chip on his shoulder. The passion was still there. But with his final tour beginning and Murphy's soon to come, Zell Miller was reaching out to The Speaker. "I like a good fight, but I would rather it not be so personal between me, The Speaker, and the Democratic leadership," Miller says. "In 1997, as always, I did what I had to do. I had to threaten The Speaker. I had to threaten the Democratic leadership. That's the only way I know how to play. It skinned some shins—mine as well as some others. Yes, I'm cranky and hard to please. We're all inadequate and petty. I believe as Hamlet, that if you gave a person what he really deserved, who would escape whipping."

Calvin Smyre is a state representative from Columbus who manages to balance a political relationship with both Miller and Murphy. Elected in 1976, he has been caught between them and at other times he has served as a magnet to draw them back together. To him, they epitomize Georgia politics of this era. "The landscape has always been Miller-Murphy," Smyre says. "I've seen Busbee. I've seen Harris. They were both leaders. But in modern days, no one will be remembered as much as Miller and Murphy. They have the best love-hate respect of anybody I have ever seen. They respect each other's political acumen. They can't bend. Deep down, I think they enjoy that relationship."

Deep down, they do.

12

MAKING A POINT

The amount stung. The decimal point drew blood. To get the full effect, it was an amount of money that had to be put into words, not numbers. That night in Savannah, in the studios of WTOC-TV, after flipping over the final page on his chart, that was just what Herman Talmadge did, stretching out his words very carefully so folks could experience every numeral and every zero.

One-hundred fifty-six *point* eight billion dollars. A Talmadge organization that hadn't run a true political campaign since 1950 was holding on by its final knuckle in a Georgia they didn't really recognize. They didn't need high-powered polls or the front page of the Atlanta Constitution to tell them what was at stake. They didn't need the steely eyes of Zell Miller cutting to the marrow in another TV ad. They knew it inside and they could see it in the tired eyes of their candidate. The age, the accusations and the alcohol had taken a toll. Unless his allies could restore some vigor in him, it was over . . . for Herman, for Gene, for Miss Mitt and for the power their last name had represented before many people in his camp were born. That night in Atlanta, the fight doctors in his corner put the 67-year-old senator back together again one more time, and for that hour he was in an arena that he had built and he had thrived.

A slashing campaign, one of the most brutal in recent history, came down to a night in August of 1980, less than a week before Georgia voters would go back to the polls in a Democratic Party runoff. Mathis, Underwood, and all the rest were on the sidelines, and in some ways were glad to be there. Mattingly was in the wings, little more than an unknown Republican typewriter salesman. It was Talmadge-Miller, with the United States Senate seat going to the winner—or so the smart money believed. The two surviving candidates had debated in Columbus that same week. Both sides claimed victory, of course, but privately the Talmadge supporters knew that Miller was ahead on points. Now they came together in Atlanta. This wasn't one of those concocted debates with a panel of news people asking the questions. This was two men going Demo-to-Demo, nose-to-nose and question-to-question.

The Talmadge strategy for the debate came down to that obscene amount of money. His staff members had done some homework and in a meeting with each one working from a yellow legal pad, they had listed the promises and the programs that Zell Miller had been presenting around the state. One here. One there. National Health Insurance. Federalized Workers Compensation. As the list grew, someone got a calculator and crunched some numbers, putting a price tag by every one of them. Then they made the charts, holding the bottom line amount for the final one. $156.8 billion dollars.

"We played that hard and it hit Zell hard," says Rogers Wade, who was Talmadge's administrative assistant in the Senate and was a vital member of the campaign organization in 1980. "We were playing in a ballpark where Zell had no idea of the parameters. Until Talmadge flipped over that chart, he had no idea of what was coming."

As for the decimal, it was drama more than reality. "That was for effect," Wade says. "All of the numbers were rounded. The decimal was for effect and its effect was sharp." Miller tried to fight back, but his words couldn't wipe away those numbers or that decimal point. "You have tried all your life to intimidate the people of this state," Miller told the senator. "I'm not going to have you intimidating me and putting words in my mouth."

Talmadge didn't have to put words in his mouth. The words and the programs were Miller's. Rick Allen, the political editor of *The Atlanta Constitution,* was in the wings watching and listening. It was a night he can play back like a VCR. "Herman had a chart and he ripped a page off and it showed that all the things Zell wanted to do would cost $156.8 billion." For Allen, it was a watershed. "That decimal point always tore me up because you can denounce a guy as a big spending liberal, but the decimal point seemed to mean he was really going to do it."

Zell Miller came to learn this, even if he didn't know it standing in the heat of the moment and the TV lights. "That debate was devastating," he says. "It's one thing to talk about all those great plans you have. It's another to tell people how you're going to pay for them. You've never seen me make that mistake again."

It was a year and a summer that all of the characters who played a role will remember. For Talmadge, it was the culmination of several years of personal tragedy and political attacks. His son, Bobby, had drowned in 1975. His wife Betty divorced him in 1977. His alcoholism and his rehabilitation was front page news in 1979. Three grand juries investigated missing funds in his office in 1979 and 1980 but never came down with an indictment. His colleagues in the Senate voted 81-15 to denounce him for reprehensible conduct that brought them dishonor. The smell of political blood was in the air. For the first time in his life, Herman Talmadge was vulnerable. It was more than political vulnerability. For the first time in his life, Herman Talmadge seemed human.

Always he was Ole Gene's boy, reared to be the tobacco-spitting image of his rascal father. The same fraternity. The same college. The same law school. The same political savy. The same unruly hair that had a mind of its own over his forehead. The same destiny. The same enemies. He was a Talmadge, and Talmadges knew what they were supposed to do and be.

Herman Talmadge managed his daddy's campaigns. He staked a claim for being governor after his daddy's death in 1946 and gave up that claim only after the courts ruled against him in favor of M.E. Thompson. He had run against Thompson for governor in 1948, and it was as if though Thompson had been a two-year caretaker for the Talmadges. He finished out what had been his daddy's term, then served four years of his own after a 1950 victory over that same Thompson. As his term was finishing, with the help of powerful friends, a vacancy was created in the United States Senate. With Walter F. George coming home to Georgia, Talmadge moved to Washington in 1957. By 1980, with Richard Russell gone, he was Georgia's senior Senator.

To a new generation of Georgians, Talmadge had become that man in Washington. They watched him become a star of the Watergate hearings on afternoon TV. Every six years, he came back and toyed with an unknown opponent and made speeches that had begun to run together. Now, his nasty divorce had unfurled all of his political habits, including an overcoat that Betty said was stuffed with money given her former husband as unreported campaign donations. Along the way, Georgia learned what its elected delegation in Washington already knew, that the invincible Talmadge was a full-blown alcoholic. From back in Georgia, the Talmadge office in Washington was hearing that first one, then another Democrat might challenge the senator. No one took it very seriously at the time.

Long distance, Talmadge began to hear name after name. People like Governor George Busbee, Speaker of the House Tom Murphy and former Governors Carl Sanders and Ernest Vandiver were calling with reports almost every day, telling the Talmadge people who was thinking about running. And Miller was one of them. As the senator's troubles became bigger headlines, the list of candidates grew bigger. There was Dawson Mathis of Albany, a former TV newscaster and the congressman from the Second District. There was Norman Underwood, a former aide to Busbee and a judge on the Georgia Court of Appeals. The lineup of would-be senators would grow longer, but Miller, Mathis and Underwood were soon the major candidates on the Democratic side.

Though Miller has never been accused of not having a strong mind of his own, his decision to enter the race certainly was made easier by the non-stop support he received from the Atlanta Constitution, particularly editor Hal Gulliver and political columnist Bill Shipp. As the qualifying date grew closer, both of them turned up the heat—in print and in private. Gulliver, in an editorial page column, drew a line in the sand and gave Miller a personal deadline to make a decision.

Talmadge didn't know how to handle any of this. "The Old Guard said be low-key, stay out of the way. The newspapers are mean, but stay out of the way and we'll be OK," Wade says. "Pat Caddell had been Jimmy Carter's pollster and he was working for us by then. He started telling us that it would be impossible for Talmadge to win without a runoff. He was saying Mathis or Miller. From a Washington point of view, we knew more about Mathis. He was a congressman, he was there, so we looked at him as the one to worry about."

Miller thought he knew better. Just as he had rightly sensed in 1964 that Phil Landrum was vulnerable, he also knew inside that Talmadge was. In 1978, his second campaign for lieutenant governor, he collected more votes than anyone on the ballot—including Sam Nunn—so he was feeling his oats. Inside him was still a desire to go to Washington, the big leagues, and he began to tell people around him so. He was saying that Talmadge was beatable, but few people listened. When he told a group of Fulton County Democrats that, they almost ran him out of the room. What he was saying was right, only he was sizing up the race as a duel between two candidates—him and Talmadge. That was wrong, and so was his assumption that Talmadge and his ethics would be the issue that made folks stand in line on election day.

"A speech I made at Emory University in 1979 was a prelude. I pretty well knew I was going to run but I wanted to see how such a speech would be greeted—a trial balloon so to speak. But ethics was not then an overriding issue, and still isn't. Ethics doesn't move voters. What moves people are kitchen-table issues . . . how am I going to send my kids to college . . . what if I lose my job? . . .

what am I gonna do about these utility bills? But I didn't know that then," Miller says.

Miller played his decision close to the vest, coyly playing with the media and the Talmadge camp. In June of 1979, just after the Emory speech, he called an early-morning press conference in the Senate Chambers and the media assumed this would be his announcement. A room full of reporters came to hear him end the suspense and confirm his declaration of war on Talmadge. So did an aide to the beleaguered senior senator, several party leaders and a number of capitol secretaries.

Instead, Miller got up and talked about giving teachers a pay raise and about removing the sales tax from food and drugs. After going through a six-page statement, he opened the floor for questions and reporters took target practice at the lieutenant governor for spoiling their predictions. At every question, he stood by his comment about "not burning any bridges behind him and not crossing any bridges before he gets to them."

None of that stopped the questions so Miller turned on the reporters. "You people want blood," he snapped. "You want me to attack personalities. I'm attacking problems. You took forty seconds out of a speech at Emory when I had mentioned six examples of double standards," adding that his other remarks had ended up "with the truss ads." Never did he retract anything he had said, only to admit that other Democrats had turned on him. "I have nothing to add or nothing to subtract from or apologize for what I said."

That was the middle of 1979, but in the coming months he would go forward with his plans. Recognizing that this was a different playing field than he had been in before, Miller decided he needed help. Before, he was a one-man campaign. In that first campaign against Landrum, he and Shirley even designed and set the type for his brochures at their own newspaper. This race would be different. Not only was the other name on the ballot going to be Talmadge, this would be a race for national office.

"I had always followed campaigns in other states carefully and I understood that this campaign would be on another level and that I would need help. I would need a pollster. I would need to do television. I never had done either before. I had met Bill Clinton earlier and had come to admire him as a 'comer.' I called him and he recommended Dick Morris," Miller says.

Clinton was governor of Arkansas at the time and for years Morris continued to be a member of his inner circle. Sixteen years later, in Clinton's second race for president, it was Morris whose relationship with a prostitute rocked the campaign and became headlines in publications in newspaper racks and at super market checkout lines. Miller says his relationship with Morris was rocky and uneven, although he learned from it. "He could see the campaign was a loser and I didn't have any money to pay him. I have not talked to Morris since 1980."

Morris helped push Miller into adopting many of the programs that got him into trouble when Talmadge went on TV with those charts. Ten years later, Paul Begala was one of Miller's advisers in his quest for governor and in 1992 and 1996 helped elect Clinton president. He and his former partner, James Carville, had to deal with the wreckage left behind from Miller's 1980 race. He paraphrases Miller who has said he "wanted to run for Senate in the worst way—and he did" and refers to Morris as a "snake oil salesman."

"Miller never again allowed a political consultant to try to pull him from his gut instincts as Dick Morris had conned him into running as a hard-core left-winger," says Begala, now a senior aide to President Clinton. "Dick Morris ran a campaign that was totally opposite from the man—a campaign that was both left-wing and elitist."

More than that, it was a campaign that turned Miller into a pit bull. "The Best Senator Money Can't Buy," was his slogan. By early in the summer of 1980, it was a campaign that ignored the kitchen table. It quickly moved to a level lower than Georgia had seen before. Miller, Mathis and Underwood were attacking Talmadge the man, not the senator. As it had been in decades past, either you were for Talmadge or you were not. Only now it was personal. Just as it had been when Gene Talmadge was the target, *The Atlanta Constitution* editorial pages began to go on the attack

Wrote Gulliver: "The ill-kept secret of this Georgia political season is that Sen. Herman Talmadge is the sawdust candidate, the hollow man, and even his staunchest supporters are beginning to suspect this is his 'last hurrah.'. . . Talmadge is one of the very last of the old Southern dinosaurs, a vanishing breed whose main mission for a couple of decades appeared to be to keep the Senate (and the country) safe for racial segregation."

Talmadge was responding. These words came at the Wheat Street Baptist Church, a black congregation in Atlanta: "I've been accused of being a segregationist twenty-five years ago. It's true. Do you know any white folks in Georgia who weren't segregationists twenty-five years ago?"

Wrote Shipp: "Miller is the complete negative candidate. He is after Talmadge like a hound chasing a rabbit or a cat after a rat. . . Some newspapermen say Miller is too negative. But the rebuttal that is obvious is that there is only one issue in this race. It is not inflation or National Defense. It is Herman Talmadge." Miller took issue: "I haven't slung mud. I've flung truth—and it has splattered all over this state."

For the most part, Talmadge was playing the role of the incumbent, the respected senior senator. Back in Georgia, his opponents were on the prowl. Mathis was comical, doing a private imitation of Talmadge that was stageworthy. Underwood was more acceptable and political. Miller had a razor in his mouth. Not that any of them were pulling punches. More than that, each often seemed to be trying to one-up the other in their portrayal of Talmadge. And it was Miller's darts that were finding their mark more than the others.

At a black church, Miller turned to the gospel of Luke and called the senator down out of the tree as Jesus had done the tax collector. "Now Zaccheus was up in a sycamore tree and he's lost touch with what the people down below wanted and needed. And the Lord said to him: 'Zaccheus, you gotta get down out of that tree and walk with the people. You've been living up there above them for too long.' That's why I'm running," the evangelizing candidate said. "This summer, I want to say: 'Zaccheus, come down.'"

Not every accusation was so biblical. When the subject was Talmadge's personal life, it was harsh. Talking about the overcoat and its deep pockets he said, "We have a lot of senators who go down as profiles in courage. We're going to have a senior senator from Georgia go down as a profile in cash."

Talmadge tried to dodge the bullets. His theme was "Who is the best qualified to serve the people of Georgia in the Senate?" His first TV ad included a message that "I've gone to my maker and I found forgiveness," citing his divorce and the death of his son but not the ethics questions or his alcoholism.

Miller fired back that the television ad "was like a Hollywood soap opera . . . 'As the Senator Turns.' Throw in your crying towel and put on your boxing gloves," Miller said, calling for Herman Talmadge to debate him.

As the summer rocked on, the traditional party crowd rallied around Talmadge, during the primary and later in the runoff. Labor Commissioner Sam Caldwell, the senator's former press secretary, said he thought Miller "should teach history rather than make it." Agriculture Commissioner Tommy Irvin reminded people of the seniority system in Washington and that the next in line to chair the agriculture committee behind Talmadge was George McGovern. At a press conference, Vandiver, former Sen. David Gambrell, former congressmen Phil Landrum, Jack Flynt, John W. Davis and Robert Stephens lined up in support of Talmadge. Arnall and Sanders along with ex-congressman John W. Davis couldn't be there, but sent messages of support. Senator Sam Nunn did not take part in the campaign, but issued a press release in favor of his colleague.

Miller retaliated with endorsements of his own, notably from Atlanta Mayor Maynard Jackson, State Senator Julian Bond, and Coretta Scott King. Jackson did not stop with his support of Miller. He said that "Any black voter who supports Herman Talmadge might as well walk down Auburn Avenue and spit on Martin Luther King Jr.'s grave."

Miller had called Talmadge "a stooge of big oil," and coupled with the endorsements from Bond and Jackson, this fueled comebacks from columnists and candidates. Referring to Bond, *Atlanta Journal* conservative columnist John Crown wrote that "to send Zell to the U.S. Senate would be tantamount to creating a senator indistinguishable from Ted Kennedy or George McGovern." Mathis said he couldn't argue with Miller's statement about Talmadge being a stooge of big oil, "but what's worse: to be a stooge of big oil or Maynard Jackson."

Not all of the name-calling was between Miller and Talmadge, however. It was Underwood that coined the phrase "Zigzag Zell"—three words that can still make the hairs on the back of Miller's neck stand up and salute. For the former judge, it was an attempt to be noticed in a field of candidates that were much more colorful than he was.

"I've always had a silly affinity for alliteration," he says. "Words are interesting to me, and I was trying to convey a conservative message. We were all making the point that the Talmadge Era was over. Zell was trying to put himself in a conservative position in a speech. I truly don't remember what the issue was. That's where the zigzag came in. I was accusing him of changing his position from one he had taken in the past. The alliterative, cutesy quality of it just came out. Anybody who has had as long a career as Zell has is going to stake out spots at different ends of the spectrum. All of us in politics are vulnerable because most everybody who's successful could be accused of zigzagging. Only most of them don't have a name like Zell." Say the words and Miller will explain them.

"Zigzag was a brilliant and devastating phrase—so alliterative and memorable," Miller says. "I hated it, but I love Norman. There are few people I have more respect for. One reason I hate it is that I've always thought it took courage to change your position. A person who has been in politics for more than three decades is bound to change. What's remarkable is the constant thread that runs through my career: education, food tax exemption, tough on crime. It was Herman who changed and supported a sales tax. Vandiver changed after his 'no, not one' statement. Carter changed after running a pro-George Wallace campaign then said, 'the time for racial discrimination is over.' Those were zigzags, good ones, historical ones, bigger than any of mine. And they were good, not bad."

Shipp thinks whatever zigging and zagging there was, was a matter of wanting to be elected. "It is sometimes Zell trying to gauge the public wind so he could stay in power to do some of the things he wanted to do. Jimmy Carter said to me one time that you can talk about all those great ideals and those great goals you want to accomplish. But if you can't get elected, you can't do anything. I think that's driven Zell to some extent."

The primary in July of 1980 was a busy day at the polls. More than a million Georgians voted, over 48 percent of the registered voters. As the analysts had predicted, there would be a runoff. For thirty years, the only question in a Talmadge race had been whether he would get 70 or 80 percent. That year, he got only 42 percent. Miller made the runoff with 24.1 percent. Underwood had 17.8 and Mathis was fourth at 13 percent. There were weeks to go before the two of them met in the face-off, but Miller now admits he knew it was over before the first shot had been fired in the runoff.

"It was an inept campaign—the worst I've ever run," Miller says. "I knew I was doing it all wrong, but if I was ever to have a breath of life left in me after it was over, I had to get into the runoff. So I painted myself into a corner but into a runoff. When Underwood and Mathis got in and staked out the conservative side of the anti-Talmadge voters, there was nothing to do but go to his left. I was far from being the liberal that my campaign had become and that played right into Talmadge's hands."

Not only did Herman Talmadge take advantage of the candidate Miller had become, but it would be an image Zell Miller would find difficult to shed. He was seen as an anti-establishment maverick who respected nothing old. Shipp had said the race was "the little people versus the big mules," and the mules were not very happy with Miller the apparent liberal. In a state that was shifting to the right more than anyone realized, this was a position that could have ended Miller's political career. During the runoff campaign, insiders began to wonder if he could recover in time for the 1982 gubernatorial campaign—if ever.

After months of mimicking and maligning Talmadge, Mathis stepped out and endorsed him over Miller. "Zell's big-government, big-spending big-deficit attitude is more than I can bear." Tom Murphy came out for Talmadge and so did Bert Lance, Miller's old friend from the mountains. "Get your fighting clothes on," Talmadge told Miller.

The Talmadge people were firing shots at the Miller people and the Miller people were shooting back. Gordon Roberts, Talmadge's press secretary, sent a telegram to his counterpart asking for a debate, and Joe Cowart said he would have been glad to talk on the telephone about it. Talmadge pushed for a debate that required only four people—"me, Mr. Miller, a cameraman and a timekeeper." Both of them boasted about being champion debaters in their youth, but more than a loving cup was on the line now. But as bad as the blood grew between the candidates, Wade says they were often egged on by their staffs, particularly from his side which was listening to the old-line Democrats who did not care for Miller.

One of them was Phil Landrum. He and Talmadge had become friends even though he was M.E. Thompson's executive secretary during the three governor fiasco of 1946. Just two years before, the former Ninth District Congressman had joined Mary Hitt and John Savage in support of Miller, who gathered together his former opponents. Now he was in the Talmadge campaign, telling the senator how Miller had run to both his left and his right. It was also Landrum who first told Talmadge that Miller's late father was a supporter of E.D. Rivers and that Zell Miller had written his Master's thesis on Rivers—a man Talmadge considered one of the great crooks in Georgia political history, and also the man who gave his father his last defeat.

In his own book, written in 1987, Talmadge put great stock in the connection between Miller and Rivers even though an ally of his guesses the former senator never read the 1958 thesis.

"Just as surely as I was Gene Talmadge's son, Zell was the political off-spring of Eurith Dickinson Rivers. Zell's father had worked for the Rivers Administration, and Zell idolized Ed when he was growing up. Although Ed was a likable fellow, most historians agree that he was a disaster as governor. The one notable exception was Professor Zell Miller. Zell's masters thesis is a defense of the Rivers Administration.

"Since Papa cleaned up the mess that Ed made in state government and then ruined Ed's political comeback in 1946, the triumphs of the Talmadges were also the end of Ed Rivers. What better way to avenge Ed than for his most ardent admirer to bring down the last of the Talmadges? Zell was too much of a historian not to appreciate the irony of the situation."

Zell Miller's thesis dealt with Rivers' success in public education, in the creation of a state welfare system, and in his creation of the state patrol. Yet, in an even-handed manner, it also went into detail on the charges of parole-selling and of embezzlement—charges for which Rivers was never convicted. Miller's final statement in the document said history would be Rivers' "just judge." Nor did Talmadge seem to realize that Grady Miller had been dead five years when Rivers became governor in 1937.

That squabble had been fought out in the 1930s and 1940s between a Talmadge and a Young Harris College graduate of another generation. The 1980 race came down to a series of four debates, beginning in Columbus. There, Talmadge closed with a paraphrase of the fifth chapter of Matthew, verse forty-four, a scripture that tells us "to love our enemies." He then asked everyone to join him in a prayer for the people who had been "abusing, vilifying and persecuting me."

Only the people who watched around the state would really judge the winners and losers. But both candidates along with newspapers across the state, recruited debate watchers who offered reasons why Talmadge and Miller had both won and lost. As the race drew to a close, Talmadge became more aggressive and Miller's campaign reduced its attacks and began telling voters why Zell Miller would be a good United States Senator.

In Savannah, Talmadge produced the telling charts that hit Miller like a blow below the belt. It had been just six years since Miller slapped an unwary Mrs. Hitt with his question about the state budget. Now he had been sent back to school.

Yet, Miller's remarks were optimistic to the end, even though he knew when he voted that morning in Young Harris, he would not be going to Washington. Herman Talmadge won the Democratic nomination with a sweeping 58 percent of the vote and 140 of the state's 159 counties.

Zaccheus had come down out of that tree and he came down fighting. "I'd rather be right than senator," Miller said on election night. He said he would be voting for the Democratic candidates in the fall, but that he would skip over the race for United States Senator. "There was this dead cat out in the road and the more times you run over it the flatter it gets. That's just the way I feel—flattened."

A lot has been written and said about the 1980 primary and runoff. Miller's loss has been attributed to a variety of factors, but Miller simply staked out positions on the major issues that put him to the left of most Georiga voters. Voters were clearly ready to consider someone other than Talmadge; Talmadge's poor showing in the primary was proof of that and he probably should not have run for re-election. But Miller ran a campaign that the editorial writers and academics approved of, away from his own instincts and roots, as Begala said, and he lost. He would not let that happen again.

The day after the election, Mary Beazley got a phone call in Washington. It was her former boss—Zell Miller. She had worked for him in the lieutenant governor's office just as she had worked for other Georgia political leaders. She had also worked for Jimmy Carter when he was governor and when he moved to Washington she went along. Naturally, she had followed the Senate election in Georgia. She knew what had happened when Miller called and asked if he and Shirley could come up for a visit. "He wanted to be a tourist," she recalls.

That's what he was when Beazley and her husband picked up the Millers at the Washington airport two days later. Only it turned out they were more like tourists than anyone could have imagined. "Our car wouldn't start. And believe it or not, he didn't get one bit excited. We rode the train into town and my husband had to go rent a car." Three days before he was trying to come to the nation's capital with the pomp and glory of a United States Senator. Now he was being jostled around on a subway.

The next day, the four of them toured Thomas Jefferson's home at Monticello and, as they were soaking up history, Miller decided to stay over for a few more days so they could see the home of Robert E. Lee near Fredericksburg, Virginia. "He was more satisfied and calm than I've ever seen him," says Beazley, who still helps guard the door to the governor's office. "The election and Herman Talmadge were never discussed. This was his way of dealing with all that had happened. It was a kind of closure, a renewal of his spirit, and he was doing it through history."

Now it became Mack Mattingly's turn to go after the incumbent. "The problem is inflation," the St. Simons Republican said. "The problem is not Herman Talmadge. The problem is the price of food and gas, and rent and utility bills. Just running Herman Talmadge out of office won't change things. Zell Miller, Norman Underwood and Dawson Mathis were just more of the same."

Mattingly was the epitome of the new-wave Republicans who over the years had slowly moved into the state. Democrats like to say those folks were attracted to a state that prospered because of its Democratic heritage, then after they got here they became Republicans. Mattingly, a prosperous IBM salesman, came to Georgia from Indiana. When he began to campaign in the general election, he had shed no blood. Talmadge's veins had been pumped dry.

The time was right for Mattingly. Not only did Talmadge have troubles, but also this was the year of Ronald Reagan and Reagan conservatism. Though Talmadge was anything but close to Jimmy Carter, they were both Georgia Democrats. The fact that Talmadge, one of the last of the wool-hat Democrats, had in many ways voted like a national Republican meant nothing to the new voters spread out around Atlanta. Those people had listened to the attacks of Miller and friends. But they didn't need to. All they needed to hear was the anachronistic voice of Herman Eugene Talmadge, Jr.

So it was a weary Talmadge who limped back to Washington and again tried to be senatorial. Like most people, he believed the race had been won in the summer when the Democrats came to the polls. That was Georgia as it was remembered by Herman Talmadge and his people in Washington. But this was the Georgia of 1980.

"From the beginning, Talmadge had no room to run," his friend Wade says. "He had to approach the new voter in Georgia. He was right about that. Only most of them were Republican." For one term, Mack Mattingly became the senator from Georgia. Herman Talmadge came home. The old had become new.

For Miller, it was a part of his life he would like to forget. "It left me so bloody that it took me ten years to recover. Talmadge was defeated. Underwood and Mathis were never elected after that. It was a disaster for all of us."

Politics is seldom a game of absolutes, and usually opinions come and go as often as the latest press conference. That 1980 fight for the Senate is an exception. Its wounds refuse to heal—for any of the participants. The ones who lost and the one who won.

"People close to Senator Talmadge remember what he taught us: in politics your enemies are never permanent," says Wade, who in a summer seventeen years after that Democratic Party squabble was working to bring the Republican National Convention to Atlanta. "It was that way with Ellis Arnall. Talmadge is not a sentimental man but when Governor Arnall got sick he would go and sit with him for hours. They were that close. As for Zell, he got in Talmadge's focus and it was hard to get him out of there. He blames his loss on the primary. He thinks he was pushed aside by the party after all he had done. By being the most vocal messenger, he has focused all of it on Zell."

Not that Miller and Talmadge were ever close. People like Talmadge seldom joined in the mundane game of state politics and they were also of different generations. Miller's races against Landrum could have distanced them. They had no alliances to rebuild, for all they had had in common was that great umbrella, the Georgia Democratic Party.

In recent years, Miller began to reach out to Talmadge people, trying to arrange a meeting with the aging senator whose health had begun to fade rapidly. Miller, who doesn't often say such things, said "Yes, I'd like to heal the wounds with Talmadge. He took my hide off in the election and then in his book. I don't blame him. It was war. But I don't want us to go to our graves without making amends. Every single person I've ever run against later became a good friend—except for Talmadge and Guy Millner. I'd like to be better friends to both of them." Circumstance threw the two of them together in late 1996 when a formal dinner was held in Cobb County for Sam Nunn, whose own Senate career was coming to a close.

Governor Miller and his party were at one table. Nunn, joined by Talmadge, was seated nearby. Photographers were wandering among the well-appointed tables posing pictures. Miller saw one of them coming his way and he moved toward Talmadge, who slowly got to his feet. Nunn, seeing what was happening, joined them. As that photographer focused, others joined him, recognizing that this was magic. For a moment, it wasn't politics, it was history. The next morning, wearing their neatly-pressed tuxedos, the three of them were on the front page of the *Constitution*.

As that race was recorded in 1980, Zell Miller had many bridges to build. "There was a period that I agreed with the conventional wisdom that I was dead politically, that I could never win the big one," he says. "But the more I thought about it, the more obvious it was to me what had gone wrong. I didn't have the financial resources and I needed someone who understood polls, media, strategy, and … me. I was not as smart as I thought I was."

There would be a governor's race in 1982 and George Busbee had served his two terms so there would not be an incumbent on the ballot. But at that moment, two years seemed a long way off to Miller. Whatever came in the future, he was still the lieutenant governor of Georgia and in January of 1981 he needed to be ready to preside over a body that he had been neglecting.

"The office of lieutenant governor in Georgia is one of the most powerful legislative offices in the country and I had never used it to its full potential. I realized that if one did use that office fully he could gain the respect of those who finance campaigns," he says. First he had to reaffirm the respect of a number of senators.

He had been in that office longer than anyone. To him, it was the best office in government. Even after being governor, he gave thought to running for it again after he was out of office—"More thought than you or anyone would expect." There was enough politics to make it interesting and enough power to feed an ego. Yet there were also times to pursue other interests such as teaching, reading, and writing.

Only like him, it was changing. Al Holloway and John Riley—two- thirds of the committee on committees, which Miller had established were no longer as powerful. He could not take the chance that he could work as well with their replacements. He could lose his influence. As a friend told him, "If you do, you'd be a cut dog." So Miller decided to take back the power he had relinquished in the early days of his first term. He was licking his wounds from one fight while he picked another one on his own turf—the Georgia Senate.

Frank Eldridge had been a member of the Senate since 1965. The Waycross Democrat had served under four lieutenant governors—the late Peter Zack Geer, George T. Smith, Lester Maddox and Miller. He had seen Miller come in and make it more inclusive and open, then he had seen the demise of the so-called "super senator." Under Miller, authority had been more even-handed.

"Yet there was never any doubt who was in charge," Eldridge says. "He didn't back away from the Al Holloways, the Gene Holleys or the Culver Kidds if he thought something needed to be done. I remember one time when he was sitting over to the side with a very influential member of the senate who was giving him a very hard time. He had heard enough, and Zell said, 'Well, son, get you up an automobile and a million dollars so you can run around this state, and if you get enough people to vote for you then you'll be lieutenant governor and you can do what you want to do. Until then, I'm going to do it.' Zell got up and went back to the podium and that particular member of the senate sat there for several minutes to collect himself because he had had his feet jerked out from under him and he had hit the floor like he hadn't experienced it since he'd been in the senate."

Eldridge says Miller's approach to getting a vote was masterful. First, he would say what this bill would do was good for Georgia. Second, he would say it was good for the senator's district. Third, he might say it was good for the senator politically. Finally, he would get personal and say it was something he would like for the senator to do. All of that came before the vote got to the floor. However, much of the power and influence came through the committee process and in 1981 Miller decided to retake the power to select and appoint the committee chairmen.

From the outside that was a major step, and it certainly was controversial to the two members who would have joined the lieutenant governor on the old committee on committees. But Eldridge says it wasn't that important internally, that the true power had always been in the referral of the bills—which Miller had all along.

"I don't want to minimize the change, but it was more symbolic than substance. Even a member of that old committee supported it because he needed the lieutenant governor to be on his side. Zell was just reclaiming power that was inherently his," says Eldridge, now the Secretary of the Senate.

Wayne Garner was a freshman senator that year. He knew Miller only from a distance. Looking around, he learned quickly that this was a Senate where the older heads were strong, that they could deliver the votes. There was also a number of younger members coming in and the "Young Turks," as they came to call themselves, were beginning to be the balance of power. As the fight to restore the lieutenant governor's power was about to come to the floor, Garner got a phone call at his home in Carrollton.

"I'm going to move to get my power back," he said. "That's a great idea," Garner told him, for he thought giving it up was crazy. "I need you to write me a letter telling me you will vote with me." Garner says this is one of Miller's strongest traits—his ability to build a consensus and hold it in place. That's why he wanted a letter. It not only sealed a senator's support, it was a symbol. Garner also had to survive on the floor so he called Senator Tom Allgood of Augusta, who at the time was the Senate Majority leader, to tell him he was voting with Miller.

"Mr. Leader, the lieutenant governor just called and said he's going to move to abolish the committee on committees," Garner said. "Isn't that foolish, Wayne?" said Allgood. "He doesn't have the votes to do that."

"Well, he's got mine, Mr. Leader. If I catch hell, I catch hell."

Miller prevailed. That proved something to people who thought there was no more fight in him. It also served notice that he was back, and that he intended to be lieutenant governor of Georgia. Eldridge says this renewed vigor did not end with the effort to reclaim his power.

"After he lost that race, he became more assertive on the issues he believed in. He took a more dominant position on the appropriations bills. He was more engaged in the day to day activity of the senate. It was as if he was saying, 'I've been elected to this job. I'm here to do this job. I'm going to do the best I can do at this job because I may never be anything but lieutenant governor'," Eldridge says.

Marti Fullerton says the Talmadge experience made him even tougher. "He took back the Senate. Some of them may have thought he was brooding and that they would have a Palace Coup. Wrong," she laughs. "He made up his mind that nothing was going to get by him again."

No one as competitive as Miller can just walk away from a fight and not look back. Nor can a political scientist and historian not want to conduct a study of the events. Shirley Miller says he dissects and he had done a lot of that along the way in the Talmadge race because he could see defeat around the corner. "He was worrying with it and there is a lot of difference in worrying with and worrying about something," she says. "If you're worrying with it, you're looking for an answer. If you worry about it, you're just wasting time."

Zell Miller had other things to worry about that had nothing to do with that summer on the senate stump. His mother was dying. She had been what folks used to call a shut-in since 1979. But in 1983 she suffered a stroke, and on September 19, 1986, at the age of 93, Birdie Bryan Miller died.

She had been too busy to be there in 1974 when her son qualified to run for lieutenant governor of Georgia. He was going to send a car for her, but she said no. Miss Birdie didn't have time for a ceremony. She was building a "Zell Miller for Lieutenant Governor" sign in front of the house she had put together a stone at a time.

Her son's and daughter's handprints were in the walls of the side porch, put there when the cement was wet and they were small. Using a nail, she had written in "Built in honor of Stephen Grady Miller, for Jane and Zell." Later, her son added a plaque in the living room that said: "This house was built in memory of Stephen Grady Miller, outstanding educator and Dean of Young Harris College, who died at age 40. It is also a monument to his brave widow, Birdie Bryan Miller, who designed it, gathered the rocks from the creek, dug and cemented the basement and made a rocky field into this beautiful place."

Celestine Sibley had met Miss Birdie even before she met her son. She had written about her in the Constitution then, and after her death Sibley wrote again, describing a Southern woman "who most refutes the silly image that creeps into books from time to time. You've seen the stories about pampered, flirtatious, sugar-mouthed so called tough Southern belles. I like to think that Birdie Miller, tough and accomplishing and full of laughter, was far more atypical."

The Rev. John Kay, her pastor, says she ministered to him more than he did to her. She was also petulant. "I grew sideburns for a part as the narrator of 'John Brown's Body.' That was back in the 1960s when people around Young Harris took great exception to long hair, beards and sideburns. Mrs. Miller especially disliked my sideburns. Every Sunday after church she'd come to me and ask: 'Now when does that play start?' "

Her memorial was held at Sharp Memorial Methodist, a church named for her old friend where the chimes rang in honor of her late husband. The governor and Mrs. Joe Frank Harris were there. So was her son, the lieutenant governor. So was her daughter, the teacher. The Rev. Dow Kirkpatrick gave the eulogy, and one thing he says still strikes Zell Miller as unusual. "As a minister, maybe I shouldn't say this, but Birdie Miller was so strong, she would have been courageous even if she had no faith in God," the pastor said.

Sibley, who in a long career as a reporter and columnist, had even then interviewed and written about a variety of people most would call famous. But then and now, she has a special memory of this simple mountain woman. "She was a strong woman of the hill country," she wrote as she remembered her first visit. "We won't see her likes again, but for some of us, she will ever be the person we would most like to be like."

For Zell Miller, there were also stones left to tote.

For Birdie's son, it was a decade in which the values she had taught were tested. She always had expectations for him and along the way he had come up with some of his own. He wanted to be a congressman and twice he failed. He thought he would try to be governor, but when he did, the rules were changed. He had tried to be a United States Senator and again he failed. He considered quitting politics, going back to the mountains and returning to the classroom where he had started. But when they buried Birdie next to his father, he remembered that she never quit. If there was a stone left in the creek, she wouldn't quit until it was up the hill. Now Zell Miller had hills of his own.

Political wounds were soon healed and the healing had begun with Ovid Davis. For decades, Davis had been the voice of Coca-Cola around the Georgia capitol. He was the soft drink company's chief government relations officer and a close adviser of Herman Talmadge. Yet, soon after the Senate race, he arranged for Coca-Cola patriarch Robert Woodruff to make a $1,000 donation to Miller – a step that was worth more in symbolism than buying power. But until an afternoon in April of 1997, Miller had found no personal closure of all that had happened in 1980. When closure finally came, the room was filled with generations of old Georgia leaders, but the TV lights were not burning and there were few reporters present to record the event.

The event was born with Miller in the governor's office. He had told people close to the retired senator that he wanted to name a stretch of Highway 41 for Talmadge—a road that ran near the old family place in Lovejoy. It was nostalgia, but it was also a gesture for the then and now since it was an occasion when once more the Old Guard could come together and honor Talmadge whose failing health had been taking him back and forth to Emory University Hospital for months. Since spring weather could be unpredictable and because many of the guests were elderly, the decision was made to move the ceremony to a ballroom at Atlanta International Raceway in Hampton.

Around the room that Spring afternoon leaders of the past and present were joined by people who enjoy passing the bread and butter to the powerful—"The wannabes," said Agriculture Commissioner Tommy Irvin, the emcee for the luncheon. Most of the faces were no longer young. Most had been around for the years when the name Talmadge meant magic and power. But now Herman Talmadge had to cup his hands over his ears to hear and every step was carefully planned. Knees that walked the marble halls of influence no longer work. But there he was at the head table, shaking hands with the endless line of nameless people who for some reason thought he would remember the first time they had met. Two seats away, with Linda Talmadge between them, sat Zell Miller. Those who came forward to speak to the former

Senator spoke to the governor out of courtesy, but many of them were restrained and reserved. This was Herman Talmadge's day and this was his crowd.

Third District Congressman Mac Collins, who represents Talmadge's district in Washington, spoke first. His remarks were more resume than personal. He was little more than a warm-up. Over lunch, many of the guests had wondered what Miller would say, how he would handle his hard-nosed history with the guest of honor. Now it was time, and Irvin went back to the podium to introduce his old mountain neighbor, reminding the crowd that he knew Miller "when he was a crew-cut boy from Towns County."

Miller came to the microphone and, acknowledging the history that sat at tables around the room, he moved into his text. The elders in the crowd remembered the Georgia he described. Younger people were painted a picture by Miller's words. "When he became governor, Georgia still had more than 1,750 one-room school houses, and many other school buildings were in a dilapidated state. The major school construction program undertaken by the Talmadge administration was badly needed," Miller said, going into more detail about what his former foe had accomplished for education and school children.

Then he talked about an education of another kind. "While I'm talking about Senator Talmadge and education, he certainly gave me one. I hold a Ph.D. from Herman Talmadge University. And although it took me a few years to realize it, I've been a stronger man and better governor because of what I learned at Herman Talmadge University. For example, since 1980—the year I got my degree—I have never proposed a program or let anyone else propose a pie-in-the-sky idea without asking: 'How much does it cost, and how are we going to pay for it?' "

In an aside, Miller remembered a phone call he had made seventeen years before to former lieutenant governor Peter Zack Geer, who had died only a few weeks before that program. Geer looked at Talmadge as his mentor, his hero, and Miller was calling to tell him that he was going to run against Talmadge. Geer minced no words. "Zell, have you lost your mind? Don't you know you're taking on the He-Dog?" People in the room were relaxed and laughing. Any question they had about why Zell Miller had come were washed away in the casual way he turned the laughter toward himself. But as soon as he had them walking down that road, he turned his attention back to Herman Talmadge and what he had meant to Georgia. He had let the audience know and—more pointedly—he had let Herman Talmadge know why he was there. He never said he was sorry, but by the tribute he paid the message was delivered. As Miller returned to his seat, Herman Talmadge reached in front of his wife and shook Zell Miller's hand.

Department of Transportation Director Wayne Shackelford followed with the dedication of the Herman Talmadge Highway. It is that stretch of Highway 19-41 that spans from Tara Boulevard in Jonesboro to the city limits of Griffin. "May it remind all who travel this way of his contributions to their way of life," Shackelford said. Slowly getting out of his chair, Talmadge and DOT board member Sam Wellborn of Columbus unveiled the road sign that had been covered by a dropcloth. Then, with Irvin helping him up the steps, Talmadge went to the podium. A stool was put behind him. As he started to talk, the familiar voice was a whisper. For the people in the room, it was a reminder of mortality for this frail man had once been Georgia's boy governor. He wasn't a boy anymore, even though that unruly shock of hair over his forehead still had a mind of its own. But as the people cheered and as he looked into the faces of so many old friends, the stool wasn't needed and the voice grew stronger with every phrase.

He began with Miller.

"Governor Miller was extremely generous in his remarks," Talmadge told the people fanned in front of him. "As he mentioned, we had a particularly bitter campaign against one another. Since that time, I have not made many kind remarks about the governor. I will say this about him: the older he gets, the wiser he gets."

As the ceremony ended, people crowded around the head table. There was little time for the people at the head table to say their good-byes. For just a moment, Linda Talmadge whispered in

Miller's ear and used both of her hands to hold on to his. They were planning a private lunch for the Millers and Talmadges. Herman Talmadge was using his stool by then, shaking the hand of everyone who passed, patiently posing for snapshots. Excusing himself, Zell Miller moved to the back of the room. He was the governor, but this wasn't his party and he knew it. Stopping to talk for just a moment, he downplayed the events of the day. "I don't want to put words into his mouth, but I think this made us both feel good," he said. There was no ceremony, just a few quiet good-byes and Zell Miller was gone.

Rogers Wade and John Thomas could finally relax. The two of them had helped bring together this ceremony which despite the laughter seemed to be a farewell gathering for many of the political legends in the room. Wade and Thomas are former aides to Herman Talmadge and they remembered too well all that had transpired between him and Miller seventeen years before. "This was closure for two real strong individuals," said Thomas, an Atlanta lobbyist. "This was two people who had been circling themselves for too long." Wade talked about how much Talmadge had anticipated this day. "Linda kept him away from three funerals in the past few weeks," he said. "When he's up this much, it puts him in bed for days. He wanted to be strong today."

The room was almost empty now, except for waiters and waitresses who were clearing away the tables. Leaving a cart piled high with dirty dishes, one of the waiters went to shake the senator's hand. Herman Talmadge leaned back in his stool and talked about the day. "Governor Miller sure had some generous things to say about me and I tried to be generous to him," he said. "I guess we kind of buried the hatchet."

Seventeen years later, 1980 was finally over.

13

BETTING ON THE LOTTERY

Feet in the air, James Carville looked like he was created from an erector set as he unhinged his denim-covered legs on the couch in the rear of the "Zell Miller for Governor" headquarters. With a body that could have belonged to Ichabod Crane and an accent that overdoses on Tabasco, he would put on a pair of headsets and march around the crowded room as he carried on endless phone conversations, seldom finishing a sentence, never using comma or period.

His partner was Paul Begala. When Carville would lapse into a who's-on-first kind of monologue, the much calmer Texan would finish the sentence, interpreting what his flamboyant Cajun colleague *meant* to say. When Begala moved to Atlanta, he knew very little about the gubernatorial candidate they had been hired to tutor and direct. Carville, working out of a Baton Rouge agency, had helped Miller with some television spots on his ill-fated race for the United States Senate in 1980, so they had at least met. Begala came in cold and out of work.

"I didn't do any homework on him," he says. "I had just gone four months without a paycheck—the result of Dick Gephardt's broke and collapsing presidential campaign. So all the homework I needed was that he was fool enough to want to hire a broke hack like me."

As the 1980s came to a close, the Carville-Begala team was a hot item in Democratic Party circles. They not only understood Democratic candidates, they were winning which, in the Reagan Era, certainly drew attention to them. Two particular campaigns they had directed caught Miller's eyes—the victory of Gov. Robert P. Casey in Pennsylvania and the victory of Gov. Wallace Wilkinson in Kentucky. Casey had lost three times in statewide races before his victory and that impressed Miller, whose critics said he couldn't win the big one. Wilkinson had used a statewide lottery as part of his platform in a Baptist-dominated state, which impressed Miller for other reasons.

An unlikely match, Carville and Begala met in 1983 while working separately for Lloyd Doggett, an unsuccessful candidate for the United States Senate from Texas. Among other miscalculations, Doggett had conducted a fund-raiser at a gay bar. Carville had parachuted into the campaign from a short stint with Gary Hart's failed presidential campaign. It was an organization that believed in meetings and Carville noticed a red-haired fellow at the table who kept working at his word processor while people around the table were talking furiously but saying nothing. It was Begala—fresh out of the University of Texas and a person into action more than theory, a fellow who had ideas and the ability to carry them out. Once they got together, they worked off a philosophy that said: "Those who can, do. Those who can't, meet." They were brass-knuckle advisers who stressed the message, not just the style.

Their common passion for baseball and country music along with their assorted resumes fit perfectly with Zell Miller. Carville came out of a small town in Louisiana, had trouble in college, then joined the Marine Corps, an experience that changed his life. After coming back and finishing college, he was a junior high science teacher. He worked on his first political campaign in 1959, the same year Miller got involved in politics. The fact that Carville and Begala had an aversion for the small talk of meetings and the endless pontificating of scholarly experts would also endear them to Miller who hired them in 1988.

Finally in the spring of 1990, after more than a year of long-distance assistance, Carville and Begala moved into Miller's headquarters, a one-story office near the Brookhaven MARTA station in Atlanta. It was a large room filled with desks instead of walls. In the back of the room sat Carville, chattering, pacing, sometimes reclining on the couch and randomly firing a BB gun at the dots in the Tilex ceiling.

When Carville would call for a brief meeting and he was holding court, no one was sure exactly what he was saying, but they knew he was in charge. Those who knew Zell Miller feared that the light at the end of the tunnel was a train, not the lights of the governor's mansion. They knew that except for his disastrous experience with Dick Morris in 1980, Miller had run single engine campaigns, and after the Talmadge debacle they wondered if he really would be able to turn his fate over to this political team from the west.

In the years since that Talmadge race, Miller had run two more successful campaigns for lieutenant governor, but that was another playing field. This was the governor's race, and in 1988 and 1989, there were already rumors flying about who would be on the 1990 ballot. Unlike the past, the list of viable candidates now included both Democrats and Republicans. Miller was on everybody's short list, which surprised no one. For fifteen years, observers had been touting him as a future governor. Only now he was fifty-eight years old and with the possibility in Georgia of a two-term governor, it took neither a political nor mathematical genius to conclude that 1990 would be his last realistic run at an office that had eluded him for so long.

It seemed inevitable there would be a clash between the pollmeisters and the politician, and Marti Fullerton remembers an early lecture Carville gave Miller when the campaign veteran seemed to forget that he was the candidate and others were calling the day-to-day shots: "He told Miller, 'You're paying us big bucks, and if you want to run the show you're wasting our time. And if you do, I'm outta here.'"

It was a clash of an ex-Marine from the Bayou and an ex-Marine from the hills. But from their relationship and from those exchanges a different Zell Miller began to emerge. More than political changes, they were tweaks in a personality you could set your watch by. It didn't come out of explosive debates, though all of the personalities involved were capable of them. It didn't come because Carville and Begala were out-of-town experts. More than anything, they were forging a bond built on respect for what one could do for the other. Miller's long-time co-workers could sense the changes and Carville says Georgia needed to see this resurrected candidate. "This was a reinvigorated Zell Miller. It wasn't your father's Oldsmobile."

Many of the workers who surrounded Miller in that race were veterans of his other campaigns, going all the way back to his forays against Phil Landrum for Congress. Even if they understood what Carville and Begala were trying to do, they couldn't believe it would take. They knew Miller was listening, but could a man so stubbornly proud really turn his life over to anyone?

One of the watersheds for the group came in a meeting of the campaign leadership. Carville and Begala had been hammering out a point and Miller was responding in his familiar style. He took what they said very personally, and with the nub of his missing left index finger waving at them as he chopped his hand up and down, he was on one of his rolls. He was talking about himself, almost in a third-person style, assuring everyone that he was an easygoing fellow who would do what was suggested.

"James, you tell me where to go and I'll go. You tell me when to go and I'll go. You tell me what to say and I'll say it. You tell me how to act and I'll act that way. All you have to do is just tell me." Leaning back in his chair, Carville had heard enough. "Fuck, governor," he said, stretching the single-syllable word like a piece of bubble gum. It wasn't just the profanity. It was a whimsical challenge to everything Miller had said.

Everyone in the room laughed, including Miller. It was a ridiculous statement and Carville called him on it in a very funny way. Miller laughed at himself and everyone laughed with him.

This was a new twist for a man who was boot camp tough. Maybe Carville and Begala would be able to assemble a new Oldsmobile, and more importantly to put it in the showroom so a state that thought he was the liberal in cowboy boots they had seen before could see there were other sides to him.

None of this was done to change the man that was. Dick Morris had tried that ten years before and it was a mortal disaster. Among them was a strategic unanimity which Begala says is not often the case in a campaign where the candidate is so strong-willed and so experienced, having been on eleven statewide ballots at that point and having come away with more votes than his opponents on nine of them.

"I had the sense that he had learned from some of the mistakes that he had observed in the past. We did not 'control' Zell. He has an enormous amount of self-control, and an unbreakable, unshakable will. James does too. And although I may be more easygoing than they are, I ain't exactly a shrinking violet. So there was always the potential for conflict. But it never erupted, since all of us were relentlessly focused on winning," Begala says.

Miller says it was respect. "I have never had any trouble listening or taking orders from someone I thought knew more than I did. It is fools that I do not suffer gladly. And Carville and Begala knew a helluva lot more than I did. I came to trust them completely and totally. I could not have won without them. Today, they remain among my closest friends. I want Paul to do the eulogy at my funeral. He understands so very well what's in my heart and in my head."

While Carville and Begala came to understand the nuances of their latest candidate, the younger people around them did not. They couldn't understand why a candidate would want to be involved in the fine print. They just didn't know Zell Miller, a man who thrives on control down to the most minute detail.

"He just loves the details of an event," Carville laughs. "Like when he was going to announce his campaign up at Young Harris. He knew where everybody was going to sit and what the menu was going to be. The caterers were saying, 'he's in there with all the details.' You know what I said? Let him do it. The man is fifty-seven, fifty-eight years old. I don't care and neither should you. Just let him do it."

Miller pleads guilty. "You should hear about the time I questioned how thick they were carving the roast beef," he says, laughing at his own habits. Carville accepts this as Zell Miller. "We have this ritual of going to Spring Training every year and he plans where we are going to eat every night. I guess one of the reasons I understand him is that he's an older Southern guy and so am I. I understand hard-headed people."

Miller's own experiences and the honing of his two new friends fine-tuned the campaign style of a man who always had an edge and a bite when the bell rang. Miller explains that reputation, quoting political philosophers and comparing his hardness to a pitcher from the Baseball Hall of Fame. "I can be whatever the situation calls for, call it adaptable or call it a chameleon. Most politicians understand two things very well: what you can do *for* them and what you can do *to* them. Machiavelli was right, you have to be a fox *and* a lion and I believe as he did that the leader who is feared is able to achieve more than the leader who is loved. 'Screw me and ye shall be screwed,' is not a bad game plan and is the same as a pitcher throwing at a batter to move him off the plate. It is the way the game is played. 'Politics ain't bean bag,' someone once said. You ask if I'm mean. Was Bob Gibson mean because he wouldn't let you dig in on him? I am hard, not mean. As the country song goes, 'Life's turned me that way.' Politics is combat, brutal combat, and I've been in it a long time and survived. I have calluses on my personality just like hitters develop them on their hands over the years. Am I impatient? Has anyone waited longer to make a race for governor and listened to the ridicule of being a loser as long as I did?"

Those calluses were there because Zell Miller had been around. "His long track record in Georgia politics was both a help and a hindrance," Begala says. "A help because he was so dang smart. He had a deep reservoir of knowledge, contacts and friends that could not be replaced. But it was a hindrance because he truly wanted to change his state—and it was a challenge to get that change message out there when the messenger was such an established figure."

Those were major challenges because this was a messenger that Georgians thought they knew and understood. Miller had sensed that long before Carville and Begala brought their act to town. It went all the way back to early 1988, when he and Shirley decided he would leave the comfort of the lieutenant governor's office and go after the big job. He could not be the candidate he was perceived by many to be. He had to find a way to put his view of his Georgia on the screen if he was going to be elected.

He had lunch with George Busbee, who after leaving the capitol had begun practicing international law at King & Spalding, for generations the premier corporate law firm in Atlanta—a firm closely aligned with the history of Coca-Cola. Its political connections were also important. In the 1930s, it began an alliance with Richard B. Russell, and in the 1960s, through partner Charles Kirbo's friendship with Jimmy Carter, was close to Carter as governor of Georgia and as president. This is the firm where former United States Attorney General Griffin Bell practices law, and was where Sen. Sam Nunn would hang his shingle after leaving Washington in 1996. So not only would Busbee offer the perspective of a former governor, he also could help to gauge the reaction of the business community to a Miller candidacy. Busbee, who knew Miller's assets and liabilities, was supportive. "You can not only be elected, you can govern after you're elected," Busbee told him. Their meeting was one of the key ones in making up his mind.

It was a plan indicative of the thought process Miller follows in making a major decision. Running for governor was crystallized by a visit from Gwinnett County multi-millionaire Virgil Williams in the fall of 1987.

Shirley Miller had been pushing him toward that decision for some time. She hadn't talked that much about him being governor in the 1970s, but she did now, feeling the time was right. She had worked for C&S Bank in Atlanta for nine years, but by 1987 she had helped found the Mountain Bank in Hiawassee, a second bank in the Towns County seat. She was president of the bank. Late one Saturday morning Zell had joined her at her office and was helping her close out the day when there was a knock at the front door. Waiting outside was Williams, the chief executive of the Williams Group, a company that made its mark and its money in the engineering business.

Williams took the Millers to lunch at the Georgia Mountain Restaurant. He said plainly that he wanted Miller to run for governor. More importantly, he would support him financially, a factor that was becoming an imperative for successful statewide races. Though certainly there was a small cadre of high-powered business people who had been with Miller from his first races for lieutenant governor, he had never made inroads into the kind of established support it would take to run for governor in 1990. Coca-Cola executive Ovid Davis had shown him how to open the door to the business community. J. Mack Robinson was an old friend. Now Williams was offering such support, and in Miller's first race he would raise more than $6 million.

The role of Williams was unmistakable. Not only did he have money, he also knew other people who could help. But it was in a tiny office in the corner of Williams' business that the key work would be done. Not only by big number checks, but through a style of political fund-raising that Miller knew very well, the kind where many people give little checks. From the mistakes he had made in the Talmadge race, he had learned a lesson. He had to be himself, so he not only fell back on an old style of campaigning, he once again called on an old friend and student who had worked on his campaigns since 1964.

Marti Fullerton had worked in a variety of jobs at the lieutenant governor's office, but after the 1988 General Assembly he asked her to take a leave of absence from the state payroll and take on a new job. "I never thought he'd finish his career as lieutenant governor. I always knew he'd go for all the marbles," she says. "Some people had written him off, but I never did. When he asked me to go to work for the campaign, I couldn't wait."

Fullerton went on unpaid leave, but Williams picked up her salary and gave her an office that was not much more than a closet. Within a few weeks, Keith Mason joined her. He had worked on Miller campaigns when he was in high school and college and had been a legislative aide to the lieutenant governor. His father Wayne and his uncle Jimmy were key supporters of the lieutenant governor and were powerful players in politics that went beyond their Gwinnett County base. Wayne Mason had been chairman of the Gwinnett County Commission, and Jimmy Mason was a former state representative. The younger Mason had graduated from law school and was ready for bigger assignments than riding over the state in a camper putting up signs as he had done in 1978. Soon he would be named campaign manager for the 1990 race. But his first assignment was to help Fullerton raise a million dollars by the end of 1988. When Miller threw out the figure, it was not a casual goal. There were financial and political reasons for wanting the figures they filed on December 31 to reflect those six zeros.

Fullerton, who for six years was deputy commissioner of labor, and now is with Miller as a senior aide, is still amazed at what they accomplished out of that tiny room at Virgil Williams' office. "We did something that I don't know if any candidate will ever do again," she says. "It's the way Zell Miller likes to campaign, and it was the right thing to do. We went all over the state having little fund raisers with $10 and $25 tickets. Lots of work for very little money. But it cemented his support. If somebody puts on a little event for you, you've got 'em. A barbecue, a fish fry, or even up on a flatbed truck in the middle of the Okefenokee. I think that is the last time you will ever see that type of campaigning. Now it's all just big bucks and TV."

Miller believes that was when the race was really won. "Marti, Keith, Virgil, we just ground it out. No one will ever again pay that kind of price—a fund raiser every other night, sometimes five a week, $800 here, $2400 there. All over Georgia—195 in less than 250 days. I'd leave the capitol at 4 or 5 o'clock, pick one of them up at Virgil's office and we'd drive here and fly there. It was a marathon," he says.

Observers said the folks who used to come to Miller's country music birthday parties weren't enough to win the big one. Maybe they weren't, but that was where they started. Fullerton started with old friends, Young Harris College grads who remembered their old teacher. Senators helped, arranging functions back in their districts. Williams was constantly on the phone. Fullerton and friends were learning the ins and outs as they went along, concluding such little known facts as the fact that Tuesdays, Wednesdays and Thursdays were the nights when people were more generous. She was constantly scrounging for money, for hosts and even for single-engine airplanes that could get them there and back. It was back-breaking and unglamorous. There were no Carvilles or Begalas, no George Jones singing the race was on. No splashes on the six o'clock news and no six-figure checks. But a foundation was being laid and a signal was being sent.

It was with this first million dollars that Miller was able to attract and contract with the Carville-Begala team. It was with this money that he began to organize his statewide network of support. It was this money that sent a signal to the business community that he was a viable candidate. It was this money and all that it bought that signaled the other candidates who were in the race or thinking about jumping into it that he was very serious about being governor of Georgia. It was a new Oldsmobile, but still Zell Miller.

A campaign structure had evolved. Between Carville and Begala, the Cajun was the senior partner. He set the strategy, the focus and the research. Begala worked on the "message." Mason, the campaign manager, supervised the staff and rode herd on the fund-raising. Steve Wrigley, whom Miller had hired from the Senate research staff, was in charge of the lieutenant governor's staff and anything pertaining to the substance of the race. Bill Stephens was Press Secretary, Howard Meade was a key aide, Toni Brown was the scheduler, and Martha Gilland and Marti Fullerton combined working on fund raisers.

One by one, other candidates either joined the race or considered it. Former University of Georgia football coach Vince Dooley was in the race briefly, but withdrew. Secretary of State Max Cleland flirted with the idea. State Representative Lauren "Bubba" McDonald of Commerce, the favorite of Speaker of the House Tom Murphy, was in to stay—bringing back memories of former House members George Busbee and Joe Frank Harris. There was former Atlanta Mayor and United Nations Ambassador Andrew Young, the first serious statewide black candidate. There was State Senator Roy Barnes of Cobb County, a witty lawyer who, because of his solid financial support and the fact that he was a new face on the ballot, was the candidate the Miller camp feared most. Even Lester Maddox tried to recycle his ideas of the past for another run.

Miller was on everyone's short list of favorites. He had been Georgia's lieutenant governor since 1974, and by being on the ballot twice against Talmadge he had solidified his name recognition in the state. Miller's history didn't impress Carville; rather, it concerned him.

"He had been elected mayor of Young Harris in 1959, so that was his fifth decade in politics. In 1990, that was when the whole change thing was coming up in America. What worried me was the way that Georgia operated we would have a heated primary, a heated runoff then a heated general election. It gnawed at me that we'd be on television all that year, and he had already been visible for so long that people wouldn't identify him with change. He had a lot of ideas, but he had been around so long that I was afraid people wouldn't look at them—not for just one more spot but for one more anything," Carville says.

Miller knew what the basics of his campaign would be. So did anyone who knew him very well. His platform would begin with education and all that it entails. He would talk about being tough on crime. He would support lifting the sales tax on food as a means of tax relief, especially for senior citizens. He would talk about the environment and economic development, and how the two connected.

Those issues had been part of the Zell Miller portfolio from the beginning. They were predictable to him. But, in a crowded field and with an uneven track record at the ballot box, the Miller team needed something new and dramatic to better define their candidate.

It was the candidate himself who brought that idea to the table. Georgians were not aware of the creative side of Zell Miller. As lieutenant governor, he reflected the ideas and administrations of Busbee and Harris. Reporters asked his opinions on what the governors were doing and too often he expressed them. The talents of Busbee and Harris did not include the gift for glib.

Miller on the other hand was never short on quotes, so he had always been a newsmaker even though his headlines did not reflect his own political creativity. He had restructured the job of lieutenant governor in his own image and had become a key player in industrial development, but these did not allow him to present a personal platform. Having Tom Murphy as his antagonist and his foil had helped, for in the media Miller was usually seen as new, different and progressive. Even so, when it came time to line up the candidates for 1990, Zell Miller could easily have been seen as another tired name with a trunk full of baggage in his Oldsmobile.

The spark he needed was the lottery. It was no secret that Georgians played the lottery, particularly in Florida where Georgia money was crossing the state line every day estimated at $200 million a year. Nor was a lottery a new idea. It dated back to the birth of the nation. The Revolutionary War was fought with cannon paid for by a lottery created by Benjamin Franklin. A lottery bought the shingles for the roof of the building in which the first regular United States Congress convened. Down in Dixie, the Confederate States of America used lotteries to raise money to conduct the Civil War. A lottery had even supported the Georgia Children's Home. Nevertheless, the state Constitution of 1868 said a lottery was illegal and specified that the legislature would impose appropriate punishments if one were conducted—provisions repeated when that document was revised in 1877, 1945, 1973, 1981 and 1983.

Times were changing, however. Georgia was one of only sixteen states that did not have a state-run lottery in 1990. Certainly, it had been successful in Florida, though there were debates about how much of the proceeds actually made it into education. The history and the contemporary success of lotteries were part of the message when Miller said he wanted Georgia voters to decide whether they wanted a lottery.

Despite the reality of what was happening in Florida and thirty-three other states, this was Georgia and this was the Bible Belt. As recently as six years earlier, Miller had said that "a lottery would undermine morals more than pari-mutuel betting"—a stance with which most Georgia politicians would agree. No one knew how voters would judge a candidate who suggested the state not only endorse, but operate any form of gambling. But Miller believed he had seen a change in that attitude.

"After Florida put the lottery in, I began to sense a strong interest I had not seen before," he says. "I can remember coming back from south Georgia and telling Shirley something is happening out there." At speeches around the state, when he asked if there were questions, hands would go up and people would ask about a lottery. "Never before had people asked me about a lottery. I thought —I didn't have any polling data but this is an issue."

Beyond the political was the financial. Miller knew the state economy was slowing drastically and if he were elected governor, the money would not be there to do the things he wanted to do— particularly in education. By then he was in touch with Carville and asked him about a lottery since he had worked on the Wilkinson race in Kentucky where a lottery was among his major issues. Off the top of his head, he told Miller he should take a poll, but that Georgia would favor it two-to-one

"I polled and he was right. The people of Georgia—across the board—wanted a lottery, and they didn't care what the money was used for. I had found my new source for my education programs, and I had found an issue that would set me apart from all the other candidates. A poll would have showed the others the same thing, but because my gut had told me Florida had changed things—coupled with James' experience in Kentucky and the modern method of political polling—I had the issue we had been looking for," Miller says.

Not that there wouldn't be obstacles. Pollster Allen Secrest warned Miller that those who were opposed felt very strongly, and that such opponents could turn into a huge negative factor. "You'll have to be willing to take their wrath and it could get very rough," Secrest told his client. He was right. It got very, very tough—from some of Miller's best friends and supporters. But it set him apart from the other candidates. It became his issue. "More than any one single thing, it elected me," Miller says.

One of the first times all of the would-be governors assembled on one stage was at that summer's annual convention of the Georgia Press Association. The publishers were meeting, of all places, in Fernandino Beach, Florida. Many of the people attending the luncheon where the candidates would speak had bought lottery tickets while they were in Florida and were lamenting their losses during the convention.

Yet, when Miller talked about a lottery for Georgia, the editors and publishers took issue with him, just as they would later in the year when they wrote editorials against the proposal. But at that session, it was obvious that the lottery issue forced the others on the podium to deal with Miller and the lottery. Not a single one would say he supported it. Some favored a vote on it, some outright opposed it. Only Miller gave an unqualified "Yes, I'm for it." He had broken out of the pack, just as he wanted to do.

Young Harris College had been a breeding ground for Methodist ministers, so many of them were well acquainted with Zell Miller, who had been reared in that denomination. The United Methodist Church in Georgia became one of his staunchest opponents on the lottery, pitting him against many old friends around the state. Don Harp and John Kay, both of whom had been Miller's pastor and friend, were among the opponents. They were against the lottery, but they still supported the candidate who was pushing it.

"That's an issue, not a matter of personality," says Harp, a member of the Young Harris baseball team when Miller was its coach. Though they disagreed on the lottery and on some other issues in the gubernatorial platform, Harp appeared on a Miller campaign ad and was roundly criticized by his fellow ministers. "But friendship goes deeper than issues. He just thought education was more important than the lottery issue."

Kay, the former pastor of Sharp Memorial United Methodist Church in Young Harris, where Miller had once served as Lay Leader, also differed with Miller on the lottery issue. They did not discuss the issue at the time but if they had, Kay would have told him how he felt. Even then he never doubted his friend's commitment to education. Now, looking back at the results, he knows that the lottery and how the money has been used will be part of the Miller legacy. "Some condemn him for it, but I look at the total picture," he says. "There was no question that Zell's heart was in the right place, so I voted for him."

Begala calls the decision to embrace the lottery courageous "for a devout Methodist like Zell, not to mention someone who has a deep understanding of his state's culture." He says Miller saw it as a non-tax source for education funds, but he was "especially concerned about all those Georgia dollars bleeding into Florida across the border and argued that if for no other reason, Georgia needed a lottery of its own for self-defense. Today it seems so obvious, and the lottery has been so successful—educating hundreds of thousands of young people—but his courage in pushing the lottery for education was truly admirable."

Carville says it was the lottery that gave Miller the ticket to talk about not only education but also the other things he wanted to accomplish. "He could talk about those things, and he could do so without talking about raising taxes because of the lottery. It showed him as somebody who was willing to embrace something new, even after all those years in Georgia politics. Frankly, the lottery was just an idea whose time had come, but at that time it sent a significant signal to people that Zell Miller was somebody who was tired of doing things the same way that they had always been done."

In 1990, while he was still lieutenant governor, he was faced with the challenge of getting through the House the amendment calling for the referendum. Murphy blocked it, as Miller knew he would. It was part of a political strategy to make it clear that it was Miller who was favoring the lottery, that he was progressive. In the eyes of lottery supporters, it sealed McDonald into the anti-lottery camp since he was closely identified with the speaker. It also clearly defined that Miller wanted to keep lottery proceeds out of the state's general fund—something that Murphy was adamant about. The Miller message was that lottery proceeds would be controlled by a separate agency and that profits would go toward special programs such as a statewide pre-kindergarten for 4-year-olds, scholarships, and a high-tech linkup for Georgia schools. Miller was never specific about what programs would be implemented, only that it would go for new and different programs and not supplant existing funds. Because he was not sure how much money would be generated, he tried to be general and vague.

Among the candidates, Barnes became the chief critic of the lottery. He was staking out a spot to the right of most of his opponents, and the lottery became the wedge between his platform and Miller's. He even went to the 1990 Senate committee meeting to speak against the proposed amendment, knowing that the lieutenant governor had the votes to get it out of the Senate. The Cobb County attorney saw this issue as the best way to edge into the runoff everyone was forecasting—between Miller and either Andrew Young or Barnes.

Miller also began to connect the public's natural aversion to new taxes to the idea of a lottery: "Thomas Jefferson once said a lottery 'is the fairest tax of them all, because it taxes only the willing.' That's the point Georgians need to understand: the alternative to creative revenue sources like the lottery is taxes. And folks, in the climate we live in today, taxes ain't much of an alternative. While statistical evidence shows that only a small number of poor people will play the lottery, all of them pay taxes. When they stop at a gas station or walk into a grocery store, every Georgian will have a choice about whether to buy a lottery ticket. But they have no choice about paying taxes."

Such statements were Miller's way of underscoring how strongly he favored the lottery. He wanted voters to have a chance to speak. But it went beyond that. "I could come out and be for the people having a vote on the lottery, but I don't think that's enough," he said. "I want to tie it to education because that is really why I'm for the lottery. I don't need to just be for the people having a right to vote on it. I need to be solidly behind it—all the way. I'm not going to be halfway in this thing. None of that zigzag stuff."

Mason, his campaign manager, says they always knew who their opponents were. "It was the elites, the old guard," Mason says. "There were a lot of newcomers in this state, a lot of conservatives, who were for it. A lot of them were suburban Republicans. This was an issue that cut across demographic lines, except for the over sixty-five group. Our biggest pocket of support in the beginning was among older whites, so we were going against our base to some degree, but we took that risk."

To bring those demographic groups together, Miller widened his focus. Paraphrasing a theory that there was more than one Georgia, he talked about the rural, the poor, the less-developed Georgia and the urban rich. "I see the Georgia that is and the Georgia that can be. I want to close that gap."

His first political hurdle that summer was the Democratic Primary in July. Pundits were forecasting a divided ballot with no one dominating the field. That theory was blown out of the water when Miller came in with 41 percent, followed by Young with 29 and Barnes with 21 percent. McDonald trailed far behind with 6 percent. Privately, the Miller camp was relieved since they had continually thought Barnes would be tougher to deal with in a runoff than Young. In the primary, Miller showed that his historical support in black precincts had not forgotten him. As the runoff race began, it was a race run on mutual respect.

Begala says Georgia was fortunate to have two candidates of that caliber running on the same ballot. "While Zell admired Andy

Young, he was never going to concede the black vote to anyone—even Andy. It made for a fascinating race, and one that was good for Georgia since Andy made strong appeals for the white vote while Zell got a solid 20 percent of the black vote. The fact that the party and the state didn't fracture along racial lines is a tribute to both Andy and Zell. Georgia was lucky to have two guys like that running at the same time."

Miller coasted through the runoff, capturing 62 percent of the vote. This set the stage for an interesting general election that fall between Miller and Republican Johnny Isakson, a real estate executive and former member of the Georgia House from Cobb County. Not since Howard "Bo" Callaway in 1966 had state Republicans fielded a strong contender in that race, but going into the November election the Miller camp was giving Isakson strong respect.

Miller's campaign respected Isakson and feared the calendar and the clock even more. This was a campaign that had stretched through nearly two years and voters were tired of politics and politicians. Georgians could hardly turn on their TV set without seeing a candidate's face and even if that candidate was one they favored, they were ready for this election to be over with. This was also the summer the military crisis in Kuwait was escalating and there were already hints that the economy was in trouble. Since voters in many ways perceived Miller as an incumbent because of the thirty years he had spent in state government, there was a concern that he would be affected by these outside factors.

On a personal level there was no animosity between the two candidates, but the intensity began to bubble over as election day neared. Begala praises Miller's campaign for its populist style and for his "instinct that connects with real people and knows how to grab folks by the heart and soul as well as the mind." His focus is unwavering and sometimes his passion comes off as mean.

One of those times came during the campaign, and Begala takes the blame for what happened during a one-on-one debate at the Temple in Atlanta. "Before the debate, Johnny's campaign manager, Jay Morgan, was playing the usual juvenile, bush-league games that people sometimes play in a campaign, insisting that his guy go first and close last, asking which podium he was going to use, the usual things. I don't remember the specifics, but he was being kind of petty and it really got under my skin. So instead of sitting calmly with Zell, cracking jokes, talking about baseball and country music—which was what I was there to do—I wound him up. I poked him in the chest like a drill sergeant and shouted: 'Don't you take anything off this bastard. Go out there and kill him!' Bad idea."

The debate began, and it was uneventful until Isakson started ducking responsibility on certain issues. Begala remembers the steam coming out of Miller's ears. First, the Republican said his long record of supporting every appropriations bill wasn't his fault but the speaker's. Nor were his votes against abortion rights and the Equal Rights Amendment his fault. He blamed his conservative constituency. When Isakson said the fact that his real estate company was punished for redlining while he was president of it wasn't his fault but his father's, Miller pounced.

"Johnny," he said, "at some point you've got to stand up and take responsibility for your actions. You can't blame the Speaker. You can't blame your constituents and you can't blame your father." Isakson bit his lip. "You say what you want about me, Zell Miller," he said, his voice quavering and with tears in his eyes. "But don't you attack my Daddy."

Begala still remembers the TV report. "That clip ran on the news for three days straight, making Zell look mean-spirited. The fact that Zell never did attack Johnny's daddy—indeed, he was defending him—was left on the cutting room floor."

There is speculation among many observers of that race that Georgia Republicans never did understand the evolving changes among voters around the state. They may not have realized that voting was no longer a natural reflex in Georgia, that Yellow Dog Democrats were a dying breed of animals. Isakson's advisers in many ways may have seen him as just another sacrificial lamb being led to an election-night slaughter.

It was anything but that as Miller won with 52.89 percent of the vote. Isakson had a competitive 44.5. The presence of Libertarian Carol Ann Rand on the ballot had Carville squirming. That was the last election when a candidate had to get more than 50 percent of the votes to win. Miller's people figured Rand or any other Libertarian was usually good for 2 or 3 percent. That meant their candidate had to come in comfortably over 53 percent to win.

Miller was out of money, and they had been on TV that year as often as Lucy and Desi reruns. That visibility and the prospect of more campaigning concerned Carville as much as Isakson. "He was a good candidate, but in the final days it had become apparent that he would never catch us. Then somebody tapped me on the shoulder and asked what would happen if we didn't get 50 percent. The whole bottom of my stomach went out. Oh, no, I thought, I can't do this a fourth time. About 11 or 11:30 that night, nothing was certain. I just kept thinking, people can't look at us one more time. Not one more spot. Not one more anything."

Those fears never came to pass, of course. Late that night, Zell Miller was declared governor-elect of Georgia. He had come into state government as an idealistic professor. The man that was elected in 1990 had lost some of the idealism, but in its place were experiences like no other chief executive had brought to the office. It had taken longer than anyone imagined, but he soon would be governor.

Paul Begala calls it destiny: "I truly believe Zell was destined to be governor instead of a Congressman or a Senator. I think by his nature Zell is an executive. He can lead, which is different from simply persuading. He is decisive by nature, whereas many people in politics learn to be indecisive in order not to foreclose options for compromise and consensus. His skills are natural and his success will be lasting as governor."

James Carville says it was time: "Strange as it may sound, if he had been elected in 1978 or any of the years that followed, he would not have been anywhere near as good a governor as he was in 1990. Look at his resume. I doubt that there has ever been a governor as qualified to be governor as he was. I would be surprised if you could show me anyone who has had a more extensive connection with state government than he has."

The Zell Miller elected in 1990 was very different than the one who came to Atlanta in 1960, also from the one who was elected lieutenant governor in 1974. Miller sums up the difference this way: "In my early years, I was ambitious to be. In my later years, I became ambitious to do."

The very next morning, Governor-elect Miller held a meeting at 7:30 with Williams, Mason, Wrigley, and Stephens. He had already decided who was going to do what.

14

A LEGACY OF OBSCURITY

Lester Maddox's podium was an obscure street corner in downtown Atlanta, distinguished only by a straggly tree that offered comforting shade to his bald head. Ricocheting off the buildings around him was the strident, unyielding voice of a protester who had been allotted fifteen minutes on a flat-bed stage provided for dissidents to speak on whatever cause made their blood pressure rise. The street was alive with Democrats in town for the 1988 National Convention, but none were paying attention to this little old man waving at cars and speaking to everyone who came by the corner he had staked out.

Lester didn't have a microphone, only the runaway delivery of a machine gun stuck on automatic. He wore a seersucker suit and the skin on his neck no longer fit. He was seventy-two years old, but he was still a card-carrying Georgia character.

An African-American cabbie, stopped his taxi mid-street, stuck his head out the window and asked how he was doing. He called him Lester. "You make 'em tip you, you hear? Those Democrats have plenty of money," Lester said.

A woman walked past, then returned, just to shake his hand. "I appreciate what you did as governor," she said, patting his hand, and at the same time telling a reporter in an aside that Lester wasn't perfect. "Honey, what did I do wrong?" he asked.

The cabbie called out to him and the woman stopped to shake his hand, but most of the people paid him no attention, other than to snicker at his antics. To them he was nobody. That morning, it had been eighteen years since he left office as governor of Georgia and twenty-four years since he waved a gun around and shut down his Pickrick Cafeteria rather than let black customers eat his fried chicken. Once he made headlines. In 1968, he had walked out of another Democratic Convention in Chicago. In 1988, he was offering $2,000 a minute if they would let him speak to the party there in Atlanta.

"Shoot, they wouldn't let me speak for a million dollars," he said that morning. And they didn't. He was ignored. He had been elected governor of Georgia in 1966 and lieutenant governor in 1970. He ran for governor again in 1974 and 1990. He even made an alleged run for the presidency in 1976 after his old Georgia nemesis, former governor Jimmy Carter, got on the ballot.

"I still regret not endorsing Carl Sanders over Carter," he said, remembering the gubernatorial election of 1970. "I had a choice between Sanders and Carter. If I had it to do over, I'd go for Sanders 'cause he wasn't a phony." Still Lester and still a Democrat. "I don't leave my wife, I don't leave my church and I ain't gonna leave my party," he said. Vintage Lester.

But at the same time his experience on that street corner near what is now Centennial Olympic Park is indicative of the relative obscurity of so many former governors of Georgia. They had their time of power and influence, then they went away. For every irreverent Gene Talmadge in his red galluses there was a Thomas Hardwick who opposed the Ku Klux Klan or a Clifford Walker who joined the Klan. For every Jimmy Carter who went to the White House, there was a M. E. Thompson who bought Jekyll Island and went home. For every Richard Russell whose name is attached to the United States Senate Office in Washington, there is a Joe Frank Harris who has disappeared into the classroom and the corporate board room.

James F. Cook, author of *The Governors of Georgia, 1754-1995,* offers several theories on why so many of the state's chief executives have left behind faceless memories. "First there was the shortness of the terms, first two years, then four-year. Until 1978, a governor could not succeed himself so they served only one term and the public loses sight of them after that. Out of office, they have no power. They are no longer a threat. Their popularity immediately declines. There was no reason to remember many of them," Cook said.

In the introduction to his book on Georgia governors, the Floyd College history professor said Georgian's view of their chief executives is a paradox in a region that has often revered its political figures. "Southerners, with their renowned interest in politics and respect for tradition should, it seems, have a particularly high regard for their governors. But insofar as Georgia is concerned, that is not the case. Indeed, for reasons not entirely clear, many of Georgia's chief executives have become forgotten figures," Cook wrote.

That is peculiar, for Southerners traditionally have held a parallel affinity for their political icons and their beloved college football coaches. In Alabama, George Wallace's popularity was rivaled only by the legend of Bear Bryant. Georgia had the name of Talmadge in the political arena and in football there were Bobby Dodd and Vince Dooley, and Dooley once toyed with translating his recognition into a political career. Louisiana had Huey Long and Paul Dietzel. South Carolina had Strom Thurmond and the equally colorful Frank Howard. Mississippi had Johnny Vaught to lead the Ole Miss football team, but at a game in Jackson—during the tragic time James Meredith was trying to gain admission to the university—folks insisted that Ross Barnett address the fans who cheered when he told them how much he loved the customs of their state—not football, but segregation.

In many ways Sanders was seen as a breakthrough when he took office in Georgia in 1962. He was not from that old school. He was articulate. He had matinee looks. He had been a football player at the University of Georgia. He was a visible state senator. He was the state's first urban-born governor in modern times. During his four years as governor he helped strengthen higher education and his administration was free of scandal. He ran for re-election in 1970, but he was defeated by Jimmy Carter. He went on to a very successful practice of corporate law in Atlanta and often has been a confidante of Georgia's business and political leaders.

But is he remembered? Cook wrote a biography of Sanders in 1993, and his research for the book took him to the University of Georgia Law Library—a building that Sanders had helped make a reality at his alma mater. Cook frequented the library for weeks and noticed a plaque in the entranceway honoring the work Sanders had done to help make the new library possible. "People there passed it every day," Cook said.

One evening, Cook took a stack of books to the front desk to be checked out of the library. While the attendant was stamping his books and checking his card, he decided to give her a history test. She didn't know Carl Sanders, and she didn't know he had built the library. "And she worked in his building," Cook said.

Until the modern era, most of the men who served as governor have been unknown even to scholars of Georgia history. They had their moments of fame and went off the screen. Only Carter, Richard Russell and Herman Talmadge went on to national careers. While Gene Talmadge, Marvin Griffin, and Lester Maddox were colorful and flamboyant, others were mundane.

"Maddox was just a fluke," Cook said. "He was elected only because of time and circumstance. He was powerful for a time though, and I've found references to him from around the world."

Others attracted attention only at home. "Joe Frank Harris was the opposite of flamboyant and George Busbee was more dynamic than Harris, but he has also faded from view. For people my age, Carl Sanders was seen as one of our finer governors. We remember him, others don't," Cook said.

Gene Talmadge is remembered. At the time he came on the scene in 1926 as a candidate for state commissioner of agriculture, he embodied new politics. After the collapse of the populist movement, New South Progressives emerged. They believed in the power of the white elitists, and from them came the all-white primary and the County Unit System. Talmadge was considered part of that group.

He came along in the wake of the Depression and gave a measure of hope to down-and-out Georgians. They liked to hear him take on the powerful—from Ralph McGill and those "lyin' Atlanta newspapers" to the intellectuals at the University of Georgia, to the President of the United States, Franklin D. Roosevelt. His campaigns were traveling medicine shows. He would often arrive in an ox-drawn wagon, sitting atop a bale of cotton. By the time the crowds saw him they had their belly full of barbecue and moonshine and they had heard some hillbilly music from Fiddlin' John Carson and his daughter, Moonshine Kate.

> *I've gotta Eugene dog, I gotta Eugene cat*
> *I'm a Talmadge man from ma shoes to ma hat.*
> *Farmer in the cawnfield hollerin' whoa gee-haw*
> *Kain't put no thirty-dollar tag on a three-dollar car.*

With swagger and a flair for the dramatic, Talmadge would make his entrance, jerk off his coat so they could see those red galluses, pop them a few times, and start flailing. It was part politics, part tent meeting. The crowd was into it as much as he was. Sometimes they couldn't wait for him to get to their favorite part. "Tell 'em about Ruuzevelt," someone would yell. "I'm a-comin' to that," he'd say.

Talmadge was a master of the stump, using words and phrases country folks could understand. With his unruly shock of hair bouncing on his forehead, he would talk for hours and the people would listen. He belonged to them. Not to Atlanta. Not to those city people who had never seen the backside of a mule.

Talmadge was governor from 1933 to 1937, again from 1941 to 1943, and was elected once more in 1946 but died before taking office. His death just before Christmas in 1946 created the fiasco of three would-be governors walking the halls of the capitol in early 1947.

Outgoing Governor Ellis Arnall said he was staying in the office until a successor had been properly chosen by either the voters or the courts. As for Herman, he called him "a pretender."

Newly-elected lieutenant governor M.E. Thompson, who had been Arnall's executive secretary, thought he should be governor since the voters had elected him to the second spot, which had been created by the new Georgia Constitution of 1945 that went into effect that year. The Georgia Legislature said Thompson had not yet been sworn in as lieutenant governor so he had no valid claim.

The younger Talmadge said the job should be his. He had received 675 write-in votes and the Legislature, with the power to chose from among those who had been in the primary, went with Herman.

Gene Talmadge had taken ill after the Democratic Primary, which in those times meant he was all but elected since the Republican Party was not a factor. Knowing his father wasn't well, Herman took the advice of a county school superintendent who had tediously researched the election laws. Quietly, all over Georgia, Talmadge supporters wrote in Herman's name. It was an insurance policy.

Talmadge died December 21, 1946 and his funeral was a state event. All the political figures were there. President Truman wired his condolences. Talmadge's closest cronies were his pallbearers. His body lay in state under the capitol rotunda and mourners filed through in two abreast for hours. Most of them felt like one grizzled supporter who told a reporter that Gene Talmadge was always "for the poor son-of-guns like we is."

His body was taken from Atlanta to McRae, where the Baptist church was filled with four freight car loads of fresh flowers. He may have polarized the state with his politics, but his death brought it together.

In the following morning's *Atlanta Constitution,* Harold Martin vividly described how regular people had lined the roads as the hearse slowly carried his body through tiny Georgia towns: "Talmadge would have understood all that he saw along the road

... the old lady in the sunbonnet before the lonely cabin, waving as he passed ... the old men on the corners in the little towns, their hats held to their breasts ... He would have noticed that most of their heads were gray ... He would have recognized these, his own, the legions of the faithful who believed in him and who would never change."

Those were his people, and so was the political army that stormed the capitol that week in January of 1947 when the Legislature and the courts were trying to decide who the next governor would be. It was a sideshow. Secretary of State Ben Fortson, charged with protecting the Great Seal of Georgia, was so concerned he put it in his wheelchair and sat on it until the matter was settled.

As anyone who understood Georgia politics could predict, the Georgia Legislature, said that Herman Talmadge was the rightful governor. After squabbling, they decided that since no one had received a majority of votes for governor, it was their duty to do so. Rep. J. Robert Elliott of Columbus nominated Herman Talmadge. Years later, when Herman Talmadge was in the United States Senate, he returned the favor by nominating that same Elliott for a Federal judgeship. Elliott, now in his late 80s, still sits on the bench in Columbus.

At two o'clock in the morning on January 15, 1947, Herman Talmadge put his hand on the Bible and became Georgia's youngest governor. After taking the oath of office and making a short speech, Talmadge and his supporters went downstairs to the governor's office where Arnall still sat. He refused to give up the office that night but before morning Talmadge had his adjutant general, Marvin Griffin, change the locks. That didn't faze Arnall; he just sat up shop as governor at the information booth near the Washington Street entranceway.

Meanwhile, a Baptist minister and a county commissioner had told Thompson that an envelope full of write-in votes for Herman Talmadge were suspicious. Thompson tipped *The Atlanta Journal* which assigned a young reporter named George Goodwin to look into the matter of the Telfair County ballots.

Goodwin went into the Secretary of State's office and began examining the ballots. What he found was startling. Turning to Fortson, Goodwin said: "Do you know that they rose from the dead in Telfair County, marched in alphabetical order to the polls, cast their votes for Herman Talmadge, and went back to the last repose?" Talmadge was never accused of being part of the scheme and years later attributed the action to an over-zealous supporter.

Goodwin was later awarded a Pulitzer Prize for his story.

Thompson had been given that same oath office and he proclaimed himself governor. So the did the courts, which in March finally ruled that the Georgia Legislature did not have the legal right to elect a governor—a decision that would be overruled nineteen years later when that same General Assembly elected Maddox over Republican Howard "Bo" Callaway.

Herman Talmadge had been governor sixty-three days, but with the court decision he relinquished all claims to the office and M. E. Thompson became governor, holding the office until 1948. That summer, Georgia voters elected Talmadge who served the remaining two years of his father's original term and in 1950 was again elected to serve his own four years.

When the Talmadge forces stormed into the capitol in 1947, they were not just honoring the memory of their leader. At stake was more than Gene or Herman's claim to the state's highest office. In the decades that preceded his death, Talmadge people had found their way into elected offices all over Georgia. It was a syndicate of influence that would be part of state politics for years that followed. When Herman Talmadge was elected to the Senate in 1956, he led them from Washington, with lieutenants left behind to perform the day-to-day duties.

The governors who followed him were honor graduates of the Talmadge school. Marvin Griffin had been executive secretary to E. D. Rivers and adjutant general under Arnall. He had been defeated by Thompson for lieutenant governor in 1946 and became an ally to Talmadge during the three-governor controversy. He later was lieutenant governor while Talmadge was governor and succeeded him as governor in 1955. Ernest Vandiver had managed

Herman Talmadge's 1948 gubernatorial campaign, had been a top aide, had served as adjutant general in his administration as governor, and was lieutenant governor under Marvin Griffin. Vandiver became governor in 1959, carrying 156 of 159 counties in one of the most lopsided races in memory.

It was an era when the Talmadge organization had keys to most of the state's courthouses. Not that they were without detractors. Georgia was a two-party state—Talmadge and Anti-Talmadge. Gov. E. D. Rivers had led the Anti-Talmadge forces in the 1930s and passed the torch to Arnall who, many years later became a close personal friend of Herman Talmadge and would symbolically make the first campaign donation to every Senate campaign.

Herman Talmadge was not only his father's son, he had established a power base of his own, founded on the money and influence of Coca-Cola magnate Robert Woodruff. Both enjoyed a good cigar and power. Woodruff was Talmadge's corporate mentor. It was Woodruff who encouraged him to run for the United States Senate in 1955, who spelled out to the veteran Walter George that it was time to retire and vacate the seat for the younger Talmadge. In 1962 Sanders had been elected governor without the Talmadge flag. In 1966 Vandiver was supposed to retake the office, but his doctors diagnosed a serious heart condition. For a short time Talmadge toyed with the idea of marching home and taking back the office that was rightfully his. It was Woodruff who reminded him of the power of Washington seniority.

The outward influence of the Talmadge group had been diminished by Sanders' election in 1962. That year, Sanders defeated Griffin who was in many ways the last of the rural, folksy governors. Griffin had never part of the inner circle in the Talmadge camp, however. The scandals of his first administration had hurt his standing and from Washington Talmadge did little to support Griffith.

While Sanders was not directly connected to the Talmadges, he had come out of Augusta where Roy Harris was the kingmaker. Harris had been a state legislator for twenty years serving as

Speaker of the House, but after being defeated in 1946 he was content to stay behind the scenes. Harris went in and out of the Talmadge group so they did have an indirect link to the Sanders Administration. Many years later, in 1980, when Talmadge was coming home from the Senate, Sanders offered him a spot in his Atlanta law firm.

The interlocking, intertwining web that tied Georgia politics together was endless. Tracing a candidate's political heritage was a complex genealogy. Even a Republican such as Howard "Bo" Callaway, if you checked his roots, was begotten by the Talmadges for it was Gov. Herman Talmadge who had appointed him to the State Board of Regents. In the 1930s and 1940s, one of the spawning grounds was the Signa Nu Fraternity at the University of Georgia. Many would-be politicians had been accepted into the brotherhood there—including both Gene and Herman Talmadge.

Aspiring politicians changed sides as often as they changed socks but for several generations the Talmadge school graduated more potential candidates than any other. Many had never worked for Talmadge himself and were not on a first-name basis with him. Their connection was to a Talmadge disciple, and they were legion.

It was not until the early 1980s, when beleaguered Labor Commissioner Sam Caldwell was defeated, that the last of the first-generation Talmadge crowd had effectively passed from the scene. Caldwell was at one time Herman Talmadge's press secretary.

With Sanders' election, the Georgia Legislature became the breeding ground for governors. Sanders came out of the Senate. So did Jimmy Carter in 1970. George Busbee and Joe Frank Harris were creatures of the Georgia House where veteran Speaker of the House Tom Murphy had ruled since 1973. Zell Miller was a product of the Senate where he had served and presided as lieutenant governor.

It is Maddox who breaks all of the rules. He was an Atlanta cafeteria owner known as much for his free-swinging paid ad in each Saturday's Atlanta newspaper as he was for his home-cooked vegetables. His advertisements for the Pickrick attacked and teased a variety of political figures. Mainly, he was for segregation and state's rights. As his ads brought in customers who stroked his ego so much that he became more involved in Atlanta politics. A local folk hero, he ran unsuccessful campaigns for mayor, vice-mayor and lieutenant governor. In 1964 and 1965, he had made national headlines by his defiant stance against serving blacks at his cafeteria near Georgia Tech. Even so, no one took Maddox seriously when he jumped into the 1966 race for governor.

Vandiver's withdrawal from the race had created a void. This also was the race where Ellis Arnall—absent from a Georgia ballot since 1941—announced he would again be a candidate for governor. Former Lt. Gov. Garland Byrd, whose heart trouble kept him on the sidelines in 1962, was an early entry. So was Albany newspaper publisher James Gray.

So, too, was Jimmy Carter. Carter had been one of the freshmen who came to the Georgia Senate after the demise of the County Unit System in 1963. Carter's victory did not come easy. There had been vote fraud in Quitman County and it took a new election for the former Naval officer to make it the capitol. He had operated a peanut warehouse in Sumter County, but he was nevertheless one of the progressive senators who began to change the rural image of the General Assembly.

By 1966, he was planning a race for Congress from Georgia's Third District, a seat held for the first time since Reconstruction by a Republican, Howard "Bo" Callaway. Since they had been teenagers, Carter from Plains and Callaway from Pine Mountain had been long-distance competitors. Callaway was the son of Cason Callaway, a textile giant who had been a personal friend of his neighbor, Franklin D. Roosevelt of Warm Springs. His family had also gained notoriety through the creation of Callaway Gardens, a popular resort near LaGrange.

Carter had graduated from the Naval Academy. Callaway was a West Point graduate. As a state senator Carter had fought for four-year status for Georgia Southwestern College. Callaway had been a member of the University System Board of Regents at the time, and had sought similar status for Columbus College while trying to block Carter and the Americus college. Several years later, when Carter was a candidate for president against Gerald Ford, the former's vice president's campaign manager was Bo Callaway.

Then, just as Carter was about to enter the 1966 congressional race against Callaway, the Republican announced he would run for governor. Instead of the wide-open Congressional race, at the last moment Carter also became a candidate for governor.

It was a crowded race, and the old warhorse Arnall was the early favorite. Already television was playing a role in gubernatorial races and Arnall's long-winded 1940s style did not translate well the new medium. At times, he was an anachronism. He did, however, lead the pack in the Democratic Primary, with Carter finishing third. And to everyone's surprise, Maddox was second.

In the runoff, it was Maddox. He had a following and he was a relentless campaigner, but at the same time he was helped in the runoff by crossover Republicans who figured Maddox would be easy for their man to defeat.

This set the stage for Georgia's first true two-party statewide race in modern times. It was partisan and it was contrast. Maddox had only a high school education. Callaway had graduated from the military academy. Maddox came up poor. Callaway came up comfortable. Maddox's campaign was primarily the "Maddox Country" signs he personally tacked up on trees and signposts all over the state. Callaway's organization was all business.

The Republican Party had gained strength in Georgia during the early 1960s with the rise of Arizona Sen. Barry Goldwater and his conservative philosophy. Goldwater had carried the state in 1964 in his unsuccessful race against Lyndon Johnson. A group of investors and political figures, unhappy with the perceived liberal stance of the Atlanta newspapers, had started *The Atlanta Times,* a daily statewide newspaper that in its eighteen months of publication had a policy against putting photographs of black and white athletes together on its sports pages. The GOP was particularly strong in the suburbs of Atlanta and in Columbus and Macon. Callaway was their poster boy. They were encouraged when Maddox emerged from the Democratic Primary.

The Democrats were not encouraged and, Arnall—a traditional Democrat—would not dissuade a write-in campaign. His decision quickly backfired. On election day, Callaway attracted 453,665 votes but Maddox got 450,626. Arnall had more than 50,000 write-in votes, a figure that kept either of the party nominees from getting the majority that was required. The election went to the General Assembly where the predominantly Democratic House gave the election to Maddox, 182 votes to 66.

Four years later Carter returned to run again, and so did Sanders. Maddox could not succeed himself, but he offered for lieutenant governor, biding his time until he could regain the governorship four years later. Carter, painting himself as a man of the soil, outdistanced the more urbane Sanders in the primary, then ran away with the general election.

Carter was the state's 76th governor and on the day he came to the capitol steps to deliver his inaugural address, he was standing, ironically, in the shadows of statues honoring Gene Talmadge and Tom Watson. Maddox was seated behind him on the podium.

During the campaign, Carter had said he was "happy to be on the ticket" with Maddox, scarcely indicating the storms that loomed ahead as they tried to coexist in the capitol. Wearing a somber suit and a serious expression that replaced the trademark family smile, he went to the microphone. People cheered. The VIPs on the podium stood. So did Maddox.

This was a peanut farmer from Plains. His father Earl had served in the Georgia House after being handpicked by the Talmadge organization to run against Frank Myers of Americus, an anti-Talmadge legislator. Earl Carter was a Talmadge man who took his young son to rallies, where he had heard Ole Gene roar. When Herman Talmadge—at Earl's invitation—came to speak at the 1953 graduation ceremony of Plains High School, he stayed overnight with the Carters. Jimmy Carter's grand-father, Jim Jack Gordy of Richland, had been doorkeeper of the House and was an ally of Watson. Gordy was even a guard when Gene Talmadge was living at the old Governor's Mansion in Ansley Park.

Coming from that kind of background, his words put him on the cover of Time. "I say to you quite frankly that the time for racial discrimination is over," he began, fulfilling a private promise he had made to the pilot who had flown him around the state during his campaign. "Our people have already made this major and difficult decision. No poor, rural, weak or black person should ever have to bear the additional burden of being deprived of the opportunity of an education, a job or simple justice."

These are the leaders who preceded Zell Miller. Among the modern governors, Miller had served either with them or for them. He was a state senator with Vandiver and Sanders, executive secretary under Maddox, executive director of the Georgia Democratic Party with Carter and lieutenant governor with Busbee and Harris. As a Georgia historian with nearly four decades in state politics, he says he has learned from each of the governors he served.

• Ernest Vandiver—"He had the courage to change his mind on integrating the University of Georgia. If he had 'stood in the door' Georgia would be more like Alabama today. Show me a state whose governor dealt with integration forthrightly and I will show you a modern growing Southern state today. Show me a state where the governor demagogued the situation and I will show you a state still paying the price as we go into the new millennium."

• Carl Sanders—"He was one of Georgia's best governors. He knew how to use the power of the office better than anyone I've seen. There were significant improvements everywhere. Our modern University System started, especially with all our community colleges. He put a lot of airports in rural Georgia which is more important than most realize. I have studied Sanders closely and admire him greatly."

• Lester Maddox—"I learned a lot from him. No one was better at showing their respect to law enforcement officers. He showed me that you should go back into the kitchen and shake hands. Don't just sit at the head table." He taught me to not just limit your appointments to your supporters. There are many good people out there who may not have supported you.

• Jimmy Carter.—That you can win a race by starting early was a great lesson. I admire his tenacity, his work habits, and his very fine mind. Persistency and hard work can accomplish a lot.

• George Busbee—"He was great at dealing with the Legislature—much better than I am. He showed me how important it was to get the business community on your side. He taught me how to accomplish economic development. He had good instincts for doing the right thing."

• Joe Frank Harris—"He knew the budget so well. That gives one an extra strength, because only a dozen or so people know what's really in it. Knowledge is power. Knowledge of the budget is great power. He was always a gentleman, even when I had some hard questions on his Quality-based Education plan and gave him a headache with my grocery tax exemption. He's had the great courtesy and grace not to second guess or criticize me, and I'm sure he's been tempted."

This was the background Zell Miller carried with him to the governor's office in 1990. His classroom experience had given him a textbook for the theory of government. The people he had served with had given him a close look at the practical side of politics. He had studied it and he had lived it. Now it was his turn to lead.

15

COOKING HIS OWN BREAKFAST

"Take what you want, saith the Lord. Take it and pay for it."

She never cited a chapter and verse, but all his life Zell Miller figured his mama was quoting the Good Book when she used that phrase. She quoted it often, to him or to anybody who was around. It was part of a lecture on money and life. Long after the fact, he discovered that the words were Birdie rather than biblical. By then the origin of the simple beatitude didn't matter, for along the way her son had adopted the words as his own. It was a philosophy that didn't need a theologian or an economist to decipher, just an independent woman who wanted to pay her own way.

Zell Miller was just like her. Most of his life had been spent "making do." Or, as Birdie Miller put it, "Living hand to mouth." It was just part of life. You make ends meet with what you have. You take it. You pay for it. Because that was the Lord and mama had said you do.

"I got this from my mother. Every paycheck that she made, I can remember her pleasure in sending a loan payment to the Bank of Hiawassee, how proud she was when a note was clear. I grew up with that aversion to debt. Shirley will tell you that I'm almost a fanatic about it. I just plain hate debt. It bugs me. Always has. Shirley has one credit card. I have one. We don't owe any money except for a small house payment. One of the most admirable

things I've heard said about my wife was expressed by a mountaineer neighbor: 'Shirley could make a living on a flat rock.' "

Take what you want, saith the Lord. Take it and pay for it." Zell
Miller had done everything but take the oath of office. Georgia
voters had chosen him over Johnny Isakson in November of 1990
and the transition had begun between old and new, between
Harris and Miller. A hectic summer was behind him and it would
be January of the following year before by law he was the state's
79th governor. But there was no time to celebrate or rest. A honey-
moon would have to wait. He was at work at seven o'clock the
next morning. While some people were counting votes others were
still counting money, and the news wasn't good. Thirty years of
fiddling and working with state government and all he could think
about were the words of his mother, the years when he was a kid
selling coathangers and peanuts on the streets of Atlanta, the times
when he and Shirley struggled with paydays that didn't come often
enough. Like he says, life made him that way.

He wouldn't get the keys to the governor's office until January
of 1991, but soon after the votes were in Miller was looking at a
state budget that was in deep trouble. His predecessor, Joe Frank
Harris, had been tightening the belt for months, but it wasn't
enough. Georgia was facing a year when projections indicated it
might fall short of its $7.8 billion budget by 4 percent. Put another
way, they had to find $312 million. Even though there had been
an election win, Miller certainly had known there were festering
problems. States and governors all over the country had been dealing with such problems for months. It was the same everywhere.
The solutions were not. Some governors had been using the recession as an excuse to raise taxes, and Miller was determined not to
do that.

"Two things especially struck me between the eyes," Miller
says. "First, I could not do the sales tax exemption off groceries
though even then I thought I could when times got better. Second,
I had to have—just had to have—that revenue that could be generated from a lottery as soon as possible. Of course I couldn't even
do that until the Constitutional amendment was voted on in

1992. I also realized I needed legislative help very badly—there were some hard decisions ahead, and that without a shadow of a doubt included the Speaker."

Murphy was there from the beginning, and Miller welcomed him and needed him. "Like me, The Speaker is a student of the budget, one of the best. He knew the situation we were in as well as I did. He also has great respect for the office of governor. Not always the person in that office, but the office is sacrosanct to him. He reached out first. Even before I was elected, the old loyal Democrat was helping the nominee. He was in my headquarters on election night, and was one of the first to offer me congratulations after I had won. I never had any doubt that he would be there when I needed him on the budget. Now the lottery—that was a different matter."

Miller wasn't the first Georgia governor to face a budget crisis. George Busbee and Joe Frank Harris had faced similar problems. Both times the recessions had passed quickly and were followed by impressive growth spurts. They were graduates of the State House and Harris had been chairman of the Appropriations Committee, so he was especially adept at dealing with the bottom line. As lieutenant governor, Miller certainly dealt with the document, but in the early stage he was more concerned with programs than dollars. It was late in his second term—after his crushing defeat by Herman Talmadge—that he concluded he needed to be more involved with the budget process.

"I came to realize that knowing the details of what was in the budget gave one an added power. I don't know why it took me so long to realize that. Of course, some people serve twenty years in the legislature without knowing it. The truth is that the budget is almost everything in state government. It is the 'main tent,' as my father would say. Everything else is a 'sideshow.' Anyway, over the years I came to have a very good knowledge of the budget and its process," he says.

Miller aide Steve Wrigley says the governor's detailed knowledge of the budget is overlooked. "A budget isn't interesting from a political standpoint until you really delve into it. But it's the heart and soul of government, and what gets funded defines the entire operation. It's that way in business or in baseball. The Atlanta Braves have to trade David Justice and Marquis Grissom so they can afford Greg Maddox and Tom Glavine. Working with the budget is not always interesting, but it's the defining aspect of the organization. Miller's skills in this area have been underestimated, and his commitment to managing government has been over-looked."

Miller's commitment to tightfisted management lasted well past the end of the recession in mid-1993. "We will do more with less," he said in his speeches and told his staff in private. He passed two major tax cuts, one in each term. He launched a privatization initiative early in his second term that would ultimately result in several state recreational facilities and prisons, among other things, being handed over to private management. He has also been a national leader on welfare reform.

Perhaps no other proof is needed than that the number of state employees has grown very little during Miller's tenure. While Georgia's population has grown over thirteen percent and the state budget has grown forty percent since Miller took office, the number of state employees has increased only four percent. When it is considered that much of that growth has been in the hiring of employees to staff newly built prisons, the number of state employees has actually declined under Miller.

Georgia governors have gained a reputation for sound fiscal management, and, ironically, perhaps, to Miller observers of the 1970's and 1980's, Miller may be the tightest manager of them all. No less an authority than Standard and Poor's, the New York agency that rates all public bonds, in 1997 gave Georgia its first AAA bond rating in history and attributed it to "conservative financial management, strong financial position, and low debt bur-den." But this rosy outlook was several years down the road. In 1991, the Miller team was busy just trying to make the budget balance.

Harris and his staff had been trying to prepare for the situation since the 1990 fiscal year began. They knew the numbers were slow, so they weren't spending some funds that had been appropriated, knowing that revenue collections wouldn't be there to pay for them. Compounding their challenge was the fact that the state's reserve funds had been depleted to balance the previous year's budget. Meeting with the administration's budget people, Miller's team began to craft a budget based on the alarming new projections. He had a fifty-six page loose-leaf notebook with programs he wanted to install—"A blueprint for the 90s," he called it. But first things had to come first so he jumped into the budget. Time was another challenge. Sitting governors usually begin work on a routine budget in early September; this was late November and it was hardly a routine budget. Miller translated that into the lyrics of a Jerry Reed song: "I've got a long way to go and a short time to get there." By the day after the election, he had appointed Virgil Williams, his hard working finance chairman as honorary chief of staff and as chairman of a group that would oversee the transfer of power to the new administration. He later asked Williams to chair a group of private-sector leaders to tackle the problem of government waste.

Miller recalls it as a laborious process. They labored day in, day out, trying to make the numbers work. "I was more like a book-keeper with a green eye shade than a newly elected governor," he says. The bookkeeper soon realized he needed help and he also concluded that it was important that this budget they were working on become his. "I knew I had to have a budget director that everyone knew was my man—my man and no one else's. Clark Stevens was the OPB director under both Busbee and Harris and he was an able, knowledgeable man. But I wanted my own man." Hank Huckaby had once worked there and he had been a department head. When Miller named his old student to the job, it sent a message. It will be Miller's budget through and through.

Huckaby, a meticulous record keeper, began recording the rapidly changing developments. One of his early observations was especially bleak: "It became immediately apparent that the program/service goals of the Miller Administration would have to be put on hold until Georgia emerged from the recession. In fact, there was a growing concern that throughout the four years we might be faced with mediocre growth levels; that we would face relatively austere times especially when compared with the relatively robust years of the Harris Administration."

Miller's new team had two months, and it was indeed a short time to get there. They spent November working every day on the budget and the forecast was grim. They had fixed a supplemental budget and were working furiously on the 1991 budget. They were making progress, but there was still work to be done so on the first Saturday morning in December Miller once again assembled his staff for a strategy session. Gathering around the table, they opened the meeting and Hank Thomason, the governor's economic advisor, led off. It was the first of December so he had the new revenue projections. "I've got bad news," Thomason said. One hundred million dollars worth of bad news.

Numbers had been crunched and budgets already had been drafted and were on their way to the printers. One person's statement and it was back to the calculators. Others in the room were shaking their heads. Miller didn't wait for the anger to kick in, the frustration of all they had done. He just started working to find $100 million that he could cut.

Over the years, Miller has often quoted the lyrics of Georgia songwriter Joe South. His words were appropriate: "No one promised us a rose garden." And weeks before the ceremonial swearing in, there were fewer roses blooming. It was belt tightening time for the state and for the new governor himself.

It was the state's problem but it was also his, and he reacted the way he had been taught to react growing up in the mountains. He would just cut some more, a way of life he understood very well. This is a man who can get a good table anywhere in Atlanta, and sometimes it is appropriate for him to be seated at his favorite spot at the Commerce Club. Yet when he stands in the food line at the Picadilly Cafeteria on Howell Mill Road, the guy behind the counter smiles and says they have his favorite entree—stuffed bell peppers. "And we also have the rice pudding, governor."

If he was going to push state agencies to be frugal, it had to start at the top so he and Shirley had been looking at the governor's own budget—at the capitol and at the mansion. One item stood out. Twenty-two state troopers were assigned to the governor's mansion. Two of them were always to be with him personally. If he was going out of the office, one would drive and the second would go as an advance. Miller wanted only one to drive, but only after he had asked if he could travel solo.

"He wanted to know if he could drive himself," says Attorney General Michael Bowers. "Sure, I said, to the grocery store or the dry cleaners. But I told him that by law he had to have protection. He could change the law, but unless he did, he was required to have executive protection." There was also a matter of liability. What if he ran into somebody? A simple fender-bender could become a state issue. Bowers laughs at the memory of their conversation, but says, "That's just Zell Miller." There might need to be a trooper at the wheel of the unmarked state car, but Miller still cut the number of agents in half.

There was also the kitchen. There were two chefs on duty—Miller wondered why. He learned that one came in the morning to cook breakfast, the second to take care of the needs in the afternoon and evening. He didn't need two chefs. He and Shirley had always prepared their own breakfast. Sometimes, she cooks, sometimes he cooked. Why should they change? Miller thought the situation was extravagant. "Mainly, I thought here I was, asking department heads to cut back, so it would be natural for me to cut myself. Everybody had to tighten their belt."

No one knew how long the recession would last, so Miller continued to put a magnifying glass on the fine print of the budget. He was telling people all over state government that the times were shaky and uncertain, that Georgia was experiencing the slowest revenue producing time in thirty years. Recovery was not in sight. "You never know how deep a mud puddle is until you step in," he had said, but every day people were finding out just how deep this puddle was. News from other states offered no encouragement. California was predicting a budget reduction of nearly $15 billion.

Closer to home, North Carolina, with a state budget about the size of Georgia's, had a $1.2 billion shortfall. Miller, meanwhile, was laying out the largest budget cut in Georgia history—more than $700 million.

Dealing with finances was an obvious priority, but there were plenty of other chores to keep a new governor busy. He was assembling his own team. Long-time assistants Toni Brown, Mary Beazley and Martha Gilland came from the lieutenant governor's office staff. So did Keith Mason and Wrigley. Bill Stephens, and later Chuck Reece, would handle the media. Huckaby and Dan Ebersole were absorbed with the numbers and the dollars. Sarah Eby-Ebersole was busy crafting the governor's first state-of-the-state address. One by one, others from his old office were coming aboard. They all knew this man's work habits and how important the work on the budget was, but in the back of everyone's mind was the lottery legislation which had to pass the General Assembly before it could get on the ballot in November of 1992.

In the way of the lottery stood the imposing shadows of Murphy, his Rules Committee and the House that he controlled with a large gavel. Murphy knew the lottery was waiting in the wings, but meanwhile he had become a vital partner in the quandary over the budget. "I reached out to the Speaker. I talked about him, sometimes as his adversary, sometimes as his student, but always with respect," says Miller, who needed the help of Murphy as the legislature convened that January.

While the financial crunch was a threat, it was also an opportunity. Many Georgians—particularly the state's business leadership—thought of their new governor as a free-spending liberal. His campaign against Herman Talmadge ten years before had given some that image, and though he had soothed many of those concerns in the years that followed, there were still skeptics. When his plans to deal with the state's financial woes began to come together, the profile of a new Zell Miller began to unfold. This did not go unnoticed in Georgia boardrooms. Even though he was coming out of sixteen years as lieutenant governor, he was at best an unknown quantity to the state's business community. Atlanta real estate developer Tom Cousins was one of those people who had doubts. He had given tacit support to Miller's election, but he now admits he held little hope for the kind of governor he would be.

"I don't know if he had intentionally taken a backseat, but I did not know that much about him when he was elected the first time. I had no reason to think he would be anymore than a care-taker. He knew the system, but I had no idea he would be the leader that he was from the very beginning. He understands the problems and the solutions. He gives a yes or no answer and fol-lows through. People in and out of government are willing to follow someone who gets things done," Cousins says.

Cousins was part of the original team of business people who stepped forward to help streamline state agencies. During the cam-paign, he was also among a group of state leaders who came to the governor with a proposed research agency. From that evolved the Georgia Research Alliance, a coalition that is attracting nationally known figures in research who are bringing grant money with them to the state. Supporters say that in the future it will pay sig-nificant dividends in both business and education. Even with the crisis the state was facing in 1991, Miller was able to find the money needed to fund this alliance. He has added to it each and every year he has been governor. By 1997, it had brought more than $800 million in research dollars into the state. "He saw the benefit," Cousins says. "Sometimes politicians don't pay attention to what makes sense. Not Zell Miller."

As the legislators came to town for the 1991 session, Miller was ready even though revenue reports were not improving. Already, the governor and his staff were whispering about a possi-ble need for a special session that summer. They knew they could do so without causing too much alarm, since that also would be a year they reconvened to hammer out new legislative districts. To underscore his commitment, Miller told legislators that he did not shrink from this responsibility. "I welcome it," he said. "I promised as a candidate that we would change the way state government was run. So I see this as an opportunity for us to streamline and downsize Georgia's state government—to make it leaner and more efficient."

His State of the State address that year spelled out that this would be forty days of "hard choices, hard thinking and hard work." He also reached out to the Speaker, standing in the hall where Murphy had ruled under three different governors. More than anything, he directed his words to the heads of state agencies. "It is a time for a new approach to managing our resources. We need creative and innovative solutions to the problems we face. We need a bureaucracy that is lean, and focuses its resources not on sustaining and enlarging itself but on the delivery of services to the citizens of this state."

This was a group that sometimes thought itself out of the line of the governor's fire. Even though they could read the newspaper or watch the six o'clock news like everyone else, and knew the sad financial shape the state was in, they still had come to Miller with a request for $2.2 billion in increased spending! He had already announced the abolition of 2,000 vacant positions. "They don't appear in the budget and will not appear in any of my future budgets."

To temper some of the harshness of his message, he injected a personal story that reflected into the way he handled his personal finances. It involved the late columnist and author Lewis Grizzard. Grizzard and Miller shared a love of country music and stock car racing and had once been part of a country music trivia show on an Atlanta radio station along with Lee Wallburn, the editor of *Atlanta Magazine*. Miller told about a trip with Grizzard that they had made to Nashville. "We were browsing through an expensive western wear store. After being there over an hour, trying on fringed leather coats and admiring boots that cost over a thousand dollars, Lewis bought nothing and I bought a can of shoe polish and a pair of socks. As the clerk looked at us a little askance, I said to her, 'I'm from the Georgia mountains and there we look at what we'd like to have and buy what we can afford.'"

The implication was loud: Georgia was going to spend what it could afford. Going into his first legislative session, Miller and his staff were adamant that the budget he presented be one that could be passed. "The Miller Administration aspired to be a strong one in the mold of the Carl Sanders Administration," Huckaby wrote in his log. "There we could not allow the first totally Miller budget to be substantially rejected/rewritten by the General Assembly." They were successful, but not without some internal give-and-take as Huckaby described. "The requirement to propose a budget that we could pass provided the forum for long hours of discussion, debate and some arguments. These were primarily confined to those closest to the governor—myself, Ebersole, Mason, Wrigley—which probably made the discourse even more painful, because everyone had known him for many years and shared his goals for Georgia, especially in the area of education. Therefore, it was not pleasant to accept the fact that those goals and campaign promises had to be put on hold, perhaps for an extended period."

It was abundantly clear that Miller was not flying solo. Had they looked closely, people who had whispered about how much of a loner he was, would have seen that he was sharing the burden with his closest allies and that he was reaching out—to Murphy, to the House leadership and to the business community. Speaking to his newly-created Commission on Effectiveness and Economy in Government, he charged them to look into "every nook and cranny" of state government. "You are in an endless search for ways to deliver a quality product in the most efficient way possible," he told the members. "I do not want to diminish the services we provide to our citizens. I want to enhance those services." He reminded them—as he did everyone he spoke to during this time—that the goal of his administration "will be to prepare Georgia for the 21st Century."

When the idea for the commission was hatched, Miller had seen it as a thirty month study, but he didn't have thirty months to wait. Its membership included the presidents of Coca-Cola USA, Georgia-Pacific and First Financial Management Corporation, along with chairman Virgil Williams, who put them to work even before Miller's inauguration. It was this commission whose recommendation led to the hardnosed reduction in state employees. In the past, Miller had appealed to traditional Democratic Party faithful such as organized labor. With the support of the Williams Commission, as it came to be called, he went nose-to-nose with the state employees union which naturally opposed the cutbacks. "Getting things done is a shifting of alliances," he said.

This was yet another indicator that Miller had broadened his base of support beyond the special interest groups that had dominated his earlier campaigns. It was more a matter of expanding his support than it was a zig or a zag. With so many new Georgia voters thinking of themselves as conservative if not Republican, he had deduced that he needed a wider platform to survive. Though no one knew it at the time, he was foretelling a new wave of Democrat—a new wave that in less than two years would elect a President of the United States with Miller at the forefront.

To gain support for the drastic solutions that were sure to come and to underscore the severity of the budget crisis, Miller embarked on a schedule of speeches that were designed to build a consensus and to educate. He was not always greeted warmly by the special interests. At the Georgia Association of Educational Leaders, no one sat with him at the long head table. Another was the annual gathering of the Georgia Municipal Association, where every year the governor spoke to the members at a luncheon. Traditionally, it was a time for a governor to boast and the GMA to applaud him, and wearing their best political smiles, to have their pictures taken with the chief executive.

Miller went before them with a rambling speech outlining programs that were being cut and others that were being downsized. There were few smiles as he reminded them he supported no new taxes to fix the problem. "New resources are not going to come along and bail us out. We must act to change the way we have been doing things. I'm changing the rules. Spending more money, in a bygone period, was the easy, obvious answer, but it is not an answer that is open to us in 1991, for you nor me, nor will it be in the course of my administration as your governor." If they weren't somber enough after those words, he told the officials he thought their budgets were also bloated and that in the area of personnel "You could stand a little Slimfast, too."

He continued his sermonizing in an address to the Georgia Press Association, telling them he wasn't just cutting before the times were tough. "Every sacred cow in state government will be put on the table. And if it is not giving milk—if it is not providing services—I'll shoot it."

A Zell Miller speech is a compilation from two sources— namely Sarah Eby-Ebersole and the governor. Frequent readers and listeners of his speeches can usually detect the phrases that are his, and calling for the death penalty for sacred cows were words that could come only from Miller. Through his words—more importantly through his actions—he was setting the tone for an administration that was increasingly conservative in fiscal matters. It was apparent that he was a manager as well as a chief executive. He had been very clear and upfront with the state, making sure that everyone understood the gravity of what they were doing. And, less apparent from the outside, was the fact that he had waited for this moment for a long time and that he relished being in charge. Many years before, a much younger Zell Miller had written a column for the Enotah Echoes which in stilted words talked about "Carpe Diem." Now, using another platform, he intended to "seize the day."

Georgia had enjoyed several prosperous years, and during that prosperity the number of government workers had also increased. The state employment rolls had grown by ten percent every other year for the past twenty. The year before Miller became governor, in the midst of a hiring freeze, the state payroll had increased by 4,000 employees. So even as the legislative session came to a close, he was still trying to deal with his own department heads.

Nothing had changed in the economy, and a special session was ahead in August. That June, in another confrontation with the agency heads, he told them this situation would establish his administration "either as a progressive, proactive, on-the-ball operation, or a passive, passe, don't-rock-the-boat sort of outfit. And I doubt it is any surprise to you that I aim to be a progressive, proactive, governor. We are going to play hard, we are going to play rough, we are going to sweat."

By the first of July, it was obvious that a special session would be needed to trim the budget even more. The recession had finally caught up with Georgia, and Miller would have to preside over what his colleagues in California, North Carolina, Connecticut, and over thirty other states had to: a severe cut in the state budget.

In an unusual move, Miller decided to invite the key members of the legislature to weekly, sometimes twice weekly, sessions at the Governor's Mansion weeks before the start of the special session to work on the budget. This group—Lt. Governor Pierre Howard, Speaker Tom Murphy, and the members of the budget conference committees—wrote the scaled-down budget that summer at the Mansion. Miller, Howard, and Murphy all agreed that what the group produced would be introduced—and passed—during the special session.

This cooperation was very much part of Miller's strategy. At times the going was tense and difficult as the budget writers agonized over huge cuts in programs long considered sacrosanct. "There was disagreement," Wrigley says, laughing at the understatement. "There were some major cuts in some areas and obviously people lost their jobs which is always painful. Nobody likes to do that, but in situations like that there is no other choice. It was also a situation where nobody had anywhere to go to protect their own special need or project. Normally the governor, the House and the Senate are separate avenues, and a legislator might play one against the other to protect a particular program. Well, that wasn't the case here. Everyone was in agreement. There was nowhere to go."

Those meetings during the summer helped clear the air. Anybody who wanted to yell could yell. Anybody who wanted to cuss could cuss. Do it then, at these meetings at the Governor's Mansion, not later, on the floor of the General Assembly. It was an opportunity to disagree so that when the gavel sounded and they went to work, they would be ready to deal with the problems, not the special interests. There were no TV reports and few newspaper accounts, but it was an important moment. Wrigley says Murphy and the House members brought needed experience to the room. "The Speaker was a valuable partner. He understood, and so did the rest of the House members, that this was a serious situation and that if we didn't deal with it correctly it could have a negative impact on the state's image. The governor and the legislative leadership were sitting down together. And, if you're prone to deal with personalities as well as politics, it was a chance for two old foes named Miller and Murphy to put aside the past. Their work would not go unrewarded.

The most important achievement was that the special session on the budget went smoothly. Miller and his staff wanted to avoid the long, public bloodbath on the budget cuts that many states had endured. It was important to get consensus among the leadership about what had to be cut and by how much. Miller's consensus approach produced a budget with over 200 individual line items eliminated entirely. Over 200 more were reorganized, connected, or combined. As Miller put it, "I did not take a meat ax to the budget. I took a scalpel." With the long summer of work with the legislative leadership over, Miller was ready to begin the special session.

On August 18—on the eve of that special session—Miller went on state wide television to explain what was about to happen. He talked about his personal agenda, the one on which he was elected the previous summer—better schools, safer streets and a cleaner environment. Then he put those things aside and talked about the lingering recession that was crippling Georgia and the nation. It was not a speech of emotional oratory or clever phrases—except when he described the state's past prosperity as "drinking that free bubble-up and eating that rainbow stew," borrowing the lyrics of a Merle Haggard song.

This was an address that reflected a different side of Zell Miller. He put on a businessman's face. He talked in a taxpayer's language. He sounded little like a traditional liberal when he talked about getting into government because he believed that it could be an agent of change—"but that doesn't mean we have to have big government." He spelled out where the proposed cuts would come, but reassured people that the quality of education would not be compromised and that prisoners would not be set free on the streets. "I hope and believe that in the years that follow, when our children inherit this great state and this responsibility, they will look back and say that our day was not a period of retrenchment and back-pedalling, but that this was the beginning of a new era in Georgia. Let it be said that in a moment of testing and trial, we gave new meaning to the idea that government exists to serve the people, and not just to tax them. That it exists to achieve purposes, and not simply to perpetuate itself."

There was also a momentary glimpse into the frustration that he was facing. He came into the office with thirty years of plans—from lofty education programs to removing the sales tax on food. Now he was faced with a challenge that could engulf his entire four years. He had said during that first campaign that he would serve only a single term. So even that summer, he was working under a clock that was ticking much too fast. "It may well be that my destiny in the ongoing history of this great state is to grapple with a difficult time, and so to set the stage for another governor to live and lead in a future time of economic growth that comes as the fruit of our present sacrifices and labor. So be it."

None of those things came to pass. The legislature came together and grappled with the problems created by the recession which finally passed. By 1993, the dire projections had ended and the economy slowly was coming back. Since that time the state's economy has outperformed the national average each year and Georgia has been the fastest-growing state east of the Rocky Mountains. Personal income has grown by a third since 1991, and for the first time in Georgia history is approaching the national average. More Georgians are employed than at any time in the state's history. As for those depleted state reserves, in 1997 the budget shortfall reserve was full at $320 million—largest in the state's history. Many things contributed to those statistics, but, make no mistake about it, it began in 1991 when Miller effected a head-on collision with state employment, spending and taxes.

Though the financial picture had improved, he continued to push for improved services, implementing a plan to privatize specified state agencies along with a budget redirection program calling for them to identify at least 5 percent of existing expenditures each year for redirecting toward higher priority programs. So far during the Miller administration, nearly a billion dollars has been shifted by redirection. In his 1997 State of the State address, Miller was looking back at his early months as governor as "a forced march to reality—and we have kept right on marching."

None of those programs were on the screen as 1991 mercifully came to a close, a year that was hardly spent the way anyone could have imagined. Most of it was consumed with numbers or the fear of numbers. The Georgia Chamber of Commerce was kicking off its pre-legislative forums with a stop at Young Harris College, and Zell Miller would be one of the speakers on the tour. It was an appropriate place for him to look back on his first year as governor. For the old teacher, it was a chance to teach again. Those weren't students in the YHC dining hall, but nevertheless he gave them a lesson in what he was about and what was to come. No one knew that November how long the economic downturn would last, yet the governor talked about building.

Left unsaid was how much the preceding year had been a reflection of his personal experiences. He had never managed a corporation but as governor he had managed the state checkbook the same way his mother had managed hers. He bought for the present and shopped for the future, just as he had bought shoe polish and a pair of socks instead of the cowboy boots he couldn't afford at the time. He had turned out to be the kind of leader few people had anticipated, partly because it is part of his personal pattern to play an underestimated role, partly because after sixteen years around the throne, he was now in charge. As he made decisions, he had been confident, almost cocky, like the good Marine he was.

At Young Harris, most of his remarks were about the future and what was ahead for Georgia, but those words also gave a clue about what kind of governor he was going to be when he put away the ax and the scalpel. Delving into Old Testament history, Miller recalled when Jerusalem was overrun by Babylon and Jeremiah was thrown into prison. Even from that jail cell the prophet had bought land, "because he knew those problems would pass and that he needed to prepare for the future." He talked about Abraham Lincoln continuing construction on the United States capitol "even though Confederate troops and flags could be seen out his window—simply because he could see peace beyond the war."

"Here in Georgia," he said, "we have to adjust for the declining revenues of the moment ... But we cannot allow ourselves to be bogged down in the present; we cannot lose sight of where we need to go and what we need to do to prepare for the future. At the same time we are in the short-term prison of this recession, we need to be buying land for the future."

The cuts had been made and Miller was trying to make it a more efficient government, but he didn't stop there. He told the audience in his home town about the choices Georgia faced. "If we batten down the hatches, hunker down and fritter away the few resources we have, Georgia will not come out in any better shape than we were before, or in any better shape than our neighboring states. Now is the time to get a jump on some of the critical unmet needs facing this state in education and infrastructure—needs that absolutely must be addressed if we are to achieve future prosperity. Now is the time to build for the future, and I'm going to be proposing some changes along the way that will do just that." Birdie Miller would have been more brief: *"Take what you want, saith the Lord. Take it and pay for it."*

Dr. Billy Graham is among the guests who
have visited Zell at the Governor's Mansion.

Atlanta always has been an important city to
Muhammed Ali and to Zell Miller.

Zell and James Carville are both country music fans so meeting with George Jones is always an event. Nancy Jones, left, Mary Matalin, right.

On Super Bowl Sunday in 1994, Zell and Shirley joined Bill Clinton at the White House for an evening of popcorn and football. Paul Begala is behind Zell.

He may have been a Southern boy, but Zell
was always a fan of the New York Yankees.
This was taken at Mickey's fantasy camp in
1993.

Baseball Hall of Famer Mickey Mantle
became a close friend of Zell who spoke at
the former Yankee's memorial service in
Greensboro.

When Arnold Schwartzeneger was chairman
of the president's fitness program, he came to
visit Zell.

Speaking to his supporters, Zell and Shirley
celebrated his victory in the general election
in 1992.

Sam Nunn came by the Governor's Mansion
to meet with Miller and his staff on the flood
crisis in 1994.

Raising money for a new baseball field at
Young Harris College, Zell asked his friends
Hank Aaron and Mickey Mantle to help
him.

Awesome Bill is from Dawsonville and
Miller visited with Elliott at Atlanta
International Raceway.

While still lieutenant governor in 1990, Zell
was beginning to work on his plan for a
statewide lottery.

When you're running for office, you put on a
hard-hat and go out where the workers are.

Mary Beazley (left) and Toni Brown (right)
have been right outside the Governor's door
for years.

Away from the constant attention of the governor's office, Zell and Shirley enjoy their infrequent quiet moments.

As a teacher and as a political leader, Zell has always enjoyed mentoring Georgia young people.

When floods covered the area around Albany
and Bainbridge, President Clinton joined
Miller for a first-hand look.

As a boy, Zell cut school and went to The
Varsity and years later he went there with a
President of the United States.

Joining Zell at the Governor's Mansion were
Atlanta Mayor Bill Campbell, former
President Jimmy Carter, President Bill
Clinton and former Atlanta Mayor Maynard
Jackson.

Two old friends in the Oval Office at the
White House.

When Zell is trying to make a major political decision, the person he talks to first and
last is Shirley Miller.

Flamboyant James Carville – like Miller – is
a former Marine.

Shirley and Zell are parents, grand-parents and great-grand-parents.

Zell Miller liked this photograph so much that he turned it into a postcard he gives to Georgia school children.

Lt. Governor and Shirley with Governor Joe
Frank Harris and his wife Elizabeth.

Miller's HOPE Scholarship Program has created "a culture of higher expectations" for
Georgia young people.

Hall of Famers Willie Mays and Mickey
Mantle with Zell at Ted William's Hitters
Hall of Fame in Ocala, Florida.

Miller kneels to greet the late Martin Luther
King Sr.

The Possum greets the Governor: George
Jones and Zell Miller.

"To Zell without whose help we would not be riding in this car! Thanks Bill Clinton."

This Miller family portrait was on the front of Zell and Shirley's Christmas Card in 1996. Since, another great grandson has been born.

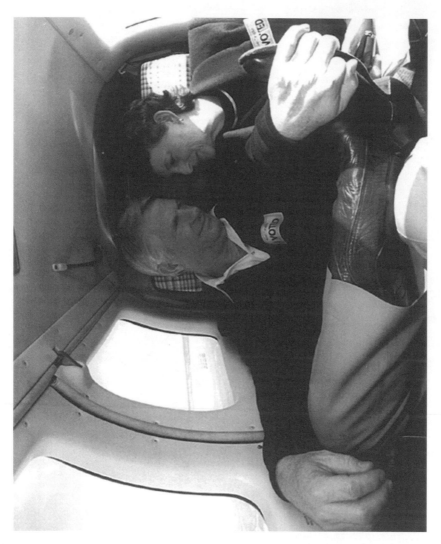

Election Day 1994: Zell and Shirley fly back to Atlanta after voting. He says that was his last time on a Georgia ballot.

16

HOPE FOR GEORGIA

N ew Age politics didn't appeal to Denmark Groover. He was a dinosaur, a throwback to the days when legislators would hang off the balcony, trying to hold back time. Only time hadn't stopped. Time kept ticking away, and Macon kept sending Denmark Groover back to the Georgia House. He was a freshman in 1953 and he was a freshman three other times. He was tough. He was independent. He was a Marine. Zell Miller couldn't help but like him.

To the public, Groover was the flamboyant legislator who had leaned over the balcony rail and moved back the hands of the House clock so a debate on reapportionment could continue. It was a scene captured on film by a photographer whose picture ran in newspapers around the world. A replica of the clock now hangs in Groover's law office in Macon. The original was shattered when it dropped to the floor of the House chambers. "And there was a switch right there so I could have turned it off," he says. "It broke into a million pieces. I sent them a check to pay for it."

To followers of Georgia politics, he was known as much for his ability to defeat a bill as his ability to pass one. When he stood to speak on a piece of legislation the authors of a bill feared that he knew more about it than they did. His skills as a legislator and a lawyer were without question. So was his toughness. Representing the late State Senator Culver Kidd, he had the gall to subpoena President Jimmy Carter to testify.

When the 1991 General Assembly convened, he seemed an unlikely ally of the new governor or his plans for a lottery. Oh, he favored a lottery, all right. But for none of the reasons Miller had preached. He believed Georgia and its political leadership was being hypocritical. "I've always said there are three things men are going to do," Groover says. "They are going to drink liquor, they are going to run around with women and they are going to gamble. The stomach is going to take care of the first, old age can take care of the second, but there ain't nothing going to stop men from gambling. So as far as I was concerned, a lottery was fine."

The lottery had helped elect Zell Miller governor. Only when he took office in 1991, his new challenge was guiding a resolution on the lottery through the General Assembly. The resolution would call for a Constitutional Amendment and if voters voiced their approval then Georgia would join thirty-three other states that had gone into the lottery business. Miller hammered on the public demand for a lottery in his State of the State Address that year. "After traveling this state from Blairsville to Brunswick, I can tell you without any doubt that the people of Georgia want a lottery, and they want their lottery to finance new education programs," Miller told the joint session of House and Senate. "I realize the lottery is an issue on which some of us disagree. I know there are strong and deeply held opinions on the subject. I want your input. But at the same time, I want you to know that I am adamant that the new lottery funds must not supplant existing funds for education. I hope you are, too."

Enter Denmark Groover.

As the final manuevering continued, both sides figured it was going to be close. Rep. DuBose Porter was handling the bill for Miller. Groover told Porter he would help if it was needed but nothing was decided. When the governor heard Groover was willing he was elated. He was obviously a part of the Old Guard. Having him speak for the resolution would carry a lot of symbolism. He had been a strong supporter of Bubba McDonald's campaign for governor, so it would be apparent that his words weren't partisan. Only when Groover was asked, he said he didn't want merely to speak. "I wanted to pull the last twenty minutes," Groover says. "I wasn't going to get up and talk then have the rest of the world parade up there. By then, whatever I said would be forgotten. Porter needed me, he just didn't know it. Finally he said yes."

Groover explained to his colleagues that he didn't support Miller's campaign for governor because he thought he had a better candidate. "But the Constitution of this state says that all government of right emanates from the people. And this man had the guts to propose a lottery and he was the only one that did. He ran on it and he was elected on it. The people wanted an opportunity to vote on it themselves. Are we going to give them that opportunity and give him the opportunity to sell it, or are we going to take our own personal prejudices and political fears and kill it here?" The enabling resolution was adopted by the House with 126 ayes and 51 nays, only six votes more than was needed. The Miller team had predicted it would pass with "about 125 to 130 votes."

On many evenings a city or an organization sponsors a dinner for the legislators. The night after the lottery vote Groover had gone to one of them. The governor was also there and came over to Groover's table and squatted down beside his chair. "I want you to know that you passed the lottery," Miller said. "While you were speaking, I had tears in my eyes." Shirley had been with him in the governor's office as they listened to it. It is one of their most unforgettable moments.

Eight days later the resolution waltzed through the Senate by a vote of 47-9. Resolutions don't require a governor's signature. Usually they go straight to the ballot. In April of that year, Miller held a ceremony, and with reporters all around him he personally signed the lottery resolution. Even the opposition was saying it would pass easily, perhaps by 70 percent. But it was a long way to 1992. Almost too long for Zell Miller.

The 1992 General Assembly created the lottery corporation. Miller's legislation spelled out that 90 percent of all lottery proceeds would be earmarked for three specific programs, college scholarships, and a voluntary Pre-Kindergarten program, tuition grants and public school capital outlay. Miller integrated the latter to include technology: satellite dishes and computers. The remaining 10 percent would be set aside in a reserve fund in the event there were fluctuations in lottery ticket sales.

In May of that year, predicting the lottery would generate from $250–$300 million a year, the governor kicked off a full-scale political campaign to be sure voters understood what was being proposed. Opposition was already marshalling, and one minister compared the dealing of crack cocaine to the promotion of lottery sales. Miller responded by saying "What I worry about are these 4-year-olds who don't even know their colors. Some don't even know the difference between an apple and an orange and they certainly don't know their letters. They are the future dropouts of this state."

Statewide lotteries were not unusual. New Hampshire had adopted the first one in 1964 and thirty-two other states had gone into the lottery business by 1992. More than anything, lotteries were the resurrection of an old idea. They were common in seventeenth-century England, and were brought to this country by the early colonists. Many Georgia schools in the 19th Century were built with lottery money, as were improvements to the state's rivers and harbors. The first hospital in Savannah and the first library at the University of Georgia were built with the game of chance. A state lottery for education was approved in 1866 as a way to provide tuition-free education for Civil War orphans. It was abolished a decade later, following widespread charges of fraud and corruption. Gambling had been illegal in the state until 1977, when Bingo was legalized.

Proponents of the 1992 amendment dwelt on the needs of education. They said passing a lottery would give needed revenue to an outdated, inadequate education system without raising taxes. They also reminded Georgia voters that people in their neighborhoods poured almost $200 million each year into the Florida lottery. "Maintaining the status quo has not worked. Bold steps must be taken if we are to enhance educational opportunities for our children. We have to invest in new ideas and new approaches to education and education funding," said David Garrett III, an Atlanta contractor and the chairman of the governor's Georgians for Better Education, a group created to advocate the passage of the amendment.

Opponents said a lottery was a sucker's game. "It's called a sucker's game for good reason. The odds of winning a typical lottery jackpot are upwards of 14 million to one," said Buddy Crowder, a Marietta advertising executive who was one of the most vocal members of the opposition. "Every legislature that has earmarked lottery money for education has within five years broken that promise . . . Can anything good be said of a lottery? Yes, indeed. As one California newsman had said when the state's lottery turned to brass: 'This is proof that the lottery does improve education. People get smart and stop playing the lottery.' "

Miller went on the road that year as if he were on the ballot himself, criss-crossing the state week-in and week-out. Many of his appearances were in schools, where he continually made the connection between the lottery, education and Georgia's children. It was a disappointing campaign for him since he found little support for his proposal among the state's educational community. "Some education leaders have either tiptoed quietly through the tulips all around the lottery or in some cases strongly opposed it. Did I expect too much from you? Maybe I did," he told a meeting of the Georgia Superintendents Association, just a week before the vote. On the other side of the issue, various religious denominations came out against the lottery, and one of the opposition ads featured former Atlanta Brave Dale Murphy. Churches all over Georgia placed anti-lottery statements on their outdoor signs. One of the strongest opponents was the United Methodist Church— and Miller was a lifelong Methodist.

Talk of a 2-1 victory for the amendment was just talk. Voters did vote yes, but it was a narrow 52-48 percent victory. The vote was split among urban and rural Georgians, with city voters being a major factor in the decision along with black voters who went 2-1 in favor of the lottery. The margin was smaller than predicted, but Miller had prevailed. By the end of the year he had a lottery commission in place and by the summer of 1993, the first lottery ticket was sold, appropriately to Zell Miller.

But more rewarding to him were the programs created with the lottery funds. During the campaign for governor, he had been general in his descriptions of what would be done with the lottery dollars. He was more specific as he advocated passage of the amendment. But it would be some time before the scholarship program he had described truly took shape.

Sarah Eby-Ebersole, his longtime speech writer, says she can trace the genesis of the program through his own words, that it was apparent HOPE was being confirmed and his plans were coming together. His chief of staff, Steve Wrigley, knows when it came. "If anybody tells you otherwise—they're wrong. I saw HOPE being born—right on that couch in the governor's office. There had been a lot of memos and papers on the table, but he sat there and described it just as it came to be."

HOPE is an anacronym for Helping Outstanding Pupils Educationally, and it belongs to Miller: "I named it and I conceived it. The paternity rights are mine." He also came up with how it would work. He wanted to keep it simple so it could be easily understood: free tuition, books and fees—got to keep a 'B' average. I wanted it to be a scholarship program built on merit—not income level. I believe strongly that one can have anything if they are willing to work and pay the price for it. That includes a college education. I also knew what the GI Bill had meant to me. This would be Georgia's GI Bill. You give something, you get something."

In a speech to the Biennial Legislative Institute in 1992 just a month after the lottery amendment was approved at the ballot box, Miller used the name HOPE for the first time in describing the tuition grants. "Today, just seven years before the dawn of the twenty-first century, we are at a critical juncture in our state's history—truly a crossroads. It has never been more important for our students to get a college education, but at the same time, it has never been more difficult for their families to pay for it. HOPE has the potential to touch the lives of 90,000 students in Georgia beginning in the fall of 1993."

There were bureaucratic problems in the beginning, some of them because Miller was so insistent that the scholarships begin that very year. Neither students nor educators knew what to expect. Nothing like this had ever been done. Miller composed it like the voyage of Columbus, not knowing exactly where it was going. Looking back, Mike Vollmer, a lawyer from Snellville and the director of HOPE, says those problems were inevitable. "Had we taken the time and talked to the education community, we would still be sitting here talking and debating. Politicians are the same way. It was good that we just jumped into it."

HOPE has its critics, most of whom argue that minority students are at a disadvantage under the program or who feel the program is merely an entitlement for the middle class that transfers wealth from the poor to the well-to-do. "HOPE tips the balance of aid too much in favor of the privileged," the College Board claims. There is no data to bear this out, and HOPE has received praise from both conservative and liberal quarters like the *Los Angeles Times, Education Week, Dallas Morning News,* and *Washington Times.* A number of states are even trying to figure out how to copy the program. Perhaps *The Philadelphia Inquirer* has best summed up how people feel about HOPE outside of Georgia: "[HOPE] is the kind of thing you look at half in amazement and half in anger, and wonder why your own bonehead state didn't think of it."

Vollmer says HOPE has changed most people's attitudes about the lottery. "I've seen that change," he says. "I remember being almost thrown out of Rotary clubs because of this thing called the lottery. Now they want to talk about HOPE and what it is doing."

The Rev. Creede Hinshaw is pastor of Mulberry Street United Methodist Church in Macon. Founded in 1826, it is known as the Mother Church of Georgia Methodists. Its dignified building with elegant stained glass windows is a landmark in downtown Macon. The headquarters of the South Georgia Conference is only a few doors away. It is as Methodist as a congregation can be. When the lottery amendment was on the ballot, Hinshaw was pastoring St. John's United Methodist Church in Columbus and was open in his opposition of the lottery, both in the pulpit and through a weekly column he wrote for *The Columbus Ledger-Enquirer.* By 1997, his opinion about the lottery had modified—not because he had altered his views about the game itself, but because of the educational program it had funded. "I was against the lottery, but you'd better believe that my son is going to college next year on a HOPE Scholarship," Hinshaw says. "But if you quote me on that, you also need to say that if the lottery was on the ballot again, I would vote against it."

Miller says the Pre-K program was more difficult to implement than HOPE. "We had to have it in the Education Department at first. They saw it as more of a daycare social program. I didn't want that. I wanted it to be pre-school with emphasis on "school." I wanted the children to learn things, not just play. Many professionals wanted it only for at-risk kids. I had to fight hard to get it for all four-year-olds. There was lots of opposition to that. Many local superintendents did not want to be bothered by it. I just went to private providers. Pre-K will have a very beneficial effect on education in our state. I'll be dead before its full impact is felt, but it will be significant."

Miller felt offering the Pre-K experience only to children who statistically are determined to be at-risk was wrong before of a Carnegie Institute study that found that 40 percent of Georgia's kindergarten kids are at risk on their first day of school. "And it's interesting that the percentage of Georgia kids who drop out of school is about the same. Most of these children are weighed down by poverty, hunger, health or emotional problems, abusive homes or violent neighborhoods—problems that get in the way of learning. They need it the most, no doubt about it, but to be fair it should be available to all."

That Miller would seek the label of an education governor isn't unusual. Other governors in Georgia and elsewhere have sought such a title. E.D. Rivers, who had been mentored by Miller's father, extended the Georgia school year and wanted public school students to have free textbooks. Carl Sanders strengthened the university system and began to build a system of two-year colleges around the state. But none have been more consistent in their rhetoric and action about the subject than Zell Miller.

It began when he was a state senator, continued while he was lieutenant governor, was the hallmark of his campaign for governor, and has been the mantra of his administration. That was why he was willing to gamble with the lottery. Not because he wanted people to stand in long lines at convenience stores and pay for Saturday night chances. Miller wanted to have the money to make significant changes in education in a state that had for decades been near the bottom in most academic categories. The problem he faced was that as he readied himself to enter the race for governor, the economy was in trouble. The lottery gave him an alternative to taxes and a pathway to action. He was well aware how much talk had been generated about Georgia schools in the past by other politicians. He wanted to do more than make speeches.

"From the standpoint of a political scientist, Georgia has a very strong governor. His appointive powers. So the office itself is strong. If the governor wants to use the bully pulpit, he can have great impact, although Georgia can be a very tough state to penetrate. It is a matter of making it a priority and saying it over and over again—and actually doing something the people can see. It is one thing to talk about the theory of education. That's easy. It is another thing when you can see a grandson or niece going to the University of Georgia on a HOPE scholarship, or see your 4-year-old grandson going to a Pre-K class. At a PTA meeting, you can see the computers or the satellite dish outside. Those things are not just theory. You can see and feel those things and that is making a difference," he says.

If the speeches of Zell Miller were available on video tape, you could stop, start and fast-forward throughout his political career. It would not be surprising to see how much he has repeated the same things over and over again. He talked about taking the sales tax off of food items to his students at Young Harris College in the early

309

1960's—and it was finally accomplished in the 1990's. He talked about tougher DUI legislation—and it finally came. He talked about the need for a system of juvenile justice—and it is a reality. He talked about toughening the approach to crime and criminals—and in Georgia it is two strikes and you're out. He talked about changes in the state's penal system—and bootcamps have been opened. But more of his time at the podium has been spent talking about his view of education than of all the other topics combined. Over and over again for three decades he pounded the same points home.

That is no accident, he says. He has treated his push for education the same way he treated his campaigns for office. "It is a matter of dwelling on it. You have to pound on it. In a political campaign you come up with a mantra and you repeat it over and over until you and your staff are tired of hearing it. When you are sick and tired of hearing it yourself, that is just about the time it is beginning to penetrate the voter. I have done education that way. I have talked about it in just about every speech. Look at my State of the State addresses. There's education. I hammer on it—over and over."

For him, it is personal as well as political. In 1932, the year of his birth, Georgia's education system was backward and so were the schools in his part of the state. When Miller finished high school, only one out of five were getting a high school diploma. Now four out of five students are graduating. Yet, he was reared in a special island that had a culture all its own. His parents were college educators. His playground was a college campus. He saw young people going to and from class for as long as he could remember. His greatest influences were teachers—his Aunt Verdie, Miss Edna Herren. That you would be educated was taken for granted in his small island that was hidden within an isolated county. Learning was expected. Miller has tried to create that same culture of higher expectations for Georgia.

With that culture in mind in 1991, Miller decided to honor the state's outstanding high school graduates. His idea was to invite them to a reception at the Governor's Mansion on a Sunday afternoon. Obtaining the names of the state's valedictorians, he sent out invitations. His invitation said they could bring along their parents and a favorite teacher from their high school. "They not only brought their parents, they brought their brothers and sisters. They all came," Miller says. "Hours before the reception was to begin, there were cars lined up to get into the parking lot. We took pictures all afternoon. The next year, we invited them in shifts." With the governor's encouragement, support, and the money generated by HOPE, young people's plans are changing.

"Not many years ago, few people expected their children to go to college. It was a dream of theirs. But when they got beyond the dreams, they didn't think college was affordable or accessible. That's no longer the case. Now they don't think *whether* their child is going to college, they think *where* they are going. I think this makes Georgia different from the other states, which makes me proud. I don't know that a high school junior or senior in Mississippi or Alabama or even a northern or midwestern state has that same HOPEful feeling—if you'll excuse the play on words. It is a feeling of what they can do in their life. I have parents come up to me with their 12-year-old children. They look at their child and say this is the governor, then they tell me that this child is going to be a HOPE scholar. And the kid's under 12 years old. That is the 'culture of higher expectation', " he says.

Miller recognizes that many of those people who are pushing their children toward college are doing so because the young person will get a better job, not learn to appreciate the classics. This does not concern him. "Once you begin to learn, it ripples out. You study Shakespeare because you have to if you're going to pass English. But with some students, something they read touches them. They go on and read more. They become broader, more educated, more knowledgable, a better-rounded individual. Again, you are creating higher expectations. You can fill up a person's brain with information just as you fill a jar with water. But I am not so sure that person has knowledge. Some teachers don't want kids to memorize the different dates, the battles. I disagree. I want students to have a skeleton, a framework of information on which to build their knowledge. Not just to parrot it back. If you don't know the importance of 1776, or 1865 or 1929, how do you put the rest together. But the most important thing you instill in a person is a desire to learn, to want to know. That's why I have so many books around me. I can't get enough of learning. A pursuit of knowledge is a wonderful thing. So as kids pursue the grades for HOPE, it will create that pursuit of learning."

Extending that drive to learn is a challenge in a state that historically had limited respect for education. Georgia was populated by a people who had a strong work ethic for the field or the mill, but did not see the need to extend that fondness for hard work to the classroom. Miller says "We were blessed with this good piece of geography ... the fertile soil of Southwest Georgia, the beautiful mountains of north Georgia and a beautiful coastline. We had so many positive things. What we didn't have was a skilled, educated work force. Now we can say that we're beginning to have that and it's a revolution—a complete change from what it was in the 1940s, 1950s and even the 1970s and 1980s."

In 1993, Steven Portch knew more about Georgia's past than he did its present. He was comfortable in his position as Vice Chancellor of the University of Wisconsin when he was contacted by an educational headhunting firm that told him he was being considered as the Chancellor of the University System of Georgia. For eighteen years, he had been working in a state where the tradition of education was strong—from grade school on in to higher education. And here was Georgia, a state that had always talked about football more than learning. As an educator, Portch began to do research on this state that was interested in him. He found a state that was dealing with its history.

"I concluded that the state of Wisconsin was in a maintenance mode, trying to maintain excellence in the face of all these outside forces—including tax cuts," he says. "And everybody I talked to in all my research about Georgia talked about its deep committment to go on to a higher level. If this had been a state that only wanted to maintain where it was in its public school system and in higher education, I would not have come. But in Georgia I felt energy and commitment—and it was coming out of the governor's office."

Still there was that lingering perception about the South and education. It was with him when he came to Atlanta to meet with the Board of Regents. The search committee had gone to Madison, Wisconsin to look him over—in sub-zero weather that sent them scurrying for topcoats. Now Portch was coming to Georgia to look them over. They were playing a peculiar game since Portch knew they were going to offer him the job and they knew that he was aware of that fact. One of his stops, though only a courtesy visit, was at the Governor's Mansion. It was spring, and the governor was packing for his annual trip to baseball's spring training. Still, he made time to meet the British-born educator he had heard so much about. Both of them had spent a lot of time in classrooms, and they prepared for meeting each other as if it were an exam.

Portch remembers the visit from the moment Miller opened the doors between the mansion's great columns. The scene couldn't have been any more Southern. The governor greeted him, and they walked into the entranceway. Miller guided him to the right, into the library, a room filled with books by Georgia authors. There are first editions there—even one of Margaret Mitchell's *Gone With the Wind.*

"He impressed me, because there are an awful lot of governors who don't have libraries. And a lot of them don't know what's in their libraries even if they have them. The second thing that impressed me was that he had read my background material, and knew that I had done a lot of my own writing and work on Flannery O'Connor. So he pulls off the shelf a first edition of one of her books to show me. In those one or two minutes, he indicated to me that this is a guy who does his homework and a guy who cares about reading, literature, and history," Portch says.

Miller candidly admits he was trying to close a deal. The search committee wanted Portch. It was more important that Portch be comfortable with the governor than the other way around. "I pulled out that Flannery O'Connor book because I wanted him to know that this was a governor who knew who Flannery O'Connor was," he says.

After leaving the library, they went upstairs above the public area, where the Miller family lives. There Portch saw more bookshelves and more books. Ones that couldn't fit on the shelves were stacked on the floor. This was part of Miller's personal library, an eclectic collection of books that range from history, to biographies, to Civil War history, to management, and even to baseball. The two men sat down and began to talk, about education certainly, but a talk with Miller often goes far afield. When Portch mentioned some of the things he thought could be accomplished in Georgia, the governor stopped him right there.

"He looked me in the eye and asked me how long some of this stuff is going to take. This was about six months before he would be up for re-election so I looked him in the eye and said, 'Well, governor, it better not be any longer than four and a half years.' He roared, and at that moment I think we cemented our relationship," says Portch, who the day after that visit did become Georgia's chancellor.

According to Miller the appointment of Portch has been "the best thing that has happened to my administration." Portch, like the governor, thrives on action. He has been a leader and a catalyst behind a plan that for the first time has opened up communications among the university system, the state board of education and the technical schools. Portch says Miller's understanding and grasp of educational issues is unequaled among the nation's governors.

"It's unrealistic to think any governor would have a deep sort of intuitive understanding of every issue, but in education he does. He has an ability to see possibilities in ideas. I went to him with a concept of one statewide library and told him I'd need ten million dollars to do it. I had the vision of connecting all of the libraries in the state by a computer network. He grasped that. He understood the connection between education, technology and serving the citizens and he saw enough potential in it that within fifteen months it was up and operating. The result was the Galileo system and we have already had more than one million users," Portch says.

Portch has noticed something personally about Miller that few have talked about over the years. Even his political friends talk about his impatience and how you had best say what you want to say quickly, because he will dismiss you either by showing you the door or by just not listening to what you say. Portch, on the other hand, says Miller has an unusual ability to listen. "He doesn't always ask a lot of questions, he listens, and when he does you can see things connect in his mind," the chancellor says.

Miller does have the ability to tune in and tune out. He abhors small talk or people who are talking a lot and saying little. Then there are the people Miller calls 'propeller heads,' a strand of people who seem to hang out around state houses just like they do around college campuses. Miller pays the highly-educated Portch a compliment by saying that despite all of his degrees, he is not a "Propeller head."

"That's someone who sits around and talks things to death," Portch says. It is with people who carry on those lengthy discussions that Miller has trouble listening—something he laughs about. "They are the ones who ponder things, who write long memos and who can talk endlessly about how to solve a problem."

Under Portch the state's university system has been active, and new presidents have been named at the University of Georgia and Georgia Tech. It has been attracting young and qualified faculty members that Portch says will be part of Miller's educational legacy. He thinks that the culture or climate for education that Miller wanted so badly to create is attracting these people and keeping them.

"That climate is terribly important," Portch says. "We have made many changes in this system over the past three years and our faculties have been terrific in their willingness to make those changes—which is not always typical of a university faculty. A lot of that has to do with the fact that they feel good about being in Georgia. They don't pick up the paper and read that the governor is calling them lazy or worthless. They pick up the paper and see a governor who expects more out of them, but also supports them. He demonstrates that by providing computers for their desks, good merit raises for high-achieving faculty, and a number of other ways. That sort of climate is extraordinary—and even if he didn't have a cent to give us, that attitude would have allowed us to do certain things."

Portch has been raising the bar for college admissions in the state, particularly at the University of Georgia. Through cooperation with the state board of education, that is bringing about an increase in standards that extends all the way down to the still-growing Pre-K program. That is also part of the education culture Miller has been creating. Though not a direct part of the university system, the Georgia Research Alliance is also part of that climate. Through it the state is able to attract high-profile research professors to the state, an effort that carries over to the needs of the state's business community. Unlike the Research Triangle in North Carolina that has built a campus, Georgia's program is built around the sophisticated laboratories and the eminent scholars it attracts and the grant money they bring with them. Miller describes it as being similar to the Atlanta Braves building a championship team going out and signing Cy Young Award winner Greg Maddox, in an effort to recognize and bring talented people who can contribute to the team, or in this case, the state.

Columbus banker Jim Blanchard is the chair of the Research Alliance. He says this group has helped increase high-tech research in the state's university system. "To me, the Research Alliance is the most outstanding economic activity that we have in our state—bar none," says Blanchard, the chief executive officer of the Synovus Financial Corporation. "It's among the finest such programs in the country. It is a mission of love and faith by Governor Miller, the General Assembly, the business community and academe, namely the state's six research universities. The early investments are now beginning to bear fruit and we're seeing the results that we originally intended—that is, to establish scholars and to pull in research dollars. We're up to about $700 million a year now and we expect to be at $1.2 billion annually by the year 2000."

Miller says there is a correlation between the steps forward Georgia has been making in education and its recent success in economic development. Since the recession of 1990, in seven years the state added an average of over 2,000 jobs every week. On buisness relocation Georgia led the nation over the past five years with twice as many as the second state, Texas. The Quick Start program, which provides adult education, has retrained more people for Georgia industries every year since 1991 Miller credits the partnership between education and business for much of the state's success.

"A man named Tal Duvall, who used to head the University of Georgia Extension Service, was one of the first people who tried to convince Rotary Clubs and Lions Clubs and the general public around the state that there was a connection between economic development and education. Now it is generally understood that a good education is the best infrastructure a community or a state can have. When I say those things now, people nod their heads. Years ago, they wouldn't have seen it that way. Back then, people thought an economic infrastructure meant helping them set up an industrial park or building a highway near their town."

As Georgia's expectations for education have increased, so has its recognition. When Portch was researching the state, he was astonished at the success of the HOPE Scholarships and what they were doing for the state's students. He was surprised that in Wisconsin he knew very little about what Georgia had been doing. That has certainly changed. For the first time in its history, Georgia is gaining a positive reputation for its educational innovations.

The national media has noticed, and continues to notice. In stuffy educational journals, and on all three network evening news shows Georgia is making headlines. Other states are looking at HOPE and Miller thinks Clinton's idea of a national scholarship program can work if the President is able to solve the challenge of how to finance it without taxes. HOPE, the Pre-K program and the state's distance learning system have all attracted national attention.

So much so that in 1996 Miller himself was approached by the search committee seeking a new president for the University of Minnesota—an opportunity he turned down and discussed only with Portch. That was long before a rumor floated around the state that Miller might become the next president of the University of Georgia—a rumor he categorically denied when it was first mentioned.

Miller wants Georgia's story to be told. Given the chance, he will tell the story himself—as he did when Bill Clinton invited several governors to the White House for a strategy session in early 1996. Things were not looking good, and Miller was unusually outspoken about the direction of the campaign and the need to emphasize education. He thought it was an issue that was vital to the voting public and would play to the President's basic strengths. He thought the Republicans talk about abolishing the Department of Education was stupid and that the only thing more stupid was bashing teachers. He ended his monologue by saying, "Mr. President, you need a big educational issue." The President shot back with a grin, "Like HOPE?" "Yes," he answered, "Like HOPE." He knew the president had been fascinated with it ever since he conceived it. Miller never had a conversation—and there were many—when he didn't want to talk about it.

It was Clinton himself, in one of their many conversations about it, who suggested what became an effective newspaper ad for Miller's re-election campaign in 1994. He thought Miller should put a list of HOPE Scholars in every county newspaper in the state. "James and Paul will think it's a waste of time, but I guarantee you it will work," Clinton said, taking a friendly jab at the political advisers he shares with Miller. He was right. James Carville and Paul Begala were not enamored with the idea—but it worked. "Bill Clinton is the best political consultant I've ever known," smiles Miller, also sending a message to their two successful friends.

That advertisement underscored the impact of the scholarship plan in individual counties, and also reminded people who had opposed the lottery how the proceeds had been spent. Miller laughs at one particular phone call he received. "It was from a preacher who had been violently opposed to the lottery. He wanted to know why we had put his child's name in the list of students getting lottery money."

Clinton continues to be interested in HOPE—which fits the man from Hope, Arkansas so well. He was scheduled to make the commencement address at Princeton University in 1996. He called Miller—typically late at night—and invited the Georgia governor to accompany him and sit in the front row. He was unveiling his plans for a national HOPE scholarship and he wanted his friend to be there. It was a memorable trip for Miller, especially when Clinton aide Leon Panetta whispered, "This thing had better work." Miller believes it can work at a national level if the President is able to fund the program without using tax dollars. Having the White House adapt a similar program is flattering—both to Miller and Georgia. But he wants knowledge of the state's story to go beyond Washington's imperial air.

Education continues to be Zell Miller's passion. People such as Jim Blanchard say Georgia will never have a governor as committed to education as Miller. It is a passion shared by Shirley Miller who is a spokesperson for adult education and a strong supporter of the state's literacy programs. As governor, Miller has pushed through annual pay raises for Georgia teachers. After three consecutive six percent increases, state teacher pay was second in the South based on 1997 figures and is approaching the national average. Many of the graduates from the state's colleges and universities in 1997 had benefitted from four years of HOPE. That program has financed 96,753 students in state colleges and universities, 111,530 in technical schools and 51,315 in private insitutions in the state. Since its beginning the Georgia Lottery had contributed $2 billion into public education. The lottery continued to prosper and was the seventh largest in the world with sales totaling more than $5 billion.

"I want our message to be out there in the country," Miller says. "I want other states to know what we're doing in Georgia. It has always bothered me—as a historian, as a Southerner, as a

Southern politician, and as a teacher of Southern politics in the 20th Century—how the rest of the country has looked at the South. Especially about education. They think we can write great literature and that we have good story tellers. They enjoy listening to our music. And that's about it. So I had dreamed forever that if I ever got in that Georgia governor's office. I was going to do something significant for education. Because education doesn't matter just a little. It doesn't even matter just a lot. It matters most of all."

To Miller, this is a message that needs to be delivered to young people as well as politicians and voters. This was something Mike Vollmer learned along with a shocked publisher of children's books in New York City. He had been the first director of the HOPE program, but was then overseeing the Pre-Kindergarten program in 157 of Georgia's 159 counties. He had been involved in two of Miller's most cherished programs. Since 1992, the Pre-K program has grown from 750 kids to the more than 60,000 who were enrolled in 1997. Georgia is the only state in the nation to operate voluntary classes for any child whose family wants to participate. It is a ground-breaking program that has become a model for school systems around the country. It carries an annual price tag of $210 million—all of it from the lottery. Working so closely with the governor, Vollmer knew of his passion for the Pre-K concept, but in 1996 he learned just how passionate he was. Vollmer had been summoned to the governor's office and he didn't know what Miller was doing when he got up out of his chair, walked across his office and got something off his desk. Whatever it was, he kept it hidden behind his back as he walked back to where the former lawyer was sitting.

"Mike, did your mother ever read to you?"

"Yes, she did," Vollmer answered, wondering where this was leading.

"Birdie used to read to me all the time and here's one of the books."

Behind his back was a copy of *The Little Engine That Could.* It is a classic children's book that was written by an unknown writer named Watty Piper in 1930. Other stories from that generation have faded away, but *The Little Engine That Could* can still be found on children's book shelves. It tells the story of a tiny engine that took a job hauling toys to children on the other side of the mountains. None of the big shiny engines in the train yard would take on the job, but the little one did, even though no others thought he could pull that heavy load. Going up the mountain side, the little engine was struggling, but all the way he kept encouraging himself.

"I think I can. I think I can. I think I can."

And of course, he did.

"Last night I was in Oxford Book Stores looking at all of the childrens' books," Miller told Vollmer. "I was wondering. Could we get one these books for the Pre-Kindergarten kids?"

Vollmer assumed he meant a book for every classroom. That would be about 1,500 books and he didn't think that would be a problem. Only Miller didn't mean a book for every Pre-K class. He meant a book for every one of the four-year-olds in the statewide program.

"That's 60,000 kids, governor."

"I know. And can I write a personal message in the front of the books?"

Vollmer is still amazed that a governor of a state would take the time to go shopping for such books himself. "I can just see him going up and down the aisle," Vollmer says. When he called Platt & Munk, the publishers of the book, they were even more amazed. It wasn't prudent for Vollmer to ask the governor if he had lost his mind, but that was basically what the publishers of the book said when he approached them with an order for 60,000 books with Miller's personal message in the front of them. They didn't know if that could be done. Of course, no one had ever asked them something like that before. And, like the little engine, they could.

"I called the governor and told him what they said and suggested that I could write a message for him. He said no, that he would do it himself," Vollmer says. "It was only a week before the Olympics were coming to Georgia and Atlanta and I knew he was busy. Then I got a call from Toni Brown, his secretary, and she said he wanted to talk to me. He got on the phone and asked when I needed it. After we hung up, I thought about all of those thousands of people from around the world who were coming to Georgia. And there was the governor, in his office, working on this message for the kids. Those words in the front of the book are straight from the heart—his heart."

Zell Miller has given out copies of the book to many people—even Bill Clinton, who has become so fond of the little engine and its persistence that he keeps Miller's copy in his desk in the Oval Office. If you pick up a copy of this special edition, there it is, near the front of the timeless little book with its simple, colorful artwork. At the top of the page is the state seal of Georgia. Below the great seal, above his scrawling signature, is Zell Miller's message to four-year-olds and their parents.

"The story of the 'The Little Engine That Could' is one of the most important stories a child can hear. Its lesson of persistence is timeless.

I believe persistence is an instinct with which all babies are born. It is the life force which teaches them to cry until someone picks them up to feed or comfort them. It is the inner nature which causes them to get up when they fall and try again until they learn to walk. It is the motivation by which we learn to ride a bicycle, catch a ball or play a musical instrument.

Unfortunately, society conditions us by the time of adolescence to equate 'failing' with 'quitting' and quitting is life's greatest failure, bar none.

That is why the lesson in this story of continuing to try is so important, and I would urge both parents and teachers to read it over and over again until they know it by heart and can draw on it for the rest of their lives.

It can work for the child. It can work for the parent. I know because it worked for me."

17

A POSSUM AND THE FLAG

George Jones had quit drinking, but the people who came to hear him sing had not. It was after 10:30 when he came on to the stage at the Silver Moon Music Hall and Buena Vista had been waiting for him since late afternoon when his tour bus made a ceremonial swing around the courthouse square. He was singing in a metal building outside of town where they used to manufacture modular prisons. By the time he sang his first notes it was as packed as a Baptist church on Easter Sunday In fact, some folks in the back were setting pitchers of beer on folding tables borrowed from, of all places, the fellowship hall of the First Baptist Church.

When Baptists lend tables and chairs to a honky tonk you know it's a big night, and that's just what it was for Buena Vista. George Jones was a legend, after all. Early that day, word had spread quickly that his buses and tractor trailers had been spotted outside of town. (Have you heard? His Silver Eagle has a satellite dish mounted on top of it.) People came from all over. Not even the fire marshal knew exactly how many people were at the concert that night, but if a census taker had counted heads the Silver Moon would have been the largest town in Marion County. Just to see if George was a no-show. Just to hear him sing one more time.

Even his friend the governor came. Zell Miller flew into Americus early that evening and a state patrolman drove him over to Buena Vista. They arrived in time for a little party that promoter Mike Moon threw for Jones and his wife in a pre-fab building behind the Silver Moon that served as a dressing room. When Miller walked in, the house was already filled with the usual local politicians and leaders, joined by the mayor of nearby Columbus. Nobody was eating much. Everybody wanted to pose for pictures with old George and the governor.

It wasn't long before Jones excused himself and went back to his bus to get ready for the show. Miller was then led to a door at the rear of the hall and whisked up the wooden stairs to a balcony seat that looked down on the corner of the stage. Miller sat down at a ringside table with Frank Martin, the mayor of Columbus.

Emcee Mark Cantrell—a Hank Williams Jr. wannabe who went by the name of Johnny Outlaw—came on to the stage and was giving the rowdy crowd a rundown of coming events. He was throwing out the hype and hoopla and, as if he needed to goad them, reminding folks there was plenty of cold beer available at the three concession stands. "And by the way, folks, the Silver Moon has a special guest tonight—the governor of Georgia, the Honorable Zell Miller." A spotlight located Miller, who stood and waved to the crowd.

People started booing. Heads turned and people looked up at him. Their reaction was neither polite nor political, just real. This was unvarnished Georgia, the kind of people who expect to hear a fiddle in the band. Forget protocol or what mama taught them. Budweiser and emotion overcame them. They kept on booing.

There were a few polite cheers, but more than anything there were catcalls and the unmistakable sound of Rebel Yells. People stood on chairs, waving their fists. A small choir near the stage broke into a rendition of "Dixie." Zell Miller might be their governor, but he better not mess with *their* flag.

The state trooper looked worried. Local folks were embarrassed. Sitting next to the governor, Martin was stunned. He couldn't believe how lusty the reaction was. Zell Miller never even sat back down. He casually moved toward the steps and hurried down them, wading into the crowd.

When folks saw him, they were totally disarmed. Hands reached out to him. There were a few hugs from old friends and a number of people made their way through the darkness to ask him to pose for just one photograph. Standing up on the balcony, he was the governor who wanted to jerk the Stars and Bars off the state flagpole. Down on the floor among them, he was the governor, their governor, the fellow they had elected just two years before.

In a few minutes, with flashbulbs exploding all over the building, George Jones finally made his entrance, singing about how they used to call him "No-Show Jones." He sang a few more songs, then gestured toward the balcony and reminded folks that the governor was there. The Possum never said he agreed with changing the flag, only that Zell Miller was his friend and he wished they would give him a big hand. And they did. Just as they had booed him a half hour before.

That night was only a few hours out of a long year for Zell Miller. The turmoil had exploded on May 28, 1992, when he called a press conference to announce that the following January he would introduce legislation calling for a return to the banner that flew over Georgia prior to 1956. That was the year that the General Assembly had adopted a new state flag that included the Rebel Cross of the Confederate battle flag. It was an era when the decisive vote on the new banner caused hardly a stir, only a few questions about how much it would cost to have it flying at schoolhouses around the state. Miller's announcement, thirty-six years later, created a barrage almost as loud as the cannons at Fort Sumter.

His decision caught many by surprise. *The Atlanta Constitution* had been focusing on the issue since early that year, pushing for a new Georgia flag to be flying when the Centennial Olympic Games came to Atlanta in the summer of 1996. They harked back to the 1956 decision, but more than anything reminding people that in recent times the Confederate battle flag had been carried by hate groups who were marching against their neighbors.

Attorney General Mike Bowers, meanwhile, had written a letter to the editor of the newspaper saying the flag ought to be changed, saying that to do so was "not a refute of our heritage." Miller had been sidestepping questions from all directions about a change of flags by saying over and over that it wasn't high on his personal priority list. In private he and his staff had been talking about it for months, trying to devise a workable plan.

"We talked about it first at a Braves game early that May," says Keith Mason, the governor's chief of staff. "He said he needed to change it if he was going to be remembered as a progressive Southern governor. And it wouldn't just happen without some leadership from the governor. But first, he wanted to build a consensus."

From the beginning, Miller knew what he wanted to do and what was right to do. He told Carville, "I don't think I can live with myself if I don't give it a try." He still thought of himself as a history teacher so he was well aware of the origin of the flag and what it symbolized. On a selfish side, since taking office he had been building an image of being a progressive deep South governor, especially in terms of managing the state and in education. He was putting together a strong record of appointing both blacks and women to positions in state government and the judiciary. The question about the flag was out there dangling, waiting for someone to deal with it.

This was not a new idea. Janet Merritt, a state representative from Americus, used to bring it up regularly in the Georgia House on behalf of the Daughters of the Confederacy. Prior to the Democratic National Convention coming to town in 1988, sensitive Atlanta spin-doctors had anticipated what sorts of negative stories the city might expect, and the state flag was on the list. Senate Majority Leader Tom Allgood of Augusta had researched the issue and circulated the findings around the legislature in the late 1980s, and Frank Redding of Decatur had authored a bill calling for a new flag that had lain dormant in the House for years.

No, it wasn't new, a fact that was not lost on the governor. Critics often accuse Miller of seat-of-the-pants decisions and of not seeking counsel from many sources. The steps he took in confronting the flag were the antithesis of such scouting reports, however. Mason and Steve Wrigley remember a series of conversations among the staff as Miller sought their input. On the phone he was bouncing ideas off James Carville. There were a few calls to Paul Begala, but he was on the road trying to get Bill Clinton elected president so his input was limited, but strongly supportive. *The Atlanta Constitution* was keeping the topic alive almost every day in its news columns and on its editorial pages. Miller was determined to keep a tight lid on the discussions, not wanting any of their inner-office conversations to leak to the press.

A plan was developing and with every phone call outside their circle the chances of it getting out were growing. One day at lunch, Miller, Mason, Wrigley, and Ed Kilgore, another aide, got in the car and headed for Houston's, a Peachtree Street restaurant that is a longtime favorite of the governor. They had talked about the issue on several occasions but now it was time to make the final decision. They were going to eat, but there was only one topic on the agenda.

"We talked it through from every possible angle," Wrigley says. "And we all said, yeah, this won't be easy. We were concerned about how you talk about it, the reasons why it ought to be done. We thought it through. We worried about it from every direction. We just fundamentally underestimated the power of the opposition."

Their game plan, as Mason describes it, appears sound, even in retrospect. "He determined that he would call in the political leadership of the state for a meeting and then have a number of business, religious and community leaders within the state at another. Then he would call all of the former governors. He wanted that consensus."

Miller remembers vividly his calls to the former governors—especially the one to Jimmy Carter, an old political friend who he had known since their days in the Georgia Senate, who was polite but non-committal. He had expected a different response from Carter. "I knew I was in for a hard time when he asked, 'What do you want to do that for? I've always thought that was a pretty flag.' I told my staff about it and we worried that if a progressive like Carter questioned it, what would others think," Miller recalls.

Anticipating a backlash as he went public with his proposal, Miller called in his office staff and announced his plan. He warned them that the phones might get busy and then gave them a list of people to invite for a meeting the next day. His spirits were boosted when he welcomed about thirty of Atlanta's best-known business and civic leaders into his office. "I sat on the edge of my desk and laid out my best argument on why to do it," he says. "They responded with a standing ovation. I was overwhelmed and my staff was encouraged.

Another gathering would include twenty of the legislative leaders and some key mayors from around the state. Wayne Garner was one of the twenty who was invited. He had been one of the "Young Turks" of the Senate when Miller was lieutenant governor. After Miller became governor, Garner served as Chairman of the Board of Pardons and Paroles and the Commissioner of Corrections. He would be totally surprised by the events of that meeting.

Garner is a mortician by trade and that morning he was preparing for an important funeral in Carrollton. He got a phone call from the late Cap Hicks, an irascible aide of the governor who was long on loyalty and short on tact. "You're to be at the governor's office at 10 o'clock," Hicks said. "I can't be there," Garner said. "I've got a big funeral and I need to be there." "No, lay all that business aside. You are to be here at 10."

When Garner argued a little more, Hicks made it clear that this one was important. In the eyes of Cap Hicks, even death and dying would have to wait if Zell Miller said so. Garner was his buddy so Hicks shared with him that he shouldn't miss this meeting.

Garner got in his car for the ride up I-20 to the capitol. All the way, he was trying to figure out what was going on. "This was about the time that Bill Shipp and Dick Pettys had started the story that Zell had prostate cancer—which he didn't. So I thought to myself: Old Buddy's sick. That's what it is. He's fixing to tell us all that he's stepping down. Well, I got to the capitol and everybody's there—the Senate leadership, the House leadership. Then I look around and there's a couple of mayors in the room. And I wondered why he called them. I mean, I had convinced myself that he was sick and he was going to tell us before he told the state."

Frank Martin, then the mayor of Columbus, was one of the city leaders who came. The day before, he had gotten a call from the governor's office and was asked to be in Atlanta the very next morning. He was new to the job and new to politics, so he asked the caller what the meeting was going to be about. "She either said she didn't know or that she wasn't at liberty to say. She said the same thing when I asked who was going to be there. When I asked again, she said I'd have to ask Governor Miller. But when the governor of the state says be there, you be there," Martin says.

Like Garner, Martin looked around the waiting room outside the governor's office the next morning and tried to figure why each one of them was there. When all of the guests filed into Miller's office, the room was filled. Since many of them didn't know one another, he went around the room and everyone introduced themselves. He got to the point quickly, telling them that when he left that room he was going straight into a press conference where he would announce he was going to propose a return to the original pre-1956 state flag.

As he finished his remarks, he asked for the support of the people in that room. A few of the legislators were saying they had to go back home and check with the people in their districts. Most of the people sat quietly in their seats. The governor was the only one standing.

Martin also stayed in his chair. "I sat there wondering why anyone would have to go home and check with anybody. Either you were for it or against it and I was for it. What he said struck me as logical and enlightened. Everything rang true. I kept waiting for someone else to speak. I finally stood up and said, 'Governor, I support you and your effort.' No one else said a word."

Miller was finished and people were leaving, grumbling as they made their way to the door and into the waiting room. Garner lingered. When Miller made his announcement he says he "could have been knocked over with a wet noodle." They knew each other pretty well and Miller could read the writing on the senator's face. "You don't look too pleased," the governor said. He was correct. Garner wasn't pleased. "You've misread this one," he told Miller. "They're going to give you hell. Now as for me, I don't give a damn. I kind of agree with you. But you have misread the politics."

Garner was right, though no one knew how right that morning. Miller thought he was prepared for a reaction, and he always enjoyed a good fight. So without blinking, he went ahead with that afternoon's press conference, thinking he was prepared for anything. His statement was brief and eloquent:

> I want the world to see Georgia as a vibrant, growing state that is moving ahead, and not as a state that is entrenched, holding fast to the symbols of a time when we resisted efforts to right the wrongs of the past. The present Georgia flag, with its stars and bars, was adopted in 1956, in the dawning days of the civil rights era. What we fly today is not an enduring symbol of our heritage, but the fighting flag of those who wanted to preserve a segregated South in the face of the civil rights movement. It is time we shake completely free of that era. The old Dixiecrats have by-and-large said they were wrong. Their one-time presidential candidate, Strom Thurmond, recently supported the nomination of Clarence Thomas to the Supreme Court. The Georgia flag is a last remaining vestige of days that are not only gone, but also days that we have no right to be proud of—days that should not be revered as one of the high points in the history of this state. We need to lay the days of segregation to rest, to let

bygones be bygones, and rest our souls. We need to do what is right.

Most of the immediate support came from predictable, traditional sources. So did the antagonism. None of that was really surprising. The raw emotions were still to come, erupting from the people in between the two extremes. Their feelings would go deeper than anyone could have anticipated—including Zell Miller who over the years had prided himself in having a political antenna as tall as an Atlanta skyscraper.

Reaction to Miller's announcement was swift:

From the Rev. E. Randel Osburn of the Southern Christian Leadership Conference: "The issue is only symbolic, but symbols create attitudes and attitudes create actions. Now, if we can just have this spirit manifested in a character change of Georgia, then we can move closer to building what the Rev. Martin Luther King Jr. called 'the beloved community.' "

From Charles Lunsford of the Sons of Confederate Veterans: "The state of Georgia is not a part of the United States of its own free will. It voted independence . . . then was invaded, subjugated and forced into the union."

From Georgia Speaker of the House Tom Murphy: "I ain't going to say but one thing. I have committed to numbers and numbers of my people ask that I would not vote to change the flag."

From U.S. Speaker of the House Newt Gingrich: "I believe the state would be better off by going back to the pre-1956 flag. Go back and look at what the segregationist Democratic Legislature said when they adopted this flag. There are more noble and historic Georgia flags. I see no reason for Republicans to stand with Tom Murphy behind what his crowd and the Democratic Legislature did."

As the governor had warned his staff, the phones would be busy. Calls were 5-1 against him. The media began conducting polls. So did the Center for Urban Policy Research at Georgia State University which indicated that a majority of the people in the state pledged allegiance to the existing flag. The survey that June showed 55 percent of the people in the state wanted to keep the flag. Among black Georgians, 54 percent supported the change. To everyone's surprise, 38 percent of black residents agreed with the current banner. Later polls conducted by Miller showed it even more one-sided against the change.

Little was written about the issue during the summer, but members of the legislature were hearing plenty. Mason says this was part of the governor's plan. "He wanted to build his consensus before the 1992 elections so that legislators would have a chance to hear from their constituents, so they wouldn't come back to Atlanta the next year and say they didn't know what the people back home thought."

Former *Atlanta Constitution* journalist Frederick Allen thinks the ploy to give legislators a chance to listen to their constituents backfired. Because what the people back home wanted was to keep their flag. His theory is echoed by a number of legislators.

Politicians were not the only ones feeling as if they were on the spot. A hard-core element in the South had always felt neglected and trodden upon. To them, the world had not only forgotten them personally, but society was forever tampering with their heritage and their history. Forget? They couldn't. They were among the people who whooped and hollered and put hand over heart when a nightclub band struck up "Dixie" as the last call approached on a Saturday night. Country rockers had written anthems that reflected these attitudes—a feeling bluntly expressed by Charlie Daniels in "The South's Gonna Do It Again."

On a much more serious vein, the feelings expressed after the flag issue crept into the psyche wasn't about a piece of cloth—it was about race relations and it was about an economy that was still in trouble. The summer of 1992 followed the Rodney King beating and the non-stop telecasting of the home video that on every newscast reminded Americans—black and white—of what those Los Angeles policemen had done. Both races were infuriated. Blacks were angry at the beating and how it represented the assaults other police had inflicted on other black suspects at other times and places. Whites were upset at the backlash that was directed at the police officers who many thoughtwere just doing their job. Attitudes and feelings that had subsided or gone away all together were again boiling over.

Late that year, on the eve of the 1993 General Assembly, Miller talked about the upcoming session and about the flag. The head-counters already were saying he didn't have the votes and since he had said he was going to be a one-term governor more than a piece of cloth was at stake. He said he planned to use history and diplomacy to persuade Georgia legislators that the Confederate emblem ought to be removed from a flag that represents a new generation of Georgians. "Politics is the process of education and persuasion," he told Dick Pettys.

After all the discussions and debates, Miller speculated that Georgians still didn't understand why the crossed bars of the rebel battle flag were added to the state flag in 1956. Most people assumed that this was a flag created right after the Civil War, out of respect to the men and boys who had died in that bloody war. Instead, it came out of a legislature that was fighting for another Lost Cause. To prove his point, the history teacher dug up quotes from politicians of the past along with newspaper clippings from 1956 and included them in a legislative memo.

Sitting down with Pettys and other capitol reporters, he showed them a copy of the 1956 State of the State address Gov. Marvin Griffin delivered to the legislators who a week later adopted that flag: "There will be no mixing of the races in the public schools and college classrooms of Georgia anywhere, any-time as long as I'm governor . . . All attempts to mix the races, whether they be in the classrooms, on the playgrounds, in public conveyances or in any other area of close public contact ... peril the mores of the South."

By then, the governor's office was suffering from a severe case of reality. Miller looks back at what was happening: "I got a very rough response from many people. I could feel it everywhere I went. Later we polled on it. 'Later' is the key word here. When we did, it was dramatic. Not a single group, age, race, income level, education level, gender, supported my position. Blue collar and white collar were against the change. Black and white were against it. Male and female. Education level didn't make any difference. I not only miscalculated, I had miscalculated badly."

Anyone as experienced as Miller could count the votes and he didn't have them. He could have backed down, but he didn't. For weeks, he crafted the words and ideas that would go into his State of the State address. "I can't live with myself just being meek about it," he told Mason. Read the text that came out of this process and it is as though the final draft was two speeches in one. The first section dealt mainly with the predictable items those kinds of addresses usually include. The last part was Miller through and through, with refinement from Paul Begala and an important opinion offered by former adviser Ed Kilgore.

The men and women in that chamber didn't need the governor to remind them of what the ensuing forty working days would be about though they came to the capitol that day wondering how he would present his case. Even those who opposed him on the issue remember the speech he delivered that day in the House chamber—particularly the 1,639 words that put into context the feelings of Zell Miller.

> In addition to the primary task of preparing our infrastructure and our programs for a new century, we should also be preparing our hearts and our attitudes for a New South. Next week, Bill Clinton will become the third consecutive Democratic president from the South. And for the first time since 1828, when Andrew Jackson and John C. Calhoun took office, two sons of the South will assume the top two positions in the United States government. The South is the fastest-growing area in the country. And our dominance in national leadership and the economy reflects our growing prominence in the world.
>
> Yet, at the very time when all southerners may rightly take pride in this region's current success, some Georgians persist in believing that the pride of the South is better defined by a

symbol of defiance and intolerance—the Confederate Battle Flag, which was imposed on our state flag in 1956.

Of all the arguments that have been made for keeping this flag, the most infuriating to me is the contention that if we don't we will somehow forget the sacrifices made by those who fought for the Confederacy. We will not forget. We cannot forget. Our graveyards, our literature and many of our own family histories will forever keep alive the memory of those who died for the Confederacy—and the memory of those whose freedom from slavery depended on the Confederacy's defeat. I certainly cannot forget my own Confederate ancestors. I will never forget my great-grandfather, Brantley Bryan, who was wounded while fighting with Stonewall Jackson at Chancellorsville, then wounded again and more severely at Gettysburg in the same battle that took his brother's life.

But I also cannot forget the millions of Georgians, my ancestors and yours, who also made sacrifices in other wars, both before and after the War Between the States. And in reverence to their memory, I cannot accept the idea that the brief, violent and tragic period of the Confederacy is the only part— the only part—of our long history that defines our identity and our traditions. Georgia will be 260 years old next month. For forty-three of those years, we were a British colony. For eleven years a sovereign state under the Articles of Confederation. And for more than 200 years a member of the United States.

For four brief years—that's 1.5 percent of our state's entire history—Georgia was a member of the Confederate States of America. Yet it is the Confederacy's most inflammatory symbol that dominates our flag today. We all know why. And it has nothing to do with the bravery of the Confederate troops. You may quibble all you want about who said what in 1956. It is clear the flag was changed in 1956 to identify Georgia with the dark side of the Confederacy—the desire to deprive some Americans of the equal rights that are the birthright of all

Americans, and yes, the determination to destroy the United States if necessary to achieve that goal.

The legislators who voted to change the flag in 1956 were prepared to eliminate our public schools Supremacy Clause of the US Constitution. They were prepared to eliminate our public schools and even prohibit our college football teams from competing in bowl games—in order to maintain segregated schools, segregated public transportation, segregated drinking fountains and segregated recreational facilities.

We have long since repudiated every element of those shameful 1956 days of defiance—except the flag they created. We now proudly send our sons and even our daughters abroad to defend the United States of America. Yet we maintain as a symbol of our state a flag that challenges the very existence of the United States of America. And a flag that exhibits pride in the enslavement of many of our ancestors.

There is one and only one argument for maintaining the current flag: the polls. The polls say it is popular. I submit to you that this one issue, by its very nature, transcends this particular session and this particular climate of opinion. It goes to our identity as a state, and it goes to our legitimacy as public officials. Very probably this one vote will be the only one for which this General Assembly is ever remembered, and the one vote for which each and every one of you will be accountable, not just by your constituents, but by posterity and history.

You will have to live with this one decision far beyond the next election—ten years from now, thirty years from now, to the end of your public career, to the end of your life. If you don't believe me, think about those Congressmen who followed the polls of their day and voted against the Civil Rights Act of 1964. Some were ruined, and the rest forever regretted it. I submit to you that you cannot escape this individual decision. You cannot hide in the crowd. This issue will not go away, and I do not believe a single one of you in this chamber really believes that the present flag will survive for very long into the future.

So, that brings it down to a matter of sheer guts. Will you do the easy thing, or the right thing? When your grandchildren read about this in school and ask you how you voted, will you be able to answer in a forthright manner, or will you say, "Well, you see, the polls looked bad back then." Or, 'I wanted a referendum first?' Will you proudly act as an individual, or will you just go along with the crowd?

My all-time favorite movie is To Kill a Mockingbird— *the Academy Award winner based on Harper Lee's story about life in the South in the early 1900s, with Gregory Peck as Atticus Finch, a lawyer raising two small children. In that movie's key scene, Atticus is defending a black man unjustly accused of rape, and a lynch mob tries to take justice into its own hands. As Atticus confronts the mob at the jailhouse door, his daughter, Scout, joins him and sees that the leader is some-one she knows. And she calls him by name. 'Hey, Mr. Cunningham. Remember me? You're Walter's daddy. Walter's a good boy. Tell him I said hello.' After a dramatic pause, Mr. Cunningham turns and says to the mob, 'Let's go, boys.' A group bent on injustice, was turned aside by one small girl who appealed to them as individuals.*

Well, my friends in this chamber, I know you. And I appeal to each of you as individuals—as fathers and mothers, as neighbors and friends, most of who were taught in Sunday School to 'Do unto others as you would have them do unto you.'

Leaders of this General Assembly, I know you. I know the love and dedication you have exhibited over the years to your children and grandchildren—and so often to the underdog in a fight. Let that love manifest itself now in a way that will crown your proud careers with the glory you deserve—not with the scorn of posterity that will obscure forever your proper respect.

Veteran legislators—those who remember the segregation-ist frenzy that changed the flag before—I know you. Rarely does one have a chance to rewrite one's own personal history and erase one great blot. You do. Take it before it is too late.

Rising stars who aspire to future leadership—I know you. I know you are doubly tempted to hedge on an issue where both popular opinion and the powers that be blow harsh against your principles. But my friends, you cannot lead with a finger raised to the wind and an ear to the ground—it's an undignified position. Lead now, or you will find it very difficult to lead in the future.

Republicans, believe it or not, I know you. I respect your traditions and the rebel yell of the lost cause sounds especially harsh and awkward in your throats. Your vote on this issue will say much about where you aim to take the party of Lincoln in a changing state.

Freshman legislators—I don't know you yet, but I do understand the desire for change that brought you here and the unlimited horizons you face. If you vote against changing the flag, then, no matter what other innovations you may promote, you will forever be cast as a member of a rear-guard faction that refused to hear change knocking on the door. Oh yes, you can be reelected, not just in 1994 but again and again. But in your quest for change, you will never overcome this one retrograde vote.

I know you members of the General Assembly. And I hope you know me well enough to know that I am dead serious about this issue. And, to paraphrase Rhett Butler, frankly my dear friends, I do give a damn. Since 1789 Georgia's motto has been: 'Wisdom, Justice, Moderation.' There is nothing wise, just or moderate in a flag that reopens old wounds and perpetuates old hatreds. Our battlefields. Our graveyards. Our monuments. Important reminders of our history, both the proud and the painful. They will and always should be there. That's history. But our flag is a symbol—a symbol of what we stand for as a state. I want to see this state live by the words of George Washington to the sexton of the Rhode Island synagogue: 'Ours is a government which gives to bigotry no sanction, to persecution no assistance.'

If you're truly proud of the South, if you're truly proud of this state, and all of its 260 years, if you look forward and want to play a significant part in what Georgia can become, then help me now to give bigotry no sanction, and persecution no assistance.

Without Ed Kilgore, the speech might not have been wise, just, or moderate. For it was he who suggested that Miller's original draft should delete a litany of names that called several legislators by name. Near the end of the speech, when he talked about the various categories of legislators, he was going to call some of them by name and say "I know you." Kilgore wisely talked him out of that tactic. Miller was emotionally spent after his speech, but the fight had just begun.

With a Super Bowl coming to Atlanta the following year and the Olympics on the horizon, the issue drew national attention. In February, the Atlanta-based Cable News Network invited Miller and Charles Lunsford of the Sons of Confederate Veterans to be on "Larry King Live" to debate the issue.

That night, Lunsford told King's TV audience that news accounts from 1956 include no remarks to substantiate that the flag was adopted in anger over court-ordered desegregation. He claimed that the NAACP was trying "to bring about the eradication of everything Confederate" and issued a warning that war monuments might be next. And yes, he admitted to Miller and the moderator, he wished the South had not lost its struggle for independence.

"We'd still be under that flag, governor, if not for the loss of a few battles as the result of an invasion," Lunsford said. "Do you really think we'd be better off if the South had won that war? asked Miller.

Lunsford said he did. "You do?" Miller said. "I can't believe that, Charles. We would not have had a United States. We would not have been able to defeat Nazism and the Japanese in World War II."

Yet, after King pointedly asked the question, the governor admitted that he still didn't have the necessary votes to change the flag, and also added that he had no problem with the Confederate cross being displayed on pickup trucks, baseball caps and T-shirts. But he emphatically said, "The state of Georgia in 1993 does not stand for slavery; it does not stand for insurrection; it does not stand for defying the Union."

It may have been 1993, but much of the talk was centering around 1956. Miller was a Marine sergeant when that all-male, all-white body conducted its business. Denmark Groover, once a heroic Marine pilot, was a member of that legislature and in 1993 the Macon lawyer also held a seat in the Georgia House. By 1997 he was out of politics again but sitting in a law office filled with souvenirs of his four different stints at the capitol, he retold the events that led to the creation of the controversial flag.

John Sammons Bell was chairman of the Georgia Democratic Party and later went on to sit on the Court of Appeals. The design for the flag was his and the proposal originated in the Senate. It was not an administration bill, but Groover—Griffin's floor leader—handled it in the House. The new flag was being introduced in advance of the Civil War centennial which was four years away.

"Of course, I can't say that there were absolutely no feelings against what was going on at the time, that *Brown v. the Board of Education* didn't influence John Bell's decision to do what he did. I never discussed it with him," Groover says. Yet, he also remembers how people were reacting to the idea that they were being trampled and how reverent they were to the generation of people who came out of the War Between the States era. "What they believed in," he emphasizes.

Asked if what happened in 1956 was inspired by the memory of the 1860s or the events of the 1950s, he says it was probably a combination of both. "What was going on in the 1950s seemed to be an attempt at a destruction of those in the 1860s and an assumption that the War Between the States was fought wholly and entirely in order to preserve slavery—which was not true."

The only controversy that arose in 1956 came out of a running feud between factions in the House, Groover says. George L. Smith was testing the thirty-three-year-old Groover and trying to embarrass Marvin Griffin when he asked if anyone was going to make any money out of the design of the flag. "I knew what he was getting at. I mean John Bell was up in the gallery. I don't know who would make any money out of it, I said. I didn't know whether the chairman of the Democratic Party would make anything or not. I just didn't know. John Bell got mad as hell at me for not explaining that nobody can make any money off the patent of a flag," he recalls. Groover did his job well in 1956 for the measure cruised through the House by a 107-32 vote with sixty-six abstentions. Earlier, it had passed in the Senate by a 41-3 margin.

In 1993, the Miller bill to restore the flag Groover and friends had removed was in the hands of Wayne Garner and Pete Robinson, two senators who in the jargon of the legislature "toted the water for the governor." Robinson was the primary sponsor, with the affable Garner as his ally. For them, this is an ugly memory—so ugly that both of them soon retired from the legislature. Garner is now commissioner of the Department of Corrections in the Miller administration and Robinson, a Columbus lawyer, is a part-time lobbyist. As the tempers got more heated, the two of them were called into the office of a Miller aide and told that state troopers were on their way to their children's schools. They would watch the two senators' children until the bill had passed or failed. It was a threat that Miller did not learn about until 1997.

Robinson knew what was coming. He couldn't even count on the support of the minority senators. "Folks were saying they're going to cover up the Confederate memorial at Stone Mountain during the Olympics," Garner says. "People were saying all kinds of stuff and none of it was true."

Robinson went to Miller with a compromise. They would revert back to the pre-1956 banner as the official state flag. The flag with the St. Andrews Cross would be legally flown over

Confederate monuments. Robinson and Garner even enlisted the aid of Gary Parker, a former Republican senator from Columbus who is black. They thought they could enlist support for the measure so Robinson presented it to the governor, who quickly said, "That's not my bill. My bill is to change the flag." Yet, he didn't stop them, knowing that somebody had to go out front and speak on the issue.

That someone was Robinson. Someone came up to Robinson right before he went into the well and said, "You don't know what you're doing. You don't know what that flag means to our state." His reaction and his speech became: "Don't tell me I don't understand."

Said Robinson: "I've never seen a horizon out my window that didn't have red clay in it. Neither did my father or his father, or his father, or his father. So don't tell me I don't understand. My great uncle served in the Senate of 1956 that changed the flag, the battle flag. My great-great-grandfather served in the House in 1878 that adopted the flag we propose to go back to. So don't tell me I don't understand. I've got a letter from an eighty-two year old man in Columbus who said that his grandfather told stories of being at Cemetery Ridge and seeing the Confederate Battle Flag, which was actually the flag of the Army of Northern Virginia, the Stars and Bars. He can tell stories of hearing his grandparents talk about the battles. So this was a battle flag—not the flag of the Confederacy. It was a symbol of war—not peace. For that reason, that old fellow wants us to change the flag." His words got only twelve votes.

Garner still thinks it was the thing to do. "I think he listened to the business community, and the people worried about the Olympics and thought that would be a good thing to do. But he's also like a lot of us new Southerners. I don't think there's a racist bone in his body. I think he felt good about what he did. He meant it when he said black children and white children ought not to have to go to school and look up and see that flag. He misread the politics, but his heart was in it."

Even with the failure in the Senate, a bill was still floating around the House and Groover had asked for some time to speak on it. Majority Leader Larry Walker was sitting next to him and as Groover rose to speak, Walker whispered that the governor had asked them to withdraw the bill from consideration. "I said it was too late for me to stop. Besides, what I'm going to say needs to be said."

Groover was the only member of the legislature who had been part of passing the revised flag in 1956. He didn't speak in support of Miller. He had in his pocket a compromise flag that he wanted to present—despite the fact that his wife said it was the ugliest flag she had ever seen. More than anything, he was the only person there who could put any perspective on the various spins of history that had been circulating around Georgia newspapers and the Georgia General Assembly. The most important message he delivered was the fact that he said he was willing to meet anyone halfway.

Sitting in his office in Macon, he reached into his desk and showed a visitor a replica of the alternative flag he suggested. He talked about his own background and why he wanted to speak that day in 1994. "You see, I went to the legislature when segregation was the number one political issue in this state. I was born and raised in a country town in South Georgia and anybody, any white, in my generation who told you they didn't have prejudice was a liar. However, one of the benefits of my being in the legislature and living through those changing times is not political advance but the opportunity to move away from some of that prejudice. I said in my speech that I didn't like Martin Luther King, Jr. He made people like myself look at ourselves and to some extent we didn't like what we saw."

Miller failed. He had scars and the battle flag was still on the staff. He gained nothing. Miller compares what he did to a Japanese Kamikaze pilot who killed himself but didn't alter the war in the slightest. "In fact, I may have made the matter worst. There was no way I could pass that bill and once I saw that I should have pulled the plug on it much sooner than I did. I'm sorry, but I left the situation where it cannot even be discussed calmly for years to come."

It took a lot of nights like the one in Buena Vista when he confronted the boo-birds, but Zell Miller the politician ultimately survived. Not that anybody really forgot. Pat Jarvis found that out in 1994 when he was on the road with Miller kicking off his reelection campaign. They were in Willacoochee for a political rally. While Miller was speaking from a flag draped platform in the middle of the deep South Georgia town, Jarvis went into a convenience store nearby.

One of the men inside recognized Jarvis and they were talking about the Atlanta Braves when the fellow looked out the front window and saw Miller. Then he scowled at the woman behind the cash register. "Look there. That's the son-of-bitch who was gonna change our flag."

"Nah," she said. "That's the son-of-a-bitch who's paying my daughter's way through college."

18

'GIVE 'EM HELL, ZELL'

Coming off the airplane in New York, Martha Gilland was loaded down like Juan Valdez. She carried 500 laminated cardboard signs. She had 500 wooden sticks that she was going to attach to the signs. She had carried all of that stuff with her on the flight from Atlanta because she was afraid to check it. For someone like her, it was a long way from Armuchee, Georgia to Madison Square Garden, but she was on her way, along with the signs and sticks.

She had gone to work for Zell Miller in 1981, coming to the lieutenant governor's office from a job with the Georgia Democratic Party. She hadn't worked there long and that was her only brush with politics. Nine years later, she left that office, and was among the earliest members of Miller's campaign staff in his first run for governor. If you work for Miller, your job description is often whatever he needs done at the moment and that would be the way it was at the 1992 Democratic National Convention. She was in charge of signs.

Zell Miller would be the keynote speaker for the convention and the signs she printed and carried were to be part of the celebration when he was at the podium. "Give 'Em Hell, Zell," they said, and she was supposed to pass them out that night for the excited Democrats on the convention floor to wave at the appropriate time. It would fire up Zell and it would sure look good on TV—provided, if Martha Gilland could get them to the arena

"I was worn out, but I got them to Madison Square Garden. Herb Mabry helped me get them into the building. We hadn't been there long when I realized that I had left the wooden sticks back at the hotel. I never did know what the hotel did with them, and don't care. People would just have to hold them in the air without a stick. It was unbelievable. I didn't have a floor pass, and they weren't going to let me get down on the floor. I told those people that if I had to catapult onto that floor I was going to do it. One way or another, I was going to be there when my boss spoke. Herb heard what was going on and got me a pass. I didn't have to jump," Gilland says.

Chuck Reece, the governor's press secretary at the time, had another assignment. During Miller's speech, he was to stand just out of camera range with a spare text—ready in case the TelePrompTer broke down. "It didn't, thanks be to God, so I never had to dash on to the podium like a water boy in the fourth quarter of a football game. But Miller, Miller was great. His delivery was dead solid perfect and no one had to be prompted to wave those 'Give 'Em Hell, Zell' signs. They knew when he was giving George Bush and his cronies hell, and they responded."

It was Zell Miller's night at Bill Clinton's convention. But it came close to not happening at all. Miller had been seriously ill all day. Both he and Shirley had a strep infection and the antibiotics were slow to take effect. His fever was alarmingly high that afternoon and he had soaked in a bathtub filled with ice to get it to go down before it was time to go to Madison Square Garden. He had stayed in bed all day and after the speech he couldn't wait to get back under the covers.

Before Miller went on to the podium that night, his good friend Ann Richards came over to him. She had to get close before he could hear her over the din of the crowd. The former Texas governor had been in that place herself, talking about how George Bush had been born with a silver foot in his mouth. She wanted to keep him loose. "Zell, honey, don't be nervous, it's just 30 million people watching every word you say, and if you do good, they'll ask who wrote it." After the speech, she would be waiting to congratulate him and to give him a Texas-sized hug.

Reece couldn't believe how outwardly calm Miller was. "Or at least how calm he appeared. In my time with him, I certainly had the opportunity to see him nervous now and then, but that night, when an average man would have been shaking in his boots, he seemed entirely confident in his. I believe he was wearing his boots. He must have been, and even if he wasn't, I prefer to remember it that way. It was a damn good thing to work for a governor who wore cowboy boots."

The moment came. Behind the podium. Looking directly into the lens of the camera. "Listen to this voice," Zell Miller began.

But the actual beginning came several years earlier. Zell Miller first met Bill Clinton in 1979, when the newly-elected governor of Arkansas came to the Georgia Governor's Mansion as the guest of Governor George Busbee. When he was elected, he was the nation's youngest governor. He had run an unsuccessful race for Congress and had served a two-year term as the state's attorney general. Miller liked him from the beginning. His wife, too. "I had read about him and thought he was a 'comer.' I watched in awe and admiration as he made his comeback after a disastrous 1980 defeat. What he did gave me hope that I could come back after losing to Talmadge," Miller says.

Though they are from two different generations, the similarities in their personal biography are uncanny. Both lost their fathers—Clinton's father died in an auto accident three months before his birth and Miller's father died seventeen days after he was born. Both were reared by headstrong, somewhat eccentric Southern women—women who were more like Scarlett O'Hara than Melanie Wilkes. Both grew up in isolated rural towns. Both were seen as whiz kids and both had an early obsession for the game of politics. Both were single-minded and driven. Both of them had more than once learned what it was like to recover from a political defeat, experiences that had changed their lives. Both had been around long enough to be considered traditional

Democrats, but several times each had gone into the closet, changed into a new suit of clothes and emerged as a new kind of Democrat.

The Miller-Clinton friendship flowered when Miller was elected governor of Georgia in 1990. Following the fall elections, the National Governor's Conference sponsored a conference for newly-elected chief executives. It was late November, in Louisville, Kentucky, and was a training session for the governors and the key members of their staffs. "Government 101," is the way Steve Wrigley describes the crash course on running an office. Wrigley was there along with Keith Mason and other members of the Miller staff. On the first night there was an informal, get-acquainted dinner and the Georgians were all at a large table enjoying their meal.

"Bill Clinton comes over to the table," Wrigley relates. "He was still the governor of Arkansas and it was obvious that he and Miller knew each other well because he stayed with us about thirty minutes. Mainly, it was he and Zell telling war stories and talking about old times. I remember as he walked away from the table the governor saying: 'That man is going to run for president.'"

By the next year, Miller was embroiled in his year-long battle with the budget and he had gathered all of the key players together at the mansion. It was in the summer of 1991—before Clinton was a candidate. "We were in the meeting and Clinton shows up at the mansion," Wrigley says. "The governor introduced him around the table, then he left, just like that."

As the two had got to know each other, they had found things they agreed on and things on which they would never agree. Miller explains: "From the start, I looked at the military and Vietnam differently than he had in his youth. We were from two different generations. I respected his views. They were familiar. I had two sons and many students with that line of thinking. I just didn't agree with it. I learned a long time ago that you can never find a politician you can agree with on every issue, unless you are that politician. I knew I would support Bill Clinton for President before he ever really decided to run. I had studied him for years. I respected his mind and his heart. I liked the way he operated as governor. Then as I really got to know him, I liked him very much. So did Shirley. We also liked Hillary. I am one of her greatest fans."

That Miller would be interested in presidential politics was not unexpected. He had been to every Democratic Convention since 1972, when he was executive director of the Georgia Democratic Party, the same year Clinton first became involved as a campaign worker for George McGovern. Miller had been an early supporter of Jimmy Carter's race and when the former Georgia governor was elected there was talk that Miller might join his administration. Then in 1984 Miller had been the statewide campaign manager for Walter Mondale. He did not take a leadership role in the 1988 race since he was already deeply involved in planning his own race for governor. So in 1991, it was not unusual for Miller to want to be involved in planning the strategy for the Democratic Party.

It was on his mind when he headed to spring training for his annual outing with James Carville, Paul Begala, Steve Wrigley and Pat Jarvis—known as "The Little Bulldog" when he was an Atlanta Braves pitcher. Things were coming together for the Braves in West Palm Beach that Spring, and things were coming together in Miller's mind about the future of the Democrats and how they could beat George Bush—who at the time was at the top of his game. They weren't talking about Bill Clinton. That came much later. They were talking about a strategy that any Democrat might follow in 1992. They all thought there was a great lesson to be learned from Miller's successful 1990 race.

Bush's approval rating might be going through the roof, but that was because of the perceived victory in the Persian Gulf. But what if somebody made Bush answer to the dismal economy? What if they talked about pocketbook issues, the kind people sit around the kitchen table and lament? What if this Democrat avoided the traditional social issues that usually dominate the platforms? What if he didn't avoid the incumbent, but challenged him on such issues? It was a plan of salvation. Do these things and ye shall be saved. By the time the group left South Florida, they had created what they called "The Blueprint for the Democrats to Win in 1992." At the time, a Democratic victory seemed as likely as the Braves winning the 1991 championship, but strange things happen in politics and in baseball.

Late in June of that year, Miller was one of the major speakers at the Democratic National Committee's Southern Caucus in Raleigh, North Carolina. His first-grade seatmate, Bert Lance, had helped arrange the invitation. Carville and Begala helped Miller craft the remarks that had been hatched in the Florida bleachers. It was not just another speech; it was the genesis of the 1992 Democratic campaign. The audience in Raleigh was hearing the governor of Georgia spell out the exact framework of a platform that another Southern governor would use to be elected President of the United States. Miller was candid and blunt:

"We can no longer escape the facts. If we ignore them, the facts will become our fate and the Democratic Party will have no future. So what can we do? I believe the answer is not to abandon our central principles, but to revive them, to return to the Democratic Party's defining purpose. You see, for too many presidential elections, we have had things backwards. We have chosen to fight on social issues rather than to run on the economic issues that shape the daily lives of American families. When the average American family stays up late in to the night, they are not worrying about whether school prayer should be voluntary or mandatory. They are worrying about how to balance the checkbook or where they will find the money for Junior's college tuition.

Our party grew up around the economic issues that concern working Americans most deeply, and that is the common bond that unites us. But instead of rallying around those basic, unifying economic issues, we have allowed ourselves to be distracted by social issues that not only divide us but also defeat us." Later, during the Clinton campaign, this would be shortened to "Its the economy, stupid," by Carville.

He called social liberalism the Democrats' Achilles heel, and even called by name two of the party's most recent failed nominees. He discussed the issues that bring the most political heat and even talked about how he had dealt with some of them in his 1990 gubernatorial campaign. "I was open about where I stood on the social issues. I said I was for sex education, and now we are implementing it. I endorsed a hate crimes bill, and I have said that I would sign legislation repealing Georgia's anti-sodomy law. I am completely committed to a woman's right to choose, and I have not equivocated in my support of the ERA. I believe Georgia has the strongest arts council in the South—and as long as I am governor, that will be the case. But you see, those issues were not the sole message of my campaign. Most of all, I stood for economic empowerment—for education, for efficiency, and instead of higher taxes, for a lottery."

More than anything, he appealed to the party's thirst for the White House. After he had outlined his views, he offered the opinion that to ignore such economic choices would be political suicide, that the party owed this to the nation since in the economic wars "Japan and Europe are kicking our butts. It's time that we Democrats kicked back." Do all of those things and the party "would be relevant again, alive again, proud again and yes, victorious again."

That September when Bill Clinton came to Atlanta to speak to the annual Richard Russell Dinner, he had a copy of the Raleigh speech in his inside coat pocket. Clinton was staying with the Millers at the Mansion, and after the dinner they settled into the upstairs study. Relaxing, they talked at length about the kind of campaign Miller had outlined. They learned they agreed on most of the points in the speech and on most of the issues. They even discussed some Clinton speeches and—like that night's speech at the Russell dinner, they were long and unfocused, a criticism that Miller shared with his friend. More than anything else, they talked about the ideas Miller had outlined in Raleigh, about the future of the party and about the future of Bill Clinton.

Miller recognized the focus and control that the Carville-Begala team had brought to his 1990 race and he thought they could do the same for Clinton. The two governors talked until nearly three in the morning. Clinton would have talked some more but Miller excused himself and went to bed. "That man has the stamina of a horse," Miller laughs.

Just before eight o'clock, the next morning Miller met Mason in the driveway outside the mansion. Mason asked how the night had gone and Miller said it was great, that they talked until the wee hours, that they had done a lot of talking about Carville and that Clinton was real interested in talking to him. There was a breakfast at the Mansion that morning so that Clinton could get to know some of the major Democratic donors in the state and Miller wanted his administrative assistant to somehow find Carville. "Can you get them in touch later this morning?" asked Miller. "Clinton's actually going to Washington today and it would be good if we could get them together." Mason reached Carville at Mary Matalin's house. "I woke him up, but he said he would be glad to, that he was involved in a race in Pennsylvania but hadn't decided if he would be involved with anybody in the presidential race. I said we'd get them together on the phone about ten o'clock," Mason recalls. After the breakfast, Miller and Clinton went back upstairs and Mason had Carville on the line.

"I got somebody on the phone," Miller said. "I've told him that he ought to hire you." "Fine, always good to get work," Carville said, as Clinton came on the line. He knew about Carville by reputation but the two had never met. Since Clinton was on his way to Washington, they agreed to meet that afternoon at a hotel lounge near Capitol Hill. Meetings like that happen in Washington every day, it's like people in Detroit who meet and talk about making automobiles. In Washington, they talk politics.

It was Clinton and his friend Bruce Lindsey sitting across from Carville and Begala. In a conversational manner, they talked about what it takes to run for President. Carville remembers very little about what was said. Begala says he begged Clinton to concentrate on his message: who you are, and why you want to be President. They talked no more than thirty minutes at the hotel and no commitments were made. Clinton was still shopping for political consultants and the other two were looking for a candidate.

Carville was being courted by two other presidential hopefuls—Sen. Bob Kerrey of Nebraska and Sen. Tom Harkin of Iowa—and he was playing hard to get. Clinton asked Miller for help. He called Carville who asked the Georgia governor if he had decided yet who he was supporting. "We talked back and forth analyzing him. We both saw him in the same way. He saw what I did, how focused this man was and how much thought he had given to running. James demands a lot from his candidates. He can't tolerate laziness and he's nobody's fool. He had seen enough to know that this man had the fire," Miller said. Within weeks, Clinton and Carville were a team.

As a foursome, they seldom get together. Mostly they talk to each other separately in long, rambling phone conversations. Usually they discuss politics, but sometimes they share something as mundane as the time Miller had an audience in Florida with baseball hitting legend Ted Williams whose first question to the Georgia governor was whether or not he was a Republican. The quartet of Miller, Clinton, Carville and Begala makes strange harmony. If they were a musical group, each one would want to sing lead. Each is driven. Each wants to be heard. Each is bright and knows it. Each detests anything but winning. They think southern. They are consumed by the gamesmanship of politics. Collectively they share a passion for sports, music, and history. The bond they share could be compared to wartime buddies who didn't know each other before the war, but are forever linked after being on the frontline together. Elections often take on the connotations of war, and that is the battlefield these four have shared. They've worked with or around each other on four political races—two of Millers and two of Clintons. Each time Georgia was involved.

They knew they enjoyed each other's company, but their political relationship was cemented during the presidential primary season of 1992. During the previous summer, the Georgia General Assembly had met in special session to discuss reapportionment and the budget crisis. Afterward Miller began to question why the state was participating in Super Tuesday. He did not think it should, because the Georgia primary was overshadowed by the big electoral payoffs in Florida and Texas, and, although he mentioned it to no one, he had another reason in the back of his mind.

One reason Georgia was part of Super Tuesday was Speaker of the House Tom Murphy, so from the outset Miller knew there would be obstacles. He sent Democratic Party chairman Ed Sims from participant to participant to remind them that any slowdown would negate the plan, since any change in the primary date would have to be approved by the United States Justice Department. Despite the varied participants, the plan was still alive and Mason said holding them together "was like holding a big beach ball. It keeps getting away."

Carville has said it was more than Clinton that inspired Miller to seek a change of date. "If you play *Family Feud* and ask a hundred people to name a southern state, I believe Georgia would come up more than any other. Georgians don't like being lumped in with everybody else. They feel they have a mystique: 'We're Georgia.' In politics, many states are important, but winning the Georgia primary establishes the candidate that's doing well in the South. There was a move afoot to separate the state and increase its influence even further." Yes, there were other reasons, but Miller admitted he made it a higher priority because of his friend Clinton.

By the time the 1992 legislative session came around, the shaky coalition formed to move the date forward a week was somehow holding firm, but there was still the problem of time. Miller then worked one of a hundred deals he had over the years with the senators' "Silver Fox," Culver Kidd, who came up with a way to hurry it through the process by substituting the language that would change the date of the primary to an existing bill that was already in his committee. That bill was the first bill of the first day that year and despite some token Republican opposition within two days after its introduction the bill was on the governor's desk for his signature. As one House Republican put it, "That bill was doomed to success."

The importance of that manipulation was obvious by the time the Georgia primary rolled around on March 3. Clinton had done anything but catch fire. Questions about the stability of his marriage and of whether or not he had improperly avoided the draft during the Vietnam War were haunting him. There had been primaries in New Hampshire, Maine and South Dakota, and he had won none of them. He was a Southerner coming South so the political oddsmakers said he could not survive a close race in Georgia. Anything less than 40 percent would not be acceptable. Anything below 35 percent would be a mortal blow to his campaign.

In Georgia, he got 57 percent of the vote. Paul Tsongas won Maryland and Jerry Brown took Colorado. But the attention had been focused on Georgia and Georgia gave the Clinton candidacy the boost it needed going into Super Tuesday. Carville gives the credit to Zell Miller.

"He really cracked the whip," Carville says. "He was to Bill Clinton what John Sununu was to George Bush in 1988. If Tsongas had even come close in Georgia, it would have been a mess for us." When he says Miller was cracking a whip during the primary, he was thinking of the homestate arm-twisting the governor used on his network of supporters. If Bill or Hillary were coming through the state, the Miller people were on the phone to assure there would be a turnout at every stop. He always showed up himself. "I'll never forget the time in Atlanta at the CNN Center when he put so many people on the platform that it collapsed. The way he put it was, 'if you ain't on that stage, you are out,'" Carville remebers.

Score one for Bill Clinton and score two for Zell Miller. Clinton got his first primary victory and the momentum he so badly needed going into the summer season. Miller had pushed for the change in the primary date which proved so vital, and he had turned out the numbers—not only for the campaign stops, but most importantly, at the ballot box. Those are things a politician doesn't forget.

A person, on the other hand, remembers a friend who takes a chance and supports you when others are reticent. And in the case of the Clintons, they remember that the day after the Gennifer

Flowers allegations went public that Hillary Clinton was spending the night at the Governor's Mansion and had a statewide fly-around scheduled with the governor for the next day. The first stop was in Columbus, Georgia and the governor of Georgia was there at her side as the first painful questions were asked about the purported affair. He stayed by her side all day as they went from one Georgia city to another. All of those things were on Zell Miller's scorecard as the Democratic Convention drew closer and the party hierarchy began to discuss who would play significant roles in New York City.

There has been speculation that the attempt to change the Georgia flag was part of a plan to propel Miller into an invitation to be the keynote speaker. Begala says not. "Zell gave the keynote because Bill Clinton wanted him to. Simple as that," he says. Miller adds to that the names of Begala and Carville. "James and Paul had heard me tell the story about Birdie and the house and thought it was powerful. Clinton had heard me speak, but hadn't heard that story. He has told me since that when he read a copy of my speech that he cried. Our mothers were dear to us, and the absence of a father he understood." Another factor was that Don Fowler, the Democratic National Committee chairman, had a daughter who graduated from the University of Georgia that spring. He told Harold Ickes and others who were working on the convention that Miller's was the finest speech on the race issue he had ever heard. Leading up to the convention, Clinton and Carville had both been dropping hints and telling reporters, 'You're going to be very surprised with Governor Miller from Georgia,' because Bill Bradley and Barbara Jordan were getting all of the publicity. Miller was in Young Harris when Clinton called and asked him to be the keynoter.

Clinton was being loyal to a long time friend who had supported him politically and personally. Yet, within the party, there were skeptics who wondered about the benefits of having a presidential candidate from Arkansas, a vice presidential candidate from Tennessee and a keynoter from Georgia. Too many southern accents, they whined. "You're right that the conventional political analysis would have called for a northeastern liberal, but (as with the Gore selection) Clinton was willing to put all that aside to get someone of sheer brilliance," Begala explains. "Mario Cuomo was nominating Clinton, and besides, he'd had his moment. Bradley and Jordan also gave mini-keynotes the night of Zell's. But history will little note nor long remember what they said. Zell just flat blew them away."

Perhaps even Clinton himself did not realize that beyond the loyalty and the political debts, his choice for the keynote address was not only a student of those speeches, but more importantly could be a stem-winder at the podium. The late Governor Marvin Griffin said that to be a successful political speaker "You have to put the saucer of milk down to where the cats can get to it." Miller has always been able to find just the right spot to put his saucer of milk. He may be the best political orator of his generation of southern politicians and he is probably the last in a long history of good, lively stump speakers, a vanishing art form in the South and in the nation.

Sarah Eby-Ebersole has been writing speeches for and with Zell Miller since his early days as lieutenant governor. They are a team. She influences his speaking and he influences her writing. When they work on a speech, it is a tedious, back-and-forth exchange of many drafts and much editing as they try and wrap the words around Miller's mountain tongue. "He's a very active participant," she says. "He goes over and over them. He edits and rewrites. It's not a matter of me sitting in the corner working on a speech and handing it to him just before he gives the speech. It's important to him to give a good speech, and he works at it."

Around Georgia he has always been known for the eclectic people he quotes in his speeches. It may the words of Franklin or Teddy Roosevelt or of Edmund Burke. It may be a predictable quote from Bartlett's Anthology. More often than not, it will be the offbeat musical poetry of a Kris Kristofferson, a Merle Haggard, or a Joe South, some of his favorite country songwriters, but not figures you would expect to be quoted in a political address. Unless the speaker is Miller.

357

Miller has been a writer since his days on the college newspaper. He and Shirley even edited a small North Georgia weekly. He has published four books, not including a narrative poem *The Legend of Hiawassee*. Already rolling around in his head are three more books that he expects to finish before or just after he leaves office in 1998. None of this includes the country song he wrote with Robert Waymer in 1979. "You Can't Ration Nothin' I Ain't Done Without" was a song lamenting the spiraling gas prices and the long lines at the pump. It made *Time* magazine but no one's Hit Parade. His most recent is one he co-wrote with the legendary Nashville songwriter, Jack Clement: "Everywhere I've Ever Been Was On My Way Back Home." Miller is fascinated by people who write lyrics and he can quote many of them like poetry. Clement has spent a lot of time with him at the mansion. His love of good writing extends to newspapers which he got in the habit of reading as a boy hanging out at The Varsity in Atlanta. He says the best writing is usually found on the sports pages. All of that should indicate that Miller wants his speeches to say something—not just string together political cliches. More than anything, it underlines Zell Miller's abiding respect for the printed and spoken word.

"He appreciates a good turned phrase, particularly if it captures a picture in people's minds. He's always looking for those phrases. He doesn't want to be like that candidate a few years ago Governor Miller said gave speeches that were oatmeal with a couple of raisins thrown in. That person got the idea the news media was only going to quote a few lines and so he put a lot of raisins in there and the rest was bland. One candidate would even hand out copies of his speech that already underlined the raisins—just to make sure the media got them. We're shooting for consistent eloquence all the way through," says Eby-Ebersole, who has been writing speeches with Miller since 1978.

Moving from Pennsylvania and joining her husband Dan on Miller's staff, she soon became a student of southern orators. Over the years, she has even read collections of speeches by Henry Grady and non-Southern speakers such as Franklin D. Roosevelt and Harry Truman, whom she compares to Miller for their love of a good quip and their plain, direct to-the-point style. She appreciates good speeches, but she seldom listens to Miller's. By the time they're delivered, she's moved on to the next one because as governor he has given more than 250 speeches a year—all of them prepared texts. Miller wants no surprises at the podium although he constantly edits and rewrites even as he waits to speak.

By the time he begins, Miller has a working knowledge of the speech and has almost memorized it. He speaks from a peculiar format, demanding that his speeches be typed on "half sheets" that are made by dividing an 8-by-10 sheet of paper. By the time the text is typed, single-spaced, the pages are filled with words. He wants it small enough that it can rest at the top of the podium so he can keep his head high and maintain eye contact, and he wants a mininum number of pages to turn. Eby-Ebersole says he reads them so many times that he knows where each word is on a given page.

Miller invests much time and effort into his speeches, but Eby-Ebersole acknowledges that his skill is one that is fading away. "The whole political process is becoming much more electronic," she says. "It is becoming a high-tech business that relies on the electronic media. It is fed to people in little blips rather than those long blocks of time. Everything revolves around the sound byte."

Begala says it is remarkable that Miller has been able to translate the power and passion of old-time stump speakers into the media age. "Some folks—Jim Wright comes to mind—can give you the old-time religion, but look cartoonish on television. Others, Richard Gephardt or Bill Bradley, are fine on TV but lack the presence to really fill up a giant convention hall. Zell can do both. Some of it is because he is so disciplined. Television is a small box, and overly-wild gesticulations, common among the old-style stump speakers, look like you're flailing about. Zell uses his voice and rhetoric and his face magnificently, but he doesn't throw his hands in the air or do any of the other histrionics that work well at a country fair but look ridiculous on TV."

Stump speaking was part of the South's oral tradition—a tradition that embraced the spoken word from the pulpit or the back of a flatbed truck and included the words of song and poetry. W.J. Cash said that throughout the South "rhetoric flourished far beyond even its American average. It early became a passion—and not only a passion but a primary standard of judgment, the *sine qua non* of leadership. The greatest man would be the man who could best wield it." More often than not, a speech was just plain entertainment, but at the same time it served a more cerebral purpose.

White southerners of the 1880s sometimes were looking for speakers who would create "mind pictures of his world or of the larger world around him—images of perfection" that would wash away the defeat of the past. A skillful speaker soothed that wounded spirit. Preachers and politics took to the stump to heal their neighbor's bruised psyche—and if they saved a soul or got a vote, all the better.

Henry Grady, the editor of *The Atlanta Constitution,* was a speaker who talked about rebuilding the old South and in the process finding a new one. Grady may have been speaking for the urban elite, but Tom Watson came along to speak for the fellows who wore wool hats whose hat bands were stained by sweat. He became one of the region's earliest demagogues, using his speeches to address the fears of the southern farmers. Scholars have written many words about how the speeches of those two Georgians created a divided mind in the South.

A more modern South followed that tradition. When Gene Talmadge came to your town for a political speech, it was an event, like the fair or the circus. He might talk all afternoon, but that was all right for between paragraphs you could eat some pork barbecue or sneak off in the background and share a snort of moonshine whisky. Marvin Griffin followed in that same pattern. He was a graduate of The Citadel and a well-read newspaper editor, but on the stump he could butcher grammar but do miracles with words. Marti Fullerton, when she was living with Zell and Shirley Miller, remembers his telling her at supper one night that after they ate they were going to Blairsville to hear Griffin in his last campaign for governor. "He may not have agreed with him, but he wanted to hear Old Marvin speak," she says.

Griffin was a standup comedian with a political text. Miller knows those days are past. "Those things don't look good on the evening news," he says. "You can't show wit, intellect and character in a thirty-second sound byte. That old style is so different from TV. If you do it on television, you sound shrill, loud, almost rude. And you must never forget you have been invited into someone's living room."

Miller is a student of those stump speakers, and long before he ever dreamed of delivering a keynote address at a national political convention he had followed the history of the keynoters. He was fascinated with political communications all the way back to listening with his mother to FDR's "Fireside Chats."

In 1956 Governor Frank Clement of Tennessee—who at that time was known as the Boy Wonder—was speaking at the convention that nominated Adlai Stevenson. Miller had just gotten out of the Marines and was living in Athens. "We had one baby, Murphy, and Matt was on the way. We had this grainy black & white TV and I was going to watch Clement's speech that night. About 4 o'clock that afternoon, Shirley went into labor. I took her to St. Mary's hospital. At 5, 6, and 7, she was still in labor and no baby. When the baby hadn't come by then, I got to wondering if I was going to miss that keynote speech so I went home. It was a great speech—'How long? Oh, how long?'—I can still remember parts of it. It was a great speech. When I got back to the hospital, Matthew had already arrived. A few years ago I met Frank Clement's son, Bob. I told him I would never forget August 13, 1956, the night his father spoke. He wondered how I could remember that date so well. I laughed and told him that was the night my second son was born."

Clinton knew nothing about Miller's interest in the history of giving a speech. He just knew he wanted him up there speaking on his behalf. Weeks ahead, Miller went to work crafting a text. Begala was working with him, and it was largely their words. Miller wrote the beginning and most of the ending—"You can get anywhere in the world from here." Begala worked on it some more, adding most of the humor. and along the way Eby-Ebersole added her touch. There were debates about whether he should outwardly attack Ross Perot. Miller and Begala wanted to keep it in, and their feelings prevailed.

Three days before the address Miller, Mason, and Chuck Reece went to New York so the governor could begin the elaborate rehearsal required for his somewhat brief appearance. The Democratic National Committee provided a limousine but Miller had his own Ford. As they were leaving their hotel for the first rehearsal, Miller suggested that Reece take the limo. The practice sessions were grueling. They worked under the same hot lights they would on the night of the speech and they wanted Miller to perfect every word and nuance. Not even Edna Herren demanded that kind of perfection. Wanting to get a break from those pressures, Miller got some theater tickets. Broadway plays have long been one of his passions and it was a good escape.

"When we got back to the Park Lane Hotel, I had a message. Mickey Mantle had called and left a phone number. I called and he was in his restaurant just a few yards away from the hotel. He wanted me to come over there. When I got to the restaurant, there was Moose Skowron and Hank Bauer. We stayed up 'til 1:30 a.m. I left them there still drinking," Miller says.

Madison Square Garden would be filled with the political headliners, but spending an evening with Mantle, Skowron and Bauer was another kind of treat. He was a southern boy, but as a boy Miller had been drawn to the New York Yankees. They dominated the world of baseball when he was a young boy in the late 1930s and 1940s. Their dominance extended into the 1950s— which was the generation of Mickey Mantle. Long after his retirement from baseball, Mantle lived part of the year next to a lush golf course in Greensboro, Georgia—between Atlanta and Augusta. He and the governor had become close. Mantle had even joined fellow Hall of Fame member Henry Aaron for a fund raiser Miller hosted at the Governor's Mansion with the proceeds going toward a new baseball field at Young Harris College.

Their friendship extended through Mantle's public admission of alcoholism, his rehabilitation at the Betty Ford Center and ultimately his death from liver cancer. Just before the death of Number 7, Miller flew to Dallas, Texas where the once-muscular star was in a hospital. He was dying, and he knew it. Doctors were allowing only family members into his room. A nurse blocked Miller at the door, but looking at his friend and flashing his familiar boyish smile, Mantle told the nurse to let him in. "That's OK. He's my Daddy."

The sadness of Mantle's death was years away that week in New York. But at the restaurant that night, the three old Yankees had invited the wide-eyed Southerner to join them again. "The next day, I went to Yankee Stadium for Old Timers Day. They took me into the dressing room, into the dugout and out on to that field. With them, mind you. What an unforgettable experience. Really, in many ways, greater than the keynote."

Finally, the rehearsals were over. Fever or not, Zell Miller left his room at the Park Lane and took the elevator. In the lobby, well-wishers were everywhere. Reece, standing off to the side, snapped a photograph of Zell and Shirley that became his souvenir of the moment. They were hustled toward Madison Square Garden.

The moment came. Behind the podium. Looking directly into the lens of the camera. "Listen to this voice," Zell Miller began. It was a speech for Bill Clinton, but it told the story of Zell Miller.

"Listen to this voice. It's a voice flavored by the Blue Ridge, a voice straight out of a remote valley hidden among the peaks and hollows of the Appalachian Mountains—a voice that has been described as more barbed wire than honeysuckle. That this kind of voice could travel from a forgotten corner of Appalachia is a testament to the grace of God and the greatness of the Democratic Party. This week we are gathered here to nominate a man from a remote, rural corner of Arkansas to be President of the United States of America. That is powerful proof that the American Dream still lives—at least in the Democratic Party. Bill Clinton is the only candidate for President who feels our pain, shares our hopes, and will work his heart out to fulfill our dreams."

He invoked the names of party legends and proclaimed that "George Bush doesn't get it." But he also told the world about a woman named Birdie Miller and said that he was a product of her dreams.

"My father, a teacher, died when I was two weeks old, leaving a young widow with two small children. But with my mother's faith in God—and Mister Roosevelt's voice on the radio—we kept going. After my father's death, my mother with her own hands cleared a small piece of rugged land. Every day she waded into a neighbor's cold mountain creek, carrying out thousands of smooth stones to build a house. I grew up watching my mother complete that house, from the rocks she'd lifted from the creek and cement she mixed in a wheelbarrow—cement that today still bears her handprints. Her son bears her handprints, too. She pressed her pride and her hopes and her dreams deep into my soul."

It was a story that, when he first saw the text, caused Bill Clinton to call his own mother, Virginia Kelley, weeping as he read the story of Birdie and Zell to his own mother over the phone. The night of the speech itself, Bill Clinton cried again as he watched the address on the television screen in his hotel suite. The review of the future president was most important, for the speech had been a gift from Miller to Clinton. But only moments after the speech was over and the cheers had quietened, the TV pundits began to react.

As Miller left the podium, a shoving match broke out between Bob Schieffer of CBS and Maria Shriver of NBC over whom would interview Miller first. Reece had to intervene. "I don't remember who won. I think it was Shriver, which was a good thing since it's not wise to make a woman angry if she's married to Arnold Schwarzenegger. Interviews would continue into the next day. Like producers after a Broadway opening night, the politicians waited anxiously to see what the critics would say and the critics said Zell Miller had been a hit."

"You just heard a classic, old-fashioned and very, very skillful political speech. The key to it, plain English. Democrats have been speaking 'Washington' for twenty years. References to Dirty Harry,

Barney Fife, Knee Deep in the Barn—that is the kind of stuff you used to hear forty and fifty years ago and you are exactly right, that it appealed directly to the Democrats who have stopped voting Democratic. They're off to a very good start on that score."—Jeff Greenfield, ABC News.

"Governor Zell Miller of Georgia blasted a home run when he delivered a keynote speech that electrified the crowded convention floor in Madison Square Garden. The folksy populist—who can turn a phrase faster than Ken Griffey, Jr. turns third base—has now all but assured himself a place in the national spotlight in the forthcoming campaign and perhaps well beyond."—National Convention News

"Signs on the floor said, 'Give 'em hell, Zell.' Zell did ... A surprising best of the three keynoters."—Edwin Newman, NBC News.

Down on the floor, Martha Gilland was cheering and waving just like the others who waved the signs she had guarded on the plane trip from Georgia. When the speech was over and they had stopped poking the signs in the air, they dropped them on the floor of the arena. Gilland started retrieving them as fast as she could. On the trip back, she would have signs to carry again. Now they're collector's items. "I got mine signed and framed," she says.

Miller's young aides were basking in the words they were hearing about their boss. Like many others who had worked for him over the years, he had become their teacher as much as he was the governor. He was the headlines in the next morning's newspaper. He was the subject for most of TV's Talking Heads. He had one big at-bat in the majors, and he had turned around on the best fast ball they could throw him.

By the next evening, most of Miller's people were seeing the sights instead of the politics. Reece had pretended he was a New York tourist, eating an expensive French dinner, taking in a Broadway show, and going to the Village Vanguard for a set of mellow jazz. Back at the hotel, it was 2:30 in the morning, but none of them could sleep. So Steve Wrigley and Frank Bates gathered in Reece's room and ordered chocolate sundaes from room service. They laughed a lot. None of them wanted this to be over.

19

A PROMISE TO SHIRLEY

Calvin Smyre was waiting. It was after three o'clock in the morning. Not much traffic was on the streets of Atlanta at that hour, but Smyre was still being careful. He doesn't move as fast as he did before his hip operation, so he took his time. Down Fourteenth Street came a line of cars leaving the parking garage at the Colony Square Hotel. One of them was about to deliver Zell Miller back to the Governor's Mansion—a return trip that many people thought was very unlikely.

Miller had been governor of Georgia four years, four generally good years. But this was 1994, and the political climate didn't agree with traditional Democrats. The Republican Movement was underway. Newt Gingrich, a former history teacher from Georgia like Miller, was one of the instigators of that movement and he lived just up the road from Atlanta. Around the country, two of Miller's closest friends in politics—Ann Richards of Texas and Mario Cuomo of New York—were in trouble. By the time those cars crept up Fourteenth Street that morning, Richards and Cuomo were on their way to new careers selling nacho chips on television. They had lost. Miller had won.

That victory was one that Smyre relished. The Columbus legislator had played a major role in the Miller campaign. Upstairs, before they left the hotel, Miller hugged him and delivered a thank you for his help. All of the insiders had been there—Shirley Miller, Steve Wrigley, Keith Mason—and the newly reelected governor had singled out Smyre. Now he was alone, on a lonely Atlanta sidewalk watching the line of cars slowly approach him.

"I was by myself," Smyre says. "His motorcade stopped on Fourteenth Street. The governor got of his car. He walked across that street. He came up to me and he said that he needed to say one more time how much he appreciated me. Shirley got out with him. Then the three of us stood there, at three in the morning, just talking. That was my proudest moment. I was just a piece of a puzzle. But there we stood. He embraced me one more time, then he got back in the car and they drove away. I just stood there."

Smyre had been in Miller's suite most of the evening before. It was election day, a long day that for the Millers had included a quick trip to Young Harris to cast their own ballots. Key supporters had gathered at the Colony Square Hotel, just as they had four years before. They weren't superstitious. They just weren't pressing their luck. Businessman Guy Millner was the opposition. He owned a temp service, but he wanted a full-time job as governor of Georgia. If he was elected, he would be the state's first Republican governor in modern times.

The nation was living through uncertain times. The economy was in turmoil. Average people feared for their jobs. Georgia had come through the crisis better than most, but the attitudes of voters were still affected dramatically. Bill Clinton, Miller's friend, was the subject of talk radio jokes. Times were tough for Democratic candidates, but Miller was running on a first term that despite the economic problems that faced him in the opening days had been a strong four years. The lottery had become a reality, leading to the HOPE scholarship program and pre-kindergarten classes throughout the state. He had started to work on welfare reform. Preservation 2000, an ambitious environmental program, had begun and some experts had said the 1991 and 1992 legislative sessions were the most important ones for the environment in their memory. He had talked about bootcamps for juvenile offenders and they were in place. All of this done in concert with an ongoing effort to cut back on spending. "Do more with less," Miller had told his staff. That had been the watchword of the first four years.

That litany of success didn't mean much when Miller began to poll the voters of Georgia in the months leading up to the election season. The numbers were not encouraging. "In the summer of 1993, it was clear that a second term was dicey, a so-so proposition," Steve Wrigley says. "So the decision to run again was a huge one. In other words, Zell and Shirley decided to run knowing that losing was as likely as winning. But there was more to do. The same poll that showed the re-election was a toss-up also revealed one insight: when voters heard about his accomplishments as governor, they liked them and they moved his numbers over the top."

Miller had been wounded by the flag issue and opponents were reminding voters that Miller had promised that he would be a one-term governor. Reports said that this came from a promise to Shirley Miller that if she would support his four years in the governor's office that they would go back to Young Harris and she could resume her banking career she enjoyed so much. That soon became part of the campaign rhetoric and was seen as a promise—not only to his wife but to the people of Georgia.

The Millers saw it otherwise.

Zell Miller: "She pushed very hard for me to run that first time. I will always remember having dinner with her at Rudolph's in Gainesville when I finally said, 'OK, I'm going to do it. If I'm defeated I'll come home and if I win I'll serve one term then you can live out your dream of being president of a bank.' To begin with, it was a promise only to Shirley. Later, in testy press conferences where no one could understand what I was saying, it became a promise for one term."

Shirley Miller: "I considered it a commitment to me—not to the people of Georgia."

Zell Miller: "I fully intended to keep the promise. First, because I really wanted to keep it and second because I thought it would be political suicide not to keep it. Again, it was Shirley more than anyone who pushed for the second term. She felt like I could win even though the polls were terrible. She was very concerned that my HOPE and preK programs were not yet enough in place."

Shirley Miller: "I did push him. It had taken longer to get HOPE and preK up and running. The sales tax had not been removed. I felt he still had a lot to do. I was still meeting people who had not heard of HOPE and who didn't believe it when you told them. I wanted to see Zell get them in place. It's not easy to push Zell Miller, but we've always discussed political decisions. He wants to know what I think. He'll ask me the same question dozens of times. He'll test me to see how strong I think about something. That's what he did about the second term."

Zell Miller says his decision to defy the polls and go after that second term was almost solely his wife's. It wasn't just the one-term dilemma. He had been crippled by his move to change the flag and had yet to recover. There was little doubt that the conservative movement was coming through Georgia. An issue like the second-term question could be inflated into a major problem. So, it wasn't about living in the Mansion a while longer. They cared little for the frills and perks. It came down to their desire to leave a legacy— that ambition to do.

"The polls were dismal. My reelection numbers were at about 30 percent. We had a lot to do and we knew it." But people such as Jim Blanchard, Virgil Williams, Don Leebern, Mack Robinson, J. B. Fuqua, and Pete Correll stayed with Miller. "The state business community all stuck with me, a real tribute considering that my opponent was one of them. I think they felt I had done a good job."

Atlanta real estate developer Tom Cousins was among those supporters. He had given Miller only token support in 1990, but for the second race became a major backer. "He had risen to the occasion during his first term. I was ready to do more. I thought it was vital that he serve again." Cousins was among the first in state business circles to come to Miller and encourage him to be in that second race. He has been impressed by his leadership, but as a builder he could not ignore the fact that under Miller Georgia had been the fastest-growing state east of the Rocky Mountains for four consecutive years, and more recently in 1996 the state ranked third in the nation in job creation over the previous five years.

Before Miller could do anything about getting reelected, he had to reconstruct his campaign organization. Keith Mason and Marti Fullerton had gone to other jobs. James Carville and Paul Begala were busy in Washington and couldn't be in Georgia on a regular basis. He hired Jim Andrews to come to work as his campaign manager and at first he wondered if this might be a repeat of 1980 when he had hired Dick Morris—a decision that haunted him long after the race. "It was rough at first," Miller says. "I missed James, who in the first race had been with me on a daily basis for over a year. Gradually, Jim and I worked out our two rough personalities, and I say very honestly that I simply could not have won it without him. He's a great political consultant, the best working today, and I came to have great respect and affection for him."

Begala continued to have input on the basic strategy of the campaign. Major decisions were bounced off him. Telephones, FAX machines, and beepers overcame his absence and made him a call away. Andrews established his role and Steve Wrigley emerged as a major figure in both the campaign and the upcoming administration. Wrigley was one of those young talents that Miller had recognized after his impressive research on the creation of the Mountain Protection Act. He had joined the lieutenant governor's staff and had been a valuable staff member in the 1990 campaign and during Miller's first term. But his expanded role in the 1994 campaign was surprising. "Wrigley was magnificent," Miller says. "No one I have ever known combines his policy and political skills. He unexpectedly became a very effective and hard-nosed fund raiser. He could cajole and twist arms with the best of them."

Begala refers to Wrigley as the MVP of the entire campaign. "Jim Andrews, with whom I've worked in several campaigns, ran a flawless race. Along with Jim, you have to give an MVP award to Wrigley who helped raise the money, focus the candidate, and kept the campaign on track. Those two deserve medals for leading that campaign to victory with all that was against it. I mean, in Miller you had a candidate people considered a twenty year incumbent in an anti-incumbent year. You had an unabashed and unapologetic Clinton friend in a virulently anti-Clinton region and an anti-Clinton year. You had a Democrat in a Republican year. And you had probably the richest opponent in American politics in Guy Millner. Other than that, it was a piece of cake. In the end, what won the race was Miller's record and his accomplishments—especially the HOPE Scholarships."

Millner was tenacious. He wasn't a warm or effective campaigner, but he worked right up to the moment the polls closed that Tuesday in November. Looking back, his perspective was that if he had poured a significant amount of money into the campaign that final week, it would have been different. Miller, despite the obstacles that went with being a Democrat that year, pulled it out, capturing 51 percent of the vote. Millner, meanwhile, was encouraged enough to make another venture into politics in 1996—losing the race for the United States Senate to Max Cleland. Then, in June of 1997, he announced that he would again run for governor in 1998.

Millner was a fighter. On election night, his party at a hotel in Cobb County was more celebratory than the victor's. While some of his supporters were downstairs in the ballroom watching results on a battery of television sets, Miller was upstairs in a suite carefully watching every result that was reported. Smyre was part of that group and he remembers how careful Miller was as the night drew on and friends began to congratulate him.

Says Smyre: "I guess 98 percent of the votes were in and he had a lead. In Cobb and Gwinnett, he had received more than 40 percent of the white votes which was a benchmark. We were on our way downstairs to claim the victory when Zell and Shriley stopped at the elevator door. They looked at each other and he warned everybody that he didn't want to go down there and say anything until it was 'abundantly clear' that he had won. We got on the elevator and got off again. Zell got back on the phones to the counties. We sat there for awhile and someone said that mathematically he couldn't lose. That's Zell. He wanted to be sure. So we got back on the elevator a second time. That showed me another side of him. He is very conscious of reality."

But the reality was that this was not 1980, but Zell Miller had mastered politics in his state in a way that had not been seen in a long time. In an anti-Democrat, anti-incumbent year, Miller beat the odds with a tough, savvy campaign, but, most of all, by having a record to run on. He had built that record not based on a worn-out philosophy or even through traditional Democratic ways. As John Head of *The Atlanta Constitution* pointed out, a constant in Miller's years as governor "has been his belief that government ought to be a positive force in people's lives."

It was largely this focus of his record that allowed Miller to survive in 1994 while such Democratic legends as Ann Richards of Texas and Mario Cuomo of New York lost. And it is this that led Miller to thrive as his second term draws to a close. Surveys indicate that seventy percent of Georgia voters approve of the job Miller is doing as governor. In short, as the *National Journal* has said of Miller, "He's writing the book on how a Democratic governor can flourish in the new Republican South."

Really, Miller had called the election a year before. Over and over he would tell his sometimes too-optimistic supporters, "This race will be settled by less than 50,000 votes. It turned out to be 33,000. He had overcome dramatic obstacles to win in a year when Democrats were falling out of trees all over the country. He had overcome the numbers in the polls. He had overcome the money of a well-heeled Republican candidate in a state that was more and more considering itself Republican. He had conducted an error-free campaign. What happened that fall was a pivotal event in his lengthy career. It opened the door to four years when he could continue his programs. It underscored Georgians support of what he had started in 1990—particularly HOPE and the lottery that financed it. It brought the hope that Georgia was committed to educating and learning.

During his final four years, Miller would have the opportunity to solidify the future of HOPE and the pre-kindergarten programs. He would be able to continue to increase the salaries of the state's teachers. He would at last accomplish two projects he had set out to do so many years before—the removal of the sales tax on groceries and the strengthening of the state's DUI law. He would make significant strides in reforming the state's welfare regulations by limiting the time a recipient would be eligible to be on the welfare rolls.

There are many accomplishments that Miller is proud of and which have been overlooked, like his record on the environment. Miller certainly has his critics in this area. Environmental lobbyist Neill Herring is one of the staunchest. Their conflicts go back many years. He calls the Georgia governor an opportunist. "He thrives on bogus conflicts. He's very creative and very dramatic. He searches for an opportunity to be on stage. Reality is not important. Legislation is explained by anecdote. I haven't talked to him in four years, and when we did, he just yelled. His mountains are being ruined. Gilmer County is being destroyed by rich Yankees and chicken houses. 'What do you want to do, sell pumpkins on the side of the road?' 'Yeah, I say, we want women to make beds for minimum wage in a motel.' His Mountain Protection Act is more eyewash than protection. He's clearly on the side of the developer."

But Herring's diatribe seems more personal than professional and a little out of touch with Miller's record. The mainstream environmental groups—The Nature Conservancy, The Georgia Wildlife Federation, The Georgia Conservancy—have largely embraced, even lauded Miller's environmental record. Major legislation and water disputes with Florida and Alabama have been undertaken with little fanfare but they will have far-reaching impact on the state. Preservation 2000, a land acquisition program designed to protect 100,000 acres of Georgia's most sensitive lands was completed early in Miller's second term. It is the largest land acquisition program of its kind undertaken by any state this decade. And the Miller Administration has updated laws to protect the Georgia coast and to bring to closure the controversy over siting a hazardous waste landfill. The Georgia Wildlife Federation in

1994 gave Miller its "Conservationist of the Year" award for these efforts.

But environmental problems do remain, and other critics charge Miller has not been as aggressive in the area of regulation. Miller himself privately acknowledges that he is unhappy about the continuing problems the City of Atlanta has with its water and sewer system and with the lack of consistency on the part of his own environmental officials to deal sternly with the city. For years the state has been accommodating to the city and in some ways is an accomplice in the city's failings to manage and modernize its system on a timely basis.

Other achievements of Miller's two terms will stand out in the years ahead. The Georgia economy has rebounded strongly under Miller, with Georgia being third in the nation in job creation. A record number of Georgians are working, and Georgia continues to be one of the fastest growing states in the nation. And the state, which like most southern states has lagged behind the nation in wealth, has seen its total buying power rise by over $50 billion during the Miller years, according to the University of Georgia. Miller brought to the Governor's Office a long history of being tough on crime and has consistently championed tougher crime laws, tougher DUI laws, and greater protection for victims.

His passion for work is on display every session as he annually introduces a lot of bills and expects his team to pass them. Each year, if the number of administration bills is forty or fourteen, Miller has managed to get at least ninety percent of them passed. It is an enviable record, probably unequaled by any other governor, and is testimony to Miller's mastery both of the legislative process and, perhaps more important, the wants of the public.

Perhaps one of the most important issues the Miller administration has worked on is the so-called "water wars" with Alabama and Florida. When Miller took office, Georgia and Alabama were in litigation over water rights to the Chattahoochee and other rivers. Water law was unclear, and an adverse legal decision could have dramatically affected Georgia's economic growth. After his election in 1990, Miller asked Joe Tanner, who had been elected

Labor Commissioner, to be his Commissioner of Natural Resources. Tanner agreed, and quickly recommended that the three states try to negotiate a settlement rather than pursue costly, unpredictable litigation. All three governors agreed, and throughout the Miller term reaching an agreement among the three states on water allocation has been a high priority. Few issues have more significance for the state's future. Ultimately, in early 1997, the negotiations produced a water compact among the three states that was going to be introduced to the Congress for its approval.

There was a long list of other issues to tackle and problems to solve. Perhaps the most difficult challenge of the first term was something beyond the control freak Miller's control: a 500 year flood. It began raining in early July of 1994, right in the middle of Miller's re-election, and in a few days Macon, Americus, Albany, and most of Southwest Georgia was under water. A natural disaster poses enormous problems for politicians. If they don't show enough interest and concern, they are criticized for being insensitive and out of touch. Just ask former President George Bush about Hurricane Andrew in South Florida. But, on the other hand, if they show too much concern and are too visible, they are criticized for trying to take political advantage of peoples' misery. Most frightening of all, the emergency management apparatus, a notoriously clumsy one at the federal level, has to work quickly and with sensitivity to aid the thousands of people displaced from their homes.

Miller literally waded into Georgia's response to the flood. He visited flooded areas, stayed on state agency heads to do everything they could to alleviate peoples' suffering, and largely put his campaign on hold until the immediate crisis passed. It was a long, difficult six weeks before the waters receded and Miller was able to put one eye back on the campaign. In the end, there were no major, public criticisms about the way the state handled the flood, and that in itself was an achievement.

But it is likely that Miller's grandest achievement will be in education. "If there were a book about education governors," Education Week said, "Mr. Miller might just be the main character." Such positive national attention and acclaim are unusual for Georgia education. The satisfaction of the folks in Georgia with Miller's initiatives is also unusual for Georgia. And it is the HOPE program that arouses the most appreciation.

That Miller brought both HOPE and hope to so many Georgia young people will be his most memorable accomplishment. The history of this program will be written by the students it educates. As college seniors in Georgia graduated in the spring of 1997, many of them were among the first class that had their way paid by the HOPE program. In 1993, Maggie Hodge graduated from Harris County High School in Hamilton and in 1997 she received a degree from the University of Georgia. She was a HOPE scholar. "In the beginning, I heard all the lottery hype and I was a cynic. I thought somebody would get the money, but I never figured it would be me," Hodge says. She remembers her principal praising the HOPE winners in 1993. Now she understands why. "I'm fortunate, and I'm indebted to Zell Miller."

Stories such as hers will be written again and again as HOPE continues to foster those new expectations that Miller has so often described. Yet, another of his accomplishments has been often overlooked. Attention was drawn to his judicial appointments in the spring of 1997 when Miller appointed Thurbert Baker, his House floor leader from Decatur, the state's new attorney general. But his record had begun years before.

Still, his appointment of Baker certainly made headlines. Mike Bowers had resigned only the day before to prepare for an anticipated campaign for the Republican nomination for governor in 1998. Miller wasted little time in declaring his choice, making Baker Georgia's first black attorney general and the only African-American holding that office in any of the fifty states. Miller maintains his choice was based on neither race nor politics.

"His name has appeared on more important legislation than anyone in Georgia history," Miller says of Baker. "He described those bills. He fought for those bills. He passed those bills. He proved himself on the battlefield. That stuff about it helping the Democratic Party or him being the first African-American is an insult to him and his abilities. He's been tested through seven legislative sessions. I remember sitting in my office and listening to the squawk box as he described bills in the House and thinking how talented he was. He was my choice from the first moment I heard Mike Bowers had resigned."

His appointment of Baker made headlines, but during his years as governor, Miller has made more judicial appointments than any other Georgia governor. Atlanta attorney Norman Underwood, the former opponent who gave Miller the infamous nickname "Zig Zag Zell," has been part of that appointment process. He remembers how Miller inherited the lawsuit filed by Atlanta legislator Tyrone Brooks. It questioned the ability of blacks to elect superior court judges in Georgia and for the years it had been tied up in court many judgeships across Georgia had been left unfilled. Soon after taking office, Miller settled the case by asking a federal judge in Savannah to serve as a mediator on the question.

"He settled it because it was the right thing to do," Underwood says. "Since then, Governor Miller has appointed almost a third of all the judges in the state. He has put his stamp on the state's judiciary. He has appointed more women than any other governor—including the first woman on the State Supreme Court. In Fulton Superior Court, there are fifteen judges and ten of them are women. These judges are going to be on the bench long after his time as governor is passed."

Underwood is as impressed with Miller's approach to the process as he is the governor's record on race and gender. "I am the chairman of the Judicial Nominating Commission and never has he told me in advance that he has someone he wants to see on that list. When I finally give him that list it usually contains five names. He interviews them. And one of the things he does I think is indicative of why he is an outstanding leader. He knows you can't be paralyzed by analysis so he doesn't ask them judicial questions, he asks them about themselves, their life experiences. After he's talked to everyone on the list, he typically takes two nights. Then, very early, often before seven in the morning, he'll call the person at home and tell them he's decided to appoint them. He doesn't brood. He knows you have to make decisions."

Miller is responsible for making Georgia's judiciary among the most diverse in the nation when race and gender are considered. During his administration, he has appointed more women and minorities to judicial positions than all of Georgia's other governors combined. Underwood says Miller's efforts also have led to the appointments of people who would not have been considered in the past because they weren't from a major law firm. He said Miller has expanded the process to people whose mind extends beyond their legal education and experience. "And these people are going to be affecting the lives of Georgians for years to come. This will be an influence of Zell Miller that may extend for decades after he is gone from office," Underwood says.

While his influence in Georgia continued to grow, Miller also kept alive his role in national politics. President Bill Clinton asked him to chair the Democrats' platform drafting committee in 1996. When Clinton told Harold Ickes that he wanted the Georgia governor, his deputy chief of staff resisted. "I want Zell," Clinton said. "He's the best bullshit detector I know." Clinton set a pattern and Miller pushed it through for him. This job set Miller up for conflict with organized labor which wanted to oppose the North American Free Trade Act which Clinton had proposed and passed. Miller found a middle course on that as he did on abortion and gay rights. This was important in Clinton's re-election efforts since while Miller's committee was working smoothly, Republicans were visible every night on the evening news squabbling among themselves over abortion.

As Miller's second term comes to an end, the 1998 gubernatorial campaign is taking shape. Georgia Republicans are increasingly powerful and some observers have theorized that Miller may be the last governor Georgia Democrats will elect for the forseeable future—ending 120 years of Democratic control. Few Democrats can claim to understand the GOP better than Miller. They were his neighbors growing up in Young Harris and some of them were his kin.

"Neighbors on either side of me were Republicans, but they were loving, personal friends. Election day is just one day out of the year. We lived together the other 364. We seldom even discussed partisan politics, just understood that we belonged to different parties," Miller says. Towns was a two-party county but in the years Miller was first in politics Georgia was hardly a two-party state. Georgia Republicans played bit roles. They had random success at the local level and even in the legislature, but statewide they weren't a factor. It wasn't until the 1990s that the party had enough strength to become major contenders in statewide elections. By the time Miller and Millner met in 1994, the days of one-party domination had ended.

"We are a two-party state in every sense of the word," Miller says. "We're not trending that way. We are that way. More people (40 percent) say they are Republican than say they're Democrat (38 percent). Who is elected the next governor will not depend on what party they belong to. It will depend on what issues are emphasized. People do not vote by party label alone. They vote where the candidate stands. That's why I was elected and reelected—not because I was a Democrat. I was elected because of where I was on the issues. The next governor will be also."

The populist who once scared the pocketbooks off of business people was elected with their support in 1994 even though an informed leader such as Tom Cousins admits that four years before he thought Miller would be nothing more than a caretaker. Some in the business community had been scared of Miller in the past and he says he was leery of some of them.

Among old friends, he had been able to discuss some of these feelings—especially if they understood what it meant to be a mountaineer. George Berry understood. He grew up in Blairsville, but had two sets of aunts in Young Harris. He can't remember when he didn't know Zell Miller, who is four years older than him, an event that kept them apart as boys. Berry graduated from Young Harris College and in a far-reaching career that has moved in and out of the private and public sector, eventually became head of the Department of Industry and Trade under Gov. Joe Frank Harris.

"We used to kid about the fact that I was on the Board of Young Harris College and he was not and he was our most famous graduate. I always said it was because they were wary of that 'liberal.' When Zell supported John Lewis for Congress over Wyche Fowler in 1977, he really did rile one of the board members. This man was an Atlanta business leader and he said he didn't mind the lieutenant governor supporting Mr. Lewis, but he doesn't have to hand out literature outside the door of my building," Berry says.

Those feelings were both real and perceived, but Miller couldn't ignore them. So in 1994, when throngs of Georgia's top business leaders came to a large meeting room near the State Capitol for a photo session with the governor, Berry shared with Miller what both of them were thinking: "Zell, would you ever have believed this?"

Receiving support and respect from a group of voters who once shunned him was satisfying. "I think I was more in awe of those people than I was uncomfortable around them. Now, I find myself having a lot in common with them. They are usually very focused individuals who work very, very hard. That's me. I'm focused. I work hard. I watch how I spend money. I find that a lot of my traits are their traits."

Berry says the similarities go beyond personal traits. "Business has realized that his agenda is the New South agenda which is a philosophy that says the way you lead people out of poverty is through Free Enterprise. Zell lives by business principles. He knows that education and income track one another."

Miller's strengthened relationship with the business leadership contributed to the state's involvement with the Centennial Olympics that came to Georgia and Atlanta halfway through Miller's second term. Though he talks about mistakes made during the Olympics, he thinks the games were good for Georgia in ways that don't show up on a profit and loss sheet. "The rest of the nation has always kind of looked down its nose at the South. That's one reason Jimmy Carter and Bill Clinton were never accepted by the elitists in the national media. They will never admit it—'We have prejudices? Heavens, no. It's you Southerners who have prejudices and stereotypes.' So I discount what some of the writers from *The New York Times* and others have said about Georgia. Sure, there were some bad glitches. Munson Steed's stuff with the street vendors was a terrible eyesore. Bus drivers should have been better trained on the routes and the 911 response to the bomb threat was a disgrace."

Miller also played a large role in Olympic security during the Centennial Games in 1996. The state committed over 5,000 law-enforcement personnel to the Games. It is safe to say the Games could not have been conducted without the state's effort. Most of the competitions, nearly three-fourths, were on state property like the Georgia Dome, and the Olympic Village was on the campus of Georgia Tech. The logistical and operational issues were mind boggling in themselves, and early in 1996 Miller created the State Olympic Law Enforcement Command (SOLEC) to pull together the state's disparate efforts on security planning and named his emergency management director, Gary McConnell, as its chief of staff. The planning involved over fifty different state and local agencies plus the FBI and numerous federal agencies.

In spite of the planning, tragedy did stike. About 1:30 A.M. on July 27, a bomb exploded in Centennial Olympic Park, the new park that had become the most popular public gathering place for the huge Olympic crowds. Within minutes after the explosion, Miller and Wrigley were called. They immediately dressed and went to SOLEC headquarters on Confederate Avenue where they stayed around the clock. There followed several days of constant conference calls with the White House and City of Atlanta officials, including discussions about whether to reopen the park and if so, when and under what conditions. It was decided that the park would reopen as soon as the FBI cleared the crime scene and that a ceremony would be held to remember those who were killed and injured but also to renew the Olympic spirit. Thousands attended, including Miller. "The bomb certainly hurt [the Olympic Spirit] in the beginning, but the 'coming back' ceremony at Centennial Park was one of Atlanta's and Georgia's finest hours.

Andy Young delivered a wonderful message. That comeback enhanced our reputation," he says.

The Olympics also enhanced Miller's ongoing efforts to stimulate Georgia tourism and to promote the state in countries around the world. "It was the largest peacetime event in the history of the world. I was in Copenhagen and London right after the games and Georgia got a very good response. When I first started traveling on economic trade missions, in the 1970's no one knew where Georgia or Atlanta was. They knew about Coca-Cola. In Tokyo they knew about 'Gone With the Wind.' Now, thanks to CNN, what we've done with our trade missions and overseas offices, and the fact that the South is booming, all this has changed. The Olympics further increased our visibility."

These things also increased Zell Miller's visibility. The governor's office always has been a revolving door through which a cross-section of Georgia passes, usually pausing for the obligatory photograph with the chief executive. A staff photographer is on call to snap the grip-and-grin photo of groups that range from school kids to visiting dignitaries. Miller is not the people person that a Lester Maddox was, but nevertheless the people who come through the office marvel at how he personalizes the visit by sharing some obscure piece of knowledge about the guests or their hometown.

When a legislator showed up outside with his son who was a Marine just out of Parris Island and a friend who was a Marine recruiter in Cobb County, Mary Beazley looked at the uniforms and knocked on his closed door, usually a signal that he is busy. When Miller saw their uniforms, he was enthralled. For nearly ten minutes, they talked about boot camp. "It'll be an experience you never forget." Those kinds of visits almost come naturally. But when a group of touring Chinese students came in, it was different. They left impressed that he had visited their country and he knew something about their culture and even compared it to that of the American South.

But there's still the boots and there's still country music. For years, Miller encouraged and supported the Georgia Music Hall of

Fame. At first it was a hall that didn't have walls on which to hang its plaques. The ceremonies began in the Garden Room, a small reception area that was located across the street from the capitol. From there, it graduated to the Georgia World Congress Center and was even telecast on GPTV. But still it had no home. Miller, who had been voted into that hall of fame himself as a supporter of Georgia music, even donated the royalties from *They Heard Georgia Singing,* a book he wrote on Georgia musicians to help pay for a home. Finally, through a partnership between corporate donors and the state, the Georgia Music Hall of Fame became a reality, opening in Macon in 1996. It is an impressive tribute to the people who made the music and the governor who wanted them honored.

Singer-songwriter Bill Anderson says that it would never have happened without Zell Miller. "He's given more than lip service, he has pushed for it. Some people wanted to keep it on the back burner, but by George, he saw to it that it happened. He's been a friend of mine and a friend of music. I bet he's been to a bejillion shows in this state, just to be there for the performer," says Anderson, a native of Avondale Estates who has been the host of the Hall of Fame Awards show since 1984. He says Miller's love of music is genuine, remembering the years when Miller's friends in music would help him celebrate his birthday by putting on a show during the legislature.

Miller doesn't sing, but he is a closet songwriter. He's written a number of songs, but none of them have made anybody's "Hit Parade." He has been on the stage of the Grand Ole Opry and one of those times was to help celebrate Bill Anderson's 30th anniversary with the legendary show. Speaking to the audience, Miller told them and his old friend Anderson that he would give it all up—the title, the power, the influence—just to be able to play the banjo at the Grand Ole Opry.

"Governor," Anderson said, "I promise to stay out of politics if you'll promise to stay off the stage."

So far, both have kept their word.

20

HOME TO THE HILLS

All the way over to the television studio that morning, he was scribbling numbers on a sheet of yellow paper ripped from a legal pad. Keith Sorrells was driving and Zell Miller was counting. One by one. The primaries and the general elections. Tallying the number of times the name of Zell Miller had been on a ballot in Georgia. "My last batting average," he laughs. He was up at four that morning, an hour earlier than usual, and he had scribbled down the words he wanted to say well before the 8:30 A.M. taping. He figured the question would be asked. After that many years in politics, he knew the questions as well as the answers.

That morning, he was taping "Georgia Week in Review," a thirty minute show that airs weekly on Georgia Public Television. Bill Nigut of WSB-TV is the host of the show, and like the governor, he must have felt he had done this before. It was December, a Friday the 13th of all days, just three predictable weeks before the 1997 General Assembly convened and Nigut had prepared the usual questions about what legislation was on the horizon. Nothing meaningful was asked and nothing important was answered. That week, Miller had fired one school board and hired another—mostly Republicans—and as Nigut followed up on the appointment of those Republicans Miller's body language was way ahead of his words. He threw his head back and closed his eyes for just a second.

Nigut was speculating that Miller's choice of GOP board members might indicate the governor had plans for himself in 1998. That was the year he would leave office and also the year Paul Coverdell's seat in the United States Senate would be on the market. Did all that mean Miller had any plans after he left the governor's office?

It was the question Zell Miller had been answering since four A.M.on that folded page out of the legal pad. It was the one he had been discussing with Shirley for weeks. If he was tense about what he was going to say he took care of that with some expected Miller humor. "I plan to do something after I'm governor. I hope I have a long and healthy life and write some books." Then the words he had been scribbling kicked in. "You know, I figured you were going to ask that question, Bill, and I knew how I was going to answer. I woke up about four this morning—an hour earlier than I usually do. The finality of what I'm gonna tell you flashed through my mind. They say a man's life flashes in front of him just before he dies and my political life flashed in front of me. But it's something I'm very comfortable with. Bill, I will never be a candidate again."

Nigut wanted to interrupt with qualifying questions, but Miller kept going. "I have run my last race—unequivocally. I will not be a candidate ever again and we might as well go a step farther and also say that I will not take a job or an appointment in Washington. As for this latest rumor, I'm not interested in nor do I want to be a candidate for the presidency of the University of Georgia."

Then, for a moment, he talked about how hard he was going to work in the upcoming session in 1997 and how many things he still had left to do. He was going to work for those goals until his final term as governor is over at the end of 1998. "Then I'm going home."

From the onset, that revelation on December 13, 1996 was met with a raised eyebrow, as if another campaign would soon follow. As far back as 1975, in his first term as lieutenant governor, he talked about leaving it all behind and going back to the mountains and teach. He had said he'd be home in Young Harris after one term as governor. According to his tally in the car, Miller had been on the ballot in Georgia twenty-two times—counting primaries, runoffs and general elections—more than any other person who has served in the executive branch. As the GPTV tape was running, he said he expected both friends and enemies to be skeptical about what he was saying because, "Everyone thinks it's hard for Zell to pass up an election." And it has been difficult. He has been a public servant during parts of five decades. "I love the chase and I love the idea of making a race, and no one has loved being governor more than I have. I enjoy coming to work, but there comes a time to pass the torch and that time has come for me."

His 1997 State of the State address followed a few weeks after that show was broadcast and after the news stories that followed. Standing in the House Chambers with the room packed with familiar faces, he was reflective. "I am now in the late autumn of my political career, my administration, and my life. It is a time when one reflects and thinks seriously about what is really important, what really matters." What mattered in the forty days of governing that followed was that old legislative process he had enjoyed since that idealistic professor with a flattop and a suitcase full of ideas first walked into the Georgia capitol. The stars in his eyes could still twinkle and the engine could still crank. Miller was Miller. He didn't stay on the sideline living up to the line he seemed to enjoy, the observation that he would not be a lame duck but the *same* duck.

He arrived as a teacher and he'll leave as a teacher. The packaging has changed, but he will leave with the same traits he arrived with. He has zigged and he has zagged because he was practical, as practical a politician as anyone who has played the game. He has never been understood, often because he didn't want to be. Sometimes it was part of his game to hike up the leg of his pants and show off his monogrammed boots. Sometimes it was a shield to use his best Towns County twang and roll out a clever mountain metaphor. Sometimes it was wise to quote Haggard and other times he might refer to Gershwin. Sometimes he was a person who explained the ballet of a double play and other times he could lecture an auditorium of college presidents about the genetic development of a child's brain before the child started to school.

Miller's is a story that twists and twirls like the road you take to the top of Brasstown Bald. He is the boy who never knew his father and then spent a lifetime chasing him. He is the boy proud that his mother could build a house but puzzled why she never sat on the porch with him like his friends' mothers did with them. He is the ten year old mountain boy with funny words who was so uncomfortable in school, he attended the Varsity instead of class. He was so near the streets that he stole Coca-Colas off a truck parked at a traffic light. He is the drunk in a county jail who didn't think he could live up to other people's expectations. He is the Marine with boot camp values who began to find out who he wanted to be. He is that state senator who was in a hurry, and he is the ambitious professor who thought he could take on a congressman and a president. He is the lieutenant governor, the man who fussed with Murphy, the man who by toppling Talmadge almost doomed himself. He is a two-term governor and all the things he accomplished in that office, many of them the things that the naive history teacher started when he came to town. He is a husband who doesn't hide his emotions as he says his biggest disappointment is that his wife never had the career she deserved. He is a grandfather who gets teary as he tells you that his twin grandsons drew pictures for his 65th birthday, and that one of their pieces of childish art put him in a picture with Washington and Lincoln. He is the friend who tells an aspiring president that his speeches are too long and later is invited to spend the night in Lincoln's Bedroom, not because he donated money to a campaign, but because he *saved* that campaign.

Yet he has consistently been depicted as a hillbilly intellectual who listens to hillbilly music, and that rankles him. Most reporters weren't interested in that other side. The weird, different colorful side was more interesting and much easier to write about. For every 100 articles on the cowboy boots/country–music Miller, there was one on this man who has written books, has a Master's degree, two years work on a Ph.D., and been a professor at four colleges and universities. He would not forsake his cowboy boots because he thought it would be giving in to the establishment. He was saying "Take me as I am. I'm not going to change for you. And don't look at how funny I talk, look at how good I can talk." The country music was how he grew up. He wore it like a chip on his shoulders for the elitists. The truth was, he also knew a lot about, and liked, classical music. Miss Edna Herren gave him a season ticket to the Atlanta Symphony when he was a student at Emory and he wrote her what he liked about each performance. As a young man, he had more classical records than country music records.

Paul Begala met Miller as an out-of-work consultant, helped elect him governor, and stayed around as a friend. "What can I say? I love the guy," he says. He acknowledges that Miller has not been understood, and that most of the journalism around him has often reflected a narrow view. "And some of that is because, like all great leaders, Zell understands the advantages that accrue from being underestimated. In terms of his character, his personal story is so very compelling, so Lincolnesque, that I think it would make a helluva movie—tragic and heroic and inspirational. The circumstances surrounding his birth, his upbringing in Young Harris, his first foray into the big city of Atlanta and subsequent tailspin, landing his ass in Parris Island and turning his life around forever. Not a bad yarn, I'd say."

To understand his career they will need to know the man who lived it, but historians won't look much at that yarn Begala is talking about. They will look at Miller's years of service, at what kind of Georgia he inherited and what kind of Georgia he leaves behind as he concludes an unprecedented twenty-four years as a member of the state's executive branch—eight of them as governor. And it will be an impressive resumé. His legacy of education will be noted—the HOPE Scholarship, the statewide PreKindergarten classes, the computers, the satellite dishes, and the improvement of the salaries and wages of teachers. His ability to help Georgia be a place where the nation and the world like to do business will be applauded. His contributions to the safety of the state will be recorded—the philosophy that after two strikes a criminal is out, the boot camps so unruly kids will have a place to stop for a moment and taste some discipline, the changes in DUI laws that will mean a grownup driver will no longer be able to plead no-contest and keep his license, and the zero tolerance for underage drivers who drink. His unmatched ability to manage and reduce government will not go overlooked, particularly the leadership he showed in dealing with the recession that came with his first oath of office. His compassion for people will not go unnoticed, especially his endless quest to take the sales tax off of items in a person's grocery cart.

Many of these things are products of his own experiences. They were a part of him when he arrived. But what has changed dramatically over the years is his style, the way he goes about both the practice of politics and the art of governing. The petulance is still there, but it has been tempered. The one-man-band still plays, but he has cautiously expanded his band to other players. The energy has always been there, but it has been better focused. The creativity is evident, but it has been sobered by practicality. The need to control has never left, but the demands of the office have forced him to give up a few. The political instincts have now been blended with data and opinion though he has remained a person.

Dick Pettys of the Associated Press has observed Miller longer than any active capitol reporter. He calls him a renaissance governor. "Miller encompasses the broad view of government, as intricate as Jimmy Carter; the global view of a George Busbee who let government run itself, who tinkers but doesn't meddle; the ability to deal with a budget the way Joe Frank Harris always had. He has the best qualities of his immediate predecessors. Miller is the master of the deal. He knows it. He studies it. It's his life. He thinks about it a lot and he has spent a lot of time thinking about it. He understands what motivates political people better than anyone."

Bill Shipp is another reporter who has followed most of Miller's time at the capitol. He describes Miller as a progressive and enlightened leader. "He is a guy who has been very creative and imaginative. He was a person who started out very much a populist, but has modified that stance so that the business community finally trusted him. He is a governor who has made contributions particularly to higher education and he has broken Georgia out of the mold, for better or worse, of being a Bible Belt state that was against everything. I don't believe he's a hillbilly. I think if you scratch Zell Miller you will find one of the more vain governors we've ever had. He's not comfortable with himself, not secure with himself. He's a man who when he gets out of bed every morning has to prove himself all over again that day. That's been behind the drive that's always been behind him."

Ken Edelstein has reported on Miller as the Atlanta Bureau reporter for the *Columbus Ledger-Enquirer* and more recently for *Creative Loafing,* a weekly news magazine in Atlanta. His specialty has been environmental reporting and Edelstein says Miller's record has been mixed, that the state has exploited its natural resources because of its economic success. "But even if you don't like what he did, you like the way he did it. He knows this state like a chess board and can see so many moves ahead of anyone else. He's a master at governing this state, the political genius of this century."

Former aide Keith Mason says Miller uses all of the tools at his disposal. "He understands the powers of the governor's office: the power of appointment; the power of the line item veto; the other discretionary tools that are available to him. He has had legislators and their wives and husbands over to the mansion for black-tie so they would feel special. He sometimes walks the halls at the capitol, just to be seen. He will go to a committee meeting if needs to. He'll have private meetings with a legislator and send them a message. Before he launches any major initiative, he thinks through all the facets necessary to build public support, whether it's a poll or a phone call to the newspaper editorial boards. He figures out the pressure points, public and private, and he uses them."

Wayne Garner was a member of the Senate when Miller was lieutenant governor, and more recently has served as the commissioner of the state's Department of Corrections. He was appointed to that job by Miller—a man he did not originally support for governor, going instead with his friend from the Senate, Roy Barnes. Garner remembers a conversation where Miller talked about them being alike. "You know Garner," he said, "you are like me in a lot of ways. You'll jump off into some empty swimming pools but you are never guilty of just bouncing up and down on the board wondering whether you should jump." "That's the way Zell is. He's never afraid to jump, to try something. To me, he's been a better governor than he was lieutenant governor. He's decisive. He's got that mean streak in him so he's not afraid of a fight. As far as running this state, he hasn't done any zigzagging. He's made decisions. I guess he always knew he'd make a great bride because he had been a bridesmaid all his life."

Steven Portch, the chancellor of the state's University System, hasn't known Miller as long as the others and most of their dealings have been over their shared passion for education. Portch thinks education is the key to understanding him. "It's really deep in his soul. I think there's still a wonderment in his eyes at times when he realizes where his life has led him and the role that education has played in that."

Former State Attorney General Mike Bowers has, as a Democrat and a Republican, known Miller and said his change of parties didn't change their relationship. At times Bowers has been at odds with the governor as well as joining him as a target of Tom Murphy. Bowers was reared in a rough part of Atlanta then went on to graduate from West Point, thus he shares the governor's drive to overcome a poor upbringing and his affinity for military structure. "If I tried to define myself, it would be my education. It was very removed from Georgia. That broadens you, deepens you, and gives you a different look at yourself. Mine was a military education. It teaches you to focus on merit—not who a person is but what they can produce. Zell can be defined by the Marine Corps. That's where he found the things I've just described. He came out with the idea that you judge a person by how well they can shoot, how much they carry, how well do they produce."

Mike Vollmer, called Miller's Mr. Fix-It, headed the Office of School Readiness which oversees the pre-school program. Previously, he directed the HOPE Scholarship program. One of the reasons he thinks Georgians accepted HOPE so readily was a trusting relationship with the governor, a trust that the proceeds from the lottery would be spent on education. "Our state did not put a premium on education, but Zell Miller has started changing that mindset. Now people are beginning to understand that education will be the key to our future."

Michael Thurmond was director of the Department of Family and Children's Services. When he was a member of the Georgia House, he fought aspects of Miller's tax exemption on food. As a compromise, then Governor Joe Frank Harris suggested a compromise and one would have exempted fresh seafood, but not fish in a can. Thurmond went to the well of the House with a lobster and a can of sardines, held them up and asked, "Are we supposed to be helping poor people." It was a scene Miller often reminds him of but is also indicative of his first views of Miller. "When I first got to know him, I thought he was unconcerned for poor people. But I'm also a historian, and I realized that mountain people have a different view of the poor. They're fiercely independent, suspicious of government. That made me understand him better. Later on, after I was in this job, we went on a statewide tour of DFCS offices. He was the first governor to ever visit a welfare office. I watched him that day. He talked to those people. He told them he knew what it was like to be poor, to grow up without a father. He became a human being."

Author Terry Kay says much of Miller's success can be traced to those roots that Thurmond mentions. Kay's novels deal with people and places he knew as a boy in North Georgia and, he says, so does Miller's politics. "'Look at me. I'm here. I'm willing to work. I have ability.' He wants those things proclaimed from the mountain tops, that he made it—against all odds. Whatever you think about his politics, he came from red clay furrows and a background he can't escape."

Court of Appeals Judge Ed Johnson has never really known of a time in his life when Miller wasn't part of Georgia politics. He met him when he was in college, worked on his first campaign for lieutenant governor as he finished law school, was a 28-year-old senator under him, was appointed to the Court of Appeals by Miller, and gave him the oath of office as lieutenant governor in 1982—the year Miller became the longest-serving person in that office. "For me, seeing him leave office is a poignant sadness. It's the end of an era for an old war horse that I still see as a young stallion." Johnson is one of many who graduated from Zell Miller University, a school without a building, but one that has taught many young people about government. His alumni are scattered throughout state government and some have moved into the national arena.

Sarah Eby-Ebersole and her husband Dan are among those graduates and she sees this nurturing of young talent as one of Miller's often unseen gifts. "That's part of the teacher personality of Zell Miller," she says. "To identify, to be able to see potential in young people, to sort that out and to say, OK, here is a young person who really has potential. He wants a person who will take the initiative to learn things, who will see a job as an opportunity to learn, as a learning experience. He has a knack, one of the gifts that make him a good teacher, of sensing who will grow."

Begala, a native Texan, laughingly counts himself as an alumnus of ZMU. He came to Georgia to work for the man. Now he comes back often to visit or join the governor on their annual outing to baseball's spring training. "Some politicians look down on hired help like me—especially high-dollar out-of-state consultants who get their face on TV a lot. They can't wait to win the race and never see them again. Not Zell. I've learned more from him— about life, politics and everything else—than from nearly anyone I've ever known. I mean that. He's had a big effect on my life. He has high standards, and demands that you meet them. He has true-blue populist instincts—not condescending, paternalistic views, nor arrogant, uncaring, callous opinions. He has played a major role in shaping my politics, beliefs, and my thoughts on strategy. The speech he gave back in 1991 to the North Carolina Democratic Party served as the strategic blueprint for my work on Harris Wofford's 1991 Senate election and Bill Clinton's 1992 election."

Martha Gilland is one of the many women who have played meaningful rolls in Miller's campaigns and in his administrations as lieutenant governor and governor. She sees that as a natural progression for a person who, when he talks about personal influences, starts with his mother, a teacher, and his wife. More than anything, she talks about his energy and how a person going to work for him better have a big dose of it. "He demands. But the man will not ask you to do anything he won't do. He gives 100 percent and if you don't you won't last long. He always knows what he wants. He's a stick-your-thumb-in-the-pie kind of guy. He wants to know about everything."

James Carville, Begala's former partner, says Miller is in one sense a simple man and in another a very complex man. "His exterior is easy to read, but he has a steelish, steelish interior. He is the ultimate sort of a guy who has learned to forgive but not forget. If he gets on something or someone, he can't let go."

Miller's experience with the media has been a love–hate experience. Reporters have seen him as a frustrated writer and he has looked at them as writers who frustrate. Early in his career, when he was first elected to the state senate, he was the one reporters sought out for quotes. That isn't unusual, since capitol reporters, as a means of survival, gravitate toward any legislator who can speak English instead of government jargon. He was identified as a progressive, so editorial writers took notice of some of his early bills. Even then, he benefited from comparison. Zell versus the Old Guard. Zell versus Landrum. Later it was Zell versus Murphy and Zell versus Talmadge. This put him in the role of the Good Guy, and his press reflected that though it is often unhealthy and always inflated. Like most politicians, his skin was thin, and coupled with a fuse that was short, there were explosions. Early in his career, he would particularly explode over anything he construed as a put-down of mountain people. Over the years, he came to detest the oft-repeated profile of him that deals with his boots instead of his abilities.

Miller describes this as a love-hate thing. "I admire writers. I hate lazy reporters, and often, like birds on a wire, one flies off to another line then here comes the rest, they're like cows in a pasture, all pointed in the same direction; they're scared to death of the race issue and are very timid in their writing about it but so is every-body else. They love "process." They will always write about it over policy. Most of them are very puzzled about budgetary and mone-tary issues. But, having said that, there's not a one over the years who I did not really like or who I thought regularly did me wrong. They didn't misquote me, just reported what I should never have said in the first place."

Miller's concern about his image is in contrast with his resis-tance to become a personality at the national level. He made the keynote address for Bill Clinton in 1992. He was recognized by the President at his State of the Union address in 1997 for his inspired creation of the HOPE Scholarships and closer to home Clinton came to Georgia and praised his friend at a speech in Augusta. "That's why I came to Georgia—because Governor Miller with the HOPE Scholarship, with the pre-kindergarten pro-gram, with the commitment to hook up all your schools to the Internet, with all the other initiatives, has turned the lights on, and America is seeing the light," Clinton said, harking back to Franklin Delano Roosevelt, the President who turned the lights on in Georgia in the thirties. "It is no secret that I am a great admirer of your governor. He spoke for me in New York in 1992 and talked about the house his mother built with her own hands. And with his thick Georgia accent, he pierced the deafest of ears who never heard anybody talk like that before. And no one who heard that speech will ever forget the vivid image of his mother crossing the creek with the rocks in her hands. Governor Miller is the son of a teacher. He became a teacher himself. He's given his life to bring-ing education to every child here. But he has something else that's very important and embodied in that Marine Corps pin he wears on his lapel every day. Whatever he decides to do, he does with the same conviction and intensity and doggedness that he showed when he was a member of the United States Marines. And I'm glad he's fighting for you and your future. And I'm grateful that he's fought for me."

Presidents are usually effusive about their praise of officials in whatever state they are visiting, but the mutual regard between Clinton and the Georgia governor extends beyond bouquets from a podium. There is a debt there—the kind politicians typically enjoy collecting. He did fight for Clinton, at a time and in a place that helped rebuild the engine that propelled the former Arkansas governor into the White House. It is one Miller has never collected. Around the time that Clinton unveiled his plans for a national scholarship plan at Princeton University, Miller shut that door. "Before he could even ask me or even think about it, I guess, I let him know that I had no desire to go to Washington. Having been a governor, he understood it. I reiterated it to him again in a long call he made to me the Sunday evening after the election in 1996. Carville wanted me to go by the way, and this was one time I didn't listen to James," Miller says.

Begala won't say what his advice was, invoking sort of a consultant/client relationship. "Advice I would have given Zell about a hypothetical Clinton cabinet job I'd rather keep confidential. Advice published in a book isn't useful," he says. "But I will say this: Zell Miller has run as large and complex an organization as I can imagine and he's run it efficiently and effectively. His expertise in education and the environment are especially impressive. I don't know if he'd be willing to play the Washington game, however— the sucking-up and grandstanding so common in that city. Then again, I think a lot of that stuff is posturing anyway and plenty of people in Washington succeed remarkably without succumbing to that nonsense—Dick Riley for one. So, yes, I think Zell would have done a terrific job in the cabinet. What I won't discuss is whether the President inquired about such an eventuality."

The fact that such discussions were held indicates the depth of respect Miller has yet his national profile hardly exists—at least not among the national media. He may get a phone call on an educational issue or on his views on crime, but isn't on the list when the topic is national politics. This isn't surprising since Miller has consistently refused national appearances, other than the 1992 keynote address. While other governors openly lobby for such dates, Miller for years has consistently turned down the opportunity. He has done *Face the Nation, Nightline,* and the *The Capitol Gang,* but it was only when he thought he could promote Clinton or Georgia's advances in education. When the National Governor's Conference is being held, his peers go in days in advance and make themselves available for the press or other appearances. Miller refuses to engage in the smoozing.

Begala says this is by design, that Miller doesn't play the national media game or the Washington power game. "But," he says, "among those who follow politics with passion and interest and intensity, Miller is something of a legend. His 1992 convention speech is part of a class at the University of California San Diego; his 1994 re-election when other Democratic governors were being defeated; his HOPE scholarship—that's the kind of stuff real pols, big-time politicos talk about with awe and envy."

Miller is unique among his political peers because he enjoys the chase *and* the office. Many political figures are one-dimensional. Some enjoy getting elected. Some enjoy the service. Miller has been adept at both. People around him say his line about enjoying coming to the office every day as governor is not a throw–away phrase, that he enjoys being governor. Even in the 1997 session, at a time when he could have been beginning his victory lap toward the finish line, he was aggressive with a long legislative agenda. Lame duck? No, the same duck.

He has evolved into a chief executive who leads more than he persuades. He works hard, but he always worked hard. He has good ideas, but they were there all the time. Steve Wrigley is Miller's right arm, his chief of staff and his confidante. They talk dozens of times a day and every evening on the phone whether there's a reason or not. Wrigley is close to Miller, but left over from his quest for a Ph.D. is an analytical approach that allows him to be as detached as someone can be in an office at the back door of your boss's office. Wrigley believes it was a matter of meeting a challenge. "Frankly, you don't have the opportunity to display these things as lieutenant governor or any lesser office. The challenges just aren't there. It's natural that you wonder what it will be like when it's you, when you're put in the game as the quarterback. And for him, this office has just fit. He's very, very good at it. He came into office at a difficult time financially, and without any hesitation on his part tackled everything that came. People claimed he used to fly by the seat of his pants and at a point in his career, he did. My theory is that that was also an institutional thing. Being lieutenant governor just wasn't enough for him; you don't set the agenda in that office, and he's more comfortable at setting the agenda. In that situation, he might not have been as disciplined, deliberate, and careful as he naturally is. I didn't work for him in the seventies and eighties, but my evaluation is that his MO has changed since the beginning of '89 or '90. I admire a man who can reach a little higher and is willing to tweak some things in the way he does things in order to operate at a higher level," says Wrigley, putting his boss on the political couch.

Overlooked in the assumption that Miller is distant and aloof are the personal traits that are also part of his leadership. Mary Beazley has worked around the state capitol since the days when Miller was a state senator and has worked for him since he was lieutenant governor. She's been there consistently except for four years when she worked for Carter at the White House. She says that he has always been "his own think tank." She also talks about the family atmosphere, how she isn't part of his administration or his staff—she's part of his family. Toni Brown, his scheduler, has been with him eleven years and she gets emotional when she tells about the governor coming to *her* Christmas party. Two years ago, he gave her a Christmas card and talked about their common interest in the Braves and in baseball. In addition to the message, there was an invitation and a plane ticket so she could join Miller,

Carville, Begala, Wrigley, and friends on their jaunt to spring training.

Wayne Garner summarizes all of this by saying that Miller is blessed with "good funeral etiquette," which to a former funeral director like the corrections chief is vitally important. Down South, you go to weddings and funerals and good etiquette might also involve a nice floral display and a dish of fried chicken delivered to the family home. Garner tells of the death of his own father and how Zell and Shirley Miller came early and stayed late at the funeral home the night before the burial. "That meant a lot to me. That was all he needed to do," Garner says. "But the next day at the funeral, there he was, on the front row." Garner remembers the burial of long-time Miller aide Cap Hicks and how Miller gave a moving, personal eulogy.

Eulogies aren't part of that basic etiquette, but they are for Miller. He tried to get through a storm to speak at former Lt. Gov. Peter Zack Geer's services. College friends talk about the words he said for his mentor and teacher, Miss Edna Herren. At a Greene County memorial for baseball great Mickey Mantle, Miller remembered visiting No. 7 not long before he died of liver cancer. Mantle shook his head about the muscle bound legs that could get to first base faster than a sprinter had faded away. "Look at those wheels," he said to Miller.

People closest to Miller remember the personal tribute he gave—in the rain—when Charlie Jenkins died. He was the father of United States Congressman Ed Jenkins and two other sons. Jenkins, Miller said, "was a true mountain man, 100 percent authentic, the genuine article." He also played and coached the game of baseball. "When it comes to baseball legends, when it comes to boyhood heroes, it is not a Mantle or an Aaron that touches my soul and sends shivers of excitement up and down my spine. No, my boyhood heroes were not named Mickey or Willie or Babe. They were named Quentin and Hoyle, Tom and Skud, Arnold, and Charlie."

These personal things in his life that are as much a part of the legacy Zell Miller leaves behind as the accomplishments of his two administrations and the decades he has spent in public office. These things were the foundation of a political leader whose road to power took so many turns. There is a serendipitous aura about his life in the mountains without a father, about the troubled kid cutting school and stealing Cokes, about the rebellion against the plan others had for his life and about his turnaround in the Marines. Those are old events, but as an adult, every incident in his political career served a purpose, every one prepared him, redirected him and pushed him toward one job—governor of Georgia.

Carville didn't know him well until 1988, but he suspects the Miller he knows has come back to himself. "The Zell Miller you see as governor of Georgia is pretty close to what he wants to be. If he had been elected in 1978, he wouldn't be nowhere near as good a governor as he is now. I doubt there has ever been a governor anywhere as prepared as he was." "I believe Zell truly was destined to be governor," Begala says. Miller has been governor at a time of transition. This is fitting since he got into the game during a period of other changes—most of them dealing with segregation and the urgency to keep Georgia schools open. He will be judged as a governor against different standards than those who served in the past, a past that always began with race. Race was the definer. It defined Herman Talmadge, Ernest Vandiver, even Jimmy Carter. Certainly it is the consuming memory of Lester Maddox. After Carter, governors acted from a new agenda, one where race was not dominant. Neither George Busbee nor Joe Frank Harris will be judged because of how they played the race card. It is the same around the South. The past had George Wallace, Ross Barnett, and Orval Faubus. The present has had Lamar Alexander, Richard Riley, and Bill Clinton. This generation of leaders has looked to education and economic development—as has Zell Miller who followed them.

Dr. Dan Carter, a professor of history at Emory University says Georgia has been fortunate that race was never as defining as it was in Alabama. Carter, who is well versed in the history of Georgia's neighbor, wrote *Politics of Rage,* an acclaimed biography of George Wallace. "In Alabama, the Big Mules had their faces turned to the

19th Century and would not bend. Georgia had an urban business class that did not want the things to happen here that happened in Alabama or Mississippi. They found a dignified retreat because there were people who wanted to do the right thing," says Carter, who describes Georgia's history of progressive governors—a lineage that includes Miller.

"He goes back to an Ellis Arnall. Zell sees his roots in the progressive tradition. The Hoke Smiths, the others who were flawed by racism but wanted to improve education and the road system. Arnall and E. D. Rivers set the standard for modern governors who wanted to keep an optimistic outlook, one where you talk about your problems with a can-do manner," Carter says.

James Cook wrote his book on Georgia governors in 1995, just as Miller's second term was beginning. In *The Governors of Georgia, 1754-1995*, the Floyd College history professor writes: "With a booming economy and the state lottery providing unprecedented revenue, Miller is poised at the beginning of his second term to achieve his goal of becoming 'Georgia's education governor' and may become one of the most influential governors in the state's history." In an interview two years later, Cook hadn't altered that opinion. "He is one of the most influential. He has set the agenda for this state for years to come," he says. "Miller has always been committed to education. He is a teacher, who understands the necessity of education if Georgia is to have its place in modern society. The lottery brought HOPE and he is paying teachers more money at a time when others have had doubts."

Carl Sanders was another member of that progressive tradition. He has known Miller since he arrived at the capitol as a freshman senator. Sanders praises Miller's willingness to take risks. "I give Zell high marks for having courage and a willingness to take on controversial issues. I was really surprised when he made the lottery the centerpiece of his first campaign, but he got elected on it. Frankly, I think he has surprised many people with how well he has administered the office of governor and I think Zell will go down in history as one of the great governors of Georgia."

Because he is a wire service reporter, Dick Pettys of the Associated Press draws little attention. As the primary political writer for AP in Atlanta, he cranks out the news like a machine. He has been reporting on Miller since he was with *The Gainesville News* and Miller was running for Congress, Pettys is a storehouse of Miller anecdotes. Asked for his assessment of Miller, Pettys doesn't pause. "He is the best governor I've seen. He gets what he wants. He understands government and he understands politics. He ain't perfect, but he's damn good."

But what will history say about Zell Miller?

Miller's answer is the same as Winston Churchill's: he will take care of the history by writing it himself. He is at work on a pictorial scrapbook of his time as governor, a compilation of speeches he has delivered while he's been in public life, and another book that will offer his views on Southern governors who have made a difference. So while people who heard what Miller said to Bill Nigut at the end of 1996 may have pictured him sitting in a rocking chair and looking out the mountains, that is not his forecast for himself. "The decision not to run was the easiest political decision I've ever made, no joking. People who imagine me sitting in a rocking chair simply don't understand. I don't have any intention of sitting on a porch in a rocker. I may be sitting in the stands watching my grandsons play baseball or watching the Young Harris College team play. I plan to write, speak, and teach—at Young Harris, and probably some other places," Miller says.

It is a decision that seems to have made him more peaceful. But before it was made there were other considerations to consider. Popular opinion was that in 1998 he would run against Paul Coverdell for the United States Senate. Coverdell defeated Democrat Wyche Fowler who had ended the brief career of Mack Mattingly—the man who sent Herman Talmadge back to Lovejoy. After Coverdell's election, some state Republicans whispered that if they had known Fowler didn't want to get reelected they would have run a stronger candidate. He has grown, and he is now the state's senior senator. But being a Senator no longer has the appeal it once held for Miller. After being in an office where there is action and challenge, the lingering debates of Washington were not enticing and, therefore, ruling out a run against Coverdell in 1998 came quickly. Returning to the lieutenant governor's office, however, was a decision he thought about at much greater length.

As the 1997 General Assembly drew to a close, Miller followed the tradition of the past and made courtesy calls on both the House and the Senate. When he mounted the podium in the Senate, it felt natural, the old chamber looked good to him. "This will always be my home," he told the senators.

It is obvious when you talk with them, that both Zell and Shirley relish the thought of being with their growing brood which now includes Murphy and Susan, Matt and Katie, grandchildren: teenager Justin and the twins Bryan and Andrew, age nine. Their oldest grandchild, Asia is married to Shane Martin and is mother to the great-grandsons Jacob and Joshua.

Wistfully, Miller talks about how that life will be. He says he will always vote and be interested in current political matters and that if candidates come through Towns County, he will take them to the coffee shop. The only thing that would bring him out of the bleachers would be for a future politician to tamper with the lottery or with the HOPE Scholarship or pre-kindergarten programs.

"I doubt anybody will ever do away with the lottery or with HOPE," Miller says. "My concern is that some well-meaning person will come up with another program that sounds good. Then another and another until HOPE and pre-K are diluted or narrowed. I also fear politicians will try and take control of the lottery and the history of state lotteries is that as they become politicized, they fail." Miller has seen enough guards change to know there are right ways and wrong ways to leave office. He greatly admires the way Joe Frank Harris made a new life away from the capitol. "I also admire the way he has never second-guessed me even though I'm sure he's wanted to. I hope I can show that kind of graciousness." On his mind more than a concern about things such as that is a desire to welcome Young Harris freshmen to Political Science 101.

Marti Fullerton and Hank Huckaby remember that class, but it will be different for the next group of students who see Miller walk into a room and scratch his outline out on a chalk board. The core hasn't changed. There is the same number of people in Congress. The federal government still has a system of checks and balances and there are still the same branches in that government. It is the attitude about that government that has changed since the days of Fullerton and Huckaby. "When I was teaching it in the 1960s, political figures were heroes. People looked at them favorably and with honor. It was the time of John F. Kennedy. Then, the more we saw them on TV, the more we came to see that they weren't stars. They were like us, with all our human failures. I worry about that cynicism and the growing numbers of people who distrust government and the people who serve in government—as if government were something bad and threatening. I hope I can restore some faith," he says.

Begala laughs at the thought of Miller being retired. Here is a political leader that the Texas political consultant contends has done more to advance and improve public education than anyone since Horace Mann ... and he's teaching Poly Sci 101. "I'm not altogether convinced Miller will never be a candidate in the future," he says. "I think one day Young Harris may have the most aggressive coach in college baseball. Really, I figure one day I'll get a call saying, 'I'm running for mayor of Young Harris. Can you help me?' " On a serious note, Begala hopes Miller will finally jump into the national spotlight and teach Democrats how to run, win and govern. "I'd like him to go on the lecture circuit, but I also want him to teach, coach baseball, and inspire another generation of kids."

Zell Miller laughs at the people who call themselves close friends of his in one sentence, and then question whether or not he can be happy after he packs up his books on West Paces Ferry Road. "No matter what they say, they really don't know me. Young Harris has always been at the center of my soul. He knows his history. He knows people's memory include his promise of a single term as governor and the other times he gave into the urge to be part of the chase. But this time he is 66 years old, with grandchildren and great-grandchildren to scold when they don't get down on a ground ball or when they don't know the significance of an important date in the history books. There's also Young Harris and those mountains.

"What some of those fail to understand is that I have always known where I came from and where I was going back to. There has never been any other thought in the equation—for me or for Shirley. Really, we have never left Young Harris. When my mother was living, we were there three or four times a week. Shirley was there full-time during most of the 1980s and I joined her sometime every week. It's where our children and grandchildren are. We're going home."

When he does, he'll be back in that rock house with the handprints in the cement, the one Birdie Miller built. He'll teach on the same campus where Grady Miller encouraged a generation that has almost passed away to get under the big tent. They're gone, but Zell Miller says he's coming home. He's led the tenth largest state in the nation, managed a budget larger than most fortune 500 companies, counseled the leader of the free world, met with U.S.S.R. foreign minister Eduard Shevardnadze in Moscow, had breakfast with Archbishop Desmond Tutu in Cape Town, South Africa, and delivered a critically acclaimed speech to thirty million viewers, but inside he is that mountain kid who was never more comfortable than when he was where he could go to a window and see those familiar mountains. People back home will be glad to see him, as Bettye Sellers, a retired Young Harris professor says, "He's a politician, but he's been our politician."

And what about those parents who passed on those lofty expectations? What would Birdie say about her only son? "Birdie would be pleased in many ways. She'd like HOPE and PreK. The lottery would not have bothered her at all and she would have liked the toughness on crime and welfare reform. She believed in paying your own way. But, really, if she were alive, she'd be paying more attention to those grandkids and great grandchildren than me. She believed in molding young lives and getting them started off right."

When he comes home, he'll be old enough to qualify for Social Security, looking back on one career and renewing another. Will this mean he has finally caught up with the ghost of Grady Miller?

"Perhaps not. I have been more successful than he was in politics, true, but I lived a lot longer than he did. If I had died at age forty like he did, I would never have lived to be elected lieutenant governor—much less governor. So maybe a better politician, but a better man, a better person—never!"

There are milestones left to pass before Zell Miller sits in the bleachers. The final legislative session. The final speeches. The final ceremonies and the final signature as governor of Georgia. His plans are made. So are Shirley Miller's.

Only as she walked a guest to the upstairs elevator at the Governor's Mansion she paused to look at large color photograph that is matted and framed and hangs next to the elevator door. It is Zell and Shirley, cramped into the back of a small airplane. Moments after the picture was taken, they would be taking off from a small airstrip in Blairsville, not far from home. It was Election Day 1994. It was cool and they were wearing sweaters. Stuck to their sweaters were those little "I Have Voted" stickers people are given after they have turned in their ballots and cast their votes.

Pointing to those stickers, she smiled.

"That was the last time I voted for Zell. I think."

AUTHOR'S NOTES

Chapter 1

When State Court of Appeals Judge Ed Johnson described the scene in Birdie Miller's room at the Hiawassee, Georgia nursing home his memories were both vivid and emotional. They underscored the effect this mountain woman had on the people who met her. Descriptions of Grady Miller's death came primarily from the Enotah Echoes, the school newspaper at Young Harris College. Other information on Grady and Birdie Miller came from *Young Harris College: Its Development, Resources and Programs* by Robert P. Andress, *Centennial Chronicle: Young Harris College, 1886-1986* by Louisa Franklin and Jeffrey S. Moody and from a Master's Thesis by Joseph M. Brogdon on the history of the college. Bert Lance shared his own recollections and loaned a copy of his late father Thomas Jackson Lance's memoirs, *The Education of a Georgia Mountain Man.* He also shared an unpublished manuscript written by his father entitled "M. D. Collins: A Great Man." T. J. Lance's *History of Young L. G. Harris College* was also helpful. The works of poet Byron Herbert Reece offer a literary glimpse at Choestoe, the mountain settlement that spawned the generation of Grady Miller and the people around him. Raymond A. Cook's *Mountain Singer: The Life and the Legacy of Byron Herbert Reece* can help an outsider better understand the poet and the region. Zell Miller's *Mountains*

Within Me brings many of these things into context. And, as they would throughout this book, the personal conversations and interviews with Zell Miller were the road map for all of this information.

Chapter 2

Novelist Terry Kay may be a hill person, but he understands the mountains and its people. His observations were pointed, but equally important was the support he offered on a Saturday morning when the keyboard was silent. His brother, the Reverend John Kay, also is gifted with eye and ear. He was also able to describe the people and places. Perhaps the best source of traditional journalistic reporting on this region comes from Ralph McGill, the late editor of *The Atlanta Constitution* and a frequent visitor to Young Harris. His columns and books are filled with memories of the Georgia mountains. Bob Richardson of the Duckworth Libraries at Young Harris College can guide a lost researcher through a variety of sources. Foremost are the various histories of the college that were mentioned in the notes for Chapter 1. Some of the essays in *The New Georgia Guide* also paint a good picture of this remote area of the state.

Chapter 3

Zell Miller's own memories of wartime Atlanta, The Varsity, and the old ball park on Ponce de Leon Avenue were better than any other resources available. Gordon Muir of The Varsity offered official documentation on that historic drive-in, but a pair of amateur Varsity historians, Richard and Casey Thomason of Columbus, kicked in with information that would make you thirst for a large PC.

Chapter 4

Zell and Shirley Miller described their old teacher well. Not that I needed anyone to help me remember Edna Herren. She had helped Zell Miller be governor when she taught him at Young Harris College. She had sent me to remedial English when she was my instructor in freshman English at Georgia State University. Hilda Dyches was Miss Herren's seat mate at GSU basketball games and was my speech teacher. She offered personal memories of this teacher who was a mentor to so many. O. V. Lewis, still an accounting teacher at Young Harris, explained how the college and the village interacts. And when it came time to describe the importance of debate on the mountain campus, former United States Congressman Jack Brinkley and legendary Atlanta TV weatherman Guy Sharpe shared memories that were amazingly fresh. Bob Short, who talks about as much as he used to shoot the basketball, recalled in an entertaining manner the role sports played in their lives long before he and Miller moved into politics.

Chapter 5

Anyone who wants to understand the impact of the Marine Corps on Zell Miller need only read his own words in *Corps Values: Everything You Need to Know I Learned in the Marines*. Understand the Marines and you understand so much about Miller. Shirley Carver Miller came into his life during this period and her influence should not be overlooked. The interviews she gave for this chapter and the ones that followed were helpful. George Berry, now an Atlanta business leader but in the past a youngster whose aunts and uncles were neighbors of Birdie Miller, offered a look at his old friend that was as frank as the governor's himself. Hank Huckaby and Marti Pingree Fullerton registered for a class with Miller at Young Harris and still see him as their teacher and friend. Their support cannot be measured.

Chapter 6

The Reverend Don Harp was a baseball player at Young Harris and he described the time when their coach first became a politician. Like others, Harp continues to come in and out of Miller's life. Years later, when the Methodist preacher's image was seen in a political ad that called for passage of the state lottery, their friendship was attacked, but the pastor continued to support his former teacher and coach. Agriculture Commissioner Tommy Irvin tried to explain the details of mountain politics and how he has been both a supporter and opponent of his mountain neighbor.

Chapter 7

Understanding the dynamics of 1961 is difficult without reliving the circumstances and the chronology. This was accomplished by reading through microfilms of the newspapers in Atlanta, Macon and Columbus leading up to the January gavel of the Georgia General Assembly. Calvin Trillin's *An Education in Georgia* was a source for the events on the campus of the University of Georgia—events that shaped the daily agenda of the Georgia House and Senate in Atlanta. *The Stem of Jesse* (Mercer University Press) by Will Campbell tells the story of integration at Mercer University and introduces the personality of Judge William Bootle, a key jurist of that era. Again, various writings of Ralph McGill were helpful. The insightful memories of former Governor Carl Sanders and former legislators Hamilton McWhorter, Bob Smalley and Tommy Irvin described Miller when he first arrived at the State Capitol. Former Atlanta newspaper reporters Bill Shipp, Sam Hopkins, and Billy Winn gave a view of Georgia politics from the press gallery.

Chapter 8

Old newspaper accounts were the primary source of description for this volatile session of the Georgia Legislature. Reading those reports decades later is a reminder how important the role of reporters such as Celestine Sibley really were. Description and context such as hers and others are missing from today's political pages. Readers are being shortchanged and so is the political process. The book *Atlanta Rising* (Longstreet) by Frederick Allen, put many of the events of this era into perspective. So did the recollections of the former legislators already cited.

Chapter 9

The 1964 race for Phil Landrum's congressional seat is history, but to Phil Gailey it was yesterday. When he described the visit of

Lyndon Johnson to the town square in Gainesville he still had the college passion he had that day as LBJ spoke on behalf of Landrum. Gailey is now editor of editorials for *The St. Petersburg Times.* In 1964, Gailey, Hank Huckaby and Marti Fullerton were volunteers for Zell Miller's congressional campaign. Their memories brought back to life this colorful campaign. Country music performer Bill Anderson was also part of that era, helping the young candidate try and attract a crowd. He also remembered the songs he sang and the unknown singer he recommended to Miller.

Chapter 10

When he first entered politics, Zell Miller's friends and staff members began to compile large scrapbooks. They contain newspaper and magazine clippings on him from around the state and nation. They were valuable resources for the chapters that follow. Many of the articles found in these scrapbooks were not cited as to day and date, but nevertheless document what was being written and said about Miller. Georgia Court of Appeals Judge Ed Johnson was a campaign volunteer during Miller's first race for lieutenant governor and he shared valuable memories. Over the years, I have had many opportunities to talk with former Governor Lester Maddox and his colorful recollections, as usual, added a flavor to the times.

Chapter 11

Listening to the interview I had conducted with Speaker of the House Tom Murphy, it seemed the old had been buried and the new was harmony. Word had gotten out around the state captiol that I had interviewed Murphy and Zell Miller's staff wanted to know what had been said. That afternoon, with the tape from the Murphy interview still in the recorder, I noticed the commotion in the halls outside the House. People were shoulder to shoulder, looking up at the mounted televisions. Murphy was in the well. He was blistering the governor. The old was new again. Veteran observers around the capitol don't get excited about such events. Reporters such as Dick Pettys of the Associated Press have seen them before. Pettys, Bill Shipp and Frederick Allen noted the similarities between the two men. Murphy ally Larry Walker shared that same observation. Walker offered candid comments on the two men as did First Lady Shirley Miller who shares a surprising mutual fondness with the Speaker.

Chapter 12

Through the research on this chapter describing the relationship of Herman Talmadge and Zell Miller, the name of Ovid Davis consistently was mentioned. Davis was an official with Coca-Cola who for years had been a powerful lobbyist for the soft drink company. He was close to Talmadge and had reached out to Miller after the two candidates had tried to pick up the pieces after their bloody race for the United States Senate. Everyone said I needed to talk to Davis and before Christmas in 1996 I left several messages on his answering machine. I talked to his wife twice in the spring of 1997 and intended to get back to him later. In April of 1997, I read that Ovid Davis was dead. A lot of information died with him—which I regret. Thankfully, Rogers Wade was able to recreate much of that information. Wade is Talmadge's former administrative assistant. It was he who shared months before that Miller was going to name a stretch of Highway 41 for his former opponent. That ceremony validated feelings that had been described to me and it was there that the two political legends reached out to one another after years of animosity. Wade was an important resource for this chapter as was Talmadge's autobiography—*Talmadge: A Political Legacy, A Politician's Life*. To fully understand the rancor between Miller and Talmadge, you must know about E. D. Rivers. Information about Rivers was found in William Anderson's book on Eugene Talmadge—*The Wild Man from Sugar Creek* and in James F. Cook's *The Governors of Georgia* (Mercer University Press). It is also interesting to read Zell Miller's own words in his University of Georgia thesis, "The Administration of E.D. Rivers as Governor of Georgia." As for the Senate race between Miller and Talmadge, a search through the microfilm of the *Atlanta Constitution* was vital as were the surprising memories of Bill Shipp and Frederick Allen, the two lead reporters on the campaign. Norman Underwood, who was also a candidate in the race, described the evolution of "Zig Zag Zell," a slogan that still haunts Miller. Finally, there was the opportunity to see and hear the feelings of Talmadge himself and to hear the kind words that many thought would never come.

Chapter 13

James Carville was an experience and Paul Begala was an encouragement. My interview with Carville was as advertised. Nancy Stubbs, a Mercer University secretary who transcribed my tapes, noticed that he never finished a thought. He didn't. But he still showed needed insight into the subject. As for Begala, we couldn't schedule an appropriate time for an interview so I sent him questions by FAX and he returned his answers the same way. His answer was nine single-spaced pages and every answer was useful. It was during this time in the research that the value and knowledge of Steve Wrigley became evident. He is Zell Miller's alter ego. In many areas, the same can be said for Keith Mason, who was part of Miller's inner circle from the time he joined his campaign for lieutenant governor as a high school student. Direct quotes from them are sprinkled through this and other chapters, but their observations were just as important as the words found between quotation marks.

Chapter 14

In 1988, I worked out of the Knight-Ridder Newspapers bureau at the Democratic National Convention in Atlanta. I was writing a daily column for the *Columbus Ledger-Enquirer* and on the way to the World Congress Center one morning I saw Lester Maddox on the sidewalk waving at cars. I had known of Maddox since my folks used to take me to the Pickrick for after-church fried chicken. Now, pedestrians were passing him by and back at the bureau people I told about it didn't know who Maddox was either. The editors did. They put my column out on the wire and it was used by newspapers around the country. Next year, it won an award from the Georgia Press Association. It is peculiar that among so many non descript governors, Lester Maddox continues to draw attention. James F. Cook's book *Governors of Georgia,* along with an interview with the Floyd College history professor, was a needed resource for this chapter which was an essay on the office of governor in the state. University of Mississippi historian Charles Reagan Wilson's book, *Judge & Grace in Dixie: Southern Faiths from Faulkner to Elvis* (University of Georgia Press), offered a firm foundation for the idea that Southerners put their heroes on a pedestal—especially their politicians and their football coaches. Past conversations with United States District Judge J. Robert Elliott of Columbus and Atlanta advertising executive George Goodwin gave me perspective on the three governors fiasco and previous conversations with Howard "Bo" Callaway of Pine Mountain and Maddox were the basis for many of the descriptions surrounding their gubernatorial campaign. My journalistic experiences with Jimmy Carter—as governor, president and neighbor—were also helpful.

Chapter 15

Steve Wrigley and Keith Mason were there, so their memory was extremely useful. So was Hank Huckaby's diary. He kept those notes during the early days of Zell Miller's first administration. Since his old student was at the forefront of the budget crisis, his words proved very important. Atlanta real estate developer Tom Cousins confirmed that he was a lukewarm supporter of Miller in the beginning but that the manner in which the new governor handled the budget shortages was impressive and helped solidify his future support of Miller. Sarah Eby-Ebersole helped locate many of the speeches she and Miller crafted on the budget situation and they showed the evolution of the issue and the governor's attempts to deal with the crisis.

Chapter 16

An interview with Denmark Groover is like leafing through a Georgia history book. He talked about the 1961 political season and he talked about 1991, when passage of the lottery legislation was at issue. Groover, according to Zell Miller, was the man who saved the lottery. When the lottery was in place, it was Mike Vollmer who directed the HOPE Scholarship program. His observations about HOPE and the Pre-Kindergarten program were looks into two of Miller's lasting legacies. As an anecdote, Vollmer's story about Miller writing a personal message to children who read *The Little Engine That Could* may be as descriptive as any other about Miller's obsession with learning. If an examination of education in Georgia is being undertaken, an interview with University Chancellor Steven Portch is important. He praised HOPE Scholarships but his description of his first meeting with the governor is a clue to the makeup of both men. Jim Blanchard's views about Miller and education were covered by *Georgia Trend* when the magazine named the Columbus banker its "Man of the Year" for 1997.

Chapter 17

When former State Senator Pete Robinson told me that state troopers had to trail his children to elementary school, I understood the flag issue at a different level than ever before. I had lived through Zell Miller's attempt to change the state flag. Pete Robinson and Wayne Garner had survived it. Their interviews along with the detached manner in which Michael Thurmond described the issue are important observations about what happened during that volatile period. Former Columbus Mayor Frank Martin's memory of the meeting Miller had with leaders from around the state portrayed how alone the governor was in the issue. Again, it was left to an interview with former legislator Denmark Groover to put it into historical perspective.

Chapter 18

At issue in this chapter was solidifying the facts that surround the friendship of Zell Miller and Bill Clinton. Was this only a figment of Georgia's imagination or has Miller really been a key player in Clinton's election and his platform? It soon became evident that Miller's role was a major one—going far beyond the keynote speech he made at Madison Square Garden in 1992. Keith Mason and Steve Wrigley told how Miller got to know Bill Clinton so well. Interviews with James Carville and Paul Begala solidified the story of that relationship. Just after finishing this chapter, I came in the middle of a television documentary on the Clinton-Bush campaign. The eccentric Carville emerged as the star of the drama. The histrionics I saw on the screen brought back descriptions Wrigley had shared about Carville. Late in the show, the numbers were rolling in and it was apparent that Clinton was about to be elected. Results from Georgia came in along with another key state. Looking at the Georgia figures, Carville stopped what he was doing. "Damn, I gotta call Zell," he said. That episode confirmed what others had said. As for his keynote address speech, the memories that his staff members carry with them about it are more effusive than their boss carries. An interview with Martha Gilland proved that as she told the story of how the "Give 'Em Hell, Zell" signs got to Madison Square Garden. And when former press secretary Chuck Reece was asked for his memories, he took the time to send along a descriptive memo. The most disappointing aspect of this chapter and the effort to tell this story was the fact that Bill Clinton did not contribute. At the advice of Carville and Begala, I sent a FAX to the White House with detailed questions. The request to the president made it as far as the press secretary's office. But unfortunately, Clinton never responded.

Chapter 19

State Representative Calvin Smyre's descriptions of what happened during Zell Miller's second campaign for governor were insightful. His words captured how important that race was to Miller and the Democratic Party—in Georgia and nationwide. Anyone looking at his decision to seek a second term must begin their conversation with Shirley Miller. She has always been there. The information provided by Norman Underwood gave another side to the Miller Administration in an area that has often gone unreported. On the fourth anniversary of HOPE, I talked with a number of college graduates who had gone to college all four years on lottery funds. Maggie Hodge of Pine Mountain was one. She, like the others, is grateful—but not nearly as grateful as the parents.

Chapter 20

Watching a videotape of Zell Miller's interview with Bill Nigut when he announced his plans to go back to teaching after he leaves the governor's office is a lesson in Miller and in body language. He was so prepared and seemed so pleased that he had anticipated the WSB-TV reporter's question. The months that have followed that interview have been filled with rumors about his plans – most revolving around Paul Coverdell's seat in the United States Senate. Most of this chapter is based on conclusions drawn from interviews that have been cited previously.

BIBLIOGRAPHY

Books

Allen, Frederick. *Atlanta Rising: The Invention of an International City.* Atlanta: Longstreet Press, 1996.

Anderson, William. *The Wild Man From Sugar Creek: The Political Career of Eugene Talmadge.* Baton Rouge: Louisiana State University Press, 1975.

Arnall, Ellis Gibbs. *The Shore Dimly Seen.* New York and Philadelphia: J.B. Lippincott Company, 1946.

Bartley, Numan V. *The Creation of Modern Georgia,* Second Edition. Athens: University of Georgia Press, 1990.

Bass, Jack and Walter DeVries. *The Transformation of Southern Politics: Social Change and Political Consequences Since 1945.* New York: Basic Books, 1976.

Bowles, Billy and Tyson, Remer. *They Love a Man in the Country: Saints and Sinners in the South.* Atlanta: Peachtree Publishers, 1989.

Bryan, Ferald. *Henry Grady or Tom Watson? The Rhetorical Struggle for the New South, 1880-1890.* Macon: Mercer University Press, 1994.

Bunnen, Lucinda and Coxe, Frankie. *Movers and Shakers in Georgia.* New York: Simon and Schuster, 1978.

Campbell, Will. *The Stem of Jesse: The Costs of Community at a 1960s Southern School.* Macon: Mercer University Press, 1995.

Carter, Jimmy. *Turning Point: A Candidate, A State and A Nation Come of Age.* New York: Times Books, Random House, 1992.

Carter, Jimmy. *Why Not the Best?* Nashville: Broadman Press, 1975.

Cleland, Max. *Strong at the Broken Places.* Atlanta: Cherokee Publishing Company, 1989.

Cook James F. *Carl Sanders: Spokesman of the New South.* Macon: Mercer University Press, 1993.

Cook, James F. *The Governors of Georgia, 1754-1995.* Macon: Mercer University Press, 1995.

Cook, Raymond A. *Mountain Singer: The Life and the Legacy of Byron Herbert Reece.* Atlanta: Cherokee Publishing Company, 1980.

Egerton, John. *The Americanization of Dixie.* New York: Harper & Row, 1974.

Galpin Bruce. *The Riddle of Lester Maddox.* Atlanta: Camelot Publishing Company, 1968.

Gulliver, Hal. *A Friendly Tongue.* Macon: Mercer University Press, 1984.

Henderson, Harold Paul and Roberts, Gary, editors. *Georgia Governors in an Age of Change.* Athens: University of Georgia Press, 1988.

Henderson, Harold Paulk. *The Politics of Change in Georgia: A Political Biography of Ellis Arnall.* Athens: University of Georgia Press, 1991.

Hyatt, Richard. *Lewis, Jack & Me.* Columbus: Shinkle & Walden Publishers Ltd. 1994.

Hyatt, Richard. *Nothin' But Fine: The Music and the Gospel According to Jake Hess.* Columbus: Buckland Press, 1995.

Hyatt, Richard. *The Carters of Plains.* Huntsville: Strode Publishing Company, 1977.

Hyatt, Richard. *Those Trees Are Mine.* Pine Mountain: Callaway Gardens, 1991.

Lance, Bert. *The Truth of the Matter.* New York: Summitt Books, 1991.

Lance, Thomas Jackson. *The Education of a Georgia Mountaineer.* Columbus: Quill Publications, 1995.

Maddox, Lester. *Speaking Out: The Autobiography of Lester Garfield Maddox.* Garden City: Doubleday & Company, 1975.

Matalin, Mary and Carville, James with Peter Knobler. *All's Fair: Love, War and Running for President.* New York: Random House, 1994; and Touchstone, 1995.

McGill, Ralph. *The South and the Southerner.* New York: Atlantic, Little Brown and Company, 1959.

McGill, Ralph and Logue, Calvin M. *Southern Encounters: Southerners of Note in Ralph McGill's South.* Macon: Mercer University Press, 1983.

Miller, Zell. *Corps Values: Everything You Need to Know I learned in the Marines.* Atlanta: Longstreet Press, 1997.

Miller, Zell. *Great Georgians.* Franklin Springs: Advocate Press, 1983.

Miller, Zell. *The Mountains Within Me.* Toccoa: Commercial Printing Company, 1976.

Miller, Zell. *They Heard Georgia Singing.* Macon: Mercer University Press, 1996.

Parks, Joseph H. *Joseph Brown of Georgia.* Baton Rouge: Baton Rouge: Louisiana State University Press, 1977.

Reese, Byron Herbert. *Better A Dinner of Herbs.* New York: E.P. Dutton and Company, 1950.

Talmadge, Herman E. with Mark Winchell. *Talmadge: A Political Legacy, A Politician's Life.* Atlanta: Peachtree Publishers Ltd., 1987.

Trillin, Calvin. *An Education in Georgia.* New York: Viking, 1964.

Tyrell, R. Emmett, Jr. *Boy Clinton: The Political Biography.* Washington: Regency Publishing Inc., 1996.

Weldon, Jane Powers, ed. *The New Georgia Guide,* Athens: University of Georgia Press, 1996.

Wilson, Charles Reagan. *Judgment and Grace in Dixie: Southern Faiths from Faulkner to Elvis.* Athens: University of Georgia Press, 1995.

Unpublished Documents

Andress, Robert P. "Young Harris College: Its Development, Resources and Program." 1959

Franklin, Louisa and Moody, Jeffery S. "Centennial Chronicle: Young Harris College, 1886-1986."

Huckaby, Hank. "Diary of Zell Miller's first months as governor." 1991.

Lance, Thomas Jackson. "M.D. Collins: A Great Man."

Lance, Thomas Jackson. "History of Young L.G. Harris College." 1936

Maddox, Lester. "Prelude to One of a Kind." 1994.

Personal Scrapbooks of Zell Miller

Reece, Chuck. "Memories of the 1992 Democratic National Convention."

Rowan, Bobby. "32 Years of Public Life (1962-1994)

Theses and Dissertations

Brogdon, Joseph Milton. "A History of Young L.G. College." Master's Thesis, University of Georgia, 1938.

Miller, Zell. "The Administration of E.D. Rivers as Governor of Georgia." Master's Thesis, University of Georgia, 1958.

Magazines and Journals

Atlanta Historical Journal
Atlanta History: A Journal of Georgia and the South
Atlanta Magazine
The Atlanta Weekly
Georgia Journal
Georgia Trend

The Nation
Georgia History Journal

Newspapers

The Atlanta Constitution, Atlanta, Georgia
The Atlanta Journal, Atlanta, Georgia
The Augusta Chronicle, Augusta, Georgia
The Columbus Enquirer, Columbus, Georgia
The Columbus Ledger, Columbus, Georgia
Creative Loafing, Atlanta, Georgia
The Enotah Echoes, Young Harris College, Young Harris, Georgia
The Macon News, Macon, Georgia
The Macon Telegraph, Macon, Georgia

Personal Interviews

Frederick Allen, December, 1996 in Atlanta, Georgia
Bill Anderson, (Telephone) March 7, 1997
Mary Beazley, March, 19, 1997 in Atlanta, Georgia
Paul Begala, (Telephone) February, March, 1997
George Berry, (Telephone) March 13, 1997
Mike Bowers, (Telephone) March 24, 1997
Jack Brinkley, December, 1996 in Columbus, Georgia
Toni Brown, various times 1996-1997, in Atlanta, Georgia
Howard "Bo" Callaway, (Based on previous interviews with the
    author)
Dr. Dan Carter, (Telephone) March 8, 1997
Jimmy Carter (Based on previous interviews with the author)
James Carville (Telephone) March 14, 1997
Terry Coleman in Atlanta, Georgia
Marcus Collins in Atlanta, Georgia
Dr. James F. Cook (Telephone) March, 1997
Tom Cousins, (Telephone) March 18, 1997
Paul Coverdell, April 4, 1997 in Columbus, Georgia
Rick Dent, various times 1996 and 1997 in Atlanta, Georgia.

Billy Dillworth, (Based on previous interviews with the author)
Hilda Dyches, (Telephone) February, 1997
Sarah Eby-Ebersole, (Telephone) December 1996
Ken Edelstein, (Telephone) March 9, 1997
Frank Eldridge, December 1996 in Atlanta, Georgia
Ken Englade (telephone) March, 1997
Marti Fullerton, March, 1997 in Atlanta, Georgia
Phil Gailey, (Telephone) December 1996.
Wayne Garner, December 1996 in Atlanta, Georgia
Martha Gilland, March 1997 in Atlanta, Georgia
Denmark Groover, March 11, 1997 in Macon Georgia
Rev. Don Harp, (Telephone) December 1996
Neill Herring, March 1997 in Atlanta, Georgia
Rev. Creede Hinshaw, March 30, 1997 in Macon, Georgia
Maggie Hodge (Telephone) June, 1997
Sam Hopkins, (Telephone) December 1996
Hank Huckaby, March 1997 in Atlanta, Georgia
Tommy Irvin, (Telephone) December 1996
Judge Ed Johnson, December 1996 in Atlanta, Georgia
Rev. John Kay, (Telephone) February 1997
Terry Kay (Telephone) February 1997
Bert Lance, (Telephone) December 1996
Don Leebern, (Based on previous interviews with the author)
O.V. Lewis (Telephone) March 1997
Hovie Lister (Based on previous interviews with the author)
Lester Maddox (Based on previous interviews with the author)
Frank Martin, (Telephone) March 25, 1997
Keith Mason, December 1996 in Atlanta, Georgia
Selby McCash, (Telephone) December 1996
Hamilton McWhorter (Telephone) December 1996
Shirley Miller, March 1997 in Atlanta, Georgia
Zell Miller, Previous interviews with the author and various interviews in 1996 and 1997 in Atlanta, Georgia
John Mitchell, various times in 1997 in Atlanta, Georgia.
Tom Murphy, March 1997 in Atlanta, Georgia
Glenn Newsome, (telephone) June 7, 1997

Dick Pettys, (Telephone) March 1997

Dr. Steven Portch (Telephone) December 1996

Bob Richardson, various times in 1996 and 1997 in Young Harris, Georgia

Pete Robinson, December 1996 in Columbus, Georgia

Carl Sanders, (Telephone) December 1996

Betty Sellers, (Telephone) December 1996

Guy Sharpe, (Telephone) December 1996

Bill Shipp, December 11, 1996 in Atlanta, Georgia

Bob Short, March 1997 in Atlanta, Georgia

Celestine Sibley, (Telephone) December 1996.

Bob Smalley, December 1996 in Griffin, Georgia

Calvin Smyrne, April 24, 1997 in Columbus, Georgia

Herman Talmadge, April 23, 1997 in Hampton, Georgia

John Thomas, April 23, 1997 in Hampton, Georgia

Michael Thurmond, (Telephone) March 26, 1997

Norman Underwood, (Telephone) December 1996

Mike Vollmer (Telephone) March 28, 1997

Rogers Wade, (Telephone) various times in 1996 and 1997

Larry Walker, March 1997 in Atlanta, Georgia

Billy Winn, various times in 1996 and 1997 in Columbus, Georgia

Steve Wrigley, various times in 1996 and 1997 in Atlanta, Georgia

Special Acknowledgements

Dr. Andy Ambrose, Atlanta History Center

Bradley Memorial Library, Columbus, Georgia

Mary Margaret Byrne Library, Columbus Ledger-Enquirer, Columbus, Georgia

Columbus State University Library, Columbus, Georgia

Duckworth Libraries, Young Harris College, Young Harris, Georgia

John Greenman, publisher, *Columbus Ledger-Enquirer*, Columbus, Georgia

Ed Grisamore, *Macon Telegraph*, Macon, Georgia

Blaine Hughes, Georgia State University, Atlanta, Georgia
Gordon Muir, The Varsity Restaurant, Atlanta, Georgia
Dusty Nix, *Columbus Ledger-Enquirer,* Columbus, Georgia
Mike Owen, *Columbus Ledger-Enquirer,* Columbus, Georgia
Barbara and Elizabeth Romey, Columbus, Georgia
Nancy Stubbs, Religion Department, Mercer University, Macon, Georgia
Sharon Sudduth, *Columbus Ledger-Enquirer*, Columbus, Georgia
Jane Summey, Mercer University Library
Ed Weldon, Gail DeLoach, Sally Mosley, Georgia State Archives
Woodruff Library, Emory University, Atlanta, Georgia

Inaugural Address
January 14, 1991

Like 78 other Georgians before me, five of whom honor us with their presence today, I have now taken a solemn oath of office as Governor of this state. The succession of democratic government in Georgia reaches back across two centuries. So in the first place, this is a day for tradition, a celebration of freedom conserved, sustained, expanded and passed on from generation to generation.

That journey of freedom is not finished; the progress we have made was not always easy. And the history of the struggle is not some relic of the past, but the challenge and hope of our future. For each memory also points to the miles we still have to travel.

In the 18th century, James Edward Oglethorpe dreamed of establishing a colony in the New World where free and equal men could build new lives for themselves and their families. Today, we know that dream must include women as well as men.

In the 19th century, Henry W. Grady dreamed of a New South where there would be a hundred homes for every one plantation. Today, we know that dream must reach to the homeless as well as the middle class.

In the 20th century, Martin Luther King, Jr. dreamed "that one day on the red clay hills of Georgia, the sons of slaves and the sons of former slave owners will be able to sit down together at the table of brotherhood." And today we must keep alive that dream of the only son of Georgia ever to be honored with the Nobel Peace Prize.

Across this country, clouds of racial prejudice and division are gathering again. Here in this state, it is our special duty to reject racism. One of Dr. King's apostles — and my friend — Andrew Young made more history last year as a candidate for governor. And Georgia took another giant step toward racial harmony by conducting a campaign remarkably free from racial resentment. We will not be divided in this state black against white.

Sadly, that is an undeniable part of our past — but it is not and must not be any part of our future. And the future is the essence of this inaugural day.

We draw strength from our heritage, but we set our course to the horizon ahead. We are entering a time of change — not only change of administrations, but a profound change in the pattern of Georgia life and the way our people make a living.

The traditional cornerstones of our economy were cheap energy, farming and manufacturing. And while farms and factories will always be a real and special part of Georgia, our survival and success in the new economy will be determined not only by the productivity of our land, but by the productivity of our people; not only by the horsepower of our machinery, but the brainpower of our workers.

Our future prosperity depends not just on strong backs, but on strong minds. Georgia faces a choice: We can plow new ground — or we can let the weeds grow. So rather than resist change, we Georgians welcome it.

Indeed, let us become a catalyst for change. Let this new administration begin a new era of imagination and innovation; effort and growth.

The driving force, the engine of the Georgia that can be, is found in the first three words or the Federal Constitution I have just sworn to uphold: "We, the people." And our fundamental directive can be found in the Georgia Constitution: "All government, of right, originates with the people, is founded on their will only. Public officers are the trustees and servants of the people."

That is government at its best, and that is the kind of Governor I will strive to be.

And so we dedicate this administration to the family farmer who plants his own crops and bales his own hay. To the small businesswoman who stays open late and calls her customers by their first name. To the bold entrepreneur who has built a better mousetrap or a smaller microchip.

We dedicate this administration to the senior citizen who opens her utility bill fearing that she will be forced to choose between being cold or being hungry. And to the young family just starting out, struggling to afford day care now and save for college later.

Listen to me: It is to every family that works and saves and sometimes comes up a little short at the end of the month, that this administration is dedicated.

So what shall we do now with the power — and the responsibility?

We, the People, have the right — if we so choose — to fund bold, new education initiatives through a Georgia lottery devoted to our schools. We, the People, have the right to reach for the finest public schools in the history of this state — or anywhere in this nation.

In building a world-class school system, we will follow the advice of a part-time Georgian named Franklin D. Roosevelt, who once said, "Try something. If it works, try more of it. If it doesn't work, try something else. But for God's sake, try something."

The central purpose of the Miller Administration will be to prepare Georgia for the 21st century. Education is the most important part of that purpose. Without it, nothing else can save us. With it, nothing else can stop us.

We, the People, must advance on other fronts as well. Our government must be made leaner and cleaner, more open and more responsive.

The environment must be preserved from those who would trade our children's health and our fragile Earth for a quick buck.

Our streets and neighborhoods must be better protected against the rising tide of crime and drugs. Something is wrong when families hide behind home security bars because criminals are released from behind maximum security bars.

Our working families must be given relief from skyrocketing insurance rates, inadequate highways, and regressive taxes on the very food they eat.

We must do all this and more to strive, to seek, to find the Georgia that can be.

It is certain that our journey will not be completed in the limited time the people of Georgia have put this public servant in office. Nor will it be completed in the limited time the Lord has put His humble servant on Earth. But we take heart from the ancient Hebrew text: "The day is short, but the work is great. It is not thy duty to complete the work. Neither art thou free to desist from it."

And so today, we take the first step of a thousand-mile journey. We launch a new administration — and we look to a new century.

By empowering our citizens, educating our children, building our prosperity, saving our environment, fighting crime, and demanding a government that works as hard as our people do, we will march toward the Georgia that can be.

A Georgia in which a little boy from a remote and impoverished mountain valley or a little girl in a dirty and dangerous urban slum can have his or her chance for greatness.

A Georgia in which all of us have the opportunity to seek our destiny, seize that shining moment, and climb as far as strength and wit and perseverance will carry us; never to be blocked by barriers of race or barricades of region, or gender, or class.

By harnessing the two most powerful forces on Earth — an educated people and an unshakable faith — let us turn now to the task of leading Georgia. And then let Georgia lead the nation into the 21st century.

God bless you, and God bless Georgia.

Democratic National Committee
Southern Caucus
Raleigh, North Carolina,
June 22, 1991

I'd like to speak to you tonight — honestly and urgently — about the present condition of our party. About why we have lost so often in presidential elections. And about the dangers and opportunities of 1992.

Let me begin by stating my blunt belief: The national Democratic problem now threatens to become state and local Democratic defeat.

Because, for too many Democratic candidates, we are losing younger voters, and with them our future. We are seeing Southern Democrats vote for Republicans in increasing numbers.

We are seeing Democratic governors and senators — good and effective leaders, in touch with their people — in electoral trouble simply because of the party label they carry.

We can no longer console ourselves that while we lose the White House again and again and again, well at least we keep the statehouse and the courthouse.

If we do not change in fundamental ways, the risk is — no, not the risk, the reality is — that our party will lose cities and states and seats that we have held for generations.

And no, we cannot just wait until 1996, because by then the South may be gone and with it any realistic chance for a presidential victory.

And we cannot cling to the unworthy hope that a worsening recession will drive the President out of office — that the working people will suffer enough to vote for us out of sheer desperation.

Nor can we delude ourselves that the problem is not us, but the process; that the problem is that we don't have enough computers or phone banks or targeting; or that changing the dates of the primaries or reshuffling the deck will somehow bring about a new deal.

What our presidential nominee says is and always will be more important than what our telemarketing says.

We can no longer escape the facts. If we ignore them, the facts will become our fate and the Democratic Party will have no future.

So ... what can we do?

I believe the answer is not to abandon our central principles, but to revive them; to return to the Democratic Party's defining purpose.

You see, for too many presidential elections, we have had things backwards. We have chosen to fight on social issues rather than to run on the economic issues that shape the daily lives of American families.

When the average American family stays up late into the night, they are not worrying about whether school prayer should be voluntary or mandatory. They are worrying about how to balance the checkbook or where they will find the money for junior's college tuition.

Our party grew up around the economic issues that concern working Americans most deeply, and that is the common bond that unites us.

But instead of rallying around those basic, unifying economic issues, we have allowed ourselves to be distracted by social issues that not only divide us but also defeat us.

And because we failed to give people good reasons to vote for our nominee, the opposition was able to give them bad reasons to vote against him.

Dukakis and Mondale suffered similar fates, because, in the end, they conducted similar campaigns. Why weren't they focusing on the sky-rocketing cost of health care and demanding change? Why weren't they questioning a tax system that favors the rich at the expense of the average American? Why weren't they focusing on the loss of jobs to unfair foreign trade and demanding reciprocity?

Incredibly, our national party has replaced the cornerstone of our strength — economic populism — with out Achilles heel — social liberalism.

We also have a series of very active special interest groups, organized around liberal causes, that have imposed a filter through which only the purest of the politically pure can pass.

To some, it is not enough to be pro-choice; it is demanded that the candidates favor taxpayer funding, even for abortion on demand.

To others, it is not enough to endorse government support for the arts; it is demanded that candidates oppose any restrictions on the uses of arts funding, even if they are obscene.

To still others, it is not enough to stand up for education; it is also demanded that candidates stand against every innovative idea that in any way infringes on the status quo — from teacher testing to merit pay.

Don't get me wrong. I believe in a lot of the social issues which so many want our party to profess. But I also believe they cannot be the centerpiece of our presidential campaigns.

And to the extent that they are, we will not only continue to lose elections; ironically, we will also lose the very social goals that these Democratic elites regard as so important.

As a candidate for Governor of Georgia, I was open about where I stood on social issues. I said I was for sex education, and now we are implementing it. I endorsed a hate crimes bill, and I have said that I would sign legislation repealing Georgia's anti-sodomy law.

I am completely committed to a woman's right to choose, and I have never equivocated in my support of the E.R.A. I believe Georgia has the strongest arts council in the South — and as long as I am Governor, that will continue to be the case.

435

But, you see, those issues were not the sole message of my campaign. Most of all, I stood for economic empowerment — for education, for efficiency, and, instead of higher taxes, for a lottery.

You see, I did not become a Democrat to be a social liberal while ignoring fundamental economic choices.

We have to again appeal to working families and the middle class. We have to again advance an economic agenda. We have to define it. We have to run on it. Because, my friends, that is the only way we will ever win.

And by economic issues, I do not mean just marginal criticism of the other side's competence — or just marginal differences with the other side's priorities.

I mean a major commitment to address larger questions, like a tax code that robs from the middle class and enriches the upper class; a trade policy that robs our workers while letting our corporations export jobs instead of exporting products.

A silly education policy that threatens to take student aid away from anyone whose family earns over ten thousand dollars a year, so that the best schools in America will be open only to the poorest of the poor and the wealthy.

On all these things, we have to fight — and we also have to offer an alternative.

We have to fight for a health care policy that cuts costs, not coverage. A health care policy that does something about the undeniable unfairness of America's medical system.

You know, today if you're homeless, you can get at least a minimum of care. And if you're rich, you can go to the best private hospital. But if you're middle class, and you or someone in your family gets very sick, you can go ... very broke.

So next year, I don't care how long the Democratic Party platform is. I just care that it speaks to economic choices — that it speaks to real people and not to a narrow elite.

You see, I don't want our platform to be politically correct as much as I want it to politically connect with working Americans.

And to any of my fellow Democrats who may be distressed to hear me say all this, let me reply — that for us and for all our ideals, nothing would be more distressing than losing again in 1992.

Let me suggest that unless we talk about education and jobs, trade and economic development, we won't be able to fill positions on the Supreme Court — because we won't win.

Unless we address the increasing tax burden of the middle class, we won't be able to stop the Republican effort to exploit racial divisions

— because we won't win. Unless we deal with what is the first drop in middle class home ownership in 30 years, we won't be able to help the homeless — because we won't win.

Unless we can build a Democratic economic case, we will never be able to rebuild a Democratic electoral majority. And unless we do that, our social policy will become mere social posturing.

We will not have the power to pass the Equal Rights Amendment, we will not have the power to protect civil liberties or to end discrimination — and most of all, we will not have the power to protect the people who do the work, pay the taxes, raise the children, fight the wars and build the nation; the people who work hard every day and still come up a little short at the end of the month — the people who are the heart and soul of the Democratic Party.

But this is not just important to our party. It is also vital to our country. For under the Republicans, our standard of living has slipped to 9th in the world and is still dropping.

Our students are last in the industrial nations in math and science — not because they are not good enough, but because the people who are running America today don't care enough. If the Democratic Party doesn't fight to change these things, then no one will.

It's time for the Democratic Party to say again to the working men and women of this country: We will fight your fight, we will ease your burden, we will carry your cause.

We will raise Cain. Raise Cain against a status quo that far too many Democrats are far too comfortable with; a status quo that is paradoxically sending working people to the poorhouse and to the Republican Party at the same time.

We must stand for a strong America. Not only in force of arms — although we must never be too timid to do that — but also strong in economic might.

We must recognize the obvious: that even as the ticker-tape from our military victory was falling from the sky, so was our position falling as the strongest nation on earth.

In the economic wars that will determine who leads the world in the next century, Japan and Europe are kicking our butts. It's time that we Democrats kicked back.

We should tell the Japanese to let Louisiana farmers sell their rice in Osaka and Tokyo; and we should tell the Europeans to accept beef from Kansas and Texas.

Americans fought for their freedom; we spilled our blood for their liberty; the least they can do is give us a level playing field in return. The Administration that brags about the "Smart Bombs" has the dumbest trade policy the world has ever seen.

We must ask why CEO's make 90 times what their shopworkers can earn; why big executives have golden parachutes while working people have no health insurance; why a family that makes $10,000 a year is too rich to get a college grant, but a corporate raider that makes $10 million a year is so poor that he needs a capital gains tax cut.

We must ask why George Bush rushes to bail out S&L bandits, but turns a blind eye to honest, decent family farmers who've lost their land to predatory banks. Why he moves heaven and earth, and rightly so, to oppose aggression, but won't lift a finger to stop a recession.

These issues are the bottom line for the pocket book of working Americans, and they are the issues that made us the party of the middle class. From Franklin Roosevelt on, the economic issue was the engine that pulled the Democratic train up the hill. Social issues were the caboose.

In recent presidential elections, we have too often attempted to turn the caboose into the engine. It is no wonder that the train keeps sliding down the hill.

We have a proud history that is powerfully relevant to a changing nation in a changing world.

Working men and women look to us for leadership, but too often we seem to look away. Too often, we seem enthralled with other voices, and there is no one to speak for the middle class.

We must become that voice — for that is the best reason I can think of for being a Democrat. We must make the Democratic Party true again to its overriding economic purposes — so that we can be relevant again, alive again, proud again and yes, victorious again — for ourselves, and for our country.

National Conference of Lieutenant Governors
August 7, 1991

I am happy to be back among the Lieutenant Governors of this nation. I was one of you for 16 years — not long enough to set the record, but long enough to be invited back, and I thank you.

Although each of your jobs differs to a degree, you all have one thing in common: Your concern for the good health of your constituents, and especially the good health of the Chief Executive of your state.

And in case you don't know how a Lt. Governor shakes hands with his Governor, let an old-timer show you how to do it.

Each day, greet your Governor with hand outstretched and a smile on your face. As you shake hands, extend two fingers up under his sleeve until you can feel his pulse. . . . That's the way a Lt. Governor shakes hands with his Governor.

My Governors always had a strong pulse. They were healthy as horses. And so I stayed Lieutenant Governor through four terms. But that period was only half of my political career. I've been in an elective office now in five different decades.

Before and during much of that time, I was a history professor at four of Georgia's colleges and universities.

So I've taught history and I've lived history, and now in the autumn of my career let me tell you a little of what that combination of teacher and realistic practitioner has taught me. Let me begin with a little history lesson.

1

All of you know that in the summer of 1787, a group of political leaders met in Philadelphia's Independence Hall. They were a
diverse group — just as diverse in their time as this nation's
Governors and Lt. Governors are today.

They represented 13 independent colonies — not only newly
independent of England, but also independent of each other.
Many thought they had gathered simply to rewrite the Articles of
Confederation.

The idea that they might actually join together in one nation
under one central government was a radical shock to many, sprung
on them by the leadership after they arrived.

Debate raged throughout the summer. Some threw up their
hands and left before it was over. Others hung around to see the
final document, but then refused to sign it.

In the end, it contained only 39 signatures of more than 100
original delegates. But over the past 200 years, the Constitution of
the United States has proved to be one of the most remarkable
political documents the world has ever seen.

Its precepts have proven so fundamental, so very true, that it
has continued to be viable with only 22 changes through a Civil
War, two World Wars, presidential assassinations and even one
presidential resignation — viable through the growth of 13 little,
isolated states into a 50-state, highly industrialized world power.

You see, what is so remarkable about the Constitution is not
that it espouses a particular political ideology, but that it crafts a
delicate balance among several ideologies that on the surface seem
incompatible.

2

Somehow, in the midst of the uproar and disgruntlement that
surrounded its birth, its framers came to the realization that
democracy is a healthy tension among several things . . . some of
which today we would label liberal, and others of which we would
call conservative.

The central balance in the Constitution reflects the central struggle of the convention: The 13 colonies wanted to maintain their independence on the one hand, while on the other hand they wanted to gain the benefits of community.

The compromise they finally reached on this issue permeates the entire document. And our nation has grown up around this delicate balance.

As a people, we have a split personality — glorifying individual freedom while at the same time demanding allegiance to community.

And it has worked. It has worked because it is practical and realistic. It recognizes that our daily lives are a constant collision of various forces and beliefs that have to be reconciled.

Because, as we in politics know all too well: Pure ideologies exist only in the abstract.

In real life, most Americans are in the middle, and they mix both conservative and liberal ideologies in their practical political beliefs.

On the liberal side, we Americans believe in helping those who have fallen on hard times, in fostering equal opportunity and equal rights, in providing broad access to housing, education and health care.

3

But we also believe that traditional families do the best job of raising children, that hard work and self-reliance should be encouraged and rewarded, that destructive behavior should be punished.

And that institutions do a better job when they are small and close to home rather than large and run from afar. These ideas are a page from conservative ideology.

We believe in balancing welfare with personal initiative, in balancing rights against obligations. We don't like either permissiveness or selfishness in their extremes.

We are a nation of moderates. The political institutions and processes set up by that same Constitution are full of checks and balances that aim for a moderate, middle-ground result.

But the past 30 years of American politics have left middle Americans disillusioned and disengaged. They are skeptical. When political debates are aired, they change the channel. When the polls open, they do not bother to vote.

The reason is that instead of using the political process as intended, to move toward the middle in reconciling the issues, American politicians, forced by vocal and well-financed special interests, have moved outward toward the edges and become entrenched in ideological extremes.

Take abortion, for example. Many would have us believe it is a hard, yes/no question. And for the individual woman it is — there is no such thing as being halfway pregnant.

4

But taken as a question of public policy, our split personality exerts itself. Our commitment to individual liberty balks at the idea of government stepping in to make such a private decision.

But our shared moral values cry out against large numbers of abortions and their use as a means of birth control.

As a result, middle Americans long ago compromised on the middle ground. They support some government restrictions such as parental permission for minors, while preferring to leave the actual, bottom-line decision to the individual.

But many politicians ignore the middle-ground compromise on which the majority of Americans have already settled. They continue to argue the issue over and over in its extremes.

Or take the issue of women. In their everyday lives, most Americans are both feminists and traditionalists . . . simultaneously.

They recognize that a family of father, mother and children under one roof is the best way to raise children. And they worry about what is happening to our children with so many one-parent families and two-career families.

At the same time, however, they know that many women are finding fulfillment in their careers. And even more basic: Working mothers are an economic necessity. They are needed in our work-force, and they provide critical income to their families.

Fully half of America's two-career families would slip below the poverty level if the mother quit her job and stayed home.

5

Or, look at economic issues. Hard-line conservatives want a free market with no government intervention. Hard-line liberals expect government to force the market to behave in a fashion that offsets injustice and demands compassion.

Well, middle America sees the former as benefitting the rich and the latter as benefitting the poor. And either way, they see nothing in it for themselves.

Middle America is tired of liberal-conservative confrontations that prolong, seemingly forever, fruitless arguments between two extremes, both of which have their points, but neither of which is acceptable in its entirety.

One way middle America has tried to regain an ideological balance at the polls is by electing a Republican President and a Democratic Congress . . . but the stalemate remains.

And I'm here to tell you that middle Americans are sick and tired of it. Liberal extremists have spit on their values. And conservative extremists have given lip-service to their work ethic, but then glorified those who grabbed instant wealth in questionable ways.

Middle America is ready to move on. And what does middle America want?

Middle Americans want to do the best for their children, but they also need two incomes to maintain their standard of living. And they want help in reconciling their jobs with their family responsibilities.

Middle Americans are willing to pay their fair share of taxes, but they are worried about maintaining their standard of living in the face of an uncertain economy and sky-rocketing costs in areas like health care and college tuition.

6

Middle Americans want a balance between welfare and self-reliance. They want a little encouragement in pulling themselves up by their own bootstraps. They want a few incentives to invest in themselves.

And they want their own hard work recognized in the form of tax structures that treat them equitably with the rich . . . and health care benefits that treat them equitably with the poor.

They do not want government to do everything for — or to — them, as die-hard liberals suppose. Nor do they want significantly less government, as die-hard conservatives believe. What they want is simply for government to work. For them.

Middle Americans look at the new world order and see the dangerously shifting sands of the Middle East, the changing face of the Soviet Union and Eastern Europe, the growing economic superiority of Japan.

They worry that the world's number one nation is doomed to become a waning and diminishing power in this reconfigured world.

And they want an economic policy that addresses the fact that we now live in a global economy in which our standard of living is inextricably linked with that of other countries.

The bottom line, as far as middle Americans are concerned, is that this country is in desperate need of a new approach to politics by both parties.

We must recapture a political process that preserves the delicate balances upon which democracy rests, rather than fixating, then stagnating on opposite, 180-degree, polar ideological extremes.

7

Both parties must make politics a process that moves us forward by resolving the problems, rather than continuing endlessly, ad nauseam, to rehash them.

We must use the political process to help us find the practical, day-to-day, middle ground on the substantive issues we face, rather than to fight over the trivialized issues that middle America left behind long ago.

Middle Americans want political parties that look ahead and move forward on the important issues we all agree must be addressed — issues like maintaining our standard of living, reducing the pressure on the middle class, restoring hope for the poor, defining our role in a new world.

And that process also demands political leaders who will spend their time solving the problems that matter, instead of spending millions of dollars on personal attacks in an effort to recast each other into the same old irrelevant, extremist liberal or conservative molds.

And if you, as political leaders from around this nation, can help to restore the political process to its best tradition, then another vision of the framers of our Constitution will also come true.

Middle Americans will once again consider those of us engaged in politics to be in an honorable and respected calling.

And for themselves, their active participation can then become an expression of enlightened self-interest to be treasured, rather than an irrelevancy to be either endured or completely avoided.

Statewide Television Address
August 18, 1991

Tomorrow morning the Georgia General Assembly will convene in a special session I have called to cut the state budget. It is a task none of us wanted, but which none of us can escape.

And I appreciate this opportunity to talk with you about why we need to act—and how we propose to get the job done.

But even before the General Assembly convenes tomorrow, one very important decision has already been made. We are coming together to make cuts, not to raise taxes. From the first day of this administration, I have said I would not use the recession as an excuse to raise your taxes.

That decision has surprised some. They note — accurately —that I am a progressive Governor with a long agenda for action: better schools, safer streets, a cleaner environment.

But the working people of this state — the very people I pledged to help—are already facing enough economic pain. I cannot do enough to relieve that pain, but I certainly am not going to add to it.

I consider the members of the General Assembly to be partners in this process. I have consulted closely with the Speaker of the House, the Lieutenant Governor and other legislative leaders in preparing these budget revisions. And I thank them for their efforts and their cooperation.

You, the people of Georgia, are also partners in this process. None of us should ever forget that budgets are not just written on paper, but in people's lives.

The entire country is in a prolonged recession that has caused state tax revenues to drop sharply all across the United States.

Many economists did not recognize the recession's true depth and length. And many states based their budgets on economic projections that were more optimistic than has proven to be the case.

As the recession has dragged on, the number eligible for federally mandated welfare and Medicaid has steadily risen, placing a further demand on state resources.

We at the state level are now feeling the severe effects of the federal government's decision over the past decade to deal with its own deficit by shifting increased costs onto the shoulders of the states. In Georgia, federal Medicaid mandates now take ten percent of our total state budget.

And, as if that were not enough, the state also carries another heavy burden for which the fault rests not in Washington but in Atlanta. For too long, state government used — and misused — the strong revenue growth of the heady 1980s to bloat the state payroll.

The number of state jobs increased by 21,000 in just the past five years. Put another way, that means more than one in five state employees holds a job that did not exist five years ago.

2

The year before I became Governor, with a hiring freeze supposedly in effect for much of the time, the state payroll still grew by 4,000 employees.

The number of state employees has grown more than twice as fast as Georgia's population in the past five years, and in so doing, it has outgrown the taxpayers' ability to support it.

This growth in government has to stop . . . and it will. Some of it has to be rolled back . . . and it will be.

The decisions won't all be politically popular. None of them will be easy . . . and many of them will hurt.

But we have to do what's right. We have to streamline, reorganize and downsize Georgia's government now. And we have to strengthen Georgia's economy for the future.

We do begin in a better place than most of the other 35 or so states that are in the midst of a budget shortfall.

Our next-door neighbor, North Carolina, which has a budget about our size, had a 1.2 billion dollar shortfall — a deficit more than double the size of ours.

Our six percent deficit may be less, but we take it no less seriously. Georgia may be in better shape than other states, but it will not stay that way if we do not take decisive action.

And in planning that action, one priority has been uppermost in my mind.

Seven months ago, when I became Governor, I talked about those to whom I wanted to dedicate this administration.

3

The family farmer who plants his own crops and bales his own hay. The small businesswoman who stays open late and calls her customers by their first names. The senior citizen who opens her utility bill with trembling hands, afraid that enjoying heat will mean enduring hunger.

I dedicated this administration to the young family, struggling to pay for day care and save for college at the same time. I dedicated it to every household that works and saves and sometimes comes up a little short at the end of the month.

And I mean to keep my word to all of them . . . to all of you.

I have stayed up late many an evening, just as you have, worrying over how to make ends meet in our state. Searching for ways to scrimp and save so that we can balance the state's checkbook, just as you have to balance your own.

The budget I deal with is bigger, but so is the gap between what we spend and what we can afford.

Tomorrow morning, in the halls of the State Capitol, you, the taxpaying citizens of Georgia, will have no paid lobbyist to buttonhole legislators on your behalf. But you are the heart and soul of Georgia. You, not government, are what makes this state great.

The Chinese character that stands for the word crisis is a combination of two symbols. One means danger. The other, opportunity. And beyond the obvious dangers of the moment, there are great opportunities.

4

Georgia is entering a time of profound change. And I want my administration as Governor to be a catalyst in anticipating that change and meeting it with foresight and imagination.

I got into government because I've always believed that government can be an agent of change to accomplish positive good for the benefit of the public. But that doesn't mean we have to have big government.

The issue is not whether we have more government or less government. We need wise government that provides fundamental services to its citizens in the most efficient way possible and not in an indifferent, wasteful fashion.

I look at our current situation as an opportunity to improve state government, to make it leaner and more efficient.

We must set a new course for Georgia. We should be asking not only how much we spend, but also how sound are the purposes we are spending it for. This is a time to reduce the budget . . . and to rethink it.

Georgia saw unprecedented growth in state revenues during the 1980s. And state government ate the whole thing. It was a time, as Merle Haggard sang, of "drinking that free bubble-up and eating that rainbow stew."

Now we are faced with a crash diet.

But we are going to do more than shed just enough excess government to get us through the present fiscal year.

5

Instead, we are going to go on a serious, long-term diet that will change the habits and patterns of government on a permanent basis. We are going to embark on a ongoing program of fiscal fitness.

We are going to set the stage for a healthier, more stable economy, and pave the way for economic recovery and growth.

State revenues will improve, not because we have raised taxes to get us through, but because we are taking strong medicine, swallowing hard when times are tough.

There is an easy way to cut a budget. And a hard way. A right way, and a wrong way. And keeping the same old spending patterns but just at a lower level is the easy, and the wrong way. I do not want to make just simple percentage cuts in the broad categories that appear in the state budget document.

My Commission on Effectiveness and Economy in Government has spend six months looking closely at every agency in state government, scrutinizing the operations within departments. And I have placed a high priority on reorganizing and streamlining administration. More than half of the positions that have been cut are administrative.

For instance, improvements in office technology over the past decade have streamlined paper pushing tremendously. Yet we have continued to fund administration as if we were still taking shorthand on note pads and typing letters with carbon paper on manual typewriters. The positions have been continued routinely, year after year simply because they were there.

6

We can dismantle the auditing unit in the Public Service Commission that reviewed construction costs for Plants Vogtle, Scherer and Hatch, because its mission has been completed.

We do not need an office to review architectural plans and oversee construction of prisons in the Department of Corrections, because the Georgia State Financing and Investment Commission is doing the very same thing in the process of managing the bond financing for those facilities.

Clearly jobs we do not need are jobs we cannot afford.

I've also made deep cuts in luxuries we cannot afford, like personal cars for employees — I have cut 235. Workers in private enterprise do not have these perks. Why should state government employees have them at taxpayers' expense?

We are also going to sell two of the eight state aircraft and cut back on pilots. We will restrict travel, and we will save an additional half-million dollars on necessary travel by using point-to-point contracts with several airlines.

We have to cut some things so we can keep the others that Georgia must have to grow and improve and more forward.

Plainly, education is at the top of the list. Georgia's future well-being depends on a skilled and literate workforce.

We live in a global economy. Money and jobs flow easily across national boundaries, and our workforce must compete not only with Alabama and North Carolina, but with Germany and Japan. Short-changing education today mortgages our economy tomorrow.

7

In reworking the budget, I have insisted on preserving as much as possible the funds we send to the classrooms of this state. We will not cut teacher salaries, and my recommendations cut the Quality Basic Education formula by about two percent in non-instructional areas.

In this revised budget, a higher percentage goes into funding kindergarten through twelfth grade, than in the original budget passed last session.

But I am equally insistent that we will not be content with the same old ways of doing business in the education bureaucracy. Excess layers of middle management will be reduced. We are going to become clearer about the outcomes we want from our education programs and more rigorous about measuring and evaluating the results.

But at the same time, we must and will give local educators more flexibility to find the best way to do the job, and will encourage innovation and creativity by rewarding excellence.

Our University System, too, deserves nothing less than a new commitment to excellence. I am proud of the level of distinction it has achieved, and I am making every effort to guard the quality of our college classrooms by giving the Board of Regents great flexibility in targeting cuts toward non-essential areas.

But in other places in the University System, bureaucracy is at its worst and the winds of efficiency need to blow.

8

For example, my budget reorganizes the Cooperative Extension Service, returning it to its original mission of serving farmers and streamlining it to fulfill that mission with a new level of efficiency.

Another critical area is our prison system. I am proposing some deep cuts in the Department of Corrections, but they are targeted at reorganizing management.

The positions that will be eliminated are deputy commissioners, assistant commissioners, deputy assistant commissioners and assistant executive deputy commissioners.

Let me reassure you right now that we are not going to close the budget gap by putting criminals back on the streets. And we are not going to increase the backlog of state prisoners waiting in local jails to move into the state system.

We are going to proceed in an orderly fashion with construction, and by next summer we will be ready with six new boot camps and five new prisons. That means we will be able to end the early release of prisoners on schedule next summer.

We will put new technology into place to secure the walls around 13 prison compounds, reducing the need for tower guards. And we will use those 175 displaced tower guards to help staff other prisons.

We are going to make wider use of inmate labor in places where we have other state institutions nearby. In the Miller Administration, every able-bodied inmate who can work is going to work. We will cut operating costs at Central State Hospital, for example, by using inmate labor to do the laundry.

455

And, speaking of mental health hospitals, let me reassure you that we are not closing any state health institutions.

The thrust of the budget cuts in the huge Department of Human Resources is to reorganize administration for efficiency, while preserving direct services.

For example, we are saving millions of dollars by reorganizing and consolidating office functions on Capitol Hill and in the county offices, while at the same time preserving

9.3 million dollars for a new program for handicapped infants, toddlers and preschoolers.

It is clearly time to reorganize and eliminate projects that are not cost-effective, not generating results or whose time is past.

But I am also mindful of the human costs of change. Eight hundred of the 3,000 jobs we have eliminated are vacant as a result of the hiring freeze I put into effect. But there are still nearly 2,200 state employees whose jobs will be ended. Some of them work in my office.

I know it is a difficult time to be looking for a new job, and I am going to be working closely with our State Merit System and Department of Labor to provide as much assistance as we can to the state employees who are displaced by these cuts.

They are victims of a state government that too long failed to cast a critical eye at its own operations.

9

I am confident that state government will be stronger and that as the economy improves, we will be poised to take advantage of it.

This is a great state with a great people, and you deserve a state government that spends your tax money wisely.

It may well be that my destiny in the ongoing history of this great state is to grapple with a difficult time, and so to set the stage for another Governor to live and lead in a future time of economic growth that comes as the fruit of our present sacrifice and labor. So be it.

I hope and believe that in the years that follow, when our children inherit this great state and this responsibility, they will look back and say that our day was not a period of retrenchment and back-pedalling, but that it was the beginning of a new era in Georgia.

Let it be said that in a moment of testing and trial, we gave new meaning to the ideal that government exists to serve the people, and not just to tax them. That it exists to achieve purposes, and not simply to perpetuate itself.

Thank you. God bless you. And good night.

University of Georgia Commencement, June 13, 1992

A few weeks ago, events in southern California rocked this nation back on its heels.

Both the Rodney King trial and the riots that followed demonstrated the terrible tendency of many Americans — white and black — to see skin color first and foremost — to look at everything through skin-colored glasses.

That shocking videotape raised the question of whether those four policemen were able to see beyond the color of Rodney King's skin.

And then we wondered whether it was the color of the skin that took precedence in the mind of that jury, when it failed to convict those officers of excessive force.

But then, in the violence that followed, we saw the same thing in the other direction. People were attacked and injured, simply because they were white. Some of those protestors, like the policemen, like that jury, did not look beyond the color of skin.

When that happens in either direction, we deny the other person's humanity. We deny the fact that there is a fellow human being underneath that skin.

We deny the fact that we all feel the same emotions, that the tears we all cry know no color.

Far too often race has been used to distract our attention away from the fact that the rich are getting richer and the poor are getting poorer.

1

The fact is that during the 1980s, a new economic order has been emerging in this nation that is more unequal, more divided than ever before.

During the 1980s, the richest 1 percent of our population, got 75 percent of the growth in wealth.

While at the same time, the average American increased the amount of time on the job by 158 hours a year — the equivalent of another full month — just to maintain the same income.

And the working poor — those who work full-time but earn less than the poverty level — the working poor increased in the 80s by a third.

This is the exact opposite of what should be happening. But racism was used to cover it over; to make working white people think they have more in common with the rich than they do with the African-American person who may work beside them on the job.

I grew up poor. I grew up without a father, without indoor plumbing, for years without electricity, without a car in the family.

But I also grew up with hope. I grew up believing that if you worked hard and played by the rules, you could get somewhere; you could become somebody.

But today, many Americans have no hope. They have no hope of escaping poverty, no hope of taking control of their own destiny, no hope of becoming somebody.

Kids are not going to study and say no to drugs if the only possibility they can see ahead of them is unemployment and death from a gunshot on the streets of a housing project.

2

The young Leah Sears-Collinses of Georgia need to grow up knowing that it really is possible for an African-American woman to become a justice on the Supreme Court of Georgia.

When violence marred what could have been meaningful, peaceful protests in Atlanta it distracted attention away from the deeper issues the students were raising.

One of the points made by the Atlanta University students was that this is not the 1960s. They are right. It isn't.

In the struggle during that time, the aim was to achieve civil rights. That was the right place to begin. And we must continue to guard against those injustices, and not preserve the symbol of those times on our state flag.

But on the opposite side of the same coin from civil rights is economic rights. And that ... economic rights ... is what our challenge is today.

For example, as a result of the civil rights movement, African Americans can now sit wherever they want on the bus, but 43 percent of their children are born in poverty.

For example, as a result of the civil rights movement, African Americans can now use whatever drinking fountain or restroom is most convenient, but their rates of unemployment are double those of whites.

For example, as a result of the civil rights movement, African Americans can now eat at the restaurant of their choice, but their infants die at a rate twice that of whites.

You see, America has not yet addressed the economic side of that coin.

3

The social programs created in the 60s were designed to compensate the victims of poverty rather than solve the problems that cause it.

They give poor people just enough in the way of Medicaid and welfare and food stamps and housing subsidies to keep and sustain them in their poverty, rather than giving them the skills and opportunities they needed to break out of their poverty.

The world has undergone tremendous change since the 1960s. The industrial age, on which those old social programs were modeled, has given way to a new era of microelectronics, satellites and fiber optic cables — a world of modern technology.

Today the critical infrastructure required to generate economic growth is intellectual. It is a better educated, more highly skilled workforce.

We must change from spending money to sustain people in their poverty, to investing money in training and educating them and providing them with economic opportunity.

Theodore Roosevelt once said that "this country will not be a good place for *any* of us to live in unless we make it a good place for *all* of us to live in."

Little did he know how very true those words would become.

What all of us have got to realize, and realize pretty quickly, is that, regardless of skin color, we are all Americans. The greater the social and economic equity among us, the more successful we all are going to be.

By the year 2000, half of those who enter the workforce will be African American, Asian, Hispanic or of Middle Eastern descent.

And if all of our children are not equally well trained, well educated and able to move into the mainstream of a forward-looking economy, we are all in big, big trouble.

You who graduate here today, I believe, understand that. You have sought out and acquired an education, and you are the leaders of your generation. You are the trail blazers. You will become the role models for the next generation.

With your help we must turn our backs on an era where one race is pitted against another while the rich get richer and the poor get poorer. And we must turn our faces toward an era in which the barriers to economic opportunity are finally removed.

Because, my young friends, if all of us do not advance together, then, surely, all of us will diminish together.

Keynote Address,
Democratic National Convention
July 13, 1992

Listen to this voice.

It's a voice flavored by the Blue Ridge; a voice straight out of a remote valley hidden among the peaks and hollows of the Appalachian Mountains; a voice that's been described as more barbed wire than honeysuckle.

That this kind of voice could travel from a forgotten corner of Appalachia is a testament to the grace of God and the greatness of the Democratic Party.

This week we are gathered here to nominate a man from a remote, rural corner of Arkansas to be President of the United States of America.

That is powerful proof that the American Dream still lives ... at least in the Democratic Party.

Bill Clinton is the only candidate for President who feels our pain, shares our hopes and will work his heart out to fulfill our dreams.

You see, I understand why Bill Clinton is so eager to see the American Dream kept alive for a new generation.

Because I, too, was a product of that dream.

I was born during the worst of the Depression on a cold winter's day in the drafty bedroom of a rented house, and I was my parent's hope for the future.

Franklin Roosevelt was elected that year, and would soon replace generations of neglect with a whirlwind of activity, bringing to our little valley a very welcome supply of God's most precious commodity: hope.

1

My father — a teacher — died when I was two weeks old, leaving a young widow with two small children.

But with my mother's faith in God — and Mister Roosevelt's voice on the radio — we kept going.

After my father's death, my mother with her own hands cleared a small piece of rugged land. Every day she waded into a neighbor's cold mountain creek, carrying out thousands of smooth stones to build a house.

I grew up watching my mother complete that house, from the rocks she'd lifted from the creek and cement she mixed in a wheelbarrow — cement that today still bears her handprints.

Her son bears her handprints, too. She pressed her pride and her hopes and her dreams deep into my soul.

So, you see, I know what Dan Quayle means when he says it's best for children to have two parents. You bet it is! And it would be nice for them to have trust funds, too.

But we can't all be born handsome, rich and lucky. That's why we have a Democratic Party.

My family would still be isolated and destitute if we had not had FDR's Democratic brand of government.

I made it because Franklin Delano Roosevelt energized this nation. I made it because Harry Truman fought for working families like mine. I made it because John Kennedy's rising tide lifted even our tiny boat.

I made it because Lyndon Johnson showed America that people who were born poor didn't have to die poor. And I made it because a man with whom I served in the Georgia Senate — a man named Jimmy Carter — brought honesty and decency and integrity to public service.

But what of the kids of today? Who fights for the child of a single mother today? Because without a government that is on their side, those children have no hope. And when a child has no hope, a nation has no future.

I am a Democrat because we are the party of hope. For 12 dark years the Republicans have dealt in cynicism and skepticism. They've mastered the art of division and diversion, and they have robbed us of our hope.

Too many mothers today cannot tell their children what my mother told me — that working hard and playing by the rules can make your dreams come true.

2

For millions, the American dream has become what the poet called "a dream deferred." And if you recall the words of that poet-prophet, he warned us that a dream deferred can explode.

Robbed of hope, the voices of anger rise up from working Americans, who are tired of paying more in taxes and getting less in services. And George Bush doesn't get it?

Americans cannot understand why some can buy the best health care in the world, but all the rest of us get is rising cost and cuts in coverage — or no health insurance at all. And George Bush doesn't get it?

Americans cannot walk our streets in safety, because our "tough-on-crime" President has waged a phony photo-op war on drugs, posing for pictures while cutting police, prosecutors and prisons. And George Bush doesn't get it?

Americans have seen plants closed down, jobs shipped overseas and our hopes fade away as our economic position collapses right before our very eyes.

And George Bush doesn't get it!

Four years ago, Mr. Bush told us he was a quiet man, who hears the voices of quiet people. Today, we know the truth: George Bush is a timid man who hears only the voices of caution and the status quo.

Let's face facts: George Bush just doesn't get it. He doesn't see it; he doesn't feel it, and he's done nothing about it.

That's why we cannot afford four more years.

If the "education president" gets another term, even our kids won't be able to spell potato.

If the "law and order president" gets another term, the criminals will run wild, because our commander-in-chief talks like Dirty Harry, but acts like Barney Fife.

If the "environmental president" gets another term, the fish he catches off Kennebunkport will have three eyes.

So much for the millionaire. But we've still got ourselves a billionaire ... A billionaire!

He *says* he's an outsider, who will shake up the system in Washington. But as far back as 1974 he was lobbying Congress for tax breaks. He tried to turn $55,000 in contributions into a special $15 million tax loophole that was tailor-made for him.

3

Sounds to me like instead of shaking the system up, Mr. Perot's been shaking it down.

Ross says he'll clean out the barn, but he's been knee deep in it for years.

If Ross Perot's an outsider, folks, I'm from Brooklyn.

Mr. Perot's giving us salesmanship, not leadership. And we're not buying it.

I know who I'm for.

I'm for Bill Clinton because he is a Democrat who does not have to read a book or be briefed about the struggles of single-parent families, or what it means to work hard for everything he's ever received in life.

There was no silver spoon in sight when he was born, three months after his father died. No one ever gave Bill Clinton a free ride as he worked his way through college and law school.

And the people at Yale couldn't believe it when he turned down a good job in Washington to return to Arkansas and teach.

Bill Clinton is a Democrat who has the courage to tell some of those liberals who think welfare should continue forever, and some of those conservatives who think there should be no welfare at all, that they're both wrong. He's a Democrat who will move people off the welfare rolls and onto the job rolls.

Bill Clinton is a Democrat who has the courage to lead a real war on crime here at home. And around the world he will be the kind of commander-in-chief this old Marine sergeant would be proud to follow.

That either one of us was able, one growing up in an Appalachian valley and the other in rural Arkansas, to eventually become governors of our states is a tribute to the American dream and yes, the Democratic Party that makes it a reality.

When I was growing up back in the mountains, whenever I felt like one of life's losers, my mother used to point to the one and only paved road in our valley — a narrow little strip that disappeared winding its way through a distant gap — and she'd say, "You know what's so great about this place? You can get anywhere in the world from here."

Thanks to her and to God, the United States Marine Corps and the Democratic Party, I did go somewhere. But I've never really left that mountain valley, either.

4

Shirley and I, our children and their children still live in the Appalachian town of Young Harris, Georgia. And tonight, one of my sons is sitting in front of the television set in the living room of that same rock house my mother and her neighbors built so many years ago.

Tonight, let our message be heard in every living room in every home in America. Wherever families and friends are gathered, let them know this:

We have a leader and a party and a platform that says to the everyday working people of this country: we will fight your fight; we will ease your burden; we will carry your cause.

We will hear *all* the voices of America — from the silky harmonies of the Gospel choirs to the rough-edged rhythms of a hot country band; from the razor's edge rap of the inner city to the soaring beauty of the finest soprano.

We hear your voice, America.

We hear your voice. We will answer your call. We will keep the faith. And we will restore your hope.

Thank you. God bless you. And God bless America.

1995 Inaugural Address
January 9, 1995

Lt. Governor Howard, Speaker Murphy, Governors Harris, Busbee, and Maddox, Members of the General Assembly, Members of the Judiciary, Members of the Consular Corps, my fellow Georgians:

I come before you again as your Governor with a deep sense of humility, gratitude and responsibility. Your repeated confidence in me fuels my determination to work on your behalf to the full extent of my energy, capacity and passion.

For you see, I not only remember from where I have come, but I also see the new heights I want Georgia to reach.

About 40 miles from Young Harris, the three states of North Carolina, Georgia and Tennessee all come together. On the Georgia side is the town of McCaysville... Fannin County. Right across the state line is Copperhill... Polk County, Tennessee.

As a young man, I played a lot of baseball in that area. And back then it was a place unlike anything you'd ever seen. There were no trees. There was no grass. No foliage of any kind, not even kudzu.

There was only a huge, vast ugly scar covering miles and miles of what had once been lush, green, beautiful mountains.

That shameful wasteland was created by human beings in the early 1900's. They cut the trees and fed the fires under simmering copper ore, whose toxic fumes laid bare whatever other vegetation remained.

To the traveler spending the night at the Sahara Motel, or even to a young lad mostly interested in baseball, it was a depressing example of human destruction...of putting short term gains ahead of long term benefits.

Fortunately, that land has been largely reclaimed since those days, although you still can see signs of how it once was.

In Copperhill and all across this nation, Americans, somehow, collectively, almost unanimously, arrived at the conclusion that we cannot afford to waste or destroy our soil or our rivers or our woodlands. And protecting our natural environment has come to be part of a "common mindset" about the legacy we must leave.

Today we face a similar question that requires a similar response: What about the waste of our children? Or as Carl Sandberg called them, "the human reserves that shape history."

What about the thousands of children in the inner-cities and the remote rural areas of Georgia, whose lives are dominated by poverty and whose futures are as barren as Copperhill used to be?

What about those young Georgians who are not trained to take part in our rapidly changing economic life and are condemned to live on the outer fringes of Georgia's growing prosperity?

Is this waste not also an ugly scar? Is this waste not also a painful indictment of our neglect? Are not our children even more important to our future than our natural environment? Are not our children the "ultimate" legacy that we leave here on this earth?

Can we not somehow arrive at the conclusion that we cannot afford to neglect, to waste or to destroy our children? And then move from that conclusion into bold action, so that together we make "that" human wasteland...green and growing?

I am at heart a teacher. Perhaps its genetic, for I am the son of teachers. Whatever its source, a commitment to education runs deep in my soul. And I want to leave a long-term legacy that outlasts all the short-term political gains. I want the children of

Georgia to have better lives, more productive careers and be finer citizens.

This is why as Governor I have chosen to focus on education. For all our other challenges in this state be it crime or welfare, economic development or environmental responsibility have at their root the "same solution"... children who are loved and educated.

Of course, the starting point must be with parents mothers and fathers who take responsibility for the young lives they have created.

The traditional values... the values that have built this nation and made it better for each successive generation...honesty, integrity, hard work, self reliance, respect for others...are not embedded in DNA and somehow passed biologically from one generation to the next. They must be taught at home by parents who devote love, time and resources to raising their children.

But government also has a role to play in the future of the next generation. And today there's a lot of conversation about what that role should be. Government has indispensable functions... from public safety and prisons to transportation and public health, from environmental protection and water resources to, most certainly, economic development.

And here in Georgia, we are moving on all those fronts. And we are moving with a sense of urgency and a spirit of innovation.

We are aggressive in attacking crime, and Georgia now has the toughest laws in the nation for violent criminals. We have cut income taxes, and I want to take the sales tax off groceries.

Georgia is a national model in fiscal responsibility. Our economy is healthy... we are at the national forefront in many economic indicators. All of these are important.

But I believe that those of us who are entrusted to lead are charged with an even more fundamental mission: ensuring that all our citizens have the opportunity to develop fully the talents they were given by God.

The starting point for government must be education...sound and meaningful education. I believe education is everything. A good education provides each person the capacity to add a gift and make a contribution to their generation, thereby becoming part of the progress of humankind.

It is the educated individual who makes this state stronger. It is the educated individual who adds to its wealth, protects it against enemies and carries forward its ideals and faith. H.G. Wells had it right when he said, "Human history becomes more and more a race between education and catastrophe."

And, if we are to win that race, we must work together, putting aside party and politics, geography and gender, to form a partnership... each trusting the other, all committed to using education as the instrument for the creative development of our human resources.

And if we all make that commitment, keep that commitment and honor that commitment, Georgia will fulfill the fondest dream any Governor or legislator or citizen can dream: Georgia will give our students opportunities that cannot be found anywhere else. Georgia will lead the nation. Georgia will be the best there is.

We have made some truly significant gains in education in the past few years... landmark achievements. No other state has anything like the HOPE Scholarship Program. It has been called Georgia's G.I. Bill. It is the most far reaching program in the United States. And we are about to make it even more far reaching.

Our pre-kindergarten program for four-year-olds is also unique. No other state has reached out to such a high percentage of its at-risk four-year-olds as Georgia has. And no other state provides voluntary pre-kindergarten for all four-year-olds, as I am recommending.

It will be many years before we reap all the benefits of investing in young children. I will no longer be in the Governor's Office. I'll probably be back up in Young Harris coaching third base for some Little League team.

But I know today what the statisticians will tell us tomorrow. Our investment will have its returns in fewer dropouts and higher college participation rates. It will produce happier, smarter children. It will produce adults with higher earnings, lower criminal arrests and a greater commitment to marriage and parenthood.

It is our responsibility to begin, and we must not shirk that responsibility.

The Latin phrase "alma mater" means "nourishing mother," and that is a pretty good description of what our schools should be for our children. Teaching is much more than pouring a certain volume of factual information into young heads like tea into a cup. Teachers are the architects who guide and shape the building of young lives, with a special emphasis on creating a strong foundation for life-long learning.

Teachers are the key ingredient to improving education. Teachers are the ones who call forth the best from our children and inspire them to new heights of achievement.

If we are to build a first-class education system in Georgia, we must have at least a fighting chance to attract and hold good teachers. That's why my goal during this administration is to raise Georgia teacher salaries at least to the national average and to attract the best and brightest to become teachers.

I know money alone is not the answer. It is a matter of quality and value. In the classroom, like everywhere else, you get what you pay for. And as we raise teachers' salaries at our schools and yes, at our colleges, we will also raise our expectations of excellence in the classroom.

And I am confident that our teachers and professors will rise to that challenge.

And as our students are called to new levels of achievement, I want them to know, in the words of that old song, "You'll never walk alone." Because I want to create a mentoring program which pairs adults with students who are at risk.

I know from experience this can make a difference. It worked on me when I was a wayward young teenager and Edna Herren, my teacher and mentor, helped put me on the right path.

And I want to give those high school students who are not headed for college some real hands-on experience in the work place. The youth apprenticeship program I have started and want to expand will build a partnership between business and education that will make training for a job part of the classroom experience.

I believe it's time our schools gave a warranty on their product: the student. A diploma must be more than just a measure of attendance. That is why I will propose a guaranteed high school diploma, where employers can get additional education at no cost for recent graduates whose skills do not live up to their high school diploma.

I want to give our children and their parents more choices. I want to give our schools more flexibility...with fewer top-down regulations and paperwork. I believe in the philosophy of charter schools — free from all state regulations — and I want to make it a lot easier for local schools to set them up and get them going.

We are putting classroom computers, media center technology, satellite dishes, distance learning networks into all our schools — technology in amounts unheard of before in Georgia, and unheard of still in many other states.

But it is not enough to lead the nation in new technology. We must also lead our children to enduring values. Yes, our children must know about gigabytes and CD-ROM. But it's even more important that they know about the Golden Rule, and right and wrong.

Yes, I believe that schools should join with parents and churches as bearers of society's standards.

Students should be taught morality as well as math, ethics as well as English.

You see, our children are as strong or as weak, as intelligent or as frivolous, as serious or as silly, as disciplined or as wild, as we have taught them to be.

And if our children don't have the values that we or our parents cherished, it is because someone has failed to teach them their meaning...and help make those values a part of their young lives.

Stronger schools will allow our technical institutes and our colleges and universities to concentrate on higher learning. The University System of Georgia right now is poised and ready, and I'm going to be the best partner I can be to Chancellor Portch to propel our University system to national preeminence.

And I believe we must help older students who want to return to college or to a technical institute. For, you see, I want a more highly educated Georgia.

These are the new heights I want Georgia to reach. But, my friends, I know we will not finish the job of improving education in the next four years or even in my or your lifetime.

Someone once said that one of the things education does for you is to open your eyes to the vast wealth of knowledge that still remains for you to learn.

It's like that with improving education. The further you get into it, the more your eyes are opened to how much there is yet to do. It will always be an on-going, never ending process.

In the race that H.G. Wells mentioned...between education and catastrophe, Georgia is moving fast. But this race is not a hundred-yard dash. It is more like a series of marathons: each generation carries the torch as far as it can, then passes it on to the next. Our job, as the Apostle Paul put it, is to fix our eyes on the prize and run with patience the race that is set before us.

And if we do our job, if we honor our commitment, then the torch we pass will burn brighter, the course our children run will be smoother, and our ultimate goal of giving the sons and daughters of Georgia the boldest dreams and the broadest opportunities will be closer than ever before.

That is the Georgia we seek. We shall not see it tomorrow or the next day or the next. But if our children and their children are ever to see it, we must carry on the work we have begun.

After all, the hope of a better future is why young people dream dreams, and old people plant trees.

I'm working to turn my dreams into trees. With your help and God's, the trees we plant will grow strong, nourished by virtue and the values we hold dear, and they will bear fruit for generations to come.

Thank you. God bless you. And God bless Georgia.

Dedication Address
Georgia Center for Advanced
Telecommunications Technology,
July 17, 1996

Thank you, Mr. (Horace) Sibley. President Clough, Bill Todd, distinguished guests, ladies and gentlemen...

The first thing I want to say is that I am not a scientist, and I don't pretend to understand the technical aspects of the research that will go on in this remarkable building. Rather I am a historian, and I look at this research center and our growing prominence in telecommunications from that perspective.

If you look at the 25 largest cities in the United States, virtually every one grew up around some natural resource. Most of them are port cities — Boston, New York, Philadelphia and Miami on the East Coast; Seattle, Portland, San Francisco and Los Angeles on the West Coast; New Orleans and Houston on the Gulf; Chicago on the Great Lakes.

The few that are inland can also be explained, for the most part, by major natural resources. Dallas has oil; Denver has mining. Kansas City and Minneapolis are markets for the rich grains of the Midwestern prairies. And Washington, D.C., of course, is our nation's capital.

Of the 25 largest cities in the United States, only Atlanta has no natural, logical reason for its existence.

Atlanta was built on sheer human ingenuity and persistence. And the resource around which this city has grown up, is purely man-made transportation infrastructure and a knack for knowing how to leverage it.

Its very first expression, of course, was the railroad. In the 1830s, three railroads came together in a remote spot out in the Georgia woods. They formed a major junction that linked the East Coast with the Midwest. And Atlanta grew up around that railroad junction.

A century later, Atlanta was in the vanguard of the next generation of transportation, building an airport in the early days of commercial aviation. In 1940, Atlanta had the nation's busiest airport with 41 flights a day.

Two decades later, we became one of the few American cities to be located at the intersection of three major interstate highways.

Today, on the threshold of the 21st century, transportation is taking yet another leap, this time into cyberspace and onto the information superhighway, as telecommunications technology makes location increasingly irrelevant.

And true to our historical roots, Atlanta is once again deliberately building the infrastructure we need to establish prominence in this newest form of "transportation."

In two days, the biggest single event in world history will begin here in Atlanta. It will also be the greatest single telecommunications event in world history, because in the process of putting on the 1996 Olympics, Atlanta will present the world with a vision of 21st century telecommunications technology in action.

And a more important Olympic legacy than a swimming pool here or a stadium there, will be the telecommunications infrastructure that these Games have given us.

In preparation for the Olympics, Atlanta increased its cellular capacity by eightfold, making this the best city in the world for wireless portable phone connections. We already had three times more fiber-optic trunk lines than New York City, and the Olympics will leave us with more broadband fiber-optic connections than Manhattan — another essential piece of 21st century infrastructure that high-tech industry requires. Our new Integrated Services Digital Network provides internet connections several times faster than conventional modems, at a cost that is among the lowest anywhere.

The Olympics have given us a technological leg up. And this new telecommunications research center positions us to build on it, and continue to run out on the cutting edge of telecommunications technology.

This state-of-the-art research center, with its labs, high-tech demonstrations and incubator for new ventures, is magnificent in its own right. But it also serves as an icon for our vast telecommunications infrastructure and expertise. You can see rail yards and highways and runways. You can see cars and ships and trains and planes. But you cannot see a satellite or a digital network. Telecommunications infrastucture is largely invisible.

And this research center is tangible evidence that Georgia has the both resources and the determination to become the global center for advanced telecommunications in the 21st century.

The Georgia Center for Advanced Telecommunications Technology, like its parent body, the Georgia Research Alliance, is a public-private partnership that brings together academia, private industry and state government.

State government's role is to provide seed capital at the front end — funding to build this research center, matching funds to provide endowments for the eminent research scholars who will work here and to equip their labs. Because we believe that the collaborative research and incubator programs that the academic and industrial partners carry out in this building, are the engine that will power our telecommunications industry to world prominence.

In addition, the Governor's Development Council — another public-private partnership between industry and state government — has adopted global leadership in telecommunications as one of its goals in guiding the development of Georgia's public economic policy.

Someone once said that the biggest sin is not failure, but low aim. That's one sin we are not going to be guilty of. Our aim is high: By the end of the first decade of the new century, we intend to be the premier center in the world for advanced telecommunications.

We have the infrastructure; we have the industrial base; we have the intellectual capital. We have the resources. And in this magnificent building they will converge with a synergy that is greater than the sum of their parts, to carry Atlanta and Georgia forward to world leadership in advanced telecommunications in the 21st century.

Accept Blue Key Award
University of Georgia,
September 20, 1996

Thank you, President Knapp.

I am humbled to be chosen to receive the Blue Key Award. And to receive it together with Dick Yarbrough, a remarkable man whom I have admired greatly for a long time, is a special pleasure.

I also extend my congratulations to Kathy Rogers Pharr, as recipient of the Young Alumnus Award, and to Maggie Hodge, Andrew DeVooght and Julie Mickle.

Being chosen for this high honor and as your keynote speaker, gave me a chance to step back from the day-to-day details of being Governor and reflect on higher education as a historian and as one who is at heart a teacher.

Perhaps it's genetic, for I am the son of two teachers. Whatever its source, a commitment to education runs deep in my soul. And my goal as Governor has not been some short-term political gain, but a long-term educational gain.

I want us to establish in this state a culture of higher expectations. I want the question to be not "whether" to go to college, but "where" to go to college or technical school. I want Georgians to move into the new millennium with more productive careers and as better citizens.

Throughout American history, education has always been an over-riding preoccupation. And we have always steadfastly refused to allow other crises to distract us from it. In fact, it seems that unsettled times have often given us the push we needed to improve and expand education.

Two years before George Washington was even inaugurated, the Continental Congress passed a law requiring every new township to set aside land for a public school.

Even as the Civil War swirled around him and our nation's Capitol was often in peril, President Lincoln signed the Morrill Act, creating a system of land-grant colleges.

Right in the middle of World War I, Congress took time to pass the Smith-Hughes Act – sponsored by two Georgians, Hoke Smith and Dudley Hughes – to establish a new system of vocational education.

With World War II raging on both the European and Pacific fronts, Congress passed the GI Bill, assuring over two million returning veterans the chance of an education.

See what I mean? And we are the inheritors of those traditions. All that was strong and iron-hearted in the past has come down to us, and we must use our time to meet the challenges of our day, just as those who bequeathed it to us used theirs.

Today, as we stand on the threshold of a new millennium, we are in the middle of one of the greatest shifts in world history.

Not only has our economy become global in its scope, but the technology all around us is changing by the day. There is more computer power in the Ford Taurus we now drive to the supermarket, than there was in the Apollo 11 rocket that Neil Armstrong flew to the moon.

Today, the combined forces of changing technology and global competition are bringing about a transformation that literally dwarfs the industrial revolution in its impact.

And these powerful forces are changing more than just our jobs. They are changing the neighborhoods we live in. They are changing the institutions that shape our lives, and even our hopes and dreams for the future.

Since the birth of this nation, the defining elements of American society have been the idea of opportunity for all and the freedom to seize it and work to make our dreams come true.

But today, for the first time in our history, people aren't so sure about their ability to do that. While some see this as a time of profound opportunity, for many others it is a time of profound insecurity... a time in which the very plates of the earth seem to be shifting under their feet.

And the difference... the difference between those who see opportunity and those who see insecurity... is education.

Consider these facts: Fifteen years ago, the typical employee with a college degree made 38 percent more money than the employee with only a high school diploma. Today that gap has widened to 73 percent.

Half of our population today is working harder than ever before and making less money. And half of the people who lose their jobs today will never, ever find another job in which they will do as well.

The unemployment rate for high school dropouts is now about 10 percent. For those with a high school diploma, it is half that. For college graduates, it is one-fourth that.

So you can see, Education doesn't matter just a little. It doesn't even matter just a lot. It matters most of all. Education is everything.

And increasingly, it is "post-secondary" education that is everything. A high school diploma is increasingly losing its economic value. The median income of young men ages 25-34 with a high school diploma has fallen by $14,000 over the past two decades. In the economy of the 21st century, students with only a high school diploma will be worse off than the dropouts of this century.

So, what a high school diploma has become today, is only a ticket to the post-secondary education or training that will give you value on the job market.

See why I said in the beginning that I want to create a culture of higher expectations in this state? I don't want the question to be "whether," but "where" to go to college or technical school. Two years beyond high school must be expected. It must be a given. Because today as never before, higher education is the key to economic growth and development. Higher education is the most important economic infrastructure a state can have.

In Georgia, we are on the right track, and headed in the right direction. Our citizens are becoming better educated than ever before. In 1949 when I finished high school, only one out of five Georgians were high school graduates. Twenty years later, in 1970, we were up to two out of five. Today, almost four out of five of our citizens are high school graduates.

Between 1970 and 1990, the percentage of Georgians with at least one year of college more than doubled, and the percentage of Georgians with a college degree has almost doubled. Minority southerners now complete high school at the same rate as white southerners, and the percentage of minority southerners with college degrees nearly tripled in the past 25 years.

But while we've been climbing up the mountain, the mountain itself has been growing. A lot more Georgians have college degrees, but it's still only 21 percent, instead of the 30 percent we need.

One of the most encouraging trends in the past decade is that the number of our high school students taking the college prep curriculum has almost tripled, and Georgia is now outstripping the national average.

Here at The University of Georgia, last fall's freshmen averaged 1108 on the SAT – a UGA record that was about 200 points above the national average. And this institution is ranked by *US News and World Report* as among the top 20 public universities in the nation.

But these days, technology is changing so fast that you can't just go through college once and be done with it. The shelf-life of a technical degree is now down to five years. And this reality of lifelong learning means that we're going to have to adapt to the needs of growing numbers of older, non-traditional students.

Many still have this image of college as a place full of 18-22 year-olds. But today, four of every 10 students in the University System of Georgia, as well as around the nation, are over the age of

25. And the percentage of college students over age 35 has doubled in just the past decade and is going to keep growing.

And it's not just enough to keep up a well-trained workforce. We also have to be on the cutting edge of research and innovation, and that is the second economic development function of higher education.

Half of all basic research in the United States today is conducted at our universities. It is where polio vaccines, heart pacemakers, digital computers, municipal water purification systems, space-based weather forecasting, and disease-resistant grain and vegetables, just to name a few, have been invented.

University research has become critical to economic development. And the classroom and the research lab must be more closely connected than ever before. A great challenge for university faculty must be to become more adept at combining those two roles.

The future will belong to those that can put hand-in-hand: one, the ideas that will drive technology forward, and two, the educated workers who can make something of those ideas.

And here, the South in general and The University of Georgia in particular have been doing well. The National Research Council ranked nearly a fourth of the South's doctoral programs in the top 20 in the nation in their particular fields. And The University of Georgia conducts the largest volume of research of any American university that does not have an engineering or a medical college.

Tonight, I have deliberately focused on the growing economic significance of higher education. It is absolutely critical to the future prosperity of this state. But I want close by saying that we must also never mistake technology for culture.

At the same time I have been emphasizing that higher education prepares students to "earn a living," I also want to make it clear that by itself, earning is not living. And we need to educate students not only to earn, but also to live. That is the higher calling of higher education.

Because, you see, our students are not only tomorrow's employees. They are also tomorrow's citizens, parents, customers and neighbors. And higher education must enrich their ability to function in those capacities as well as on the job market.

The business of higher education is more than mere information. The business of higher education is knowledge. And unlike information, knowledge cannot be poured into the minds of students like water into a glass. Knowledge is not a destination; it is a process. It is learned and accumulated over a period of time through continuous study, thought and experience.

I believe that being "educated" means that one has learned to think, to reason, to compare, to analyze. I believe that "educated" persons are continually shaping and refining their mental visions, judgments and tastes.

Which brings me full circle to where I began... Because as the shelf life of technical information becomes ever shorter, those thinking and analyzing skills are coming to be in ever higher demand in the workforce. Employers today want workers who are continually re-evaluating what they know, continually learning new things, and continually integrating what they learn with what they already know.

As we look to the 21st century, we must continually strengthen and enhance our higher education programs to meet the demands of a technology-driven global economy. But while we are doing that, we dare not forget that higher education is about more than money. And what you do here on this campus must be as essential to living as it is to earning.

INDEX

Zell: The Governor Who Gave Georgia HOPE
by Richard Hyatt
Published by Mercer University Press,
1 November 1997
Production Editor: Marc A. Jolley
Book Design by Jay Polk
Jacket Design by Jim Burt
Jacket produced by Phoenix Color
Book printed and bound by Braun-Brumfield, Inc.
Text font: Adobe® Garamond